DATE DUE

DEC 0 4 2001	
FEB 2 5 2003	

MINORITIES IN THE MIDDLE EAST

MINORITIES IN THE MIDDLE EAST

A History of Struggle and Self-Expression

by Mordechai Nisan

McFarland & Company, Inc., Publishers
Jefferson, North Carolina, and London

British Library Cataloguing-in-Publication data are available

Library of Congress Cataloguing-in-Publication Data

Nisan, Mordechai.
    Minorities in the Middle East : a history of struggle and self-
expression / by Mordechai Nisan.
      p.   cm.
    Includes bibliographical references and index.
    ISBN 0-89950-564-3 (lib. bdg. : 50# alk. paper) ∞
    1. Minorities—Middle East—History. 2. Middle East—History.
3. Ethnology—Middle East. I. Title.
DS58.N57 1991
956′.004—dc20
                             91-52512
                              CIP

Manufactured in the United States of America

McFarland & Company, Inc., Publishers
  Box 611, Jefferson, North Carolina 28640

To Malka

Contents

Part II: Heterodox Muslim Minorities

Part III: Christian Minorities

Part IV: Jews, Israel, and Other Middle Eastern Minorities

Preface

The source of this study was in feeling and mind. A primary impetus was related to special people I met who shared my deep interest in the minority peoples of the Middle East. They proved of inestimable importance in offering their familiarity and insight on the communities with whom this book deals. Let me thank Shula Cohen, Benjamin Daniel, Salman Falah, George Hentilian, Selim Naguib, and Vera Beaudin Saeedpour for their helpful comments. In addition I want to thank Rivka Yadlin, of the Hebrew University, whose expertise on Egypt I benefited from. The role of Robert J. Loewenberg was significant too as a catalyst of my writing this book, for which I thank him. Norma Schneider provided important editorial assistance and contributed to improving the style of the final work. Lastly, I acknowledge my students at the Hebrew University, who participated in my course Middle Eastern Minorities and provided me with an attentive and critical audience as I developed many ideas later incorporated in this study.

This is a study in the spirit of narrative history. Because of its wide scope, both in chronology and in geography, it can enlighten both the professional and the lay reader. As a comprehensive work, it brings together the record of the past and links it with the contemporary political scene. It also combines some terminology and literature of the social sciences with the chronicles of history. The particular minority case studies offered are parts of a wider whole. Indeed, underlying many of this book's themes is an effort to bind loose ends and search out the more comprehensive connections among them. One very substantive question guiding the quest is whether there exists among all the significant historic minority peoples across the Mideast terrain a linkage that can serve to redefine the political character of the region as a whole.

It is my hope that this work will contribute to an appreciation of

the value of an examination of Middle East minorities, highlight some
pertinent questions concerning their survival and future, and call attention to their tale as a living human saga over the millennia.

Mordichai Nisan
Hebrew University
Rothberg School for Overseas Students
Jerusalem, 1991

CHAPTER 1

Introduction:
The Middle Eastern Mosaic

The image of a totally Arab Muslim Middle East reflects only a partial picture of reality. This strategically critical and historically significant region of humanity has been the home of many diverse peoples, some of whom should be considered indigenous inhabitants, others as foreign conquerors, still others as travelers across its formidable expanse that serves as an international crossroad. Empires have come and gone, and the remnants of earlier epochs resonate in archaeological fossils and places of epic and mythological memory. The spiritual flights of mankind hover above, and the military exploits of warriors are not forgotten. The past is never completely out of sight, and indeed the present may only be the most contemporary chapter of the past, which never dies.

Central to the saga of the Middle East is human and cultural diversity, not always divorced from great political consequences until today. The power of ancient civilizations like the Hellenic, Byzantine, and Christian is no longer with us. Nor do ancient languages like Aramaic, Greek, or Coptic beam out in the region. Old maps that show Baluchistan and Armenia would appear to be out of touch with twentieth-century developments across the region. Old religions faded, and old languages passed away as the force of Islam and Arabic burst onto the peoples of the Middle East beginning in the seventh century. From that time on, the image of a basically monolithic terrain from the Sahara and Morocco in the west to southern Asia and the Indus valley in the east grew into an indelible stereotype. It became customary to see this geographic expanse as inhabited by Muslims alone. It became customary as well to see the area from North Africa to the Persian Gulf as inhabited by Arabs speaking the Arabic tongue and overwhelmingly Muslim.

1

Yet even into this century non–Muslims and non–Arabs continued to provide evidence of the historic heterogeneity that was the hallmark of this region. Michel Aflaq, a Greek Orthodox Christian from Damascus, was the main founder and ideological thinker of the formidable Ba'th pan–Arab nationalist party, a party that continued to rule for decades in Syria and in Iraq. Nubar Gulbenkian, of Armenian descent, played a primary role as an oil magnate in developing that vital regional resource around the turn of the twentieth century. Ezekiel Sassoon, a Baghdadi Jew, served as finance minister of newly founded Iraq from 1921 to 1925. Belkacem Krim, a Kabylian Berber in Algeria, in 1954 helped found the FLN movement that led the struggle for independence from France. Makram Ebeid, a Copt Christian, was a very senior member in, and intermittently the leader of, the Egyptian Wafd party after the First World War, which provided the nationalist movement with effective leadership for some twenty-five years. Assadullah Alam, a Baluch in Iran, served Reza Shah as prime minister in the early 1960s. In earlier historic periods there is no dearth of great personalities belonging to the mosaic of Mideastern peoples. The famed Muslim warrior who defeated the Christian Crusaders in the twelfth century was none other than the Kurd general Saladin (Salah al-Din). And the renowned sage, philosopher, and doctor of the Muslim sultan in Egypt was Maimonides, the Jewish scholar of memorable noteworthiness. Both the history of the region and its contemporary landscape are too rich to ignore Christians, Jews, and various non–Arab communities in sketching out the variety of peoples who have made a mark. We are therefore led necessarily to consider the region as something less than a religious or ethnic monolithic zone. We are led to examine more carefully the variegated quality of the Middle East, and some basic statistical data will clarify the subject.

In the some twenty Arab-defined countries there are approximately 180 million people of whom, nonetheless, about 35 million could be defined as non–Arabs ethnically or nationally, or non–Muslims religiously.[1] Thus about 20 percent of the inhabitants of Arab countries are not religiously or nationally affiliated with them. This substantial minority includes about 10 million Christians, particularly Copts in Egypt, and large ethnic collectivities, particularly Kurds and Berbers. Of the 35 million some 17 million speak a language other than, or in addition to, Arabic. Beyond the Arab core area are four non–Arab Muslim countries — Turkey, Iran, Pakistan, and Afghanistan — which are generally and of late more commonly included in geographic definitions of the Middle East. These countries alone contain about 210 million people, the largest being Pakistan with 100 million. The significance of this is that in the wide region of the Middle East the Arab Muslims represent only slightly more than one-third of the entire population. True, the

Muslims as a whole are well over 90 percent of the region's population, but the Arab national proportion is significantly less.

The backdrop of history is relevant at the point when the image of homogeneity begins to fade and a more complex understanding of the Mideast's mosaic character becomes apparent. The notable Arab historian Ibn Khaldun, who, Franz Rosenthal said, "may have had Berber and Spanish blood in his veins," felt no compunction to record in his great and seminal work that Copts and Berbers were conspicuous already at the "time of Moses."[2] Indeed Christians, Berbers, and certainly Jews chronologically preceded Muslims in history. The Kurds were considered the original inhabitants of the area known as Kurdistan in the northern Euphrates-Tigris Valley and mountainous terrain. Likewise, the Berbers were considered the original population of the Maghreb, that is, North Africa. The Jews were the biblically legitimate national community in Canaan, or land of Israel, already a millennium prior to the birth of Christianity. Maronites were in the Lebanese mountain stronghold practicing their Christian faith a few centuries before Muhammad founded Islam. It was therefore appropriate for Carleton Coon to emphasize the mosaic of peoples as the "most conspicuous fact about Middle Eastern civilization."[3]

It is almost begging the point to ask why the image of uniformity diverges markedly from the reality of diversity. At root, the factor of power must be introduced, and in particular Sunni Muslim power. This is not to imply that history is immoral (quite another mode of discourse, alien to this analysis); rather, the question relates to why Sunni Islam, particularly Sunni Arab Islam in such countries as Morocco, Algeria, Egypt, and Iraq, succeeded in dominating other peoples and all but eliminating their place in the Middle East. It is this question that shall underpin much of the investigation incorporated in this study. Moreover, it is "the very suppression of submerged Middle Eastern nationalities by the dominant ruling elites in the area," as one author described the situation,[4] that permits us to query whether the Arab Muslims are native inhabitants or perhaps foreign conquerors. After all, the geographic origin of Arabs, historically Bedouin nomads, is in the Arabian peninsula and not in the Fertile Crescent area. It was undoubtedly this nomenclature that prompted Mark Sykes, a globe-trotting British diplomat in the World War I period, to sloganize his postwar territorial solution as follows: "There is one Palestine for the Jews that is the home of the Jewish nation. But there is a Palestine for the Armenians, it is Armenia. There is a Palestine for the Arabs, it is Arabia."[5] Yet, both in the seventh century when Islam was born and in the twentieth century when Arab nationalism was activated, the aspiration for power dominance extended far beyond the Arabian peninsula and deep into the heart of the Middle East, and even beyond it.

It is a compelling dilemma, and quite controversial from the political point of view, to work out a definition of the Arab Muslim. Members of the Arab ethnos, according to Maxime Rodinson, fulfill the following criteria: they speak Arabic; they live their lives in an Arab cultural environment that is unalterably Islamic; and they claim a primary Arab identity that includes a sense of pan–Arab collective solidarity.[6] It is this Arab people that seems to predominate pervasively in the core heartland of the Middle East.

But according to the above definition, doubts may arise about the authentic Arabness of pivotal, or at least quixotic, historical personalities. Was George Antonius, Christian by religion yet active in the Palestinian Arab campaign against Zionism, a true Arab? Or what shall we conclude about Fawzi el-Kawakji, perhaps of Turkish or Kurdish origin, but appearing in the annals of Mideastern events as an Arab nationalist or even Palestinian patriot? Confusion is often due to popular narratives that serve as political advocacy statements more than as valid documentary evidence of historical affairs. In ancient times the only true Arab was the Bedouin nomad. Now the Arab is almost anyone who speaks Arabic as his native tongue. But this would be far too simplistic and partial a definition in the modern political context, and it may be necessary to revert to Rodinson's triple typology that relies on linguistic, cultural-religious, and national criteria. It is interesting to recall that until the 1930s in Egypt, only the Bedouins were referred to as Arabs.[7] To mention that the so-called modern founder of Egypt in the beginning of the nineteenth century was himself an Albanian-born European Muslim (probably of Christian descent) — the famed Mohammed 'Ali — is only to magnify the object lesson.

The value of the Arab identification is in offering a cohesive national label for diverse Arabic-speaking individuals and peoples. The first secretary-general of the Arab League, with its capital in Cairo, was Abdul Rahman Azzam, allegedly a true Egyptian but whose family origins were in Libya. Likewise King Hussein of Jordan was the last surviving monarch from his Hashemite clan whose historic hearth into the twentieth century was in the Hejaz, present Saudi Arabia. In both these cases the comprehensive solution to their identification is found in the Arab identity, because their territorial residence was not indicative of any authentic local patriotic consciousness of any longevity. Therefore, building on language, culture, and solidarity within the region, the idea of the Arab developed in our historical period.

Yet, as shown already, there are various permutations of identity that cannot simply be subsumed under the Arab or Muslim heading. The Copts are Eastern, but of course not Muslims. The Kurds are Muslim, but not of the Arab ethnos. A Lebanese Christian, perhaps a Greek Orthodox, may consider himself an Arab, but he is obviously not of the

Islamic faith. A Druze is Eastern, but not an Arab, nor necessarily even resembling one, looking more like an Italian, thought Carleton Coon with an eye to anthropology.[8] Nestorian Christians or Assyrians are certainly Eastern, and the Berbers are of course Muslim, but the Israeli Jews are for the most part neither. The region's latecomers, the Arab Muslims, have overwhelmed its older inhabitants, not only by numbers and power but by coercing others to define themselves in relation to the dominant Arab Muslim norm. The minority peoples are irrefutably dwelling in a world not of their own making.

In the early nineteenth century, foreign missionary activity, particularly in Lebanon, suggested the possibility of a Christian revival of regional importance. Toward the end of the century Lebanese Christians, like Butrus al Bustani and Farah Antun, were in the forefront of pan–Arab intellectual fermentation.[9] In 1912, of some forty bankers in Istanbul, not one bore a Muslim name, many being Armenians and Greeks, some Jews.[10] In the spirit of an old struggle, and perhaps aware of a certain historical opportunity that he was helping to revive, British General Allenby was not satisfied just to conquer Muslim Middle Eastern lands and leave it at that. In the flush of victory he gave vent to his enthusiasm by declaring, "Now end the Crusades." In Damascus, French General Gouraud felt it proper to remind the defeated Muslims in 1920, "We've returned, Saladin." (Saladin is buried in the Syrian capital.) But was it reasonable to imagine that the dominant Arab Muslim norm would be threatened by a Christian rejuvenation? Or indeed was it likely that other challenges would arise to undermine that dominance? For the moment, as we edge toward the end of the twentieth century, we shall leave this central question in abeyance until the evidence is in and duly evaluated.

States and Nations

In contrast to the modern idea of territorial nationalism in Europe, Middle Eastern peoples have articulated their collective identities and organized their political lives around other ideas. The only exception to this may be the Jewish people, whose national history from biblical times focused on statehood in "Eretz-Israel," separate from other peoples. But the Muslim community, the entire Umma, had no territorial delimitation in principle. The extent of the Sultana, the authority of Islamic power, extended as far as Muslims lived across the inhabited world. True sovereignty belonged of course to God and earthly power to his Muslim representative on earth. The elastic notion of Dar el-Islam, the Abode of Islam, suggested its changing geographic scope dependent upon the ultimate incorporation of more lands and more peoples under the Muhammadan banner. Religion, not territory, served as the organizing principle of power, this always distinct from lower levels of community solidarity rooted in tribal, ethnic, or clannish ties. Nationalism, as a doctrine that posited a criterion of peoplehood to legitimize power, was unknown in the Middle East.

Yet it was the national idea that nonetheless swept across the world, including the Middle East, in the modern political history of mankind. The nation, as a group bound by linguistic affinity, ethnic sentiment, and collective solidarity, arose to claim its rightful place in the organization of power among men. It declared the natural division of mankind into distinct communities as a sign from on high and let the nationalist logic carry the argument to the point of demanding that each nation have its own separate state.[11] This notion fostered innate patriotic feelings based on national cohesion, and now in the name of sovereign statehood. If the state becomes monoethnic, as the nationalist logic implies, then it is an integral nation-state. Social and ethnic ties harmonize with the organization of political power, this conducive to internal stability and national fulfillment. However, if the state is polyethnic, including more than one ethnic group, what is to become of it?

The process of moving from nationhood to statehood may alternatively move in the opposite direction, from statehood to nationhood. With the political framework established and integrationist policies in operation, the state institution can try to cultivate the sense of a newly cohesive people. The articulation of a fresh collective consciousness based on an original political loyalty is known in history. Switzerland would seem to be an example; the United States is another one. The state definition of the nation, perhaps Hegelian in spirit, can in principle overcome ethnic diversity in the name of a new political value.[12] It is here that the territorial factor becomes a compelling political force, arousing a common feeling among diverse ethnic groups, granting them equal citizenship, and hoping that older "primordial sentiments" can be subsumed under a shared civil sentiment for all.[13]

The incongruence between state and nation has been viewed in contradictory ways—as a human blessing or as a bitter curse. John Stuart Mill, spokesman for classic liberalism, was a strong believer in uniting diversity.

> Whatever really tends to the admixture of nationalities, and the blending of their attributes and peculiarities in a common union, is a benefit to the human race.... The united people, like a crossed breed of animals, inherits the special aptitudes and excellencies of all its progenitors.[14]

It is interesting to recall that Mill went on to affirm conclusively that in the relationship between the English and the Irish, there is next to nothing "to keep apart two races, perhaps the most fitted of any two in the world to be the completing counterpart of one another." This was written in 1861 after Irish resentment at British rule and policy had, thought Mill, been thoroughly overcome. But he did add that if in any given instance national feeling aspires to free government before the fusion of peoples has been effected, then breaking the connection is proper and necessary.

With the same optimistic liberal spirit, Lord Acton advocated the consolidation of multiethnic political entities. He saw the combination of different nations in one state "as necessary a condition of civilized life as the combination of men in society."[15] Inferior peoples will be raised up by living in concert with superior ones, this cross-fertilization acting to regenerate exhausted groups. Most significantly, liberty is assured in a multinational state because diversity and competition offset any temptation to deny some the right of equality. However the theory of nationality, whereby the state and the nation are in principle commensurate, will inevitably reduce any other resident nationalities to a subject condition. Thus, the idea of the nation-state or the monoethnic state must be rejected. Acton's premise is that only a multinational state organized around a common political loyalty can provide the human resources for the advance of civilization. He would likely have assented to Alfred North Whitehead's belief that the odyssey of mankind requires that we see other nations of different habits not as enemies, for "they are godsends."[16]

The historical judgment concerning nation-states is rendered harsh by the experiences in central Europe in the twentieth century. Repressive regimes based on the nationality principle dealt ruthlessly with minority ethnic populations. Nazi Germany serves as the most grotesque example. The mad tenacity with which the ideal of a monoethnic state was pursued was proof of the "disastrous possibilities inherent in nationalism," Elie Kedourie wrote. Majority decision, a seemingly legitimate notion rooted in democracy, was turned into the rule of force against small defenseless minority groups. It was reasonable, therefore, to point the accusing finger at the idea of the nation-state itself because it ineluctably culminated in bitter hostility and harsh measures. In the contemporary Middle East, where there is little convergence between state and nation in many new political entities, the reality of hostility and harshness is apparent as well. But the European liberal idea of ethnic pluralism in one state still constitutes if not an ideal, a legitimizing doctrine for rule by the dominant majority people. However, it is questionable if the noble vision of civilizational refineness and progress as a result of the mingling of diverse peoples applies in the Muslim Arab Mideast region.

A realistic study of polyethnic states, as opposed to a utopian idealization of them, uncovers the inherent problematics of this situation. A discontinuity between the ethnic community and the political community renders overall integration on the state level a most difficult task. Individuals belong by the nature of things to more than one community. The critical question relates to their first pole of allegiance: Is it defined by blood and kinship or by territory and citizenship? While the idea of the nation-state can breed repression and destruction, the reality of pluralistic states can also deteriorate into anarchy and unbearable disorder. As a result of this danger, minimizing the claims of secondary nationalities is seen to be necessary and consistent with affirming the primacy of the dominant nationality in state institutions. The imposition of unadulterated authority is the basis for collective existence in a divided land.[17]

At this point, ethnic pluralism must be contained, as it threatens the very survival of the state. In modern European history, the minority German population within pre–Second World War Czechoslovakia was not restrained in its nationalist machinations and actually contrived with the Nazi Reich to dismantle the state. Ethnic pluralism linked to the momentum of irredentism proved to be an insuperable challenge to the viability of Czechoslovakia. Indeed, any time a minority ethnic group in one state is itself part of a larger dominant national ethnic group in a contiguous neighboring state, it becomes an awesome problem to consolidate the first state and peacefully arrange relations between the majority and minority communities therein.[18] In this set of complicated and dangerous circumstances, Adolf Hitler addressed Neville Chamberlain in September 1938: "Would Britain agree to a secession of the Sudeten region? . . . A secession on the basis of the right of self-determination?"[19] The pluralism of Czechoslovakia had become a fatal curse eroding the marrow of the state's body politic.

The problem of polyethnic countries can sometimes be more than a benign illness, but not necessarily terminal in its consequences. National cleavages will complicate the establishment of statewide consensus on basic values. The role of religion may inhibit full integration or equality between groups if the state itself bears a religious identity in a formal or legal sense. More destabilizing and perhaps widespread can be the assertion of "an ethnic imperative" that challenges the state's regime rationale or territorial boundaries.[20] The demand for national self-expression will then extend beyond cultural autonomy as a sufficient and dignified solution for the minority community.

Of late, this problem has surged even in Western democratic countries. Earlier it had been accepted dogma that minority dissatisfaction could be effectively ameliorated through economic, political, and cultural means. However, growing ethno-regional challenges have caused stress in countries like Belgium, France, Spain, and Canada. An ethnic renaissance has led to demands, and sometimes militant action, for internal autonomy (Catalans in Spain, Scots in the United Kingdom) and even for political separatism (French Quebecois in Canada, Basques in Spain).[21] The persistence of minority nationalisms in the West, following centuries of state consolidation, should heighten our sensitivity to their vital presence in Mideastern states, which are much more recent political creations. Myron Weiner succinctly formulated the dilemma when he questioned "whether the ideal of unity and diversity, that is, political unity and cultural diversity, can be the foundation for modern states."[22]

History records important examples where peoples refused to submit to minority status as a permanent condition. The Muslims in India before 1947 and the Jews in Palestine before 1948 came to feel that their collective aspirations would be choked by a competing people that had majority predominance. This feeling, activated for Ibos in Nigeria in the 1960s and Tamils in Sri Lanka in the 1980s, is grounded in the conviction that the state cannot make the majority and the minority into one nation. The attempt to homogenize a pluralistic population may be brutal and markedly lack the political grace associated with the otherwise high ideal of matching the people with the territory in a delicate surgical operation. The goal of the nation-state is an ideal whose potentially requisite methodology is shrouded in darkness.

The dichotomy between state and nation poses profound anomalies as things stand in the Middle East. The Kurd as an ethnic identity is immeasurably more historically rooted than the Iraqi as a state or national identity. Yet the Kurd is an Iraqi, indeed a "Kurdish Iraqi," but that territorially accurate definition is much less politically meaningful for the Kurd than for a Sunni Arab citizen of Iraq. In the same way, an "Armenian Turk" would be a straightforward legal identity, but it is void of political authenticity. The same is true in the case of "Arab Israelis," whose formal citizenship is incompatible with the state's ethos, lacking the national significance that exists for the Jewish citizen of Israel. We shall later examine the Middle East state system as presently constituted to determine whether the incongruence between states and nations is a blessing or a curse.

Minorities in the Middle East

Although the use of the term *minority* indicates a quantitative inferiority alone, our investigation will probe the situation of only certain peoples, those with requisite qualitative traits as well. These peoples stand in juxtaposition to the predominant powerholders in the Mideast region: Sunni Arabs in the core zone; Sunni Turks, Pakistani Punjabi Sunnis, and Shiite Persians in Iran.

The Sunni Muslim community in particular, beyond its overwhelming majority status, is enthralled historically with a feeling of its natural or divinely granted right to rule alien populations. Mastery and hegemony characterize its collective consciousness toward weaker, smaller communities.[23] Yet such communities have persisted notwithstanding their chronic vulnerability, and the following list of traits underlies their long-term viability. While no single brief formula may be adequate to define minority peoplehood, the specific minorities to be surveyed enjoy the requisite qualitative, not just quantitative, features that make their examination an appropriate endeavor.

Essential Elements

Ethnicity

The foundation of separate peoplehood is rooted in kinship and clannishness that provide for endogamous patterns of marriage and family identity. Inbreeding within a more or less closed bloodline provides a fundamental division between those who are part of the same biological tree and those who are external to it. Without particular ethnic autonomy it becomes all but impossible to speak of separate peoplehood. Its opposite is exogamy, to the inevitable stage of assimilation within a larger absorptive community. All of the minorities to be examined maintained kinship independence from dominant Sunni Arab, Sunni Turk, Sunni (Punjabi) Pakistani, and Shiite Persian communities. As such, these minorities can in principle be defined as not belonging to the dominant peoples across the region.

Culture

Each distinct ethnic stock will undoubtedly be known by its specific collective character. Its individuality is a cherished collective product, a native identity, earthy and glowing with the authenticity of uniqueness. The aspects of culture are many in principle, and each minority retains its own mix of attributes. There is the vital mark of language, for example, as the minority maintains its own differentiated linguistic universe. It is a source of collective pride and helps define the national personality.

Indeed, speaking the alien and majority tongue is self-abusive and a step toward a loss of identity. Karl Deutsch emphasized the growth of languages in European history as a measure of national articulation.[24] The romantic touch of old languages and their utilitarian role in demarcating a community's distinctiveness is operative in the Middle East for

Kurds, Baluch, Berbers, Armenians, Assyrians, and Jews. In other cases, linguistic assimilation can symbolize a decrease of cultural particularity.

In addition to language is the role of religion. While Islam assumed hegemonic status across the entire Middle East, various communities either maintained or developed a separate or distinguishable religious life. This is true for Jews, Christian peoples including Egyptian Copts, Armenians, Assyrians or Nestorians, Lebanese Maronites, and southern Sudanese. As well, religious particularity characterizes the semi–Muslim sects or heretical offshoots, specifically the Druzes and the 'Alawites. To the degree that religion remains a core aspect of regional culture, these minorities will continue to enjoy a high degree of collective specificity.

Geography

The factor of territoriality in the case of minorities provides a relatively sharp delimitation in human settlement patterns. Such peoples have generally lived on the geographic periphery of the political entities within which they reside. Their hinterland stands juxtaposed to the core center of the country.[25] As such, the very choice of distant geographic locales may result from a long alienation from the dominant majority in the country. Moreover, the distant locale may serve as appropriate military terrain for minority warfare against the ruling power. Mountain regions in particular are the territorial hearth for almost all Mideast minorities. In fact, even the largely Islamized mountain areas of the Arab world remain, as Manfred Wenner noted, in the hands of non–Arab peoples like Berbers, Kurds, Druzes, and 'Alawites.[26] The role of geography thus provides an important spatial criterion for Mideastern minorities who maintained distance from the dominant Sunni Arab forces in particular. The relative inaccessibility of minority territory will naturally strengthen their potential viability over time. Frontier zones may be foreboding for the enemy but home for the native population.

History

The sense of a common past, composed of the glory to celebrate and the grief to commemorate, is at the core of separate peoplehood. In recollecting the historical record, a people enjoins its members in educating their children to store up the collective memories and carry them on to the next generation. In this fashion the people strengthens the conviction of a shared fate. More recent items in its collective experience thereby become part of the fund of continuous national self-crystallization. Mideastern minorities, almost all of whom chronologically precede the birth of Islam, have a wealth of famous heroes and sacred dates, memorable places and unforgettable events, that fill the historical catalog in many volumes. An oral tradition may preserve the history; some peoples record it in written form. The general continuity of their living patterns — in ethnic, cultural, and geographic terms — gives historical depth to the minorities' collective existence.

Energizing Elements

Back in 1837, Lord Durham claimed that French Canadians have "no history and no literature." In the same century, Metternich, highly suspicious of nationalism, derided Italy as only "a geographical expression." In 1936, Ferhat Abbas, leader of Algerian Muslims, stated that there was no Algerian nation.[27] Meanwhile, as we well know, the French Canadians consolidated a distinct nationalist sentiment and even stood, or so it seemed in the 1970s, on the verge of independence in the Quebec homeland. Italy became a nation-state, not just a piece of geography. Ferhat Abbas went on to become the prime minister of the Algerian provisional government in 1958, and Algeria became a state in 1962. In these cases and many others, the past was not a sure guide to the future.

Beyond the essential elements that define separate peoplehood, there are energizing elements that arouse a national awakening in a previously nonexistent or dormant community. From this perspective, the process of collective group fermentation can suggest the newness of peoplehood and seem sterile historically, without roots in the distant past. But we should concede that even the more mature and older national communities also had their beginnings at certain points in time. Here we shall illustrate different sets of circumstances that may catalyze a national "takeoff stage" in a somewhat revolutionary manner.

Social Change and Mobilization

The formation of a new social grid composed of people from different classes and occupations, settling in an urban environment and engaging in new and intensive communication systems, is a general constellation for ethnic mobilization. By contrast, the drowsiness of rural life is without a high degree of human interaction and lacks the required context for generating new aspirations or social institutions. The countryside is a static field and is unsuitable for energetic and vast enterprises. But the city and its urban vitality is the space for binding people to imaginative and liberating projects.[28] Their ethnic consciousness may surge forward, modernity assisting nationalism and not blocking its development. Social communication in towns and cities, and newly consummated economic relations among larger numbers of people, will generate common norms and symbols. Formerly estranged individuals will discover shared links as a people moves to articulate its new birth.[29]

In this social scenario, progress is abounding, and nationalism is not far behind. Both Rupert Emerson and Stein Rokkan concluded that educational and economic advance will contribute to, and be a veritable condition for, nationalist movements and their new political aspirations.[30] In this environment of deep changes in social patterns and personal attitudes, new leaders will be the spokespeople and organizers of a new sentiment. Through this process a community will sense new-found self-assuredness and seek to translate it into national power. We shall later discover whether such changes occurred in the history of Middle Eastern minorities.

Repression and Conflict

In contrast to the above explanation, an experience of common despair can catalyze nationalist consolidation in the face of shared enemies or irresolvable problems. The notion of the "internal colony" refers to a deprived economic zone whose population is dismally abandoned by a central government or whose resources are unjustifiably exploited by it.[31] Ted Robert Gurr developed the category of *relative deprivation* to indicate the gap between human expectations and material achievements, arguing that frustrated peoples in such a situation inevitably use violence to signify their break with passivity.[32] Discontent rather than ideology accounts for ethnic mobilization and a nationalist struggle. Indeed, the successful secession of Bangladesh from Pakistan in 1971 was based in part on this circumstance. Likewise, the Ibo military campaign against Nigeria from 1967 to 1970 drew upon a bitter conflict with the Yoruba, interlaced with persecution and pogroms in the 1950s and 1960s.[33] In such circumstances, the collective identity of a people sharpens considerably, though this cannot in itself guarantee political or military success. It can, however, demonstrate a heightened collective determination to take up the fight. This phenomenon too will be examined in our Middle East case studies.

Foreign Assistance

External intervention on the side of a weak community or at its behest may provide the necessary catalyzing input to generate a national movement. While the foreign power may have other than altruistic motives, the positive impact for mobilizing latent energies remains the important issue. France supported the American Revolution against the British Crown, and Egypt supported Algeria's independence war against France, even though in both cases the indigenous struggle had its own political roots and revolutionary momentum distinct from external support. Yet there may be peoples whose decision to campaign may be stillborn. We shall search in the Middle East for the external variable in the nationalist mix. For Zionism and Armenian nationalism, foreign support was not irrelevant in the decision to seek political autonomy. In these and other instances, foreign assistance can inoculate a dormant national dream with the impetus for collective struggle.

Concluding Remarks

Peoples can raise their level of collective existence along the route toward statehood in a dynamic process of self-articulation. It is true that certain societies have little capacity for full statehood because the reality of rule and coercion is alien to their needs or sensitivities. A society can function without also being a state; it may erect a governmental apparatus for transitory or partial purposes, far below the level of formal political sovereignty.[34] But whether or not statehood is the desired goal, a national minority can decidedly be transformed into a relatively more cohesive and politically conscious community. In order to illustrate this development whereby an ethnic group becomes a nationality graphically, let us visualize the dynamic movement advancing as follows: tribe — ethnic community — cultural group — society — community — people — nationality — nation-state. No claim is offered for conceptual exactitude; rather the trend alone is captured in this process called "the growth of nations" by Karl Deutsch. The terminology serves to project the direction of collective self-articulation. This will be helpful in our attempt to gauge the position of various Mideastern minorities in terms of their collective self-articulation, both in the more distant past and during the twentieth century.

At this juncture it is appropriate and possible to identify the specific minorities that will elicit our attention. They all possess the four essential elements noted earlier: ethnicity, culture, geography, and history. The impact of the three energizing elements — social changes, conflict situations, and foreign involvement — is uneven in the various minorities' experience but apparent as a subsidiary factor in particular cases. Of specific importance is that the chosen minorities all maintained a collective vitality into this century. In the language of Ibn Khaldun, they demonstrated the cohesive kinship determination implied by the term *asabiyya,* and many of them in fact expressed the spirit of national movements following the First World War. This development assumed political and/or military forms as many Mideastern minorities advanced claims for autonomy or independence. The decade of the 1920s was in particular racked with minority militancy in some cases, political progress in others, even national recognition in certain instances. Likewise, minority tenacity was exhibited in different forms during the 1970s and 1980s, some in fiery resurgence, some as historical embers burning on a low flame.

We shall analyze five non–Arab Muslim and heterodox Muslim communities, five Christian communities, and the Jewish people. The first group includes Kurds, Berbers, Baluch, Druzes, and 'Alawites. The second group includes Copts, Armenians, Assyrians, Maronites, and the Christian population in Sudan. Altogether we have posited ten minority communities in the region, in addition to another historic minority people, the Jews, who became a majority with the founding of the state of Israel. Our list does not include very small groups like Bahais, Yezidis, or Circassians who have been marginal from the broad perspective of Middle Eastern history. In particular, none have generated anything resembling coherent national aspirations. Christian denominations with no common geographic base or national aspirations, for example, the Greek Orthodox sect, are also excluded from this review. We shall also ignore Bedouins who lack any organizational solidity above the tribe and display no rootedness in any specific territorial sense. The Shiites remain beyond our ken since they have no particular ethnic dimension or single geographic heartland. Also, they are hardly a minority, being a predominant majority in Iran and a slight majority in Iraq and Bahrain.

The Palestinian Arabs are a particular case, a minority within Israel, Lebanon, and Kuwait but a majority in Jordan and part of the Arab Nation throughout the region. They are an integral element in the Sunni Arab community, illustrative of which is the PLO declaration in Article 14 of its Covenant that "the destiny of the Arab nation, and indeed Arab existence itself, depends upon the destiny of the Palestine cause." It is reasonable, therefore, that the Arab nation should support the Palestinian campaign against Zionism and Israel, as in fact it does. In the political dialectic of Palestinian relations with the wider Arab world, the Arabs assist the PLO, and then the PLO participates in pan–Arab efforts. One of them is the task of whittling away at Maronite Christian power in Lebanon. Another is the PLO role of providing the rhetoric of national self-determination to legitimize ideologically the Arab Nation's campaign against Israel. Rather than being a pitiful and poor minority, the PLO vanguard of the Palestinians enjoys global support and international coverage. The annual Saudi Arabian financial contribution of at least $70 million to the PLO was indicative of the latter's leverage in the Middle East. In 1983, the Malaysian Islamic Youth Movement gave the PLO a check for $80,000, not the usual good fortune in the lives of typical regional minority peoples.[35]

Palestinian identity is most definitely, as Crawford Young pointed out, "a novel phenomenon."[36] The very idea of a separate country called Palestine was never politically salient in Arab history. Ibn Khaldun, writing in the fourteenth century, considered "Palestine in Syria" to reflect the true state of affairs. Arnold Toynbee, writing in the twentieth century, felt it appropriate to refer to "the Syro-Palestinian people" as a known national quantity, leaving a distinct Palestinian people nowhere to be found.[37] The Arabs of historic Palestine (i.e., the land of Israel, or Eretz-Israel) never developed national particularity. Lacking tight ethnic ties, bearing no cultural individuality or religious different-ness, without territorial rootedness or any national history, the com-munity known today as Palestinians does not fit the criteria of the Mideastern minorities under examination here.

The apparent reason why it nonetheless became widespread to consider the Palestinians a national minority is that their activities re-sound with a powerful echo in the region and the world. But that echo resounded in response to certain factors, the likes of which we earlier defined as *energizing elements*. True, various social changes, situations of conflict, and foreign assistance affected various dimensions in Pale-stinian Arab life. These developments engendered a hypnotic impres-sion that the Palestinians were indeed an old integrated national com-munity. But all the while a more profound reality predominated. The basic *essential elements* in true Mideastern minority communities — based in ethnicity, culture, geography, and history — were not apparent to demarcate Palestinian particularity in any authentic sense. Things may change in the future, but the facts of the past are unalterable.

The Debate about Minorities

Few writers and researchers on Mideastern minorities have been able or willing to contend with this subject in an attitude of emotional distance and intellectual objectivity. The potential political significance of minority groups, in terms of national rights and human suffering or state stability and external intervention, has made problematic a detached search for enlightenment. One exception is R. D. McLaurin, whose essay served to highlight the political role of minorities in the region, their power position in Lebanon and Syria, and the persistent vitality of ethnonationalism generally.[38] In his case, description re-placed propaganda, analysis ruled, and advocacy was abandoned. But in most cases a sharp division separates those who see the minorities as divisive and militant and others whose eyes perceive their pitiful condi-tion and unrecognized claims.

Arnold Toynbee provided a stark statement of utter opposition to minorities when he perceived Jews, Druzes, Maronites, and 'Alawites as mere "fossils of ancient faiths."[39] This was not a pure historical judg-ment but an expression of highbrow pompous hostility. With careful consistency, Toynbee defined minorities with negative stereotypes: Berbers were "primitive barbarians." 'Alawites were nothing but "wild highlanders." And the Baluch were stamped with the mark of "savagery."[40] By contrast, the Sunni Arabs were the epitome of civilization and culture, yet the unfortunate targets of vicious Western aggression in the Mideast homeland.

Others have been more politic in their choice of language though no less harsh in their attitude. Majority-minority controversies and conflicts have provided an opportunity to castigate the smaller peoples and justify the Sunni-Muslim hegemonic rulers. William L. Langer blamed Armenian revolutionaries explicitly for the Turkish massacre of their brethren in the 1890s. For him, the vicious reprisals, resulting in hundreds of thousands of Armenian dead, were due wholly to agitators whose strategy was doomed to failure.[41] In no way is Turkish atrocity isolated as an independent factor in the terrible chain of events. H. A. R. Gibb was not averse to portraying the Arab massacre of Assyrians in the 1930s as due to the obstinacy of the victims.[42] A. H. Hourani was less circumspect in his narrative on the region's minorities when he initially blamed the problem on "sectarian loyalties." In order to avoid any doubt whatsoever, he went on to conclude that minorities must assimilate into the Arab nation by cultivating a genuine Arab feeling just like the Sunni Muslims'. Anything less than that was, for Hourani, to retain a "persecution-mania," which is indeed "a cause no less than a result of persecution."[43] The victim had become the reason for his own vulnerability, and aggression had been vindicated. As for the minorities, they must "modify the abnormal state of mind into which they have been thrown" and learn Arabic in order to constitute a single community with the majority population. Being different is sinful in this monolithic view of the Middle East.

There is therefore very little room for minority maneuverability. With guilt branded on their foreheads and barbarism reeking from their hands, the minorities' penchant for ethnic dissension must be repressed. When realized, the benefit will accrue to the majority Sunnis. Edward Said was unrestrained in turning history on its head when he decreed that "militant minorities in the Near East have almost always been aggressors."[44] This definitive judgment could serve as a veritable call to war — a war of defense no less — for the majority whose fate is now threatened by aggressive minorities.

An alternative and positive image of Mideastern minorities is a salutary balance to the partisanship that favors the powerful Sunni majority. Riffian tribesmen, part of the wider Berber community, were praised for their "extreme bravery" by Carleton Coon.[45] The Kurds were considered to possess "the national and social characteristics that entitle a people to statehood," according to Moshe Zeltzer.[46] In these descriptions minorities are portrayed in vivid colors, with sympathy, or minimally with respect.

The perception of minority pain and majority oppression characterizes the work of various authors. Pierre Rondot, while hoping for rapprochement between the two sides, did not refrain from pointing to Kurdish and Assyrian suffering.[47] Gil Carl AlRoy discussed the suppression of minorities, including the black population in the southern Sudan.[48] The absolutist idea and trenchant policy of imposing a monolithic reality on the Middle East, over and against its inherent pluralism, was rejected by some observers. Eliezer Be'eri recognized the aggressive and destructive potential burning within "Arab-Islamic-Sunni-urban domination" throughout the Middle East. Repressive Arab nationalism, he believed, would be unacceptable and rejected by Druzes, 'Alawites, Kurds, Israelis, Lebanese Christians, and others. Be'eri concluded his work by expressing a hope for cooperation among all regional peoples, but a hope, judging by his own analysis, lacking much foundation.[49]

But beyond the moral question of responsibility the real problem of majority-minority tension hangs as an albatross in the search for stability and peace in Middle Eastern countries. Examining this from a practical point of view is a political question of the utmost regional importance.

Principles and Means of Conflict Resolution

Two traditional historical approaches and two utilitarian modern ones will be primarily identified as modes of resolution in majority-minority or interethnic conflicts. The Middle East may consider more native solutions that reflect the indigenous cultural forms of the region, or it may seek to apply foreign techniques deriving from Western political experience. In either case, the failure to succeed in the effort at conflict resolution portends bitter struggles. Repression or secession will conceivably await the moment of such failures.

Arabism

With a sweeping generality, D. G. Hogarth, a World War I British diplomatic officer in Cairo, conferred upon the Arabs the title of being "among the great assimilating races of history."[50] Peoples with no Arabian blood in their veins had over the centuries been absorbed into the expansive Arab nation, learning its language, living its culture, marrying with its sons and daughters. In fact this process of intercommunal convergence appeared so thorough that non–Arabs came to lose their past or other identity completely. As far as Michael Hudson was concerned, Jews were no more than "non–Muslim Arabs," making them Arabs of the "Mosaic persuasion" in the Middle East.[51] In a particular instance of smothering any non–Arab identity, Abdel-Rahim Omran turned Maimonides, the great Jewish legal codifier and sage, into an Arab scholar called Musa Ibn Maimun. Now Maimonides, stripped of his particular Jewish vocations and made to pass as just a physician and a philosopher, was recast into a type convenient for this Arab rewriting of history.[52]

The assimilating capacity of Arabism partially became a minority choice in the context of the modern Arab nationalist movement. Some Christians, fearing political marginality and charges of alien loyalties, decided to identify with Islam and thereby authenticate their Arab identity. K. I. Qubrusi, a Christian, actually called on Arab Christians to become Muslims because Islam is an Arab religion whereas Christianity is a foreign one.[53] Less pejorative was the contention that many minorities, like Kurds, Berbers, and Copts, had joined "the Arab entity" and thereby prevented any "sectional differences" in the region.[54]

Yet the notion that cultural and political reasons had compelled many non–Arab Muslims to integrate with or assimilate into the majority community was not seen as wholly positive by everyone. One interesting critique of this phenomenon came from Sa'id Al-Din Ibrahim, who argued that the modern Arab national idea *(Qawmiyya)* had ignored the ethnic pluralism of the area. By consequence, he explained the failure of the national idea to become a practical political reality. Buoyed by a romantic flight toward a monolithic Arab nationalism, the theoretical underpinnings of this idea were unrelated to the realities of the social and ethnic regional map.[55] The compelling power of assimilation could go only so far in overcoming majority-minority tensions and indeed served as the cause of such tensions. The demand for Arab unity could easily become a repressive measure based on historical impulses now turned into institutional mechanisms within the modern Arab states. The idea that "a Kurd who lives in an Arab country becomes an Arab" may be an enticing prescription for equality and integration, but it also threatens to eliminate smaller cultural communities by fully enveloping them in the Arab fold. The virtue of openness becomes the vice of oppression.

Islam

The normative structure of relations between Muslims and non–Muslims is founded on the primacy of Islam over any other religious community, including the Jews and the Christians. Based on the *dhimmi* pact attributed to the period of Caliph Umar in early Islamic

history, non–Muslims were classified as subordinate to Muslims, defined as tolerated religious peoples who had the compensating fortune
to be "peoples of the book," *ahl al-kitab.* The bond of *dhimma* provided
for Jewish and Christian protection and security, religious autonomy,
and local cultural independence.[56] In the formative circumstances of a
new universal and revolutionary religious community, the Muslims
aspired to imprint their stamp on the world at the same time that they
were willing to tolerate older religious forces. Islamic decency extended that far but not further.

Both the law and spirit of Islam established *dhimmi* inferiority as
the logical counterpart to Muslim superiority. Coexistence was not to
be of mutual gratification to the two sides. Jews and Christians were
obligated to pay a poll tax, the *jizya,* as financial tribute in submission
and disgrace. The Koran had itself decreed that the *dhimmis* must be
humiliated as a sign of their stubborn rejection of Muhammad's revela-
tion, and the ceremonial payment of the *jizya* provided the opportunity
to strike the *dhimmi,* demean him in public, and impoverish him as
well.[57] The historical record is full of instances of Islam's abusing Jews
who came to pay the poll tax.[58] Tolerance of minority existence did not
include respect for their human dignity. Islam limited *dhimmi* freedom
in such matters as the clothes they could wear, the places they could
live, the animals upon which they could ride. The Muslim-dominated
environment in Arab countries and in Persia was saturated with ideas
of *dhimmi* inferiority and degradation, and they were the vulnerable
victims of mass abuse. Any idea of equal rights, wrote Bernard Lewis,
was a later mythical invention and never approached anything resembling historical reality.[59]

Classical Islam was rooted in the militant imperative of the holy
war *(jihad)* against the alien lands known as *Dar el-Harb* (the Abode of
War). Indeed, "only one kind of war was lawful," and it was the *jihad.*[60]
But it provided a broad, if not absolute, mandate to attack any non–Muslim territory and incorporate it into the Abode of Islam. There could
therefore never be permanent peace or true mutual recognition between Muslim and non–Muslim countries. It was only a matter of time
until Islam would mobilize anew for war in the name of Allah and his
prophet Muhammad. Yet until that time non–Muslims might enjoy a
period of relative quiet, a temporary armistice, and reflect on the
benefits of coexistence with mighty Islam.

Islam as the supreme authority offered an inegalitarian prescription for Muslim relations with non–Muslims and their joint integration
within a single political entity. The fragility and volatility of this situation existed from the seventh century on. In the nineteenth century, the
European impact on the Muslim lands extended to the realm of political
ideas and institutions. The Turkish Ottoman Empire proclaimed the

era of reforms, *Tanzimat,* and in 1839 and again in 1856 Constantinople affirmed a policy of religious liberty, physical security, fair taxation, and communal equality for non–Muslim communities within the realm.[61] The organizational idea of the *millet,* denoting autonomous religious peoples, suggested that minority groups might also play a public role in the affairs of the empire; in fact, many Jews, Armenians, and Greek Orthodox Christians were active in areas of finance, administration, industry, and diplomacy. Yet the native *dhimmi* peoples did not experience all of the positive benefits promised by the reforms, for the empire's word and deed did not fully overlap. Muslim superiority feelings balked at raising *dhimmis* to a plane of equality. While the historical origins of the *millet* system are unclear, as indeed are those pertaining to the Pact of Umar and the *dhimmi* status, the central and unambiguous fact fixes non–Muslim inferiority under the singular authority of the Muslim powers.[62]

It is more than questionable whether classic Islamic principles like *dhimmi, jihad,* and *millet* can offer a satisfactory formula for mutually accommodating relations between Muslims and the non–Muslim minorities in the Middle East. The modern era of national self-determination aspires to more freedom than merely a grant of religious autonomy. The threat of ongoing holy war is certainly a formidable obstacle to intercommunal peace. As the Muslims seek spiritual solace within Islam, they tend to political intolerance toward those of other faiths.

Moreover, even Muslims of other than Arab identity — Berbers and Kurds, for example — feel that Islamic fundamentalism is tinged with the predominant national spirit of its country of origin. In Algeria this might mean that only Arab Muslims are true representatives of the rising tide of Islam; in Iraq it could mean that Kurds are not considered legitimate purveyors of the religion, as are Arabs. Therefore, in cases of Muslim relations with non–Muslims and Arab-Muslim relations with non–Arab Muslims, or Persian Shiite relations with non–Iranian Muslim peoples, religion can serve to divide more than it can unite. The search for intercommunal harmony may require alternative nonideological answers to the quandary of conflict.

Civil Politics

The task of integration within new states calls for delegitimizing older tribal or ethnic identities to fabricate a more all-inclusive sense of collective solidarity. To the extent that the state is the structure for a coherent and single political idea, its inner stability will be firmer. In moving to realize this, the folklore of the past must be abandoned or minimally blurred in favor of the more sterile and emotionally neutral civil idea represented by the new state. Clifford Geertz argued that the maintenance of pristine "primordial loyalties" would necessarily undermine pluralistic political entities and perhaps generate demands for ethnic separatism. The answer, he believed, was to inaugurate an "integrative revolution" via a "civic politics of primordial compromise." The golden mean lay between ethnic fanaticism on the one hand and forcible centralized suppression on the other.[63] Determining that middle course (and demonstrating the requisite political ingenuity to have it draw the ideological map of a new political community) was to be a big responsibility. Perhaps inevitably, the dominant community would project its own distinctive ethos as the statewide national norm.

This notion of leveling identities, or at least cutting their rough edges, is pivotal to strategies of modernization and modernity. Industrialization, urbanization, democratization, and universal education are some of the key measures believed effective in creating common sentiments and norms for previously heterogeneous population groups. New institutional forms, such as labor unions and universities, can successfully propagate a new collective identity. Yet some have questioned whether this paradigm fits Third World countries, and for our purposes it will be vital to evaluate the vitality of older ethnic identities in the new Mideastern states.[64] Taking the tribe out of the public realm, or taking religion out of politics, would seem to strengthen the likelihood of intercommunal accommodation. In this way the minority may feel at ease with the majority.

Fouad Ajami advocated the separation of religion from politics, believing this would be conducive to national unity in Arab countries. But he felt forced by historical events to conclude that "people remain tied to old chains."[65] Those old chains, otherwise known as Islam or tribalism, were the threads that connected people to a meaningful life of spiritual symbolism and identity. The challenge to create out of citizenship and patriotism an enchanting civil religion, and to unify diverse groups in a new state, will be formidable for years to come. States tend to solidify around common and mysterious myths, and the civil polity seems hardly to offer them up to its people.

Institutional Adjustment

If politics is indeed the appropriate salvation for group aspirations, then the proper mix of power sharing may overcome domestic conflict. A new political structure, or a new pattern of dealing with old grievances based on bitter communal feuds, is suggestive of technical solutions for substantive problems. Yet this may be the most feasible alternative available under the circumstances. Arend Lijphart developed the idea of elite cooperation in situations of deep cleavages dividing groups within a state. Coalition politics at the highest governmental levels would thereby diminish the negative impact of social heterogeneity, avoid the perils of fragmentation, and unify subcultures within the overall state system.[66] Needless to say, this formula for conflict resolution necessitates a political environment that supports less than fully centralized hegemonic power structures. Open regimes may enable formerly hostile groups to learn to live together if in fact they all feel that they have a stake in the state. In democratic polities this will, or should, be the case. There the effort to integrate divided societies may work, but in nondemocratic ones the effort cannot be undertaken as plausibly. Majority rule without minority rights is a prescription for repression or rebellion.

Whether it is easier simply to grant rights to an obstreperous minority or to create new common overarching identities with it remains a hard question. It would appear abstractly true that the grant of rights is of course a more uncomplicated political operation. However, without a culture milieu for authentic coexistence, and lacking the value of compromise, the technical task of power sharing or minority rights may be a total nonstarter. If the political culture does not support conciliation, conflict regulation may never materialize. Because of this, the only or last resort may be to develop institutional instruments for conflict regulation, as any hope for emotional accommodation is not feasible.[67]

In the Middle East, governmental measures to contend with pluralism have not reaped significant success over the years. Power sharing based on federal solutions failed to last in Libya (and Ethiopia) and remains open to the future judgment of history in the United Arab Emirates. Other forms of devolving authority, as in the grant of regional autonomy, were tried in Iraq. The notion of formal confessionally based power distribution in Lebanon has been in part a working relationship, in part a matter of bitter and long intercommunal controversy and conflict. Overall, Middle Eastern Islamic political civilization has never been very congenial to dividing power in any territorial or governmental way. The absence of Western-style democracy with its softer give-and-take texture of political culture will also complicate the task. Nonetheless, we cannot rule out the possibility that institutional reforms can alleviate the incongruence between regime and society and thereby help resolve majority-minority conflicts.

Secession

The need is obvious and real for some effective principle or mode of conflict resolution in the case of minority presence in majority-based states. Ideological and institutional solutions may theoretically work;

perhaps old conflicts can be resolved by new techniques. But the memory of historical antipathy will not easily be erased. Ethnic incompatibility touches on the deepest sentiments in the lives of traditional peoples. In like manner, new states will jealously guard their sovereignty and hesitate to share power with smaller contenders. Ancient patterns of political repression, in the spirit of "oriental despotism," offer little room for compromise. Enduring deprivation by a marginal minority can easily become a veritable permanent law of history in the eyes of the weak. Religion may in these circumstances become an escapist route for collective emotional relief.

But the logic of separation remains a latent possibility in the political equation. Where state-level compromise and conciliation do not exist or do not succeed, it is worth reflecting on the conclusion arrived at by Karl Deutsch. After reviewing the record of history, he came to recognize "the very serious difficulties of different peoples to live together in a common state under the conditions of enforced closeness of contacts."[68] The implication was that separating peoples by possibly decomposing multinational states is the obvious resolution of such a political problem. Life for the minority may be unbearable and meaningless without a collective self-assertion of national rights. But across the region, aside from the successful instance of Bengali secession from Pakistan in 1971, the possibility of minority separation seems slim. We shall nonetheless consider this possibility where and if alternative solutions fail to overcome the antagonism and enmity in majority-minority conflicts.

Part I
Muslim Minorities

CHAPTER 2

Kurds: A Legacy of Struggle and Suffering

The Kurdish people, descendants of the ancient Gutis some four thousand years ago, are one of the oldest communities in Middle Eastern history and a vital part of Middle Eastern politics in our own time. Originating from Indo-European tribes, their genealogy is traced to the Medes who conquered Nineveh in the Tigris Valley in 612 B.C. Herodotus writes in the *Histories* that the Persians became the masters of the Medes, though they were once their slaves. Until today, the Kurds, modern Medians, have been contending bitterly with the Iranians, the ancient Persians. Alexander the Great, on passing through Asia, took a Kurdish woman and fathered a male offspring through her.

Situated vulnerably between strong empires, Greek-Hellenic to the west and Persian to the east, the Kurds continued to survive as a distinct national group. Their language was Aryan, related to Persian but uniquely Kurdish. Their geographic homeland covered the Zagros Range, stretching from the Tauras Mountains to the Iranian plain, or from Arabia to Georgia. A sixteenth-century Kurdish poet, Ehmedi Khani, unabashedly considered all this territory "Kurdish land," and proof lay in the Kurdish blood that filled its earth.[1] According to Merhdad Izady, the ultimate defining quality of the Kurds "has been their way of life, economically, as well as culturally and sociologically, which has kept them apart, independent of other ethnic groups surrounding them."[2] That distinction has been a valuable though costly national possession for all of a long Kurdish history.

The particular way of life, beyond a distinct language, touches on the organization and character of community affairs. Kurdish life was tribally structured from ancient times and allowed for the preservation of local tightly knit communities under a traditional leader, known as *agha* or *beg* (Turkish terms), *shaikh* or *sayid* (Arab terms). Tribal life inhibited integral Kurdish national unity yet augmented Kurdish particularism in relation to other groups.

Within the confines of a traditional culture, male predominance was axiomatic but without denying the role of the female in family and community life. Indeed, according to A. Hadi Hakki, Kurdish women have tremendous power and are visible in the social setting, unlike female members in classic Islamic life.[3] In addition to distinctive traditional clothing (baggy pants for men, the lack of veiling for women) or the famed dagger, Kurdish culture maintained its integrity throughout the centuries.

Kurdish Life under Islam

The Islamic-Arab conquest in the seventh century challenged the national integrity of the Kurds in their mountain strongholds from eastern Anatolia south to the Strait of Hormuz. Though resisting the Arabian advance and rejecting the Arabic language, the Kurds succumbed to the new religion and adopted its Sunni form (some are Shiites). However, even this enclosure within the dominant Muslim population of the era did not erase Kurdish particularity. In fact, and ironically, Kurds were in certain ways even more distinguishable after becoming an appendage of the Muslim world than before. The religious adoption of Islam was a double-edged cultural turn. On the one hand, the Kurdish Muslims developed their own distinctive dervish Sufi orders, the Qadiri in the eleventh century and the Naqshbandi in the fourteenth, and thus elevated their Islamic experience to mystical heights. Great Kurdish personalities emerged from this spiritual development in Kurdish life. But on the other hand, the Kurdish Muslims were not really considered serious orthodox members of the faith, fulfilling all its precepts according to the letter and spirit of Islam. Certainly few prestigious Islamic scholars or theologians emerged from their midst. C. J. Edmonds was himself somewhat bedeviled in the 1920s to learn from firsthand reporting in Iraq that Naqshbandis were prone to eccentricity, liked mixed bathing parties in an enthusiastic outburst of antinomianism.[4]

Indeed, orthodox Arab Islam tended to have a demeaning image of the Kurds all along. The denigration of a person was apparently facilitated and legitimated when, as in early Abbasid history from the eighth century, Abu Muslim was portrayed as of Kurdish origin, and this after his execution. It may not be fortuitous that in Turkish the word *Kurd* may mean "wolf," and in Arabic (though the etymology is not fully clear) *Kurd* may imply "monkey." What remains nonetheless explicit is that when the Islamic cleric Ibn Taimiyya in the fourteenth century wanted to identify peoples who were robbers deserving of death, he pointed an accusing finger at his fellow Muslims the Kurds.[5] An Arab saying identified Kurds as one of "the three plagues in the world."

The distinctive quality of tribal life, with power divided between the *mullah* (priest) and the *khan* (judge), did not preclude the emergence of major personalities and significant episodes that transcended narrow tribal boundaries. During the Islamic stage in Kurdish life, group autonomy based on independent principalities, or *hukumats,* was a demonstration of national determination. Surrounded in their mountain hearth between the Ottoman Empire and the Persian throne, the Kurds tried to exploit their position to the maximum. At times, in 1514–1515 for example, they fought with the Turks against the Persians, in compensation for which Kurdish autonomy was recognized by paying an annual tribute. In other moments, a few decades later, Kurdish forces fought with the Persians against their Uzbek enemies, again with the hope to salvage and entrench a modicum of Kurdish autonomy.[6] In Bitlis and Hakkiari, and elsewhere throughout Kurdistan, it was not unknown for tribal princes to mint their own money and have Friday prayers in the mosque praise their deeds and authority.

Yet it is the heroic personality of Saladin who is more than any other figure the hallmark of Kurdish glory in the people's national history. His impact is indeed national, not tribal, and glittered with the community's martial tradition as he led Muslim forces to ultimate victory against the Crusaders in Jerusalem in 1187. Born just north of Baghdad at Takrit in 1137, Saladin was more adept at organizing and uniting Islam for *jihad* than other Muslim warriors. He ruled in Egypt, Syria, parts of Mesopotamia and Arabia, but not to the satisfaction of all fellow Muslims. In the eyes of the Zangis, this caliph had the disagreeable quality of being a Kurd, upsetting Turkish primacy and turning his acclaim into Kurdish nepotic power.[7] He was the great Muslim liberator against the infidels, but perhaps even more, he was the great Kurdish king whose exploits fill the annals of Kurdish history and leave a lasting hope for national greatness again. At the same time, Saladin is held in high esteem by the Arabs.

There is, therefore, a solid basis for Kurdish national distinctiveness from ethnic, cultural, geographic, and historical sources. This people survived apart from other Mideastern peoples, but without transforming particularity and autonomy into national independence. Because of relatively disadvantageous strategic circumstances, situated between stronger powers and failing to generate a long-term political capacity for unity and self-articulation, the Kurds remained for millennia incidental to the main developments transpiring across the region. Still, Kurdish dynasties were known, even if a Kurdish nation-state was not consolidated.

The nineteenth century of nationalist fermentation and ideological mobilization coincided with, though not necessarily caused, a new spark in Kurdish life. Tribal rebellions erupted with great frequency against the Sublime Porte in 1826, 1834, 1850–1851, 1853–1855, and 1880. Likewise, revolts against Persia in the 1820s were part of a broad tapestry of Kurdish militancy against foreign rule. In 1840 a leader aspiring to unite all of the Kurdish people throughout Kurdistan and fight for national independence appeared as a hopeful savior, perhaps a Saladin in pure nationalist clothing. Bedrkhan Bey converted Yezidi Kurds to Islam and sought to bring other communities, like Assyrians and Armenians, into a common front for battle against the Ottomans. In 1884 Bedrkhan Bey was proclaimed the prince of Kurdistan. Instead of limiting goals to tribal autonomy and the preservation of the chiefs' privileges, the goal was now territorial freedom for all the inhabitants of Kurdistan. The empire was in a state of transition, interlaced with national dissension and military struggles, including opportunities for communal rights. But Istanbul, former Constantinople, withstood the challenge.

Toward Independence in Kurdistan

In the aftermath of Turkish defeat at the hands of Russia in 1877, a new leader with the same national message appeared. Sheikh Ubeidullah, based in the Hakkiari Mountains fastness, called for Kurdish unity. He wrote to the British consul that "the Kurdish nation is a people apart," having a rightful claim to independence. He formed the Kurdish League and took territory within Persian borders. But nothing lasting came of his efforts, and the Turks deported him to Mecca in 1881. His son was later to be hanged by the same Turks in 1925.[8]

Kurdish military insurrection, while basically a failure, was nonetheless complemented by other means appropriately suited to this "awakening stage" in the national struggle. The first Kurdish newspaper appeared in Cairo in 1892, and a Kurdish club opened in Constantinople in 1908, this in the turbulent days of the Turkish revolution. In 1910 a new society called Heviya Kurd (Kurdish Hope) was formed, and Kurdish intellectuals published newspapers to propagate a new national spirit. But the triumph was brief and short-lived. In spite of British and Russian aid during the rise of Ubeidullah, and in spite of Ottoman weakness prior to the First World War as the Committee for Unity and Progress took power, the Kurds still proved insufficient for the task.[9] Turkish repression and manipulation of the empire's minorities, in addition to inadequate and transitory foreign support, kept the Kurds helpless notwithstanding signs of a newly energized national sentiment.

The Middle East as a whole was ripe for a new political order following the fall of the Ottoman Empire and vigorous European intervention across the entire region. The Kurds, an old people with a new lease on life, were not indifferent to the moment. In 1919 Sherif Pasha, of the famed Baban Kurdish tribe, went to Paris to advocate his people's rights at the Versaille Peace Conference, and later at the conference at Sèvres in 1920. At the same time, Prince Sureya Bedrkhan, descendant of the 1840 Kurdish rebel, established in Cairo a Committee for the Independence of Kurdistan. These diplomatic and international efforts converged with military developments in the real arena of struggle at home. In 1918 Sheikh Mahmud took Sulaimaniya, the literary center of Kurdish national life, during the chaos that followed the Ottoman collapse. But the British set about installing a resolute regime and exiled the sheikh to India. After allowing him to return in 1922, a signal for Kurdish enthusiasm that led Mahmud to declare himself king of Kurdistan, the British a second time deported the sheikh.

The combined diplomatic and military initiatives seemed nonetheless vivid expressions of a true Kurdish national campaign for independence. The Allied powers, cognizant of President Wilson's support for small peoples' statehood and indignant over past Turkish oppression, were not averse to Kurdish aspirations. Section III of the Treaty of Sèvres, August 10, 1920, stipulated in Article 62 that a scheme of local autonomy be enforced for the predominantly Kurdish areas lying east of the Euphrates and south of Armenia. But Article 64 went even further and recognized the right of the Kurdish people to address a request to the Council of the League of Nations for independence, and this just one year later. Three qualifications, however, stood in the way of a grant of full independence: (1) The request would have "to show that a majority of the population of these areas desires independence from Turkey," this involving some level of Kurdish accommodation with non–Kurdish, including Arab and Turkomen groups. (2) The League Council would have to consider "that these peoples are capable of such independence" in a practical manner. (3) Turkey would have to accede to the grant of Kurdish statehood, beyond the fact that at Sèvres it had been compelled to "renounce all rights and title over these areas."[10]

Here nevertheless, and for the first time, was an international document recognizing Kurdish independence, encouraging a people without a state to seize the opportunity awaiting them. It is true that a history of struggle and deprivation had not elicited an overwhelmingly profound national mobilization. But there were sufficient signs of collective vitality that with foreign support, diplomatic or moral, served to suggest that a new beginning was at hand. The Kurdish minority stood on the threshold of Kurdish independence.

Turning diplomatic promise into political reality encountered

many formidable obstacles. On the international plane the Allies ignored the Kurds when in July 1923 they signed the Treaty of Lausanne
with Turkey under Ataturk, but now with no mention of the Kurds. The
fact that America did not join the League of Nations portended hard
times for some minority peoples, as Wilsonian altruism was put fatally
to rest. The British now in control of Iraq and indeed the veritable mid-
wife at its birth, proved more interested in imperial rule in the Middle
East and good relations with Turkey than in advancing the idea of Kurdish independence. The League of Nations, sympathetic from a distance,
could offer little pragmatic assistance in this game of state power
interests.

The Kurdish situation seemed to revert rapidly back to its prewar
pattern of rebellion and oppression, but with a significant difference.
New political entities based on recognized international authority,
jealous of their sovereignty and dedicated to fulfilling the majority people's goals, faced the Kurds in an aggressive mood. The idea of the
nation-state boded ill for minority peoples. In 1922 a Committee for
Kurdish Independence was organized in Erzerum, but its effective role
in Turkey is unclear. The Kurds broke out in active revolt under Sheikh
Sa'id in 1925, but he was soon captured and hanged in Diyarbekir.
Representing some one-fourth of the entire Turkish population and
located in the impregnable eastern mountain ranges, the revolt seemed
a not implausible strategy. But the Turanic ethnic impulse was at a
fever pitch and absolutely intolerant of competing, historically hostile
groups.

Diversity in the Ottoman Empire had been a mixed blessing; in republican Turkey it was considered a curse. Repression came fast and
furious, and exhibited the following traits: mass deportations and resettlement of more than 500,000 Kurds from 1925 to 1928 in central and
western Turkey beyond Kurdistan, destruction of hundreds of Kurdish
villages, prohibition to teach or speak the Kurdish language or even
wear the community's traditional garb.[11] Turkey's purpose targeted on
the utter dissolution of traditional Kurdish society through detribaliza-
tion and assuring total material impoverishment. The government refused to build schools and hospitals or to industrialize the economy for
the creation of new job opportunities.[12] In the throes of the 1920s'
revolt, and based also on a congress held in Paris, Kurds in Lebanon
established the Kurdish National League, *Hoyboun*. In Turkey they
raised the Kurdish flag at Ararat in the Van region and pursued the
struggle for national redemption in the face of a brutal and indomitable
foe.

To the south in Iraq, the decade offered little solace or hope for the
future. The very establishment of the Arab state in 1921 under King
Faisal, a Hijazi import with British certification, offended the nationalist

sensibilities of the native Kurdish population (and the religious sensibilities of the majority Shiites). In March 1923, with rebellion still simmering in Kurdistan, the British used the RAF to strafe villages. Under local and international circumstances existing after the Lausanne Treaty, the most that Kurds could expect to achieve in Iraq was a semi-autonomous administration, staffed by Kurds and speaking Kurdish, in Kurdish-inhabited areas in the northeastern parts of the country. This was much less than independence, and its implementation would ultimately depend on the goodwill of the Arab rulers in Baghdad.

With the termination of the Mosul controversy in Iraq's favor, this by the League of Nation's decision in 1925, the die had been cast. In 1932 Iraq became an independent Arab state with a minority Kurdish population. The League Mandates Commission conveyed the impression that respect for minority rights was guaranteed, but history would show that this was untrue.[13] In the early 1930s the Barzani brothers, Ahmad and Mustafa, led their tribe in clashes with government forces.[14] In typical Kurdish fashion, freedom *from* alien authority was at least as sacred a goal as independence *for* the people — the two being associated in practice though different in principle — especially since Kurdish independence was now removed from the political agenda.

In neighboring Iran, Kurdish chances were no brighter than elsewhere. Ismail Agha Simko of the Shikak tribe carried out insurrectionist activities against Persian forces as the Kurds apparently received some encouragement from Turkey and perhaps some aid from Russia.[15] It was to no avail, and Simko was captured in 1926 and assassinated in 1930.

The poignant lesson of the post–World War I period cast a dark gloom on the Kurds in contrast to the exciting hopes associated with the founding of new Middle Eastern states. Turkey, Iraq, and Iran all arose to concretize national ambitions of majority peoples, caring little for the impact on minority communities resident within their borders. Instead of release from political oblivion, the Kurds again faced repression and human suffering. The optimism earlier generated in Paris and Sèvres, or through the *Hoyboun* initiative in Lebanon, created but a faint echo in Kurdistan itself. Particularly irking was the division of the people, primarily among three states — Turkey, Iraq, and Iran — and their painful dispersion from Syria to the Soviet Union. When Baqr Sidqi, a Kurd, carried out a military coup against the Sherifian regime in Baghdad in 1936, he initiated an old-new norm in Mideastern political life. The Arabs followed suit in Iraq and in many other countries to install the army above the politicians. But the case of Baqr Sidqi contributed nothing to Kurdish aspirations.

The Mahabad Episode

And yet the winds of history blew forth new gusts of national resurgence in subsequent years for the Kurdish people. In August 1944 Kurdish unity was resolutely affirmed as representatives from Iran, Iraq, and Turkey met at Mount Dalanpar in a moment of national coordination. In 1945 the former Komala grouping was re-organized and renamed the Kurdish Democratic party (KDP) at Mahabad in Iran, with Qazi Mohammed its leader. A year later, its Iraqi branch was declared, under the leadership of Ibrahim Ahmed.

By far the most significant development in these years was the Mahabad Republic, a Soviet-supported government west of Lake Urmia (Raziya), set up in December 1945 and surviving until December 1946.[16] While Mahabad as a Kurdish center lacked the literary halo of Sulaimaniya in Iraq or the historical depth of Diyarbekir in Turkey, its location in northwestern Iran was of strategic value. Iran itself had been denied full sovereignty by the intervention of Britain and the Soviet Union in 1941, this leaving a partial vacuum that the Kurds, assisted by foreign communism, could beneficially exploit.

A Kurdish government under Qazi was formed, the flag was raised, and an army under Mustafa Barzani took to the field. Kurds from across the entire region gazed with hopeful disbelief on the Mahabad Republic. Perhaps the post–Second World War era would at last provide the political victory denied the Kurds after the First World War.

Yet fundamental weaknesses and chance developments combined to turn the republic into a fleeting experiment. Few Kurdish tribes actually rallied to Mahabad's defense, some because of the smell of atheistic and communistic Soviet involvement, some because of traditional divisions that inhibited full national cohesion for a common cause. At the same time, the departure of the Red Army from Iran in March 1946 and a bad economic slump further shortened the republic's political longevity. In December, the Iranian Army entered Mahabad. Qazi was imprisoned and hanged the following March, and Barzani fled back into Iraq—the beginning of a longer trek that brought him and his followers to the Soviet Union for an extended exile that lasted until 1958. The Mahabad Republic from 1945 to 1946 was nonetheless the most concrete realization of Kurdish independence in modern times. Its brevity was matched by its artificial quality, born in foreign circumstances and lacking the fully native national mobilization required for magnifying the possibility of lasting success.

Liberation as Rebellion

Thereafter, the overall Kurdish condition throughout the Middle East assumed its typical forms of cultural repression, economic impoverishment, and political powerlessness. Military skirmishes mounted against the Shah of Iran in the 1950s brought no gains. Kemalist terror and arrests aborted the efforts of the Socialist Party of Turkey (TSEKP) that was to expound the Kurdish struggle. The teaching of Turkish in Kurdish areas, among the "mountain Turks" as the Kurds were called, exemplified Ankara's linguistic coercion as part of a broad campaign of oppression.

Kurdistan, in eastern Turkey, was a classic "internal colony": Raw materials were extracted and exported, while rural poverty and underdevelopment persisted as government policy. In Syria, Husni al-Zaim, of Kurdish ancestry, elicited a new hope for his people, but his Damascene rule beginning from 1949 was of short duration and discredited in the name of Arab and Islamic principle as a "Kurdo military republic."[17]

The role of Kurds in Syrian power positions during the subsequent Shishakli period was also a fleeting interlude. In the late 1950s, Arabization of the eastern Jezira area was characterized by denial of Kurdish rights and eviction to other parts of the country. The fact that Khalid Baqdash, a Kurd, headed the Syrian Communist party was also of marginal consequence for his traditional community. Pro–Soviet sympathies no doubt spread among the Kurds because of Baqdash's efforts. In Lebanon, slum living became the norm for the Kurdish poor. For the Soviets, the Kurds were a political card to be played in manipulating affairs and exploiting opportunities in the Muslim world to the south. In Iraq, however, the clock struck for a new round of efforts to transcend the Kurds' inferior minority condition in history, efforts that signified a period of military struggle unceasing ever since.

The July 1958 revolution in Baghdad constituted a new era in modern Iraqi history and a new opportunity for Kurdish collective self-fulfillment. The provisional constitution declared that Arabs and Kurds were "partners," the latter composing about 15–20 percent of the total population, approximately 2 million Kurds out of some 10 million Iraq inhabitants. In October Mustafa Barzani, dubbed the Red Mullah, returned from his exile in the Soviet Union. In March 1959 his Kurdish forces loyally fought with the Qassem regime against the Nasserite threat expressed in the al-Shawwaf rebellion. Kurdish pride soared as a consequence of these developments.

Soviet aid for furthering national aspirations seemed available when the Kurd-Arab honeymoon quickly soured. In 1961 the Kurdish rebellion began as the goal of autonomy interchanged with that of self-determination in a never-ending controversy whether the Kurds wanted collective freedom within Iraq or separate from it.

By 1963, Kurdish guerrilla forces under Barzani, spurred on by tribal solidarity in their mountain homeland, carved out a "liberation zone" in northeastern Iraq that ran from Zakho in the north to Halabja in the east. The hills and rural highlands were in Kurdish hands, the villages and towns often under Iraqi control. This typical guerrilla format indicated the native strength of the Kurdish struggle. Its *pesh merga* warriors ("those who face death") numbered some 20,000 regular troops and 40,000 reservists. They were outfitted with small arms, contending against a conventional Iraqi military force. By mid–1963, the rebellion seemed to simmer out. While Barzani's tribal forces continued to attack enemy camps, kidnap officials, and skirmish with anti–Barzani tribes, the Iraqi army penetrated deeper into Kurdish territory. In June, Koisanjak was taken, and bombings of Kurdish targets, like the one against Sulaimaniya where 280 civilians were killed, became harsher.[18] In July the Soviets actually charged that Iraq sought the "physical elimination of the Kurdish minority."[19] During 1963, two coups d'état complicated Iraq's war against the Kurds, but the government was determined throughout to stem the internal threat by the best methods it had available — cultural suppression and physical repression.

The final coming to power of the Ba'th party in 1968 raised the possibility of a peaceful resolution of the Kurdish question in Iraq. Its primary theoretician, Michel Aflaq, had understood that ethnic minorities fear Arab nationalism (he was a member of the Greek Orthodox minority), and therefore the party's program of socialism and equality could reasonably provide a basis for integrating the Kurds into the fabric of a new Iraqi society under Ba'thist leadership. In March 1970, in fact, the Ba'thist regime presented the basis of a settlement grounded in Kurdish autonomy. The accord would recognize Kurdish as an official language in Kurdistan, both in education and local administration; provide for economic development; appoint a Kurdish vice president in Baghdad; and proclaim the country as the homeland of two peoples in which each enjoyed national rights. Celebrations swept through Kurdistan, but the joy proved premature. The immediate aftermath following the military cease-fire and the published political program was filled with the acrimony of mutual distrust and the charge of broken promises. "Don't trust the enemy's smile" is a popular Kurdish proverb. When the date for implementing the accord arrived in 1974, Barzani chose to reject it and took up the fight in full force.

Kurdish grievances were numerous and serious, covering the broken letter of the accord and its inner spirit. A policy of Arabization, evicting Kurds to the South and settling Arabs in the North, signaled

Iraq's determination to depopulate Kurdistan of its native, historical inhabitants. Low budgetary expenditures to rehabilitate the region indicated bad faith. At the same time, at least two assassination attempts in 1971 and 1972 against Mustafa Barzani, the leader and symbol of the struggle, demonstrated the methodical conviction of Baghdad that the Kurdish rebellion had to be contained and destroyed by any means. Barzani was adamant that Kirkuk, the city and the region, rich in Kurdish history and oil resources, be included in the autonomous region. The Iraqis rejected this demand outright and refrained from implementing major provisions of the 1970 accord.[20]

Barzani's rejection of the accord in 1974 was based not only on Iraqi perfidy but on a hope that the moment of Kurdish victory had arrived and that therefore any partial political settlement would suffocate the national élan that promised full success. Iranian support, in evidence through the 1960s by the provision of military supplies, girded Kurdish loins. Contacts with Israel led to advice in organizing intelligence operations and guerrilla tactics. More symbolically significant perhaps was American aid, in the form of $16 million and Soviet- and Chinese-made weapons, delivered via Iran in 1972. Weakening the Ba'thist regime that had signed a treaty of friendship and cooperation with the Soviet Union led certain U.S. officials to see the Kurds as a positive element in the wider superpower competition in the Middle East.

But Secretary of State Kissinger intervened in 1973–74 and prevented further American assistance to the Kurds, though Barzani continued to hope that this policy change would be overturned in Washington.[21] Barzani offered to turn the Kirkuk oil fields over to Western operation and have his fighting people act as a bulwark against Soviet expansion southward into Iraq and toward the Persian Gulf. The idea of an American-Kurdish alliance, rejected in the 1970s, would faintly revive in the 1980s when building up the Kurds would, along with other factors, guarantee that "Iraq and Iran are kept stewing in their own perverse juices," as one observer commented.[22]

The Kurdish rebellion, born in frustration and optimism, ran a bitter and brief course from March 1974 until March 1975. A de facto Kurdish protostate in northern Iraq all but dissolved because of Ba'thist determination and foreign abandonment. The Iraqi Army bombed Qala Diza on April 24, killing 131 civilians and wounding more than 300. Four days later, 42 civilians were killed at Halabja and more than 100 wounded. The army penetrated Kurdish-controlled terrain, pounding hard with Soviet-manufactured missiles, tanks, and bombers. Barzani's troops were still capable of harassing Iraqi forces and maintained a thin strip of territory along the northeastern Iraqi frontier, but the price in human life and material damage was heavy and rising.[23] Tribal divisions partially disappeared as the national Kurdish struggle doggedly per-

sisted. However, an unexpected foreign development cut the fight
short.

On March 6, 1975, the Algiers Accord between Iraq and Iran terminated the latter's support for the Kurdish military campaign against
Baghdad. At that point, the struggle became unfeasible, without arms
transfers or the geographic base in Iran. American aid had already been
denied, and Israeli involvement, apparently because of U.S. pressure,
had similarly ended. In Kurdistan itself, poverty and suffering were
rampant. The government had executed 227 rebel leaders and imprisoned thousands of *pesh merga* fighters, destroyed over 200 Kurdish
villages, resettled some 300,000 Kurds in southern Iraq, and evicted
over 100,000 to Iran.[24] Kurdish refugees in Iran slept in tents on the
winter snow; food was scarce, medical facilities inadequate. Over the
year, perhaps a half a million Kurdish refugees had entered Iran.[25]

Barzani had gambled with his people's fate and welfare when he
refused to accept the autonomy accord in 1974. A year later, the gamble
had failed tragically for a people who historically tended toward caution
rather than risk taking. Shortly before his death on March 1, 1979,
Mustafa Barzani plaintively said, "I am a failure."[26] His personal career
had been so tightly linked to his people's path that his failure was truly
the Kurds' as well. The rebellion never completely overcame the split
between the tribal-based Barzani-led Kurdish Democratic party and
Jalal Talabani's group, the Patriotic Union of Kurdistan (PUK), more
urban-based and socialist in its ideological orientation.

The national movement failed generally to cultivate Iraqi leftist
forces, and Kurdish efforts at a rapprochement with the Iraqi Ba'th
never succeeded, except for temporary cooperation between the two
sides. In a related fashion, Barzani's forces refrained from trying to
mobilize native Kurdish energies in the "liberated zone" to carry out
widespread educational and social programs leading to greater national
consolidation. Traditional tribal feudalistic practices and interests
prevented this as a narrow economic consideration weakened a revolutionary "takeoff." Freedom *from* Iraq was always a more meaningful objective, and perhaps more realistic than free government *over* Kurdistan. Therefore, while rebellion was undertaken, revolution was
bypassed.

Reliance on foreigners was a stigmatic benefit that underscored
fragile external dependency and the absence of a mass struggle, even
though seeds of such a struggle were sown and sprouted during the
1960s and 1970s. Some tribes continued to remain aloof from Barzani's
forces, and others, like the Zibaris, even fought as mercenaries in the
Saladin Cavalry, organized by the Iraqi Army, against fellow Kurds. Indeed, Barzani's father-in-law had opposed him in 1945, and Barzani's
son Ubaidullah joined the government side in the 1970s. Debilitating,

even humiliating factionalism undercut the national character of the Kurdish struggle.[27]

Even when the rebels gained successes, controlling the mountains and arming the peasant population, their foothold in Kurdistan was not turned into an advance base for offensive military operations at the heart of Iraqi power centers. The Kurdish guerrilla *modus operandi* ended where it should have begun. If Barzani and his fighters would not eventually penetrate Kirkuk, Mosul, or Baghdad, then eventually the Iraqi Army would bomb and capture Chouman, Amadiya, and Sulaimaniya within Kurdistan itself. Lacking a galvanizing ideological message and without full national unity, victims of an unimaginative military strategy, the Kurds were destined to lose. In a landlocked country and facing a strong central government, the Kurds would have to have done much more to turn the corner in this long struggle.

Kurdish Persistence and Powerlessness

Since the termination of the major period of rebellion in 1975, the Kurdish question remained a persistent problem in Iraq. Some 23 percent of the country is Kurdish by national identity, composing close to 3 million people concentrated in the northern and eastern areas. Notwithstanding Arabization and population transfers, the Kurdish language is still spoken, as reported by the KDP European spokesman following a visit to Khanaqin and other Kurdish towns in Iraq.[28]

This evidence of cultural vitality complements an ongoing military campaign that gained momentum particularly during Iraq's war with Iran, beginning in September 1980. Benefiting at times from Syrian and Iranian support, the Kurds of Iraq under Massoud Barzani, son of the legendary Mustafa Barzani, successfully mounted guerrilla operations against the army. In 1986 two of Iraq's seven armies, composed of some 160,000 troops, were in Kurdistan trying vainly to pacify the region. KDP forces numbered only 10,000 men under arms, but they were sufficient to control much mountain terrain and rule the area at night. The demand for Kurdish autonomy continued to constitute the core political program, though efforts by Jalal Talabani of the PUK to negotiate a settlement with Baghdad ran aground.[29] At the same time, Iraq had executed young Kurdish draft dodgers who refused to participate in the war against Iran, a war they considered alien to their national purposes.

Meanwhile, Masoud Barzani was in asylum in Turkey in 1988, as Iraq pounded away at Kurdish villages, using chemical weapons mercilessly in Sulaimaniya province, in Halabja particularly, where 4,000 people died, and elsewhere. The Saddam Hussein regime was reported to be poisoning PUK leaders and their families. PUK military com-

mander Mustafa Qader Mahmoud compared Saddam's policy with the
Pol Pot genocide in Kampuchea. Whole towns and villages in Kurdistan
were destroyed, and many thousands, perhaps ultimately 100,000, were
in flight for safety into Turkey. Amnesty International reported that
hundreds of Kurdish political prisoners had been executed in Iraq in
early 1988.[30]

The dark night of Kurdish history had yet to dawn with a bright
new morning. All the while, Iraqi methods of conflict resolution failed
to settle the issue. Arab assimilation is of course a cultural nonstarter,
and Ba'thist socialism is too nebulous a notion. Some improvements in
education were undertaken to mollify the Kurds. Noteworthy in this
context was the university in Sulaimaniya as testimony to Kurdish particularity within Arab Iraq. While autonomy is a formula that failed to
achieve agreement because each side interpreted its scope in a different
way, the idea of federalism had been discussed by some Kurds but rejected by Iraq and its leader, President Saddam Hussein. The feasibility
of secession, considered impossible by Ghareeb but possible by Hazen,
continues to depend upon a major transformation of Kurdish life.[31]
Tribalism would have to be transcended toward the organization of an
integrated community and the building of a more modern urban, literate society, moving to become a self-articulated nationality, politically prepared to establish a Kurdish nation-state. External conditions,
like the erosion of Iraqi state consolidation due to the war with Iran, or
latterly following the Gulf War in 1991, leading to a major Shiite uprising against Sunni power holders in Baghdad, would undoubtedly catalyze the feasibility of Kurdish secession.

Meanwhile, Kurdish agitation in Turkey bears the stamp of ethno-
regional vitality. Numbering some 8 million people and 15–20 percent
of the total Turkish population, the Kurdish geographic concentration
in the southeastern part of the country, contiguous with the Kurds in
Iraq and Iran, has been a target of Turkish repression since the republic
was established in 1923. Turkification has meant the abolition of the
Kurdish language by a 1924 law and the imposition of prison sentences
upon any Kurd found speaking the national tongue. The very idea of
maintaining that Kurds are a separate ethnic group, as developed by the
Turkish sociologist Ismail Besikci, is a crime against the state.[32] The
tangible reality of the Kurdish people has been twisted into a monstrous
denial by the Turkish regime. Bitlis, Van, and Diyarbekir are described
as Eastern Turkey rather than—as history, ethnicity, and language
corroborate—the heart of a Kurdish homeland for millennia. Facing
this threat of cultural, indeed physical, genocide catalyzed Kurdish
action.

Political organization and ethnic agitation developed markedly in
the 1960s. The decade witnessed the founding of Kurdish-language

magazines and Kurdish parties, like the Kurdish Democratic party of Turkey in 1965 and the Revolutionary Cultural Society of the East (DDKO) in 1969. Subsequent frameworks included the Kurdish Vanguard Workers Party (PPKK) and the National Liberation of Kurdistan (KUK), both Marxist and pro–Soviet outfits.[33]

Rebellion in Turkey took the form of both mountain-rural fighting and urban guerrilla warfare. Widespread leftist opposition to military regimes in Ankara provided a wider framework through which the Kurds expressed their particular national grievances and aspirations. The Popular Army for the Liberation of Turkey, whose Kurdish leader, Deniz Gezmis, was executed in 1972, offered a pan–Turkish democratic platform upon which to graft Kurdish aims. This group, and others like it, were suspected of receiving Soviet assistance, and indeed they bore a Marxist ideological stamp. Kurdish militancy against Turkey, a member of the NATO alliance and a beneficiary of U.S. troop presence and military and economic aid, is thought to be an arm of Soviet insurrectionism across its southern border.

It is noteworthy in this context that Kurds visited PLO camps in Lebanon prior to 1982. The Turkish Workers' party (POT), presenting a leftist ideological line, has campaigned for a Kurdish socialist republic to be established in Diyarbekir. Its members, like those in the Kurdistan Labor party, had been engaged in insurgency since the 1970s. Some 2,000 suspects were arrested in 1982,[34] though an unbelievable total of more than 80,000 people were reported arrested or detained throughout the Kurdish provinces in eastern Turkey during 1980–1981 alone.[35] From listening to Kurdish music tapes to engaging in nationalist party activity, the crimes of the Kurds pile up, and the military prisons fill up, with no end in sight. A glimpse of the Kurdish plight was conveyed in the film *Yol*, whose writer and producer lived in exile in Europe. But Y. Gurey is now dead.

Two-thirds of the Turkish army was preoccupied in the mid–1980s with Kurdish dissension in the East, where a state of emergency had been imposed for long periods of time. In 1987 Prime Minister Turgut Ozal had promised economic development for the Kurdish region, irrigation projects and the like, but this gesture is at cross-purposes with the unchangeable policy of Turkification at the cultural and linguistic levels, and resettlement schemes that threaten to empty the Kurdish provinces of their native population.[36] Kurdish guerrilla leader Abdullah Ocalan, reportedly a Marxist, promised to continue the fight. His Marxist-Leninist Kurdish Workers' party (PKK) inaugurated a wave of terrorism in mid–1984, raiding Turkish military convoys and gendarmerie stations on a regular basis. The PKK base areas were seemingly in Syria. A state of emergency in the Kurdish provinces of southeastern Anatolia was designed to suppress what Ankara believes is a separatist insurrection that threatens Turkey's political integrity. Mass imprisonments, torture, and forced migration, with a permanent pall of intimidation hovering over Kurdish society, characterized this minority's condition.[37] Yet the fight continued. From 1984 to 1988, Kurdish guerrillas had killed about nine hundred Turkish soldiers and civilians, and suffered extensive casualties themselves.

At the same time, an underlying trend toward urbanization in Ankara and other Turkish cities provides a certain momentum to Kurdish modernization that can contribute to a heightened ethnic consciousness. But this has not yet enabled the Kurdish position to move from radical opposition against Turkish rule to the establishment of a national elite leading an educated population and carrying an articulate political campaign directed to global forums. Endemic underdevelopment, lack of services, and widespread illiteracy hamper national Kurdish consolidation. Signs of a more profound awakening may nonetheless yet appear. Certainly personal gestures of Kurdish vitality abound. Giving babies Kurdish names and possessing videocassettes on Kurdish themes express native steadfastness against assimilation.

Within Iran since the Khomeini Revolution, which has abated only somewhat with his death, Kurdish fortunes followed the familiar pattern of guerrilla struggle and governmental repression. Numbering some 4 million Kurds, the Shiite principle in Persian identity could at best satisfy only those Kurds in northwestern Iran who share it, but only some do. Most Kurds, we recall, are of the Sunni orientation. Under the spiritual leadership of Sheikh Azzeddin Husseini, the Kurds demanded regional autonomy and the free use of their language. The reaction of Khomeini was to delegalize the KDPI (Iran) and undertake a campaign of oppression and pacification. The Kurdish Democratic party of Iran, headed by Dr. Abdel Rahman Qasemlu, fielded some ten thousand *pesh mergas* in an ongoing battle against the Tehran regime. Komala, a smaller Marxist group, also mounted armed resistance to Khomeini. With Iraqi aid they have attacked military bases, like the one at Piranshahr, and laid siege to the towns of Maku, Urmia, and Kamyaran, and the city of Sanandaj.[38] Mahabad, the capital of the Kurdish republic in 1946, was also the scene of a guerrilla offensive in late June 1982, during the course of which sixty-four people were killed. Meanwhile, Qasemlu (or Ghassemlou) was assassinated in 1989 in Vienna, then buried in Paris, five days prior to a planned visit to the United States. When the Iran-Iraq war persisted and Iraq continued to utilize Kurdish dissension to weaken and divert Iranian energies, the revolt against the Islamic republic continued. An integrating Iranian mechanism designed to mollify Kurdish grievances has yet to be invented.

There is no denying the fact that the Kurdistani homeland, traversing Turkey, Iraq, and Iran (perhaps also eastern Syria), is an indomitable

ethnic zone, grounded in Kurdish cultural vitality and economic potential, especially considering the large Kirkuk oil field. Yet the potential
of turning tribalism into nationalism, or communal consciousness into
political nationality, is still a challenge for the future. The geographic
aspect of their situation portends irredentist threats to the existing
regional states. The latter therefore support the Kurds when immediate
interests make exploiting the minority card advantageous; always,
however, they are aware of the dangerous precedent a Kurdish success
in one state would have upon the fate of Kurdish restlessness in contiguous states. Anti-Kurd coordination is therefore a permanent element that can be developed when required. Indeed, in 1987, Turkey
and Syria came to an agreement that committed Damascus to preventing aid to the Kurds in Turkey. Likewise, when the Iran-Iraq preoccupied Baghdad, the Turkish army was invited to patrol the northern
Iraqi border zone to prevent infiltrators from coming in or out. In May
1983 and again in October 1984, Turkey attacked Iraqi Kurdistan in collaboration with Baghdad's policy of repression. However, the Iran-Iraq
cease-fire in August 1988 released Baghdad to pursue its own vicious
offensive against the Kurds in the North. Once again, reliance on
Tehran proved a "weak reed" in Kurdish calculations.

Foreign support proves fragile and fleeting, dependent on circumstances and developments beyond Kurdish control, to be begun,
renewed, and then terminated without a moment's notice. Kurdish liberation, if it ever comes, requires native mass mobilization based on national unity across the boundaries of the region's states. Aid from
America was helpful for Iraqi Kurds, and Soviet aid may now be helpful
for Turkey's Kurds, but the games of superpowers should have taught
the Kurds that salvation is fundamentally homemade, or not at all.

Rejecting glamorous and global terrorist adventurism, the Kurdish
struggle has been accorded only meager international attention. One
exception was the mysterious murder of a West German diplomat in
Paris in January 1988. Another instance is the interest of the EEC in
minority and human rights before it will permit Turkey to join the European Common Market. In Europe, Kurdish groups have expressed their
militancy in national congresses and street demonstrations, and their
collective solidarity is fostered by trying to raise their children with
Kurdish consciousness. In America, Kurdish cultural activities have
been undertaken as a sign of a living tradition and complemented with
political revitalization in making the public aware of ancient wrongs
committed against an old Eastern people.[39] These activities beyond the
Mideast region, by what is partly a Kurdish diaspora, are not strong
enough to reverberate powerfully within Kurdistan itself.

Meanwhile, Kurdish leader Jabal Talabani was able to present his
people's tragic case in meetings held with U.S. State Department

officials and members of Congress in mid–1988. An exhibit of Kurdish history and plight was held on Capitol Hill in 1989, and the Congressional Human Rights Caucus has shown concern for the issue. Talabani was again in Washington in August 1990 to try and stir up American support for a Kurdish role in trying to overthrow the Saddam Hussein regime in Baghdad. Indeed Kurdish guerrillas made the most of the anarchy consequent to Iraq's expulsion from Kuwait and the threat to Saddam Hussein's regime, to pursue their military campaign — with some Turkish, Syrian, and Iranian coordination — towards Kirkuk in March 1991. Yet by early April, the Kurds were in desperate retreat from the advancing Iraqi army. National dispossession, refugee flight, even genocide, were ominous threats and approaching realities. A calamity of enormous proportions hovered over Kurdish fate. Along with the continuous fight at home, Kurdish efforts worldwide yet illustrated that this minority people had never abandoned its historic struggle for dignity and liberty.

CHAPTER 3

Berbers: Between
Rebellion and Co-optation

Since antiquity in North Africa, before and during the power of Carthage, Rome, Byzantium, and Islam, a Berber people has demonstrated a "virile spirit of independence."[1] Of questionable Canaanite or Phoenician origin, they have inhabited the area known as the Maghreb from remote times, without any solid traces of pre–Berber populations there. The Berbers remained ethnographically distinct even after the Arab conquest, an apparently Mediterranean race of lighter skin color, more European-looking than Arabian. But Berber history would be enmeshed with the Arabs by virtue of geographical fact and religious ties as the predominant fact of their life. St. Augustine may have been of Berber descent, but Islam, not Christianity, left a permanent mark on North Africa.

Organized in tribal formation and without a pronounced drive for national unity, Berbers may never have become "a truly distinct nation" with a cohesive political aspiration.[2] Indeed, from Egypt to the Atlantic, Berbers consolidated a living pattern that was rooted in the family, usually an extended grouping, the *vein*, practicing tight kinship ties based on endogamous marital patterns, then rising to the level of the canton, to the basic tribal unit, to a wider confederation. The latter framework included up to twelve tribes formed by distant warfare or other broad purposes. The alliance of cantons, composed of villages, was known as *leffs* (in Morocco) and *soffs* (in Algeria), but their appearance was transitory. Without a stratified social structure and clinging more to an egalitarian principle, Berber leaders seldom became "permanent and tyrannical chieftains."[3] In principle, segmented tribal society of this nature could be described, as by Hart, as "organized acephaly,"[4] a formula that conforms to Montagne's emphasis on the

45

"anarchic tendencies" in the Berber community.[5] The marked separateness of the Berbers served to ensure survival over millennia, but no higher collective goal than that.

Berber particularity derives from a number of important factors that conclusively represent their human habitat as a separate cultural zone.[6] Their ancient language, considered by T. N. Newmann in 1844 as a "Hebreo-African tongue,"[7] is composed of various dialects whose differences are such that they almost constitute separate languages. Lacking a uniform tongue naturally inhibited integral national unity of any kind, as did tribal organization. Yet Berber linguistic vitality is proof of collective solidarity: some 40 percent of Morocco and some 20 percent of Algeria, together numbering approximately 11 million people, are Berber speakers. The strength of the language is further confirmed by the fact that historically it was not even a written language. Although the Berbers were totally Islamized from the seventh century on, they have not been fully Arabicized until today.

Religiously Syncretic, Communally Exotic

The Muslim religious conquest of North Africa, beginning in A.D. 641, encountered Berbers, some of whom were Christianized, others classified as paganistic, who resisted the invaders in the spirit of freedom-loving tribes on their native soil. Berber identity had earlier survived Roman, Vandal, and Byzantine invasions; yet the Arab-Muslim invasion proved to be different. The Islamization of the Berbers proceeded apace because of the incentive of plunder that Berber warriors could enjoy by carrying the *jihad* farther afield, particularly into Spain in 711.

However, the adoption of Sunni Islam for the most part did not mean that Berbers were accepted as fully legitimate Muslims. Alongside mass conversion to Islam, older religious beliefs and practices were retained as the natural order of things in Berber life. The integrity of saint culture, based around the holy men who arbitrated communal affairs at times, was never abandoned. Notwithstanding that saints claimed Sherifian origin from Muhammad, the founder of Islam, the pre–Islamic origin of the saints was an indelible Berber cultural fact.[8] Moreover, the scriptural written character of Islam, rooted in the Koranic text, was not congenial to the largely illiterate Berber population. The Arab city was easily juxtaposed to the Berber countryside in both spatial and cultural forms. The urban 'Ulama could not see the idiosyncratic claim to saint *baraka* (divine grace) as anything but heretical.[9]

While it was the case that Berbers were sometimes religious

specialists and Arabs were illiterate warriors, the obverse remained the historical norm. The people of Fez railed against the uncouth, uneducated tribesmen of the rural areas. Perhaps it was the invective in a *hadith* (saying attributed to Muhammad himself) that best captured orthodoxy's view on this question: "There are seventy parts of wickedness. The Berbers have sixty-nine, and mankind and the Jinns have one."[10] Certainly there is no more obvious epithet of abuse than calling these people Berbers—a likely derivative of *barbarian,* beyond the pale of civilization and speaking a babbled tongue—when in fact their own collective name is *imazighen,* "free men."

It seems that the conversion of Berbers to Islam did not provide them with legitimacy and equality within that world religion. Based on the Kharijite heresy that attracted many in the early days of Arab-Berber contact,[11] or on the retention of folk beliefs notwithstanding Islam, Berbers maintained their identity in the post–Islamic era as in the past. It appears that even when Berber piety is firmly documented, as in Hart's finding that the majority of Aith Waryaghar men in the 1950s prayed the obligatory five times daily,[12] the image of Berber blasphemy remains stubbornly indelible.

Beyond linguistic and religious particularity, the Berbers possess a host of customs that demarcate their way of life from others in the region. Clan assemblies have traditionally constituted the judicial institutions, rather than the *qadi* or *shaikh* Muslim official or the *shari'a* (Islamic law) itself. Without centralized governing institutions, Berber society always seemed permanently in a state of tension. Maraboutic saints helped keep the peace, along with the council system that extended from the small village level to the tribal level. In the realm of religion, syncretic Berber ideas and practices, ancient legends, nature worship, non–Islamic feasting, and heterodox spiritual brotherhoods continued to coexist with mainstream orthodoxy. In the realm of politics, it was specifically the council institution that led Montagne and others to characterize Berber government as republican, a definition that did not contradict in principle the aristocratic or oligarchic rule by elders that tradition had sanctioned in Berber life.

Social life established the role of women in a fashion that differed significantly from classic Arab Muslim norms. While the Berber female never completely escaped from the esoteric realm of secrecy and modesty,[13] she did carve out a legitimate domain of public involvement. Unveiled women are free to meet men and openly discuss marriage in contrast to Arab custom in many Muslim societies where grooms do not see their brides unveiled until the nuptial night.[14] This difference was pointed out by Frantz Fanon in his examination of the Kabyles (Berbers) during the Algerian war against French colonialism beginning in 1954.[15] More daring yet, as Fanon wrote, is the phenomenon of the

ecstatic dance, or *hedra,* where men and women come together and
"fling themselves into a seemingly unorganized pantomime."[16] This indigenous Berber cultural form, for all its deviant significance, was yet
conducted under maraboutic patronage.[17] Sacrilegious license, while
rural in location, seems particularly Berber in spirit as the remnant of
older, pre–Islamic behavior. However, alongside female self-assertion
and public visibility, Berber women in the Algerian Kabylia remained
rugged and primitive, "naturally wild," wrote Bourdieu. From childbirth methods to participation in the FLN struggle against the French,
the Berber woman demonstrated a willingness to endure pain and contribute to the solidity of the cultural group.[18] Always she remained the
symbol of love, beauty, magic, and nature.

The Islamic conquest of the seventh century failed to erase native
Berber features across the Maghreb terrain. Always the contrast with
either the Arabs or orthodox Muslims bears emphasis and differentiation. Two additional examples pertinently illustrate this point, one
relating to the physical landscape and another to its inhabitants. After
twelve centuries of Islam, the rural calendar remained rooted in the
ancient Roman system, fit for the agricultural cycle and Berber conditions.[19] Regarding the people themselves, a noteworthy characterization of Berbers is that by Friedrich Engels, who, casting his eye for
proletarian productivity no doubt, described them as "a hardworking
people . . . excellent agriculturalists, they also work mines, smelt
metals and have workshops in which they weave wool and cotton."[20]
This was written in 1858, and the image of industriousness, as opposed
to one of Arab slothfulness, reappeared in Montagne's research in the
1920s.[21] The fact that large numbers of Kabyle Berbers have become
migrant laborers in France can further support the positive stereotype
of their work ethic.

As veritable schismatics, Berbers diverged from orthodox Islamic
behavior as proof of the durability of earlier religious, cultural, and
social forms. Coon's research on the Riffians in northern Morocco revealed that they probably keep swine, this explicitly forbidden to
Muslims. In distinction from Arabs who circumcise their boys at seven
years, it was not unknown for Riffian Berbers to do so at three months.[22]
Hart's investigations divulged an instance of Berber heterodoxy in their
practice of swearing oaths at saints' tombs and not on the Koran.[23] A further and explicit instance of an anti–Koranic norm was the
phenomenon of lending money at interest in defiance of Muslim solidarity.[24] In these and other ways it becomes clear that Berber culture
was never completely smothered in the conquest of North Africa by
Islam and Arabism.

Berber group identity rested throughout history on very important
geographical desiderata from a regional and domestic perspective. As

hardy tribesmen dwelling in nomadic and sedentary living patterns, the Berbers generally abandoned the coastal areas and sought communal welfare in the hinterlands. Traditionally, foreign conquerors—Roman, Byzantine, Muslim, and French—took the Mediterranean plains more easily than the interior, which remained overwhelmingly a Berber stronghold. Four zones have been Berber territorial hearths for millennia: the Atlas range in central Morocco, running south of major cities like Marrakesh, Meknes, and Fez; the Rif fastness in northern Morocco; the Kabylia area in Algeria alongside Tizi Ouzou east of the city of Algiers; and Djebel Aures farther southeast in the country. In these mountainous lands Berbers have guaranteed their physical security in relatively inaccessible natural fastnesses, indomitably independent within and from a wider Arab-Muslim-ruled terrain.

Urban contempt for the "hot-bloodedness of the Berbers"[25] was matched by Berber contempt, in righteous Ibn Khaldunian fashion, for the effeminate martial laxity of the city dwellers. It was in the mountains that Berbers eked out a primitive living standard and endured an inferior educational standard. But it was also in the mountains that they assured a collective existence, cultivating a native military capacity as part of Berber cultural norms. In the Rif, it was said, a male who had not taken a life before he was married was not a man. This often referred to internecine blood feuds and tribal tensions, not necessarily Berber-Arab conflict. But it demonstrated nonetheless the place of warfare in a lawless world. It is symptomatic of the tenacious seriousness involved that a Riffian Berber would be charged by customary *urf* law with a higher fine if he shot at his adversary and missed than if he wounded him in a fight.[26] The austere Berbers diligently developed a capacity for survival in the mountains of their heritage where they continue to reside in our time.

The classic geographic habitat of the Berbers was known, in Morocco particularly, as the *siba* dissident countryside facing the metropolitan city authority known as the *makhzen*. The alien invaders, like the Arab tide that washed ashore beginning in the seventh century, tried to extend their control throughout North Africa and over all its peoples. But it was traditionally at the edge of the mountains that foreigners, ruling in the cities and on the coast, discovered the topographical limits of conquest. The Berber mountaineers resisted with fervor against the Arab Muslims or the Sharifian monarchy of Morocco or the modern French. Indeed, the *Bled es-Siba* reached traditionally to the walls of Rabat and Fez, and close to Casablanca when, for example, the French landed in 1907. After over one thousand years of *makhzen* efforts to control centrally the entire country, the Berbers' *siba* territory remained unpacified into the twentieth century. It was fear of the *makhzen's* yoke, its repression and rapacity, that fortified

Berber determination against any and every alien threat based in the large cities. Conducting guerrilla-style warfare from their mountain fastnesses, Berbers usually preserved a fighting edge over larger but more vulnerable forces. Geography therefore became a vital element in strengthening Berber minority viability throughout Africa north of the Sahara. Living on the periphery of organized civilization denied them the opportunity to flourish but offered them the possibility to survive.

In spite of important transformations in Berber religious and political forms throughout their extensive collective life, it is reasonable to point to Berber history as an integral and identifiable human product. Prior to Islam, small Berber confederacies, even a Berber kingdom, dotted the map of North Africa. They persisted under the Roman Empire and after it. With the Muslim onslaught beginning in the seventh century, Berber resistance fended off the Arab invaders for a time, under a chief called Kusaila, then under the legendary queen al-Kahina. But she failed to turn effective military defense into a constructive act of state formation and was eventually defeated and killed in the Aures. Thereafter, and notwithstanding Berber adoption of heterodox Kharijite doctrines, the indigenous Maghrebians joined the Islamic wave in history. But even then, their particular identity was never smothered in the universal religious confines of Muhammad's believers and their pursuit of the *jihad.*

In 711, a Berber freedman called Tariq led a military expedition from North Africa to Gibralter and advanced into Spain. His Muslim forces were overwhelmingly Berber, and they provided the initial impetus for conquest, soon to be followed by an arriving Arab army that denied Berbers control of this new territorial addition to *Dar al-Islam.*[27]

Back home in their native terrain, Berbers seemed later to succeed in turning their military skills into further political achievements when they helped establish the Fatimid Empire in Egypt beginning in the tenth century. But these instances may merely have highlighted the effective mercenary role Berbers assumed in Islamic history. The establishment of Berber-run empires in North Africa, primarily in Morocco, first the Almoravids and later the Almohades, nonetheless suggested the recovery of Berber power as in pre–Islamic times. These entities that arose during the eleventh and twelfth centuries exhibited a staying power that defied a widespread prejudice according to which Berbers are absolutely unable "to organise themselves in a large state."[28] Governing parts of Spain like Toledo, founding Marrakesh in 1062, building unified states in the Maghreb—all demonstrated more than physical bravery, for which Berbers are famous. Yet in 1279 the last Almohadic empire fell, and Berber political power passed from history. The Ottoman Empire and the Sharifian 'Alawi dynasty were to assume control of North Africa and constantly challenge the Berbers. Losing statehood, the Berbers retreated to entrenchment in the *siba* hinterland.

The French Invasion and Riffian Independence

The nineteenth-century period of French conquest in North Africa posed new threats and presented new opportunities for the Berber tribes. Of specific moment was French colonization of Algeria following the initial military thrust in 1830. Thereafter, and until the 1870s, years of massive land seizure from the native population for settler *colons*, tribal taxes and social dissolution, epidemics, famines, and bad harvests all led to the utter impoverishment of the Arab and Berber (Kabyle) populations.[29] Under the leadership of 'Abd al-Kadir, descendant of a family originating in the Rif, a native insurrection fought the French incessantly beginning in the 1830s. At one point his protostate controlled some two-thirds of Algeria. In 1847, he was forced to surrender and was expelled to Damascus in 1855; two years later saw the Kabylia zone submitting to French rule. In 1871, the Great Kabyle Rebellion arose, then dissipated, as 200,000 Frenchmen ruled 3 million Algerians. Native uprisings, like those in 1859, 1871, and 1879, demonstrated the vibrancy of Berber-Kabyle cohesion against the European invasion. Indeed, resistance took on a Berber tribal cast more than a total national Algerian uprising. As one author said of Berbers, "They have rebellion in their blood."[30] Yet the Berber-Kabyle effort, enormously costly in life and property, would have redounded, if successful, to the benefit of Algeria's Arab population as well.

It is therefore clear that the Berbers of North Africa arrived at the threshold of the twentieth century bearing the essential elements of (minority) peoplehood in terms of ethnicity, culture, geography, and a singular collective history. Long struggles characterized their life of hardship and suffering against alien rulers and enemies. It remained to be seen whether new energizing elements would surface to generate a national awakening among the Berber tribes across the Maghreb or whether their very existence would be undermined in the face of modern challenges of a new variety.

While France solidified its rule over Algeria and Morocco, its European problems during the First World War opened up opportunities for renewed Berber self-assertion in North Africa. In 1916–1917, for example, the Kabyles adamantly opposed conscription into the French Army and deserted French ranks when drafted. In 1912, France had proclaimed Morocco a protectorate territory of metropolitan France, but Berber resistance was stiff in the middle Atlas Mountains, south of Fez and Taza particularly, until the late 1920s. In fact, the

Senhaja tribes were only and ultimately pacified by 1934 when, "probably for the first time in history," wrote Robert Montagne, Morocco became a single united country. The *makhzen* had overwhelmed the *siba,* yet this was accomplished, interestingly enough, not by the Arab Muslims but by the European French. The primary losers remained the dissident warlike Berbers.

Riffian Independence and Thereafter

The decade of the 1920s witnessed the most determined and successful Berber struggle for independence in modern times. Under the charismatic leadership of 'Abd al-Krim (b. 1881), a *sharif* (descendant of Muhammad's family) and a *qadi,* the Riffian Berbers fought the Spanish regime in northern Morocco whose presence there had begun centuries earlier. The indigenous tribes, particularly the large Aith Waryaghar, felt humiliated by Spain, which denied them autonomy and dignity, and threatened to exploit their resources for its own purposes. Animated by the call to *jihad* against the Christian enemy, "swarthy Riffians from the mountains — born cutthroats,"[31] in the picturesque language of Mark Twain, rose not only to fight against Spanish encroachment on their homeland but actually identified statehood as a positive standard to rally the tribal forces. 'Abd al-Krim, sporting a suspicion that the Spanish had poisoned his father, a *faqih* Islamic authority, proclaimed the national struggle in May 1921. Berber successes initially forced the enemy to retreat northward to Melilla. The Riffians overran Spanish military outposts and slaughtered captured soldiers. In July alone some 20,000 Spaniards were killed in battle. The *jihad* rolled on with great momentum, but instead of taking Melilla itself, the Riffians chose unwisely to allow the enemy to stay there. Freedom *from* the Spanish was a more natural instinct, perhaps military strategy, than the political impulse to forge a large state *for* the Riffian Berbers and *against* the Spanish foe.[32] An historic opportunity was missed in this otherwise marvelous minority struggle in the annals of the modern Middle East.

Nevertheless, 'Abd al-Krim did move soon thereafter to state building as a revitalized Berber venture. On February 1, 1923, the Dawla Jumhuriya Rifiya (Riffian republic) was established as the political pinnacle of the tribal struggle against the Spanish. While this development suggested the transcendence of tribal divisions in favor of national Berber-Riffian unity, the overall temper of Krim's leadership was distinctly religious. The war of liberation was a *jihad,* he himself was the Amir al-Mu'minin (commander of the faithful), and the *shari'a* was made the authoritative legal system in place of the custom-bound traditional mores, as people were ordered to pray the obligatory five daily prayers. The religious idiom was seemingly more native, also more legitimizing, vis-à-vis the local Arab Muslim population within greater Morocco than a national ethos still foreign to tribally conscious Riffians.[33]

Beyond all this, the Riffian state survived from 1923 until 1926 with a semblance of an organized administrative structure. Krim established a government with ministries, issued a Riffian currency, and tried to establish normal diplomatic relations. This embryonic effort was a commendable start but lasted only briefly and was soon aborted by a combined Spanish military thrust from the north and a French thrust coming from the south. The Riffian state was caught in the middle, still tribally divided and lacking full national mobilization, outgunned by militarily superior enemies and thus forced to surrender. True, Riffian warriors, who numbered about 100,000, fought valiantly. True as well, the Riffian politicians who administered affairs by raising taxes, sending out foreign envoys, and trying to solicit foreign aid, particularly German, demonstrated an organizing capacity of no small importance. But when all is accounted for, the goal of "liberty and independence" for the Rif, so stated by Krim in a letter published in the *London Times* on March 17, 1926, was beyond their grasp. The rebellion was crushed finally in early 1927, while al-Krim had already been exiled in late 1926. Striving for nothing less than full independence and statehood, the Riffians ended up with considerably less than even minimal autonomy.

Throughout the Krim period, the mass level of modernization remained low and static; little social change penetrated Riffian society. Deprivation and repression catalyzed Berber resistance but not adequate Berber revitalization. Statehood proved unsuccessful because beyond the combined determination of the Spanish and the French, who fielded approximately 350,000 troops in 1925, indigenous Riffian structures and norms were unfit for the challenge. A basically illiterate community, ensconced in a rural living pattern without new economic skills or relationships, stood at a formidable disadvantage against modern Western adversaries. The native strengths of an old community were impressive, though its native weaknesses were no less important in sealing the fate of the Riffian rebels in the 1920s.

While in northern Morocco Berber aspirations were stymied, particularist Berber cultural needs in the central and southern areas under the French were addressed with consideration. The mythological and romantic image of the Berber was cultivated in French ethnography as a foundation for a distinction from the Arab population. The colonial authorities instituted a policy that, while perhaps naively pursuing the far-fetched aim of Christianizing the Berbers, contributed to strengthen and legitimize their uniqueness. A Berber journal was issued in 1915, and a Comité d'Études Berbères was formed by the French in Rabat. Dividing Berbers and Arabs became not just an imperial method of rule but a cultural imperative. In 1930, the *Dahir Berbère* provided that customary law would apply for the Berbers, while the *shari'a* would operate for the Arabs. Moroccan Muslim opposition rose instantly to this threat to Islam, and the *dahir,* as much as it consolidated separate communal consciousness, led inadvertently to sparking urban-based Moroccan nationalism against the French.[34] It is important to note that as in other historical instances, the advance of Berber cultural particularity and structural autonomy was largely due to foreign assistance more than to indigenous developments. It is doubtful that this would be sufficient to create an "awakening stage" in the Berber community.

In the 1940s the focus of Berber activism and opportunity shifted to the Kabylia zone within Algeria. There the assimilation policy of the French, based on a total denaturalizing of native society and the use of colonial violence, had aroused grave domestic disturbances. Certainly the most dramatic event of the decade was the massacre of about forty-five thousand (!) insurgents at Setif, situated between Kabylia and Aures — Berber-Kabyle terrain. Algerian opposition was centered in Berber areas where peasant pauperization linked to rural raucousness combined to raise the banner of revolt. Bolstered by Kabyle intellectuals who rejected the idea that Algerian history began with Islam in the seventh century, the slogan "Algeria for Algerians" was designed to transcend Arab-Berber differences and consolidate unified ranks in the overall national struggle. Interestingly, within circles active in developing the path of modern Algerian nationalism, it was the Kabyle leader Ait Ahmed who championed the use of armed struggle and the Arab Messali Hadj who believed in political struggle. Violent insurrection would seem the natural sport of the Berbers, politics the masterful talent of the Arabs.

The FLN and the Kabyles

Already in 1949 voices were heard in Le Parti du Peuple Algerian (PPA) against what was denounced as the "sin of Berberism." Such a deviation would have divided the national movement along ethnic-linguistic lines while confirming the vitality of Kabylia particularity.[35] Belkacem Krim, the senior Berber leader, acted to eliminate Bennai Ouali and Amar Ould Hamouda from party ranks. The upshot was officially that nonsectarianism was to be the hallmark of the Algerian struggle. The realities, however, were more obstreperous than the rhetoric.

When the Front De Liberation National (FLN) began the war against France on November 1, 1954, Kabylia and Aures provided the natural guerrilla "foyers" of struggle. The hinterland Berber peasants took up arms—as they had incessantly during the previous century—as the "sectarian deviation" became in fact the spearhead of the entire Algerian war. Patriotic songs of the Amazigh (free Berbers) evoked memories of the past. Ali Yahia, head of the PPA in France, strenuously propagated the argument that to call Algeria Arab was racist. Indeed, four of the nine main FLN leaders were Kabyles in 1957, and their historical areas served as the natural bases of revolutionary warfare. William Quandt was not exaggerating but merely confirming a widespread judgment when he wrote that "Berbers were in the forefront of the fight against the French."[36] Ait Ahmed, the first "diplomat" of the revolution, and Belkacem Krim, FLN leader in the Kabylia, were only two of the prominent Berbers in the movement's leadership elite.

Without the Berbers taking the military initiative and attacking French targets, without their "romance of illegality" as Mohammed Harbi put it, without their daring to rise to the historic moment inspired by the French loss at Dien Bien Phu in May 1954—without them, Algerian independence would have been delayed. But with them the entire Algerian population stood up to fight a colonial regime that fielded 400,000 soldiers in 1956. When it was over in 1962 and Algeria became an independent state, more than 300,000 people—some estimates reach 1 million—had been killed in the bitter and vicious struggle.[37] That victory became a sign of Third World power against Western control, with remote Kabylia and Aures providing a momentous impetus to subject peoples in Africa and Asia to believe that freedom and dignity could be theirs, if necessary by a popular guerrilla war against a technically superior Western state.

But while the Berbers had plowed, planted, and pruned, it was the Arab elite in Algeria that picked the fruits of victory. The Kabyles were great fighters, but, particularly after the Arabs joined the FLN in large numbers during the mid–1950s, the independence struggle assumed more and more an Arab nationalist idiom and an Arabic verbalization. The less literate Berbers were generally no match for the urban Arab sophisticates. Put differently, the minority community, some 20 percent of Algeria's population, was no match for the Arab majority. This is specifically pertinent because in the beginning of the war, the French successfully contained the urban FLN organizations but not the FLN guerrillas in the countryside. French security forces in the Aures mountains were found wanting; in Algiers, Constantine, and Oran, however, they destroyed the FLN.[38] The rural zones carried the revolutionary struggle until 1956 when an urban front was successfully opened.

In the end, when the French-educated Algerian elite, symbolized by Ferhat Abbas, linked up with the rough soldier-bandits, symbolized by Belkacem Krim, the internal power struggle was set. It was the urban

Arab elements who would finally carry the popular war into the era of statehood. The military dimension merged with the political dimension, and the latter predominated in the end. The culmination of this process was not peaceful or fraternal, as the following Berber fates indicate: Abane Ramdane, a leading revolutionary Kabyle from 1955 to 1957, died mysteriously in 1958; Ait Ahmed, the leader of the Front des Forces Socialistes, was arrested in 1964; and, most poignantly, Belkacem Krim was assassinated in 1970 on the orders of Algerian President Boumedienne himself. Significant figures in the Kabyle leadership were ruthlessly eliminated after they had played a formidable historic role in prestate days. Opposing French colonialism and control had not necessarily contributed to elevating the political status of the Kabyles in independent Algeria.

Arab Statehood and the Berbers

Indeed, poststate days witnessed persistent Berber efforts to express their unique identity and play a rightful role in Algerian society. During 1962–1963, Ait Ahmed led the distraught Kabyles in guerrilla warfare against the state that he had helped establish, but Ben-Bella was successful in repressing this challenge to his presidency. Yet as compensation, more Kabyles were co-opted into positions of power as a sop to their collective aspirations. They had already received representation in the government, but a sense of alienation and weakness persisted. Later, in December 1967, a Berber minister of labor, along with Berbers in the army, attempted to carry out a coup but failed, leaving the Berber problem in abeyance.

Throughout the French period and continuing into the Algerian period, Kabyle society was undergoing various changes that energized their communal consciousness and activity. The historical disruption of peasant life through the destruction of villages, the loss of land, and the erosion of tribalization caused alarming and far-reaching developments. The Kabyles began to learn French as a linguistic vehicle of wider applicability and as a partial alternative to Arabic. They benefited from new educational opportunities to increase their literacy rate.[39]

Over time, though, the economic impoverishment of Kabylia compelled many to migrate to urban centers, particularly Tizi Ouzou, Algiers, and to France. It was there that a Kabyle intellectual elite appeared along with a proletarianized rural population. It was there that Berber life assumed a modern dimension: High ethnic consciousness and social mobility became, in the 1970s at the latest, the crucible for articulating a protean Berber national sentiment. In 1980, the Kabyle constituted 46 percent of all Algerian émigrés abroad, primarily to

France, when the Berbers were but 20 percent of Algeria's entire population.[40] The underdevelopment and neglect of the Kabylia and Aures regions, and labor migration and economic advance elsewhere, combined to accentuate Berber feelings of communal particularity. Repression and deprivation joined with modernist experiences and financial gains to stoke the fires of historical bitterness. It would seem that further expressions of Berber unrest could not be long in coming.

In an incisive study of modern Algeria, Rachid Tlemcani has shown how the state bureaucratic apparatus, supported by the single FLN party and the army, repressed popular forces after 1962.[41] The goal of a democratic polity was diverted into the establishment of oligarchic rule. This development became no more evident than in Algeria's treatment of the internal Berber question. Lacking the opportunity for a legitimate role in government and subject to Arabicization as a linguistic threat to their native identity, the Kabyles became restless and outwardly expressive. In 1973, a bulletin was published at the University of Paris VIII by the Group d'Études Berbères, and in 1978 L'Union du Peuple Amazighen was established. More symbolic yet were incidents at a popular level, like the booing of an Arab singer in Kabylia in May 1974 and the shouting of nationalist Kabylia slogans at a football game in 1977. "Vive la Kabylie" had come to replace the Algerian anthem in the Berber cultural repertoire.

The leading exponent of a Berber renaissance was Mouloud Mammeri, poet, historian, and anthropologist, who sought his people's origins as a backdrop to their collective revival. He taught the Berber language in Algiers but pursued his mission more freely in Paris. It was his profound conviction that Berbers possess their own way of life, philosophy, and mentality, which galvanized Kabyle energies toward communal self-expression. A powerful inspiration, Mammeri died in February 1989.[42] Kateb Yacine, a major Kabyle poet who also died in 1989, provided vivid literary expression to berberness known more authentically as *amazighité.* He wrote of the continuous war for cultural identity that echoed across the ages. Having overcome the myth of *l'Algérie française,* the Kabyles then confronted the myth of *l'Algérie arabo-islamique.* Kateb Yacine was a voice for the ancient Berber people who sought flexibility and multiplicity in an Algeria that reflected linguistic homogenization and cultural repression.

The most serious manifestations of the Berber ethos appeared in the spring of 1980. By then, Tizi Ouzou, sixty miles east of Algiers, had become a booming commercial center within Kabylia. It has an 80 percent Berber population. A native Kabyle bourgeoisie dealt in manufacturing and trade with a distinct aversion to the statist structures of the national Algerian economy.[43] Of pertinent significance was popular Berber opposition to the Arabicization program in all levels of Algerian education. On March 10 the governor of Kabylia banned a lecture on ancient Berber poetry in Tizi Ouzou, leading Berber students at Algiers University to protest and strike. Disturbances extended immediately to Kabylia itself. Incidents multiplied, and clashes took place between Berber rioters and the security forces. Some sources later claimed that thirty-two were killed and two hundred injured in the mop-up operation.[44]

Although the unrest was allegedly based on cultural grievances and not linked to political aspirations, the government was not fully convinced of the limited scope of Berber goals. It did nonetheless respond by proposing to establish a chair of Kabyle studies at Tizi Ouzou University and to reinstitute the chair at Algiers University. It failed, however, to establish a department of Berber culture and popular dialects at the University of Batna in the regional Berber capital in Aures.

Again, in 1981, new instances of Berber unrest surfaced on university campuses as government officials charged the minority with actions to "destabilize" the country toward eventual Berber secession from Algeria.[45] In April 1985, Berbers commemorated the fifth anniversary of the Tizi Ouzou events from 1980, and while the seeds of discontent and violence exist, the Kabyles still remain part of the Algeria that they helped found in 1962.

In the domain of conflict resolution, various solutions have been unable to accommodate the Kabyle question in a satisfactory fashion. Arabism is an abrasive nonstarter, as is any notion of cultural repression of the minority's particular identity. Defining Algeria as the embodiment of an "Arabic-Islamic civilization," as appeared in a draft cultural charter for the country in July 1981, did nothing to appease Berber sensitivities and fears. Likewise, President Chadli's stress on the singular use of Arabic and overcoming the lingering elite usage of French left the minority anxious about the status of the Berber language. Cultural and linguistic homogenization is feared as a recipe for ethnocide by the Berbers. Generally speaking, calls for the Berbers to abandon their particularism and become Arabs have historically never been heeded, even when, as in the case of the Kabyle 'alim (scholar) Abu Ya'la al-zawawi, they were presented as Islamically ordained.

The sacred Arabic tongue in prayer is tolerable for the Berbers, but its conquest of the social, economic, and bureaucratic spheres is potentially fatal to the native Berber dialects. At the same time, Islam as a vehicle for Arab-Berber fraternity is a reasonable foundation for coexistence, though Islamic fundamentalism has risen against Berber particularity in Algeria.[46] The integrative notion of a secular state is questionable and moreover challenged now by the assertion of Islam. Socialism as another integrative idea in the civil polity is unresponsive to Berber specificity and needs. Neither the Front des Forces Socialistes of Ait Ahmed nor the Ligue Algeriènne des Droits de l'Homme has proved effective in promoting Berber claims. Lastly, the Berbers have participated in government as a significant minority ethnic community, but more formal and accommodating institutional solutions to the Berber issue, such as regional autonomy, have not been offered. It will probably appear unacceptable to the majority Arab population and its political elite leadership. The Kabyle question may be, as Roberts argued, more vital than people generally suspected;[47] or Berber particularism will "probably decline," as Hazen and Quandt concluded.[48] In either case, it seems remote that any satisfactory political or cultural solution to the problem will be found.

While Berbers in Algeria played a primary role in the evolution of Algerian independence, Berbers in Morocco assumed a like function in their country. At first the French, after pacifying Berber areas by the 1930s, cultivated this non–Arab community as a counterweight to the numerically predominant Arabs. Yet the later French colonial struggle against Algerian independence complicated French-Arab relations within Morocco, as would be expected. Berber grievances against the French grew in relation to local community issues. Taxation, forced labor, and the nationalization of pastureland helped to arouse the Berber dissidents in the *siba* to identify with the exiled Sultan Mohammad V in 1953.

Not surprisingly, the Liberation Army that fought for Moroccan independence in the mid–1950s was markedly Berber in manpower and regional bases. For example, a Berber from the Middle Atlas led the Liberation Army in the Rif. Woolman contends that the Rif rebellion in the 1920s, and 'Abd al-Krim as the leader of the insurrection, served to inspire the Moroccan struggle prior to independence in 1956. The fact was that Krim, in exile in Cairo until his death in 1963, had remained active in Moroccan politics ever since his expulsion in 1927. Indeed the Liberation Army really crystallized initially in the Rif zone in 1954–1955 as Krim's legacy became the symbol of resistance for latter-day nationalists.[49]

We see here in Morocco the pattern earlier portrayed in Algeria regarding the Kabyle role in independence: Typical modes of Berber rural rebelliousness were exploited for a national struggle that ultimately succeeded. More than the wars of liberation expressed in their early form articulate and organized political movements, they benefited from earthy ethnic communities propelled by old cultural motives of restless agitation against what was considered illegitimate authority.

The military prowess of the Moroccan Berbers was harnessed by the political predominancy of the Moroccan Arabs and overwhelmed by it. It was in Fez and Rabat, in royal circles, among the intellectuals and *ulema,* and in the elite Istiqlal party that power devolved upon independence. True, the Berbers formed some 90 percent of the fighting core of the Moroccan Army, and a Riffian was its head. But it was primarily the urban politicians who set the tone of national life, chose the senior officials administering the Berber zones in the country, and defined economic policy often at variance with Berber preferences. One example of the latter was the sugarcane plantation plan of the 1960s, which dispossessed the Aith Waryaghar tribe of lands. Poverty and marginality remained the hallmark of Berber life, in both the Atlas Mountains and the Rif region.

Berber dissidence sparked clashes with the Rabat regime on many occasions. The Tafilalet rebellion of 1957 and the Riffian uprising of 1958 came on the heels of Moroccan independence as a manifest demonstration of rural Berber dissatisfaction. In this period Berbers developed the Mouvemente Popularie as a political counterweight to the Arab Istiqlal party. In a land of some 22 million people where 40 percent of the population is considered Berber,[50] it is perhaps not unexpected that communal unrest arose from time to time. One of the most daring instances was the coup effort of July 1971, when most of the army rebels turned out to be Berbers waxing angry against the "Fassi (Fez) Mafia." One observer, A. Coram, believes that had the coup succeeded, the Berbers would have ruled Morocco (as in the heyday of Almoravid and Almohad power).[51] But King Hassan II recovered, employed loyal Berber generals with efficacy, and kept his throne. In 1972, military elements tried to attack his plane. In 1973, an army revolt broke out in the Middle Atlas.[52] But in all instances, the 'Alawite dynasty, dating from 1664, exercised effective control of the regime, and this with Berber loyalist elements throughout. And as 'Alawite tradition would have it, King Hassan II has a Berber wife, Latifa.

In Morocco in particular, the co-optation of the Berbers into the political and military elite significantly offset the historical urge toward dissidence and alleviated its repression whenever necessary. As praetorian guards of an Arab-Islamic polity, traditional Berber capabilities strengthen the *makhzen* against their own *siba* terrain. Political passivity, notwithstanding exceptional episodes, coexists with military activism in the Berber legacy. Ruling is for the Arabs natural and normative, a divinely granted prerogative and a historical responsibility.

The mechanics for ordering relations between Arabs and Berbers in Morocco revolved around the throne of King Hassan II, himself a symbol of unity and legitimacy. But were he to fall, the subsequent situation might open a new opportunity for Berber self-expression and autonomy. While he holds power, the role of Islam as an integrating ethos cannot be decried, specifically because of the inappropriateness of Arabism as an integrating idiom. The feebleness of civil politics as an accommodating agency relates to the Berbers' rural residence and relative poverty, in addition perhaps to the very monarchic form of government. Potential pressure from below has been diverted in part through the popular recourse toward labor migration to France. Relevant also since 1975 was Moroccan military involvement in the Saharan war against the Polisario movement in which, paradoxically and perhaps typically, Berber ethnic elements conceivably fought on both sides.

Berber persistence and particularity in Morocco remain a remarkable historical achievement. Behind the Arab mask peers a Berber face.[53] A small but discernible cultural awakening appeared in the 1980s. A new bimonthly magazine *Amazigh (Free Man)* began publication, and a renaissance of the Berber language was recognizable. In fact, an attempt has been undertaken to unify the language and transcend the multiple dialects.

The émigré experience of life in France cannot but sharpen Berber self-identity, especially when opposition to foreign workers has become a real issue in French politics. France is the home of Berber-Kabyle political exiles and intellectuals who have turned a *prise de consciece* into a vital literary movement.

Various publications — *Awal, Sou'al, Tamezgha*, and others — have appeared that focus on documenting Berber folklore, expressing a renewed Berber cultural awareness that borders on a new vision of political society in the Maghreb.[54] For example, Mohammed Harbi, former FLN leader, looked to a democratic-pluralistic Algeria as a way to guarantee Berber identity and safeguard ethnic uniqueness in Arab North Africa. Exilic activism, while a sign of collective weakness beyond the territorial hearth, is an energizing phenomenon whose long-term impact on Berber possibilities should not go unnoticed.

Berber areas have at the same time experienced some development; commercial activities have extended into the major Moroccan cities, and new expectations have accelerated the desire for medical improvements, better road traffic, and electronic goods like the radio.[55] These features signal steps toward modernization and a potential heightening of ethnic consciouness, but a political breakthrough would still appear far off.

While Berber tribalism is an obvious communal fact and Berber ethnicity a real enough social fact, Berber peoplehood remains an unrealized collective goal. In both Morocco and Algeria the Berbers are a decentralized group with little horizontal communications and only a slight record of historical cooperation.[56] Snider's evaluation is supported by Young, who finds no evidence of "political Berberism," that is, a movement to achieve a shared national goal in North Africa. Berbers lack a literate tradition, though this is slowly being overcome, and are impaired for any effective cultural mobilization. Berberhood, Young concluded, is "unlikely to crystallize."[57]

In truth, there may be a linkage between literacy and unity, for the absence of a common written language with a body of national literature will inevitably hamper the cultivation of a homogeneous people. Arabization and general acculturation in the Maghreb may ensure, as Hazen suggests, that Berber "culture will be seen only in museums."[58] Therefore, both Charles Micaud and Abdel Kader Zghal concluded that there is no "Berber problem" as a militant minority challenge to the state integrity of Morocco and Algeria. The Berbers are in toto suffering from geographic separation, linguistic diversification, and segmented cleavages across the community's organizational makeup.[59] The obstacles to national consolidation are deep and formidable, and instances of inter–Berber solidarity, as when Berbers from Morocco went to assist Kabyles in Algeria in the period 1954–1962, remain infrequent.

There is no denying that the Berbers constitute a distinct ethnic community, persisting in their mountain strongholds and preserving a way of life different from that of the Arabs. There are even signs of Berber "society formation" based on economic and urban factors. The legacy of fighting and suffering contributes to a certain hostility toward the Other, usually an Arab. But enjoying only partially the prerequisites of an authoritative intellectual elite and a relatively educated population, divided by state borders and without foreign assistance, the very idea of Berber political self-clarification seems a very formidable challenge. The exile of Kabyle leaders like Ait Ahmed in France augmented group weakness, as Kabyles waited for an opportunity that may never arrive. Street disturbances in Algeria in October 1988 proved insufficient to pave the way to a political breakthrough. Without some dramatic and far-reaching changes across the Maghreb landscape—the collapse of the monarchy in Morocco or the sharpening of Arab-Kabyle tensions in Algeria—it cannot be assumed that this minority will mature into a coherent and united nationality with any reasonable chance of establishing political statehood.

And yet certain developments showed promise of a new era in Algeria. Widespread popular dissent led the government to agree to a multiparty system, and Islamic fundamentalist forces won a resounding election victory in local contests in June 1990. The Berbers began to talk politics and reemerged as a political force, with the formation of a new Berber party, the Rally for Culture and Democracy (RCD). Its major ally is the Kabyle-based FFS led by Hocine Ait Ahmed—who was permitted to return to Algeria in early 1990 after 23 years in exile.[60] Nonetheless, our conclusion remains grounded in hard realities.

CHAPTER 4

Baluch: From Obscurity to Geostrategic Importance

Among the lesser-known groups in the wider Middle East are the Baluch, who dwell primarily between Afghanistan and the Arabian Sea within a historically thinly inhabited zone separating Persia and India. It is there that regional politics and superpower conflicts, in the light of Afghan destabilization, Pakistani uncertainty, and Soviet machinations, have elevated the obscure Baluch into prominence. In the area called the arc of crisis an old people may play a formidable future role.

Their communal origins remain unclear, though they may be broadly classified as Turko-Iranian.[1] Two somewhat more specific possibilities relate Baluch beginnings to pre–Christian Chaldean peoples, subsequently banished eastward and traveling nomadically until they reached what became their Baluchistan homeland. Another interpretation sees Aleppo as their ancient residence, often linked to historical ties with Kurdish elements.[2] The ethnic particularity of the Baluch, without any affinity with Arab or Persian blood, is incontrovertible, as is their tribal organization. Marriage with kin was the unchallengeable norm, both for the Baluch and their near-fellow community known as Brahuis.

Led by traditional *sardars* and lesser chieftains, Baluch tribes engaged in petty rivalries over land and honor, seldom able or willing to act in a united fashion for common purposes. Nonaggression was usually the highest level of communal cooperation achieved among the tribes. At the same time, the *sardar* enjoyed more authority than power and exercised his role according to traditional responsibilities that fell far below the art of state formation.[3] Elusive tribal unity made national cohesion a distant dream and a political illusion.

Baluch culture is grounded in a distinct composite of ethnic

63

characteristics. Their language, Balochi, is Indo-European, resembling
Persian though unique in its own right. It was never a written language,
and educated Baluch would have to learn Urdu, Persian, or Hindi. The
overwhelming majority of Baluch are Sunni Muslims, but remnants of
earlier beliefs and rituals coexisted with the adoption of Islam.
Throughout, ethnic communal identity was never erased. Pre–Islamic
shrines were places of worship, and saints *(pirs)* were venerated. It will
not be surprising, therefore, that religious fanaticism was largely
unknown among the Baluch and laxity marked their orientation to the
shari'a.

During repeated migrations eastward across Persia into Sistan and
Makran and toward the borders of India, traditional Baluch predatory
behavior converged with the tenet of Islamic conquest. But the military
aspect in Baluch culture was more ingrained than the duty of the *jihad*
as such. With unabashed "noble and manly virtues,"[4] these lawless
nomads asserted their tribal prestige by raiding and fighting, Islam
never serving as the true propellant force. At root, Baluch ethnic identity was more natural and binding an identity than their Sunni religion.
When they asserted martial tendencies, it was a manifestation of the
Baluch way of life more than an Islamic imperative.[5]

Toward Independence in Baluchistan

The area of Baluchistan, divided primarily between Iran and
Pakistan today, is lodged between central Asia and the Indian Ocean,
and composed primarily of hill and mountain regions. Tending flocks
across barren pasturelands, the Baluch remained beyond the ken of
ordered urban civilization. Aside from Quetta, Kalat, and Sibi in central
and eastern Baluchistan, and Zahedan in western Baluchistan, known
as Makran, few were the cities inhabited by the Baluch. They lived as
nomads, subsisting on the traditional dates of the area, growing a few
basic crops, seeking out water for survival since the area boasts few
large rivers and enjoys little rainfall.

In their mountain heartland they would try to fend off Afghans
from the north, Persians from the west, and Indians from the east. Serving as a natural barrier or *glacier* between two or more powers,
Baluchistan was a fighting zone, indeed a border zone to outsiders, yet
a historical hearth for its more indigenous inhabitants. Greeks, Arabs,
Turks, Mongols, British, and others came through as conquerors in
various periods of history. Yet Baluchistan, with its rugged mountains
and arid deserts, survived as a distinct ecological territory, peripheral
to major developments though often related to them.

In addition to the essential communal elements of ethnicity, culture, and geography, Baluch history is a distinguishable legacy among Middle Eastern peoples. Aside from the vague source of tribal origin dating to early Islamic days, the most authentic shred of early history points to the arrival of Baluch in Baluchistan from the sixth to the fourteenth century. In the fifteenth century, an effort at unity by Mir Chakar Khan failed at Sibi. In 1666, there is evidence of a Baluch confederacy, bringing together various tribal groupings. However, the most famous episode of Baluch national integration was led by Nasir Khan of Kalat (himself perhaps a Brahui), who proclaimed his independence of the Afghans in 1758 and succeeded in preserving, at the very minimum, Baluch autonomy. In this confederacy the Khan symbolized Baluch freedom from alien rule more than he imposed a complete state regime. Tribes did not pay taxes to the Khan, though he had the rudiments of a bureaucracy, councils, and soldiers of his own.[6] With ups and downs throughout, the Khanate nonetheless survived until 1948.

During this long period, the British became the most formidable Baluch competitors. With India the primary imperial prize, the British felt compelled to utilize Baluchistan (and Afghanistan) as geographic barriers to the Russian threat from the north. In 1839, the British Army penetrated the Khanate emirate on the road to consolidating their Indian conquest. By 1876 Captain Sandemann had subdued most of northeast Baluchistan, including Quetta, and had reduced the Khanate of Kalat to a vassal state of British India.[7] The complete pacification of Baluchistan continued into the 1890s. Throughout this process of British conquest, the Baluch tribes, including the Brahui, failed to unite or create a central organization. This internal division facilitated the British victory. Likewise, separation among the Baluch, cut off by the border arrangements between Kalat and Iran in 1895–1896, further weakened the tribal efforts. Baluch subordination to the British led to incorporation into India of a previously dissident and backward territory. The irony was that the British were the founders of modern Baluchistan, even though that founding did not devolve to the benefit of the Baluch at that time. Captain Sandemann, who led the British conquest in the latter half of the nineteenth century, died in Las-Bela in Baluchistan and was buried there in 1892.

As in the days of old, the Baluch fought tenaciously against those seeking to impose foreign rule over them and their homeland. This was true in the twelfth century when they opposed the Seljuks in Persia and in the eighteenth century when they confronted the Afghans. Similarly, they fought the British in the nineteenth century and the Iranians under Reza Shah in the 1920s. External adversaries threatened to deny the Baluch their traditional life of plunder, while a life of political freedom and independence was an aspiration that they seldom defined as a national aim.

The Baluch undoubtedly possessed the attributes of ethnicity, culture, geography, and history, and felt their collective particularity worthy of sacrifice and suffering. But from this to clarifying a cohesive peoplehood, or political nationality, a great distance had to be traveled. And while they might try to move in that direction, competing forces were operative to undermine Baluch identity. Political events had turned them into "Indians" and "Persians," by way of territorial residence if not national self-identification.[8] The uniformist character of modern states would inevitably challenge the parochial sentiments that had carried the Baluch community through history.

A period of externally stimulated political agitation rather than trends of internal social change elicited signs of an "awakening stage" in Baluch life in the 1930s. The Indian subcontinent at that time was simmering with uncertainty about the region's future political devolution. Facing direct British control in certain parts of Baluchistan, as in Quetta, and indirect control in others, as in Kalat, the Baluch began to demand reforms in the spirit of self-government and ultimately independence. The call for a free Baluchistan separate from India was voiced in 1932. An All-India Baluch Conference was held at Jacobabad in December of that year, raising the cry for unity under the Khan of Kalat.

Subsequently, the imminent exit of the British in 1947 aroused hopes that Baluch independence could be reestablished, as before 1876 when Kalat was reduced to vassalage. Thus, when the new state of Pakistan was declared in August 1947, the Baluch proclaimed their independence. But all this was to no avail as Pakistan forcibly annexed Baluchistan within a few months.[9] Out of tribal desperation perhaps, more than a realization of the demands associated with national independence, the old pattern of repression by alien rule would again mobilize the Baluch to fight the foreigner.

The establishment of the Muslim entity called Pakistan was a national anomaly from the start. The very name *Pakistan* was an acronym of its multiple regional components: *P*unjab, *A*fghanistan, *K*ashmir, *S*ind, and Baluch*istan*. Five peoples were included in this Muslim successor state to India: Punjabis, Sindis, Bengalis (in East Pakistan), Pathans (in the northwest frontier province), and Baluch. The problematics of turning this multinational entity into a successful "nation-building" enterprise would be enormous; in fact, the eventual secession of Bengal in 1971 was symptomatic of the country's geographic oddity and political arbitrariness.[10]

State Repression and International Opportunity

From the moment of its appearance, Pakistan served as a base for Punjabi control, arrogating political and military positions (with the

Pathans) and speaking its Urdu tongue. The Baluch had been unequal to the opportunity of independence in 1947–1948 and seemed destined to endure this new Pakistani stage as the completion of "the process of colonization" begun by the British.[11] The administrative mechanism of this process was the 1955 one-unit policy, which denied any Baluch autonomy whatsoever, installed Punjabi officials in place of Baluch *sardars*, and led to a loss of tribal lands. Baluchistan, composing 43 percent of Pakistani territory, the Baluch constituting only 2 percent of Pakistan's population, was subdued rapidly and completely.

Islamabad centralized government controls and did little to overcome the endemic backwardness of Baluchistan. Little irrigated land and unexploited mineral resources were indicative of the economic state of affairs. The industry that existed in Quetta was typically in non–Baluch hands. The Baluch literacy rate hardly reached 10 percent. Many Baluch migrants found work opportunities in Karachi, while many émigrés travelled to Oman and other Persian Gulf countries to secure jobs. The repressive policy and depressive atmosphere led some tribal elements to revolt against the Pakistan regime, but this only induced the imposition of martial law in 1958. The army carried out a "pacification" strategy from 1958 to 1961 as a consequence of which seven tribal chiefs were executed in Baluchistan in 1958.

Meanwhile, the Baluch in Iran also raised the flag of revolt against Persian domination, but their legendary hero, Dad Shah, was beheaded in 1957. By the start of the 1960s, therefore, 3 million Baluch in Pakistan and close to 1 million in Iran were facing formidable political and military obstacles to realizing even a semblance of communal well-being. The future was dim, as an old minority found itself boxed into multinational states politically intolerant or wary of sensitive ethnic diversity.

The organization of Baluch guerrilla warfare against Pakistan became in the 1960s a combination of tribal audacity mixed with ideological rhetoric. The old and the new united to galvanize violent dissent under the leadership of Sher Mohammed Marri, of the largest tribe in Baluchistan. He spoke of a Marxist class struggle and encouraged Baluch city youth to join the resistance forces in the mountains, in the Sibi district, for example.

From 1963 on, the Baluchistan People's Liberation Front (BPLF) became the political movement for the guerrilla war at the same time that the National Awami [People's] Party (NAP) articulated the idea of a multinational Pakistan. These forces reaped success when in 1970 a Baluchistan province was recognized by the government and elections were held that resulted in a NAP victory. But President Bhutto demurred and dismissed the provincial administration, setting in motion the dynamics of a larger-scale liberation struggle in the 1970s than had been seen in the previous decade. The last straw came in February 1973 when Bhutto had again dismissed the provincial Baluchistan administration and arrested the main Baluch leaders—Ataullah Mengal, Ghaus Bux Bizenjo, and Khair Bux Marri. The Pakistani Constitution was suspended, and martial law was imposed.

The earlier secession of Bangladesh in 1971 did not predispose the Pakistani regime to belittle the eruption of renewed Baluch warfare in 1973. Until 1977, some 80,000 government troops contended with about 50,000 Baluch fighters, who practiced the textbook pattern of guerrilla tactics—attacking army camps, blocking roads, and interfering with various government activities like oil drilling. The major insurrectionary zone was Kalat—the historical home of Baluch independence. When the war ended in 1977, no gains had been made.

The guerrilla campaign had apparently enjoyed some foreign assistance, this evident from the Soviet arms discovered in the Iraqi embassy in Islamabad in 1973. At that time, Iraqi aid to the Baluch in both Iran and Pakistan was part of an interventionist strategy to weaken Baghdad's historic Persian adversary in the Gulf area. Undermining Iran by exploiting Baluch insurrection, with the concomitant support of Baluch warfare in Pakistan, served Iraq's interests.

But the 1975 rapprochement between Iraq and Iran through the Algiers Agreement ended Iranian aid to the Kurds in Iraq and Iraqi aid to the Baluch in Iran (and probably Pakistan as well). By 1977, Baluch leaders were exiled as Pakistan was able to ensure its territorial integrity. Concessions to the Baluch were now unnecessary. In the same year, Zia ul-Haq replaced Bhutto as president, and he adopted an even more repressive political approach toward governing than his predecessor.

But while the immediate efforts had failed, political and ideological developments demonstrated a persistent Baluch vitality. The BPLF articulated a leftist-Marxist outlook that suggested the possibility of Soviet involvement, already hinted at by some forty Baluch guerrillas training with the Habash-led Popular Front for the Liberation of Palestine (PFLP) in Beirut in 1973. Chinese assistance to the BPLF was also mentioned as a possibility.

Led by Khair Bux Marri, a committed Marxist from Quetta, the BPLF became the most visible and important militant force in the Baluch struggle. In an interview with Selig Harrison, Marri said:

> We are expected to accept the idea of Baluch here, Baluch there, scattered in a sort of international triangle. But what is the harm of the Baluch wanting to put themselves together? . . . Look at the United Nations, look at the little member states of the U.N. like Oman or the Arab Emirates. Can you wonder why we are not satisfied to talk about

provincial rights? We are told we are not viable — stretching from the Indus to Iran! Are the Maldives viable?[12]

It was this kind of outlook, rooted in the resource capacity of Baluchistan and put into the rhetoric of international politics, that carried a persuasive message of national potentiality.

The leftist strategy of linking the Baluch struggle to the Soviet Union, based on Marri's Marxist orientation, seemed reasonable in the light of regional and global factors. Since the end of World War II, Moscow had supported various surrogate forces that voiced their goals in the language of "national liberation" and "national self-determination," and certainly the Baluch case could qualify in the context of opposition against the Pakistani entity. Internally, Pakistan was portrayed as a colonialist regime repressing various minority groups, in particular the Baluch and the Pathans. Externally, Pakistan was aligned with the Western powers since its inclusion in the 1954–1955 Baghdad regional pact and then in SEATO. It was India's 1971 treaty of cooperation with the Soviet Union, which in particular made U.S.–Pakistani ties all the more strategically critical. Following the Soviet invasion and occupation of Afghanistan in December 1979, just to the north of Pakistan, the Russian threat became ever more real. Foreign Minister Gromyko abusively exemplified this with a warning on a visit to New Delhi in February 1980: "If Pakistan continues to serve as a puppet of imperialism in the future, it will jeopardize its existence and its integrity as an independent state."[13]

It was this juxtaposition of forces — India–Soviet Union and Pakistan–United States — that assumed an intense immediacy after Russia's war in Afghanistan. The reports and rumors of Pakistan's developing the "Islamic bomb," as a deterrent to India's nuclear program and plausible weaponry for the Arab-Muslim *jihad* against Israel, added more fuel to the political equation.[14]

It is worth recalling in this context the analysis of British interests by Lord Curzon, who in September 1899 opined that Russia was threatening to become a dangerous central–Asian power. That historical fear had compelled considerable British involvement in the Indian subcontinent. It now compelled, in the last quarter of the twentieth century, a major American commitment.

The U.S. Congress was thus willing to agree with President Reagan's policy, markedly divergent from that of ex–President Carter, and passed a $4-billion aid package to Pakistan for the years 1983–1987.[15] In addition, Washington supported the Mujahiddin resistance forces fighting the Soviet occupation within Afghanistan. But as would be expected, the Soviets acted in kind and were reported to be training four thousand Baluch dissidents in Kandhar province in Afghanistan in

1980, in preparation for guerrilla activities against Pakistan. Indeed, USSR subversion in Baluchistan had existed in the 1970s because the very establishment of the BPLF seems to have been a Soviet ploy.[16]

The image of the Soviet Union as liberator and the United States as repressor converged neatly into Baluch political awareness and political orientation. Richard Nixon grasped the regional significance of these developments when he wrote: "A People's Republic of Baluchistan would give the Soviets a red finger pushing through to the Indian Ocean."[17] The implications for the future of the Persian Gulf and its oil predominance are obvious. From South Yemen to Baluchistan, a Soviet naval encirclement of the Gulf would all but destroy the West's maneuverability in the Arabian Sea and Indian Ocean. Playing the "Baluch card," to use the language of Selig Harrison, would give this rather unknown national movement a political momentum whose significance was initially directed against Pakistan but ultimately critical for the United States and the West. It was Trotsky, the ideologue of internationalism in Marxist history, who affirmed that the revolutionary road to Paris and London would pass through Kabul. As this provocative warning assumed grave military proportions in 1979, perhaps Trotsky would not have disagreed to add Kalat to Kabul as the path of future victory against the West. The British historically positioned Baluchistan as a buffer state against Russian expansionism into South Asia. But a new possibility was now to position Baluchistan as a border state alongside India—and without Pakistan—to enhance Russian expansionism to the Persian Gulf.[18] In the Communist lexicon, *conquest* is the magic potion for liberation.

In addition to Marri's BPLF, the Baluch Students Organization, led by Ataullah Mengal, served as an important vehicle for presenting the Baluch case internationally. Established in 1967 and based in London, the BSO called for an independent state that would include parts of present Pakistan and Iran. Mengal reasoned that foreign assistance from whatever sources could help the Baluch struggle, and he was thus not averse to America playing a role. As he said, "Why should the U.S. let the SU [USSR] be the only champion of national liberation?"[19] But Washington's strategic calculus offered little hope that Mengal's rhetorical question would be positively addressed.

Ghaus Bux Bizenjo, the head of the National Awami party, was a third Baluch leader who articulated the political dynamic of national struggle. His worldview was primarily oriented toward the domestic Pakistani situation, though a relationship with the Soviets was also part of his tactical program. As the deposed former governor of the Baluchistan province, Bizenjo had the direct personal experience of Pakistani repression. For him, Pakistan was a colonialist and artificial entity, its ethnic diversity an unresolvable obstacle to national unity. Perhaps separate Baluch, Pathan, Sind, and Punjab entities could constitute a stable Pakistan federation, but the imposition of centralized control from Islamabad alone was the prescription for instability and, in consequence, alien occupation. Rather than a multinational state, Bizenjo thought that "the presence of one single nation in a country is necessary for its unity, stability and prosperity."[20] Baluch self-determination was therefore morally sound and politically reasonable as a solution to the problem. The Pakistani response was one of unqualified repression. In 1982 alone, the regime hanged seven Baluch leaders.

The realization that Baluch dignity was in the sword and not in letters did much to propel the struggle forward. Yet Baluch intellectuals were not unimportant in the articulation of the problems, possibilities, and policies of the people. Beyond the ideological and political leadership, other signs of revitalization were apparent. A Baluch Academy in Quetta was established in 1962, and a university was built as well. Compiling folk culture into written form was a basic task in these new developments.

While the Baluch struggle was alternatively advancing and regressing in Pakistan, it appeared to stagnate dreadfully in Iran. A Baluchistan Liberation Front was formed in 1967, along with the Democratic party of Iranian Baluchistan, an allegedly Marxist group. Iraq provided free radio broadcasts to the area which, however, ended in 1975. From 1968 to 1973, insurrectionist activities took place in the eastern Iranian Baluch-settled zone.

But repression was swift and ruthless. The Shah moved to Persianize the Baluch and prohibited their native publications. Non-Baluch peoples were sent to populate the area. Military controls and economic underdevelopment were the Baluch lot, and many youths chose to seek opportunities in the Persian Gulf states. In March 1978, just prior to the fall of the Shah, U.S. and Iranian forces carried out joint military exercises in Baluchistan, near Chah Baher on the coast. The American strategy in the Gulf was centered on a strong Iran, as it centered on a strong Pakistan in the Indian subcontinent. But the Shah's regime was soon to fall, Afghanistan was soon invaded, and the fate of Pakistan—and the Baluch therein—tottered in the balance.

The collapse of the monarchy in Iran seemed to provide the opening for a Baluch resurgence. Ayatollah Khomeini came into power in February 1979, but by December, Baluch insurrection against the Red Guards in Zahedan culminated in the imposition of martial law. In 1980, Iran closed the University of Seistan and Baluchistan. Baluch urban guerrillas continued to stoke the fires in the hope of exploiting the political turmoil to their advantage. Some advances were made through the role of the Baluchistan People's Democratic Organization (BPDO), with demands formulated for the use of the Balochi language, for the freedom to publish national literature (a new magazine, *Makran*, appeared), and for the right of Baluch to conduct their own affairs. Historically, Iran had eroded the *sardar* tribal system, yet in its place arose a more united nationalistic Baluch community that aspired to collective freedom, not elite privileges as in the old days.

Between Afghanistan and the Persian Gulf

In summarizing the rough road toward solidifying Baluch peoplehood, there is a discernible progression based on essential elements and certain energizing elements that characterize the community's life. From tribal formations and ethnic and cultural affinity, the Baluch advanced to the stage of nationality in the 1970s. Signs of popular mobilization for ideological expression and military struggle were apparent. The urbanized émigrés in Oman, Dubai, and London, in addition to the Baluch in Karachi in Pakistan, provided a modernist streak to Baluch society.

It is true that leftist class rhetoric still coexisted with tribalistic excrescences (like the primacy of the Marri tribe), yet the transition from one world to the next proceeded nonetheless. In this process political repression in Iran and Pakistan proved the crucible for turning Baluch identity and self-consciousness into a more coherent national experience. Economic data also corroborate this developing reality. Baluchistan is an identifiable "internal colony": The coal of Kalat, the gas of Sibi, the chromium of Quetta, and the potential oil wealth of Gwadar and Pasri on the Arabian Sea have never been primarily included in national Pakistani development plans for allocation to the Baluch areas. Thus some Baluch leave the impoverished homeland; others stay on to fight. And the fight, with some foreign aid arriving from the Soviet Union and Iraq in particular, continued, though it had not been consummated.

The record of conflict resolution to resolve the Baluch question, and at the same time to assure domestic peace and intercommunal integration within Pakistan and Iran, is largely unimpressive. At the level of national identity, both Persian and Punjabi ethnicity as agents of assimilation stood at cross-purposes with Baluch minority ethnicity. Symptomatic of this was the creation in 1986 of a new political party, the Sind-Baluchistan Patriotic Front, designed to focus opposition efforts against the Punjabis, who constitute nearly 60 percent of Pakistan's total population. Yet the central government saw fit to dissolve the Baluchistan Association in 1989.

At the level of religion, Islam is not only inappropriate for integrating fellow Baluch Muslims, but Islam in both countries exacerbates intercommunal problems. In Pakistan, the question of the country's *Muslim* (social) character, as opposed to its *Islamic* (religious) character, is old and divisive. The idea of a Muslim government in northern India goes back to 1883, later to be advocated by Iqbal in the 1930s and proclaimed as a goal in the Lahore Resolution of 1940. However, the idea of an Islamic government is a very different idea, reflected on the one hand in the influential writings of Maududi and on the other in the political program of Zia ul-Haq when coming to power in 1977. In July 1986, as the culmination of a progressive Islamization, the Shariat Bill established the law of Islam, as a total civilization, as the law of Pakistan. This meant, for example, the obligatory payment of the *zakat* (charity tax) and the prohibition of interest in the country's banking system. Yet it is no easy task to translate religious faith into effective social, economic, and political institutions, as V. S. Naipaul so colorfully narrated upon his visit to Pakistan.[21] The death or murder of ul-Haq in 1988 and the coming to power of Benazir Bhutto left open the future of Pakistan's Islamization.

As a basis for pan–Muslim solidarity, Islam remains insensitive to the ethnic pluralism that is at the heart of Pakistan's situation. Intercommunal tension involving various groups — Pathans, Urdu-speaking *Mohajirs* (immigrants originally from India), Sindhis, Baluch, and others — is endemic and causes deep cleavages throughout society. The purpose of Islam in Pakistani life is among other things to serve as a cover for military authoritarianism.[22] The unwillingness of small communities to sublimate nationality in religion delegitimizes Islam as the solution for the Baluch question in Pakistan.

At the same time, no remedy from the realm of civil politics is available. The economic development of Baluchistan could ease ethnic dissension and help to integrate the area into national life. But deprivation rather than development remains the mark of Baluchistan. The reform possibilities at one period of Pakistani history did include the idea of provincial Baluch autonomy as a form of institutional adjustment. This was introduced in 1970 as an improvement on the 1955 "One Unit Act." But the regional government reform was trampled upon by the centralist tendencies in Islamabad. The model of a multinational state is still the official policy, with or without a provision for provincial autonomy in the framework of a federal system. Before 1948, the Muslim League had foreseen such institutional measures, but their implementation has been marred by suspicion and bitter recrimination. The political system, in brief, is a failure in Pakistan and vis-à-vis Baluchistan specifically.

The fortunes of conflict resolution in Iran have been similarly unsatisfactory. The efforts at Persianization are a reprehensible cultural nonstarter. Islam, in its strident Shiite form beginning under Khomeini, has been antagonistic to all Sunni elements in Iran, and the Baluch are one of them. Shiism is the state religion, and consistent with this, Tehran has utilized Shiite Sistanis against the Sunni Baluch.

Faced with this religious challenge, a Baluch Islamic Unity party formed under the leadership of Moulavi Abdol Aziz Mollazadeh, a Muslim divine. All this did little to alleviate Baluch grievances and in fact accentuated their ethnic and religious particularity in Iran. Indeed Khomeini, upon coming to power, actually appointed a non–Baluch Shiite as governor of the province of Baluchistan and Seistan. The provincial capital of Zahedan, in which the Baluch were now a minority, became the traditional scene of disturbances and altercations with the Iranian Army. Without any civilian or secular strategy of national integration, intercommunal tensions are a fixed aspect of the situation in Iran.

Conclusions drawn from Baluch history and contemporary trends point to the basic arrest of their national development. Tribalism has been partially replaced by broader pantribal frameworks, but the legacies of tradition and underdevelopment weigh heavily upon this people. With little arable land in Baluchistan, many have chosen to migrate and emigrate. The dispersal of the Baluch from Pakistan to the Gulf states has weakened the territorial heartland as a locus of national endeavors. Close to 400,000 of them are in the Gulf, and many of the so-called Pakistanis in Saudi Arabia are really Baluch.[23] Moreover, a telling statistic shows that as many Baluch as in Pakistani Baluchistan live in the other provinces of the country.[24]

More telling yet is the fact that in all of Pakistani Baluchistan only one-third of the inhabitants speak the Balochi language, signifying the transformation of the Baluch elements into a veritable minority, even in their own historical terrain. An influx of large numbers of Afghani refugees into Quetta is indicative of the threat to the Baluch in their own land.[25] Demographically and linguistically, the Baluch are being challenged within their homeland, and beyond it they have no appreciable collective role to play, except perhaps that of a mercenary force in the Omani Army and that of the United Arab Emirates.

The Baluch community has at best only begun to enter into the modern grid of development regarding education and literacy, urbanization and prosperity, national sentiment and popular mobilization. Their otherwise exemplary distinctiveness still lacks sharper political articulation. The impediments of geographical separation from Iran to Afghanistan, facing a determined and autocratic foe in Punjabi-led Pakistan, and relying painfully on foreign assistance do not constitute a prescription of success. Baluch success may depend, as Plascov had written, on "their own cohesiveness, military capability, alliances with other domestic forces, aid from external forces," which could together contribute to Baluch possibilities both to survive and elevate the level of their struggle.[26] But this is a lot to ask and expect at any rate. Anthony Hyman, in a later assessment, perceived that an independent Baluchistan is a receding dream. American aid to the area and various developments illustrative of a weakened national presence in Baluchistan itself would presently suggest the unlikelihood of a separatist solution.[27]

Fundamental changes in the region, however, could make a Baluchistan state a real possibility: Soviet-supported massive guerrilla warfare (despite the Red Army's withdrawal from Afghanistan in February 1989), the erosion of Pakistani integration, or the disintegration of post–Khomeini Iran could conceivably offer the Baluch a new lease on political life. At that point, noble Kalat would again arise as the capital of an independent Baluchistan. As long as the Persian Gulf and the Indian subcontinent remain vital and contentious regional conflict zones, there is no knowing what the future may hold for the Baluch people.

Part II
Heterodox Muslim Minorities

CHAPTER 5

Druzes: Freedom without Independence

One of the most mysterious Middle Eastern communities is the Druze minority, whose origins, faith, and aspirations remain shrouded in thick webs of secrecy. The contemporary role of the Druzes in Lebanese developments in particular, and their not unimportant participation in Israeli and Syrian affairs, nevertheless suggest a public face permitting greater familiarity and study. But the solidity of a long and earthy past has generated mechanisms for adaptability that hide an inner reality not amenable to the ordinary tools of examination. One of the founders of the Druzes is said to have reminded them: "Obey every nation which passes over you, but remember me in your heart."

The ethnic identity of the Druze group, while generally accepted to be distinct from their dominant Arab Muslim surroundings, is subject to controversy. Kamal Joumblatt, the former head of the community in Lebanon and father of Walid Joumblatt, claimed that the Druzes have 5,000 years of history based on Greek, Indian, and Egyptian sources for the spiritual roots of their faith.[1] But he was confusing Druze ethnicity with earlier religious ideas later incorporated into the Druze faith. An instance of the opposite approach, dating Druze origins not too early but too late, is based on the claim that a French Crusader warrior, the comte de Dreux, gave his name to the establishment of a new people in the Lebanese mountains. Yet we know from credible sources that the Druzes predate the Crusades in the Middle East; in addition to which, as the traveler C. F. Volney noted during his roamings in the eighteenth century, no trace of French influence is found among them.[2]

Linked to the nature of their particular faith, which is tied to a Shiite heresy from the time of Fatimid rule in Egypt, it bears consideration that Persian origins may be the ethnic core of the Druze community. It was a missionary from Persia, Darazi, centrally involved in the founding of the Druze religion, who conceivably lent his name to the people's foundation in history. Philip Hitti, who rejected the notion of Arab origins, concluded that "the Druze people were a mixture of Persians, Iraqis, and Persianized Arabs."[3] Yet the idea of Berber origins is also feasible, taking account of this warrior people's position in the ruling and conquering ventures of North Africa, Egypt specifically, at the time of Druze appearance.

The argument of Arabian roots persists and was propagated in this century by the Druze leader Amir Shakib Arslan, except that his advocacy of Arab nationalism was perhaps dictating a prejudiced judgment.[4] Integrating the Druzes into the wider Arab fold became a point of politics, no longer a matter of historical validity. But beyond this problematic exercise in establishing Druze origins, the salience and integrity of Druze ethnicity has been an incontestable reality for some one thousand years.

The organization of the Druzes has never been formally tribalistic but familial and factional from the start. Grounded in a closed community structure, practicing endogamy throughout, asserting mutual security as a sacred obligation, this group is one of the most distinct the region has ever known. The division between shaikhs and peasants, based on economic stratification, was no barrier to an enduring sense of equality grounded in a profound sense of ethnicity. Leading notables, or zu'ama, led the community in war but had little permanent power or standing troops of their own. Each man brought his own arms when called upon.

The more predominant sociological reality was endemic divisiveness in factional family quarrels. In different periods of Lebanese history, the Joumblatts faced the Yazbecks, at times the Arslans; in Syrian history, the al-Atrash family was often confronted by Al-Asali kinsmen opposition organized in the Sha'abya movement. And in Palestine, the Halabi and al-Din clans contested for communal primacy. Throughout this feudal-based society, an ancient Druze proverb continued to capture and salvage the spirit of unity: "The Druzes are like a copper plate, for when you hit it anywhere, all of it will ring." In spite of divisions and feuds, the unity of the people was a noteworthy element for preparing a durable survival strategy in a threatening environment.

Religion and Its Precepts

The cultural particularity of the Druzes is due overwhelmingly to their religion, which identified them from birth. Religion and nationality are interlocked to become one in the Druze experience, and this is true notwithstanding the apparent general ignorance of the faith by most Druzes themselves. Deriving from the dissident Isma'ili Shiite sect, the origins of the faith revolve around the Egyptian Fatimid caliph al-Hakim bi-amr Allah of the early eleventh century. While mainstream Shiites elevated Ali, Muhammad's cousin and son-in-law, to the status of an incarnated divinity, the Druzes did the same with al-Hakim. In the mysterious transformation of his behavior, he went from Islamic piety, indeed fanaticism against all non–Muslims, to outright heresy. From a zealous construction of mosques and persecution of *dhimmis,* al-Hakim became a father of religious perversion. He stopped leading public prayer, opposed the Ramadan fast, and prohibited the *hajj* to Mecca.

The abrogation of the *shari'a* opened the floodgates to articulating a new religion that al-Hakim was personifying in a wild, idiosyncratic fashion. At root was the idea that God had appeared in a physical form in this last human manifestation of the divinity. Referred to as without parents or children, without proof of his death or murder, al-Hakim became the God of the Druze religion. Hidden and perfect, disdainful of all Sunni and Shiite doctrine and practice, al-Hakim personified an incarnational Muslim heresy of the utmost radicalness.[5] "The Druzes are not Muslims," wrote Peter Gubser, a mild enough judgment considering their flagrant heterodox divergence.[6] This was indeed the view of the Islamic cleric Ibn Taimiyah, who rejected them from the Muslim community in his *fatwa* from 1300. They are in fact, as further evidence will indicate, highly anti–Muslim.

The divinity of al-Hakim became the central element in the allegorical interpretation of his life and faith. Opposed to Islamic legalism and literalness, the effective founder of the religion, Hamza, built a theologic system that stressed the hidden spiritual core that constituted al-Hakim's suprahuman status. This *bateni,* or concealed doctrine, allowed for God's unity and the destruction of an externalized religion like Islam. Hamza, as the propagator and codifier of the new faith, turned al-Hakim, who disappeared mysteriously in Cairo in 1022, into a divine figure who would reappear in the "end of days." Meanwhile, his adherents would practise a radical unitarianism and abandon all orthodox Islamic precepts. *Jihad,* instead of the holy war against non–Muslims, became now a striving to know God. Even more, *jihad* could be conducted militarily against Muslims.[7]

This radical antinomianism rejected dogma and ritual, and replaced them with faith in the divine Imam, al-Hakim, and a set of beliefs that smacked of gnostic vintage. This was a philosophic religion without cultic paraphernalia. Druze solidarity grew from the idea of metempsychosis, which posited that when a Druze died, his soul reappeared in a new body elsewhere. Thus a universal far-flung Druze community existed, but its exact location and numbers were concealed. This heretical faith was absolutely beyond the boundaries of orthodox Islam, for if Shiism was already nonorthodox, its Druze offshoot must be outright non–Islamic to the core. The very status of Muhammad and the first caliphs, including Ali, was rejected; they were dismissed as erroneous ministers of God. Al-Hakim and Hamza were not.

In place of pure pillars of religion, the prophet Hamza substituted a moral code of behavior. It emphasized aspects of communal unity, mutual self-help, and collective self-defense, this a necessary requirement for a new religion that became the target of persecution.

The experience of *mihnah* put the Druze faith and people to the test. They closed the door to new adherents and fled from Egypt to Syria, seeking refuge from their pursuers in the mountains. They destroyed mosques and built a life of separateness from all others. The faith was studied by the *uqqal* (sages) and unknown to the *juhhal* (the ignorant). Some texts were written and studied, but the secrets remained privy to the few. No non–Druzes could penetrate the curtain of concealment. The appearance of al-Hakim on earth was an instance of divine illumination, but his light would leave all others in a state of spiritual and intellectual darkness. The Druzes believed that in the end, the mosques would be destroyed and the entire world revealed to be, or to become, part of the Druze people.[8]

Druze particularity derives from the religion but includes many elements whose significance goes beyond faith as such. A critical social mechanism is typified by *takiyya*, a prudence born of persecution, that legitimizes affectation, deception, and lying as defense measures in dangerous situations. Telling the truth is politeness, not obligation; a white lie is a sign of caution, not unethical behavior. In religious terms, hiding one's Druze identity can be a necessary posing in a threatening environment. Thus, as was said of the Fakhr el-Din emirs, "They were born Druzes, lived as Christians, and died as Muslims."[9] In the same spirit the famous Shihabi Druze dynasty from the nineteenth century has been referred to as "proto–Christian" because of the apparent conversion of Druzes during difficult times. This does not mean, however, that their inner faith was ever really abandoned. As the Druze proverb says, "A man's shirt does not change the color of his skin."[10]

The survivability of this community rested upon dissimulation at certain moments and upon military capabilities at other moments. Hardly any characteristic is so consistently emphasized as their martial vitality. "Vigorous fighters," wrote Volney; a "race of warriors," commented Parfit;[11] both based on their direct personal acquaintanceship with the Druzes in their native terrain. Basically a peasant people engaging in small-scale agriculture, they felt the ominous hand of foreign rulers—Mamluks and Turks—and the permanent problematic of local competitors—Muslims and Bedouins—that fortified them with a readiness for violent confrontation. Military skills were a natural educational trait, and the Druzes could mobilize an inordinate proportion of the community when the situation demanded. Since they were tough in temperament, hardy in health, fighting was second nature to this tried and tested minority. The impressive figure of the Druze man, sporting a cultivated mustache and often wearing a white cordless *keffiyya,* struck a pose of dignity and distinction in the mountains of Syria. Druze men, it was said, do not allow themselves to cry at funerals.[12]

Not all Druze life was cut from the cloth of hostility. The collage of group experience was, notwithstanding the military dimension, of variegated and colorful social strands. While patriarchal predominance rested upon the physical quality of things, Druze women were known for their visible public place. Unveiled though modest, wives were portrayed as equal to their husbands in marriage.[13] Hitti has reported that women initiates would even be permitted to attend Thursday evening religious meetings, though seated by themselves. Charges of sexual promiscuity seem to be part of the historical Muslim invective against this heterodox deviation. In law and in practice, Druze women enjoyed a notable status in the wider society. Unlike the provisions in the *shari'a,* the Druze religion permits a man's taking only one wife; either the man or the woman can cancel their engagement for marriage; and if the man is the one to initiate a break of the engagement, the woman keeps all presents granted until that moment. The verbal instantaneous divorce rite in Islam contrasts with the Druze requirement to handle this matter through the offices of the *Qadi.* Overall, Druze women enjoy rights far beyond those of their Muslim counterparts. Great deeds are recorded of Druze women, one of whom led Druze charges against the Christians in Hasbaya in 1859–1860, and the mother of Kamal Joumblatt was a ruling figure in Lebanon. Laurence Oliphant reported in the end of the nineteenth century that Druze women sit with their males and participate freely in social discourse.[14]

It is religion—and certainly not language, because the Druzes speak only Arabic—that highlights the community's particularity. Stories of visits to shrines and tombs signal divergence from Islam. The Druze center near Hasbaya in southern Lebanon and the gravesite of the prophet Shueib (Yithro) in the lower Galilee were foci of religious study and pilgrimage, respectively, with no ties to Islam in any way. Reports of eating pork (not likely) and drinking wine were not uncommon. Fasting during the month of Ramadan was unknown. Religious syncretism from Zoroastrianism (man descending from God) and Pythagorianism (transmigration of souls) was suspected. The obscurity of the doctrine and the legitimacy of remaining ignorant of it were conducive to religious laxity. Religion held the Druzes together, but it paradoxically constituted a rather marginal substantive aspect of everyday life. In this sense, the Druzes were a people more than a religious group. As one observer wrote, these people were only "nominally Druzes," not an invalid description in the theologic sense of text learning and ritual performance. In the social sphere, however, it was the Druze religion that solidified the community.

Druze Warfare Within and Without

From their earliest time of collective existence, the Druzes have been living in geographically distinct areas of high, inviolate mountain terrain. When they first sought refuge, they hid in Wadi al-Taym near Mount Hermon. Thereafter, they ensconced themselves in Mount Lebanon east of Beirut, in the Matn, and in the Shouf, and turned it effectively into the Druze Mountain — Jabal al-Duruz. Distant from the coast and its penetrability to foreign conquest, alien ideas, and cultural intermingling, the Druzes maintained a mountaineer solidity, unimpeded by the niceties of civilizational restraint and form. Some 120 small Druze villages dotted the landscape of the Lebanese range during the eighteenth century. In the following century when Druze autonomy was all but eliminated, they migrated, though not for the first time, to Hauran in southern Syria and further developed the area there into an alternative Druze Mountain homeland. Approximately 80 percent of all Druzes in Syria lived compactly in the Jabal Druze, 90 percent of whose inhabitants were Druzes. They always naturally turned to the heights, this in the Galilee and Mount Carmel of Palestine by the seventeenth century as well, and felt that security and dignity would be ensured.

Challenged by European Christians and Ottoman Turks, the Druzes often succeeded in fighting off enemy intruders or minimally survived their interference. At times, they were compelled to flee their villages, as during the rule of Ibrahim Pasha in the 1830s. Mountains and militarism were nevertheless the elemental prescription for Druze survival, as in the case of other Middle Eastern minority peoples.

The integrity of a specific Druze ethnic kinship, cultural character, and geographic location contributed to making a national history. It is a history of mythological struggles and sacrifices in circumstances of persecution and plight. It recalls how a small people not only survived but successfully established local Druze dynasties in Mount Lebanon, the most glorious being the Ma'anids (1517–1697), in particular under Fakhr al-Din II, who by 1613 ruled from Antioch in the north to Safed in the south. He was renowned for his military prowess, statesmanship, and liberality. He enjoyed the position of Amir in Mount Lebanon because of accommodation with the Ottomans, while the competing al-Tanukh Druze dynasty ruled in Sidon and Tyre. Meanwhile, confronted with a jealous Sultan in Constantinople, Fakhr al-Din traveled to Italy to seek an alliance with the Medici court in Florence. It is unlikely that the Druze leader needed to learn Machiavelli's advice to Lorenzo di' Medici in *The Prince* concerning the need for good arms, the study of the art of war, and the indispensability of faithful soldiers. Fakhr al-Din was already an experienced Eastern prince by that time. Nine years later, he returned home, without foreign assistance but inspired by the cultural delicacies of Renaissance Italy. Back in Lebanon, he built spacious gardens and adorned them (un–Islamically) with sculptures. But tensions with the Turks persisted, and the pasha of Damascus fought the Druzes and defeated them in battle in 1632. Fakhr al-Din II was executed, but the glory of his national Druze venture was never forgotten.[15]

In succeeding centuries the Druzes found a new leadership in the Shihabi dynasty with its capital at Dayr al-Kamar. Its most famous prince was Bashir II (1788–1840), who carved out an autonomous principality in Jabal al-Duruz in opposition to unilateral Ottoman rule. But inner Druze conflicts, between the Joumblatts and Arslans particularly, weakened kinship political cohesion. Confusion prevailed as the Shihabis reportedly turned from Islam to Christianity and their Druze identity assumed ambiguity. Later, though, Bashir II enjoyed Joumblatt support, now in opposition to the Yazbecki clan, and the Druze united under the near-unchallenged Shihabi emir. But cumulative internal feuds and external threats, in particular the attempt by Ibrahim Ali arriving from Egypt in Lebanon to disarm the Druzes, constituted too great a problem for Bashir. He led his people in revolt against the Egyptian invaders at the same time that he personally tried to crush feudal subordinates.[16] All of these episodes sapped the Druze capacity for unity. In the end, as the British bombed Beirut in 1840 in support of the Ottomans and against the Egyptians, the rule of Bashir II crumbled. He fled to Malta, and the Shihabi dynasty lost its primacy in national Druze life.

While subsequent decades witnessed Druze adaptability and fighting capability, their historical dominance in Mount Lebanon was no longer ensured. A far larger number of Maronite Christians than Druzes were reported to inhabit the zone by 1846.[17] Druze-Maronite civil war in 1841–1842 highlighted the bitter tension in the mountain, but the Druzes tenaciously held their ground. The French, who stood behind the Maronites, epitomized foreign determination to repel Muslim threats of all kinds against the Christian population in Lebanon. In late 1842 a dual regime, based on two *kaymakams* (deputy governors), was established in Mount Lebanon to provide an equitable administration for the Druze and Christian populations. It was during this period that Joumblatt leadership became predominant among the Druzes, and with British support, this old schismatic community enjoyed virtual independence. The partial subjugation of the Maronites on the one hand, and the distance of the Turks on the other, allowed for "a little independent republic" of the Druzes to function in the mountain.[18] This freedom often descended naturally into anarchy.

In 1859, apparently encouraged by the Turks and humiliated by what was seen as Maronite haughtiness, the Druzes struck out at Christians in Mount Lebanon and further south. Druze feudal lords were moved by a justifiable fear that peasant unrest in the mountain, apparent in Maronite society, could subvert Druze society too. All in all, sufficient grounds existed in Druze eyes to act with resolution.

The threat of Christian equality with Muslims, offered in the 1859 Ottoman reform, together with Christian power in the mountain, were too much for the Druzes to bear. They took up the fight of Islam and destroyed some sixty Christian villages. Druze military acumen and brutality were never in question. The blood of nuns and monks filled the streets of Dayr al-Kamar, Hasbaya, and Reshaya as Druze ferociousness wreaked infernal destruction on the Christians. In this orgy of violence, Druzes from the Hauran, under the leadership of the Atrash clan, joined with fellow kinsmen in Mount Lebanon. When it was over in the summer of 1860, Druze military superiority against the Maronites was a proven fact. This, though, did not prove that Druze political ascendancy would follow. Indeed, the aftermath of the civil war signaled the abrupt termination of Druze national autonomy for what would prove to be a very long period of history.

In August 1860, six thousand French soldiers landed in Lebanon to ensure domestic order and prevent the Druzes from whipping up further atrocities against the Maronites. Of greater consequence was the decision to establish a Christian-dominated *mutasarrif,* or administrative district, in the *Jabal* that demoted the Druzes from an equal partner (1841–1860) to a junior and inferior partner in Mount Lebanon affairs. Thousands of Druzes fled to the Hauran in southern Syria, turning it into the new Jabal al-Duruz of modern history. In 1879, Suwayda had become the new Druze capital, and across the land of Greater Syria—in the Lebanese Matn and Shouf, in the Hauran, and in the Carmel and Galilee—Druze life maintained its closed communal character, though without independence or integral unity. As in the past, intermittent Druze insurrections erupted, as in 1893 when the Ottomans tried to conscript them into the imperial forces.

As the idea of Arab nationalism developed toward the end of the nineteenth century, the Druzes considered throwing in with it. Getting wind of the mood prevailing in certain Druze circles, the Young Turks acted to stem the rising revolutionary tide after coming to power in

Constantinople in 1908. Some Druzes were hauled to Damascus and hanged. Yet Druze participation in Arab affairs continued unabated, as related by T. E. Lawrence regarding their participation in the Arab revolt against the tottering Ottoman Empire in 1917–1918.[19] Sultan al-Atrash, leader of Jabal al-Duruz in Hauran, actually entered into Damascus with Allied and Arab troops in October 1918.

Druze Particularity in Mideast States

The true spirit of modern nationalism had not touched, however, the deeper traditional fibers of Druze life by the beginning of the twentieth century. Bound by kinship ties and salient group particularity, no radical internal changes affected the native Druze community. Protestant missionary schools, like that at Ain Anub east of Beirut, offered them some Christianity mixed with some modernization. Education and medical care proved of benefit, and some Druzes entered the professions.[20] But rural peasant society as a whole, in Mount Lebanon and the Hauran, suffered from stagnation and impoverishment. The people could be mobilized, but only for a "good fight," not for national consolidation. The traditional elites prevailed, acting more like feudal lords than ideological catalyzers for a new awakening. At the same time, foreign involvement in Druze affairs proved marginal and inadequate to the wider challenges of political enlightenment and independence. Therefore, steeled by communal courage in the face of repression and adversity, the Druzes could survive, but no more than that. This was the situation as the First World War came to an end.

The formation of three separate states in areas of Druze settlement created seemingly impregnable barriers to any Druze national unity. In republican Lebanon, so constituted officially in 1926, the Druzes were a small minority of about 6 percent within the total population of what had become Greater Lebanon (*le Grand Liban*). The Christian-dominated entity formalized a confessional character to politics, but the Druze share was minimal. In Palestine during the same period, the Druzes were also an infinitesimal group on the periphery of a growing Jewish-Arab conflict that continued until Israel's establishment and thereafter. The most hopeful place for Druze developments was Syria where, though a tiny minority in the southern part of the country, circumstances proved favorable in an unexpected, though awkward, fashion.

Localism and particularism in Syria proved to be endemically aggravating to any reasonable possibility for comprehensive national unity.[21] Syria was a geographic area more than it ever was a distinct political entity. With Syria composed of a radical diversity of minority religious and ethnic communities, each traditionally suspicious of all others, the Druzes were able to enjoy a modicum of territorial cohesion in Jabal Druze in the South. Yet in addition to their own ethnic consolidation, the French mandatory regime after World War I chose to exploit the natural divisions in Syria for their own imperialist purposes. It is true, as in Morocco and Algeria, that the French were spurred on by a romantic sentimentality for old and rugged Mideastern peoples. The Druzes, the target of French intervention in Lebanon, now became the tool of French policy in Syria.

The Druzes in the Hauran-Jabal Druze mountain area of Syria, numbering 50,000–60,000 people around 1920, were offered regional autonomy by the French authorities. In contrast to the resolute repression of Arab nationalism in Damascus in 1920, a separate *état* (state) in Jabal Druze was proclaimed in 1921 and established in 1922. Its capital was Suwayda, and its local leadership was drawn from the feudal family of Salim al-Atrash, who became the governor. The regime was headed by Captain Carbillet, who treated the population with severity, imposing corvée labor and limiting the carrying of arms.

Local unrest led in 1925 to the arrest of Druze leaders and their expulsion to Palmyra, a step that catalyzed the beginning of revolt under the charismatic leadership of Sultan al-Atrash, who was smarting from the earlier appointment by the French of a kinsman rival. The traditional Druze elite feared French reform zeal, which threatened to undermine their power and status, this in addition to the humiliation suffered from the high-handed methods of Carbillet. In July 1925, when the Atrash forces took Suwayda and attacked French troops, the Druze revolt had begun in earnest.[22] It is interesting to note that simultaneous with the Druze insurrection in Syria was the Riffian war in Morocco. The latter's end in 1926 alleviated the burden on overseas French forces and allowed them to concentrate on the pacification of Jabal Druze, which indeed was achieved by 1927.

But the Druze revolt was a delicate ambiguity between local territorial ethnic patriotism and extended Syrian nationalism. On the one hand, the initial reasons for insurrection were lodged in Jabal Druze itself. The French reacted by bombing Suwayda, and the Druze conducted a guerrilla war against a technically superior adversary. The Druze separatist spirit, legitimized and encouraged by the French just a few years earlier, now confronted a determined French authority. Meanwhile, Druze flare-ups spread from the Jabal to Hauran and southern Lebanon as a discerning pattern of Druze peoplehood, across state borders, rose to the moment in history. The revolt that began with the Druzes remained throughout primarily a Druze affair. It seemed that the solidity of Druze peoplehood, even though its society was inchoate and divided, could overwhelm both foreign powers in the region and the new states whose political architects the French had been.

But on the other hand, the political rhetoric accompanying the Druze revolt was rooted in the idiom of pan–Syrian nationalist sentiment. Sultan Pasha al-Atrash, chief of the Syrian Revolutionary Armies, called the Syrians to arms with an enthusiastic cry. He proclaimed that the French "had divided the nation into states and religious sects." This nationalist claim was supplemented with a doubtful religious claim: "Our war is a holy war." Al-Atrash remained the symbol of the struggle, even after insurrection erupted in Damascus and north of it where he was not exercizing any appreciable influence on affairs.

Syria as a whole was approximately 70 percent Sunni Muslim by faith and even more Arab by nationality. It was prudent for the Druzes to practise *takiyya* and pose as loyal Syrians or dedicated Muslims rather than arousing the wrath not only of the French but of Syria's native population. Nonetheless, it is worth commenting that Syria as a whole was markedly quiescent. The rather rapid termination of the revolt provided painful evidence that a foreign power might cultivate a small minority people but that a native independence movement could not necessarily rely upon others to realize its goals. The Druzes had now learned the double lesson of French preference for the Maronites in Lebanon and French determination to repress the Druzes in Syria. Nothing beyond local autonomy, in the framework of the *Jabal* regime, could be expected in the future.

Still, in spite of the acrimony of the war, the French continued to play the Druze card to subvert the more comprehensive threat of Syrian nationalism. An *état* Druze lasted until 1936 when the Jabal was incorporated as a regular province within Syria, though a special administration continued there nonetheless.

Communal restlessness was not fully repressed when in 1938 local Jabal leaders raised the idea of joining Transjordan as an alternative to incorporation within Syria. In 1939 there was a brief renewal of Druze financial and administrative autonomy in the Jabal, but not for long. During 1942–1944 the inclusion of the province within Syria was completed, and this ended any idea of a Druze government.[23] Being an integral part of Syria did not erase Druze particularism as an ethno-regional fact, but now it was denied any political significance. France was finally decolonizing Syria with its full independence, realized in 1946, but it was questionable that Syria would decolonize Jabal al-Druze. Syrian nationalism demanded the unity of the entire country and inevitable rule by the majority Sunni-Arab population based in the urban elite centers.

The Druzes of Syria, who had fought the Turks and the French in successive battles, found themselves subject to the Arab capital city of

Damascus. In 1947, Sultan al-Atrash was disgruntled at the social and economic neglect of the Jabal.[24] At the same time, Druze peasants rose against that feudal family. Druze society as a whole lacked acceptable leadership; the group was collectively disoriented and frightened, without foreign protection or natural domestic allies. In this atmosphere of uncertainty and weakness there were some Druzes who talked of having the Jabal annexed to the Hashemite kingdom of Jordan to the south. But Syria was not in a concessionary mood at the moment of national independence.

The role of the Druzes, though just 3 percent of Syria's population, remained vital nonetheless. When opposition forces organized and conspired against the Shishakli regime in 1953, Jabal Druze was chosen to signal violent revolt against Damascus. But Shishakli preempted the Druze and massacred many at Suwayda. By January 1954, the revolt in all of Syria was over.[25]

In the course of modern Syrian politics, the Ba'th party, a radical pan–Arab nationalist and secular-socialist movement, became an agent for mobilizing rural minority groups into national political and military life. In 1963, the party took power, but it was not until February 1966 that its radical wing ousted all competitors. Druze army officers found that Ba'thism provided a legitimizing ideological cover for realizing their communal interests. Salim Hatum, a Druze who ruled along with the 'Alawite officer Salah Jadid, enjoyed the support of fellow Druze soldiers. In the summer of 1966 Hatum and other key Druze officers began to move against Jadid. But in September the head of the air force, the 'Alawite Hafiz al-Assad, threatened to bomb the Druze units if they tried to take Damascus for themselves. After some military units fought a number of battles, Hatum and his comrades fled to Jordan where they sought political asylum. Some, including Hatum, returned to Syria in June 1967 only to be arrested and summarily executed before the month was over.[26]

In modern Syrian history, the Druzes sometimes assumed the role of a dissident minority and sometimes that of a useful mercenary brigade. Their stubborn courage and ethnic particularity are always prominent group characteristics. It is the military vocation that captures their communal spirit; the political vocation is not their special expertise. When statehood was all but granted them in the 1920s, they failed to entrench and secure it over time. When senior army positions were won by talent and persistence in the 1960s, these were subsequently endangered by the drive for more singular success.

Throughout, during the rise and fall of their fortunes, Jabal Druze remained peripheral and relatively underdeveloped. Aside from modern military skills, the Druzes lack those of a fully modernizing society. It is this discontinuity between achievement in personal terms for some—for example, the Druze deputy chief of staff of the Syrian Army in the 1980s—and overall backwardness in collective terms for most that explains Druze inability to turn the corner in this century of turbulent developments.

The tension between Druzism and Arabism, between the Druze and Islam, and between peripheral particularism and Syrian unity has required various formulas for conflict resolution. Ba'thist Arabism strikes an ideological chord enhancing Druze integration, yet only to the extent that party membership and military position overlook the deeper dichotomy that cannot but persist ethnically between Arabs and Druzes. The socialist message, including radical political rhetoric, is a mechanism of the civil polity for integration in a pseudo-"secular" state that bypasses the domain of true belief. This has partially worked, particularly in the 1960s though somewhat less so in the 1970s as the 'Alawites began to dominate the Syrian power elite. Linked to all this was the renaming of Jabal Druze the Jabal al-'Arab (Arab Mountain) in 1947 to emphasize the Druzes' attachment to Syria.

Lastly, the religious integration of the Druzes into the world of Islam was strengthened when the Shaykh of Al-Azhar stated that Druzes are in fact Muslims. This theologically questionable evaluation could legitimize the "Ismaili hereticism" and allow the Druzes to play a respectable role in the Muslim East. Whether either side truly believed in the Islamicism of the Druze religion is a question. But perhaps both sides congenially employed the accommodating ruse of *takiyya*. In summary, the Druzes in Syria experienced a topsy-turvy twentieth century in a country that persistently moved toward consolidating national unity. The fact that this unity developed since the 1970s specifically under the direction of another minority community, the 'Alawites, suggested that the historical fate of all Syria, and the Druze minority within it, had yet to be finally decided.

To the west in Lebanon, the fragility of a confessional political system demanded careful reflection upon the ways of Druze practice. Their numbers rose from some 50,000 in the beginning of the 1930s to approximately 300,000 or more by the 1980s, at least 10 percent of Lebanon's population. Caught between the dominant Christians and the Sunni and Shiite Muslims, the Druzes under Kamal Joumblatt chose to adjust to the wider Arab parameters of the Mideast region. Engaged perhaps in traditional *takiyya*, or perhaps a true believer in political radicalism and ideological socialism, Joumblatt moved the Druze into the center of Lebanese national political affairs. Rather than steering communal existence in an inward isolationist direction, he charged into the heart of political activism. In 1948, Joumblatt established the Socialist Progressive party as an instrument of his personal role in the Arab-national movement. His outlook rested upon democracy and the

secularization of the confessional Lebanese state apparatus.[27] His
public position was opposed to minority divisiveness as he stressed the
primacy of "Lebanese" and "Arab" identities.

But it would be naive to infer that Joumblatt sought the veritable
disappearance of the Druzes through total assimilation into the wider
state and regional environments. For indeed he sharply criticized the
Syrians, the Palestinians, even the "Bedouin anarchy of the Arabs." He
spoke about revolutionary ideals but cautioned about the need "to find
one's authentic self." That could only mean that the Druzes were not
about to abandon their particular identity, even though they might participate in more general struggles. With three hundred years of family
history in Moukhtara, the strategy of Joumblatt was survival through
political deflection and ideological legitimization. This was in the spirit
of Emir Shakib Arslan, from a competing Druze aristocratic family, who
became a major leader of Arab Nationalism in the interwar years. Now,
in the era of Arab independence after the Second World War, Kamal
Joumblatt chose to play the same double-edged game.

It appeared that in confessional Lebanon an autonomous Druze
millet was a viable structure for community life, and this whether or not
a more comprehensive group strategy was adopted. Traditional families
dominated Druze political life and represented the people on the national scene.[28] It was Joumblatt who aligned the Druzes with radical
Nasserite forces in the 1958 civil war in Lebanon. It was the same
Joumblatt who aligned his people with the Palestinian-PLO forces in
the 1970s. Majid Arslan led a competing Druze camp, more committed
to system stability in Lebanon and opposed to Palestinian infiltration
into national politics. This became a particularly poignant issue in 1969
when PLO forces pressed for freedom of action within Lebanon and
against Israel.

Individual Druzes could hold major public positions, as when Majid Arslan served as minister of defense or Kamal Joumblatt served in
various governments or Nadim el-Hakim held the post of chief of staff
of the Lebanese Army in the mid–1980s. But the community as a whole
remained on the political sidelines until, and if, they were called upon
to take sides in national Lebanese conflicts. The combination of ethnic
introversion in the mountain and political involvement in Beirut served
the Druzes well for a few decades.

The outbreak of the 1975 civil war, the Syrian invasion in 1976, and
the Israeli-PLO confrontation upon Lebanese soil until and after the
1982 war could not leave the Druzes unmoved or indifferent. With
Lebanese society rent with strife and the political system in a shambles,
Druze particularity required resolute action for group survival. The
*re*incorporation of the Druzes into Syria contrasted sharply with their
somewhat *dis*incorporation vis-à-vis the national upheaval and col-

lapsed body politic of Lebanon. But the religious identity of the people was affirmed, and the Druze holy site dedicated to study and prayer at Hasbaya symbolized this. The military vibrancy of the people was also maintained in the escalation of violence toward the end of the 1970s. Yet a martial tradition could not in itself guarantee well-being. Indeed, Kamal Joumblatt was assassinated, apparently by Syrian gunmen, in 1977. His son Walid, who took over from his father, prudently chose to side with the Syrians.

The entire period of the Lebanese civil war compelled the Druzes to abandon their shell of communal introversion. They assumed prominence as effective fighters against their historical Maronite adversaries in the mountain. In the fall of 1983, for example, the Druzes handily defeated the Christian *phalangist* forces in the Shouf. Rumors of massacre surfaced, and Druze denials were unconvincing. One Druze officer involved in the fighting at Bhamdun, situated on the Beirut-Damascus highway, rejected the charges of massacring Christians. Yet he added: "We just surrounded the town and did not let anyone surrender."[29] This was a repetition of 1859 when the Druzes ferociously murdered thousands of Maronites. The Maronites now accused the Druzes of massacring 1,400 civilian Christians during 1983. The confession cleavage deepened as the Druzes proved invincible in Mount Lebanon, armed by Syria, assisted by the Sunnis, and invigorated by a hardy spirit of native militarism.

Untainted by urban softness and unprotected by a distraught central regime, the Druzes defended themselves with great prowess. Assuming the pose of Arab nationalists, radical "progressives," and Lebanese patriots suggested *takiyya* rather than a denial of self-identity.

However, it also implied relinquishing any collective Druze aspiration for political freedom. The Maronites might accuse Joumblatt of conspiring to establish a separate Druze principality or state in the Shouf. But the true reality pointed to traditional entrenchment rather than exploring the parameters of political independence. Caught between the Syrians, Palestinians, and Maronites—and caught up in native feudalism, factionalism, and stagnation—the Druzes in Lebanon would likely ensure their existence, but not more than that. Under the circumstances prevailing in Lebanon, that was not a small accomplishment. With the value of life virtually nonexistent there, Druze existence demonstrated that a historically persecuted people could still manage the arts of life with dexterity.

The smallest Druze community historically has been that in Palestine, modern Israel, where they number approximately 70,000. Living in six purely Druze villages and twelve mixed villages with Muslims and Christians, they did not possess communal juridical autonomy until Israel granted them the right to separate religious status in 1957. A Religious Council for the Druze community was established in 1961, and Druze courts were organized in 1962. This differentiation from orthodox Islam was preceded by Druze differentiation from Arab peoplehood even earlier. This was an old self-conscious group choice, to be reflected in the specific Druze educational curriculum distinct from the Arab one. But more striking was the fact that in 1948 Druze soldiers fought in the Israeli Army for the survival of Israel against the Arab invasion. In 1956, the Druzes were officially conscripted into the Israel defense forces, and this positioned them as adversaries of the Arab states with whom Israel was engaged in warfare. In Israel more than in Syria and Lebanon, the Druzes chose the path of integration in a spirit of comradeship with the Jewish majority population but with full awareness of communal specificity.[30]

Over the years a crisis of identity, more particularly of group strategy, nonetheless surfaced. Perhaps this was an inevitable consequence of intense ethnic interaction and modernist experiences in Israel. There was a profound sense of the "covenant of blood" that Jews and Druzes had inaugurated in the framework of the military, a feeling of small peoples united in a common struggle against a more powerful regional enemy. In political terms, this very human reality led to the formation of a Druze Zionist Society and to the expression of abiding Druze loyalty to the state. Amel Nasser al-Din, a Likud member of the Knesset, personified the Druze affiliation with the Jewish national endeavor. His firstborn son had been killed in the War of Attrition between Israel and Egypt in 1969. Another instance of integrating solidarity was the career of Zaidan Atsche, another Druze MK who also served as information officer in the Israeli consulate in New York.[31] Another Druze appointed to an Israeli diplomatic post was Asad Asad, a senior army officer who served at the United Nations mission of Israel in 1987–1988.

The formal incorporation of the Druzes proceeded in 1970 when, dispensing with the procedure to utilize the "Arab departments" when dealing with government offices, the Druzes could deal with them directly like the Israeli Jewish citizens. In 1975, all army units, not only the "minorities unit" or the Border Police, were opened to Druze soldiers.

But in contrast to group solidarity with the state, a feeling of alienation arose among members of the Druze youth and younger-generation leaders in particular. Some chose to resolve the dilemma of identity by claiming an Arab character as inherent in Druze peoplehood. A Druze Initiative Committee was established in 1972 by the Rakah Communist party, the voice of Palestinian Arab nationalism poised against Jewish Zionism, and it sought to solidify a Druze-Arab alliance in opposition to Israel. For example, a Communist cell was set up in the Druze village of Bet Ja'an in the northern Galilee, and some young men accepted party scholarships to study in Eastern bloc countries, as in pursuing medical studies in Hungary. One Druze proclaimed his sentiment clearly: "We are actually Arabs. Anyone who says otherwise is a liar."[32] This statement reflected linguistic ties with the Arabs and a shared feeling of "otherness" in a Jewish-defined state. Some young Druzes now openly opposed the compulsory draft into the army. Others complained about the absence of modern services in backward Druze villages. Yet this alienating sentiment and identification with Rakah was a distinctly marginal phenomenon.

Rafik Halabi, from a prestigious Druze family, gave vivid expression to this new orientation. He was an example of Druze mobility in an open society, a news correspondent for Israel television and later the editor of its news department. He defined himself as an "Arab Israeli" besides remaining a Druze. While his father was an ardent Zionist, he explicitly rejected this identification.[33] Denying the linkage between Israeliness and Zionism served as a signpost on the road to identification with the Arab community and its cause within—and against—Israel.

Greater Druze discomfort with the state of affairs surfaced with the 1982 Lebanese War and specifically the alliance between Israel and the Maronite Christian population. In the summer of 1983 the Lebanese Druzes were the victims of a mounting Israeli-Maronite momentum in the Shouf Mountains. Druze soldiers in the Israeli forces were enlisted by *their* state for a military maneuver that threatened *their* ethnic-religious community across the border. Within Israel, Druze spirits were confused and angry. When the army was preparing its withdrawal from the Shouf, Israeli Druzes were worried about the ultimate fate of their brethren in Lebanon. They hastily formed an ad hoc committee to lobby in political circles, to raise money for the Druzes in the Shouf, and to declare their readiness to join them if need be.[34] Sa'id Halabi, a reserve duty officer in the Israeli Army, explained "As a Druze, I cannot sit back and see my people destroyed."[35] Israel's close ties with the Maronite *phalangists* turned its loyal Druze soldiers into potential enemies on the Lebanese battlefield. As some thirty Druzes from Israel actually went north to join fellow Druzes fighting in the bitter civil war there, the irony of the situation made a mockery of statehood and citizenship as the inviolable ground of obligation in comparison with the emotive ties of kinship and blood.

The problematics of the Jewish-Druze relationship in Israel were further complicated by the question of the Druzes in the Golan Heights. There some 13,000 Druzes inhabiting four villages had lived under Israeli rule since 1967. They remained Syrian citizens and emphasized that famiy ties with other Druzes within Syria compelled them to dissociate from Israel. Meanwhile, the Druzes radicalized their views in the face of Israeli political hesitation. They feared being denounced as traitors were they to express loyalty with Israel only to find themselves later once again under Syrian rule. This feeling of living in political limbo did not strengthen Druze respect toward Israel. When the Israeli Knesset passed the Golan Law in December 1981 effectively incorporating the area into the juridicial framework of the state, the Druze population reacted with unrepressed dissatisfaction. They rejected the offer of Israeli citizenship, and even the head of the "Druze Zionist Circles," Salman Abu Saleh, was forced to give up his citizenship.[36] This entire episode further complicated the relations between Israel and its Galilean Druze community, which by the nature of things felt a sense of identification with the Golan Druzes. Notwithstanding, Druze soldiers did not demur in carrying out their military duties to ensure quiet in the Golan Heights.

The influence of modernization on Druze self-perception was particularly acute because of the role of Druzes in the Israeli Army. Military service acquainted Druze males with modern skills and a modern Jewish society. This raised painful questions concerning traditional values between men and women in Druze villages and posed a challenge to the status of religion in Druze life. Modern ideas about work and money, individualist goals and interethnic interaction, led to a slow pull toward urbanization linked with higher education. Falling between Jewish society and Arab nationalism, better educational standards, but not necessarily equally available job opportunities, could contribute to anomie, psychological disorientation in modern times.[37]

Expecting better services in their village communities, Druzes are expectedly disappointed and bitter if their living standards are no better than those available in Arab villages, whose male members do not, unlike the Druze males, serve in the security forces. Moving among competing identities and roles—Israeli patriots, Druze particularists, and Arab nationalists—has been an emotionally taxing experience. The divisions within Druze peoplehood all along, and within all of Israel, have strained the very notion of integral Druze peoplehood. Unable to identify fully with the Jewish spiritual vision of Israel, and unable to identify fully with Islam as the religion of the major sector of the Arab population, the Druzes were left in an awkward situation. Yet integrating experiences via the army and the Hebrew language, with greater government interest in the 1980s to improve the material conditions in Druze villages, offered a recipe for smoothing the rough edges in Jewish-Druze relations. The wisdom of Israel would still be put to the test in implementing a policy of sensitivity and decency to a minority that had put its wager on Zionism in historic Palestine.

Survival without Sovereignty

The overall character of the Druze minority rests upon instinctive brotherhood more than political nationhood. Being divided among three contiguous states prevents purposeful common action but enables moments of communal solidarity nonetheless. In 1954, Lebanese Druzes wanted to assist Syrian Druzes who were threatened by the Shishakli repression. In 1958, Syrian Druzes wanted to come to the aid of Lebanese Druzes during the civil war. In 1983, Israeli Druzes wanted to join Lebanese Druzes in the throes of the latest civil war. These instances of heartfelt solidarity demonstrated the binding ties of minority peoplehood in spite of geographic separation.

It was never obvious that the Druzes really aspired to statehood as the framework for their particular ethnic existence. Indeed the very drive toward independence could endanger their physical well-being in the event that Islamic or Arab forces saw this as sectarian deviation and an unforgivable separatist slide toward a fatal confrontation. The idea of Druze political independence has been favored in the abstract by some members of the community in Israel,[38] while in Lebanon cantonal Druze autonomy became a veritable reality of life in the Shouf Mountain.

Peter Gubser has suggested that were Syria and/or Lebanon to disintegrate completely as functioning political entities, Druze particularity could perhaps turn itself into Druze politicization on the road to separate statehood.[39] However, beyond these conjectures, the hard truth points to feudal habits of thought and community organization incongruously persistent in Druze life at the same time that modern rhetorical themes like Ba'thist ideology and Arab nationalism are adopted and modern skills are learned.

Symbols may help legitimize otherwise doubtful ideas, but they have little relationship to the core of Druze identity. This compact people never consistently developed an international diplomatic practice, never cultivated external support, and never tried to turn its traditional communal assets—group cohesion, military courage, and religious particularity—into a political goal. Druze statehood remains a post-traditional utopian notion, geopolitically implausible and apparently unnecessary for Druze survival. Only the collapse of the state system in Greater Syria could, in the subsequent disarray, raise the utopian notion of Druze statehood on the Middle East's political agenda.

CHAPTER 6

'Alawites: To Power and the Unknown

Within Syria, the home of an "unrealized nation," in Petran's phrase,[1] there dwell various particularist peoples who emerged prior to and since the coming of Islam. Among them are the 'Alawites, also known as Nusairis, whose primitive communal cohesion was successfully turned into a formidable political force in modern Syrian politics. Hafiz al-Assad, the president since 1971, and major military and security elite members, were members of this obscure religious sect. In their case, a minority had taken power in an important Arab country, and their story, along with that of modern Syria, reflected on the wider Middle East region in the last third of the twentieth century.

The multiethnic and multireligious character of Syria put an expected premium on the vitality of kinship ties within each separate group. The 'Alawites are an undeniably distinct ethnic community who have historically had little consciousness of being Arabs.[2] Their collective origin, rooted in a Shiite heterodoxy from southern Mesopotamia in the tenth century, may be related to Persian stock, though this is unclear. The idea that 'Alawites descend from Crusaders, who built fortress chateaux in the Syrian mountains where this minority has lived, is also unfounded. Similarly unsupported is the view of Renan that the 'Alawites are outright Christians, based on the etymological identity of Nusairis (an 'Alawite name) with Nazareen; closer to the truth apparently is the fact that the Crusaders, like other transient powers, persecuted the 'Alawites.[3] Claude Cahen offered the hypothesis that Nusairi origin may be rooted in the ancient Mardaites of the mountains, later developing their particular religious faith.[4] Mystery shrouds this people's formative history, and an absolutely authoritative explanation does not exist.

Yet the intense in-group feeling, based on strict endogamy during their thousand-year experience, is not in doubt. Ethnic solidarity has traditionally not been eroded by the tribal structure of 'Alawite life, which continued even during the recent period of their history. Mountain 'Alawite society divided into four tribes, which, though they have generally lacked centralized organization, were not known to engage in considerable intertribal strife. Their chiefs held no particular power, and segmentary forms of relationships predominated throughout. Tribal division did not, however, deny the wider validity of an 'Alawite kinship community vis-à-vis Arabs, Turks, Crusader Christians, and Sunni Muslims in particular. External hostility and internal secrecy accentuated the ethnic cohesion of this small minority community.

Mysterious Sectarianism

Central to the cultural identity of 'Alawites is their unique religion that transforms them from tribes into a sect, perhaps a true people. The generally accepted source of the 'Alawite religion points to Muhammad Ibn Nusair from the village of Nasaria, near Kufa in central Iraq. In 891 he was reported to have seen Christ, according to a certain source;[5] more likely, he drew upon the Shiite imamic tendency in highlighting his religious initiative. He proclaimed himself the Bab (door) of the Imams and assumed prophetic status against both Sunni and Shiite doctrines. Ibn Nusair and his followers were forced to flee Iraq and settled in the western mountains of Syria where they cultivated their separate deviationist religious community. A different, perhaps related interpretation of 'Alawite origins tells of al-Husayn ibn-Hamdan al-Khasibi (d. 968), buried north of Aleppo, who apparently helped organize the new faith.[6] Whatever the truth about the genesis of 'Alawism, the reaction of orthodox Islam was undeviating in its absolute rejection of it. Ibn Taimiyya considered 'Alawites more infidel than idolators and called for *jihad* against them. In reaction, the 'Alawites adopted the ways of silence and *takiyya*, hidden away in their refuge in the mountains.

'Alawite religious faith, or the Nusairi sect, is rooted in a doctrine whose ideas reflect multiple theological and philosophical influences. Phoenician paganism and Christian trinitarianism allegedly coexist with Islamic notions. Astral images and nature cults predominate in 'Alawite spiritual visions and experiences. Greek or Gnostic conceptions of the divinity intersperse with human incarnation as a key element in its theology. But most critical is the place of 'Ali, Muhammad's cousin and the leader of Shiism, who is the corporeal embodiment of the divine, much like Jesus in Christianity. The primacy of 'Ali, portrayed allegorically as the sky (Muhammad as the sun, Salman as the moon), makes 'Alawites an offshoot of the Shiite Islamic branch. But its other aspects make the religion a particular combination of beliefs, focusing on souls and stars, that bedevils the search for a clear picture of the group and its faith.

External sources often castigated the 'Alawite or Nusairi doctrines as excessively permissive of moral and religious deviation. Debauchery in sex, the eating of pork, the drinking of wine during seances, and worshipping the devil were some typical charges.[7] Certainly the notion that the enemies of 'Ali travel the spiritual route of metempsychosis, only to return to the world as dogs, did not endear 'Alawites to other Mid-eastern peoples. Real sinners come back as Jews, Christians, or Sunnis. Telling falsehoods ensured the hostility of surrounding neighbors. The celebration of festivals that were hardly derivative of orthodox Islam, pilgrimage rites to tombs (ziaras) and sacred spots, baptismal ceremonies near the water—all captured the extent of the aberration.[8] Ismaili influences were ascribed to the Nusairi path, besides a pagan and Christian impact, and for all these and other reasons the 'Alawite religion was beyond the pale of mainstream Islam. Ignaz Goldziher was categorical: "This religion is Islam only in appearance"—though even its appearance was hardly Islamic.[9] The 'Alawites, then, were neither Arabs nor Muslims.

The cultural contours of 'Alawite life revolved around a religious solidarity binding a peasant-based agricultural community. They grew vines, wheat, tobacco, and cotton, existing always on the social and economic margins of an external alien and antagonistic society. They reportedly remained out of the mosques, certainly out of power. With a religious life that wavered from paganism and Gnosticism to Christianity and Islam, 'Alawites rejected foreign initiation into their secret cult. In-marriage was an iron ethnic rule, and women, believed to lack souls, were known to dance with men at certain moments of celebration.[10] Orthodox Muslims, had they known, would have frowned upon this libertarian practice.

Carrying the burden of Shiite loss and founded on the legendary personalities of 'Ali and his son Husayn, the 'Alawites remained a politically and economically depressed community. The world was in darkness, and light was luminous only for the 'Alawite believers. A classic minority complex of vulnerability combined with virtue colored the group's self-consciousness. A permanent condition of poverty had compelled 'Alawite families to sell their daughters into servitude to rich Sunni households in the city. This disgrace remained a vivid experience into the twentieth century. Perhaps the only true redeeming feature of 'Alawite life, aside from a unique religious heritage, was a martial tradition of mountain fighters. These people, lacking urban finesse or intellectual refinement, did exude a rough-and-ready Mideastern robustness to survive over the centuries and during profound changes in the regional power structure.

The geographic location of the 'Alawites in the Nusairi Mountain, known as Jabal Ansariyya, effectively defined it as an 'Alawite province for some eight centuries. The coastal city of Lattakia has been ruled by various forces—Greek, Arab, Seljuk, Crusader, French, and Syrian. Its 'Alawite population was always very small, while the Sunnis constituted the majority group along with a significant Christian presence. But in the mountains a hardy 'Alawite people concentrated in some eighty tiny villages. In 1940, Weulersse reported that 224,000 of the 350,000 inhabitants, or approximately two-thirds, were 'Alawites. Lodged between the Mediterranean sea to the west and the Ghab plain to the east, the mountain homeland suffered from economic underdevelopment and political abandonment. The major inland cities of Syria were Damascus, Homs, Hama, and Aleppo. Some 'Alawites lived in Homs and Hama, usually as peasant farmers under Sunni landlords. The mountains remained an ethno-regional 'Alawite enclave, peripheral to major Syrian developments but central to minority group survival. The topography suited the physical needs of a dissident religious sect and promoted the viability of its unique collective identity. This geographic fact would later be turned into a potent social lever in the drive for 'Alawite power in Syria, but an 'Alawite power that was traditionally nurtured by group cohesion cultivated in a closed mountain environment.

The history of the 'Alawite minority is marked by seclusion and insurrection as alternative modes of group strategy against threatening external peoples and states. During the Crusades, they were suspected by Muslims to be allies of the Christians. During the modern French period in Syria, they would be similarly suspected. In the 'Alawite mountain stronghold, a degree of collective autonomy was maintained over the centuries. In the nineteenth century, they were basically independent of the Turkish pasha of Tripoli. When the Egyptians under Ibrahim Ali controlled Syria, the 'Alawites revolted against them, then later against the reconstituted Ottoman authorities. Uprisings took place in 1806 and 1811, and in 1852 when 'Alawite autonomy was declared.[11] Virtual 'Alawite autonomy continued until the very fall of the Ottoman Empire in 1918. By that date, the ethnic, religious, and geographic integrity of Jabal Nusairi was an indisputable human and historic reality, but one lacking the talents or resources to become an 'Alawite political state.

'Alawite Statehood and the French

The establishment of French mandatory rule in Syria in 1920 became the basis for a transparent policy of "divide and rule" that was of benefit to the 'Alawites. Not internal social change but external intervention energized a dormant and listless community. In fact, in the interval between the Turkish retreat and the French arrival, 'Alawite bands were already filling the vacuum in the Jabal. At the same time no less than 73 'Alawite chiefs petitioned French general Gouraud in late 1919 requesting the formation of a free Nusairi union. Perhaps not unexpected was that initial 'Alawite-French contact erupted in battles in the mountains. Shaykh Salah al-Ali led his people in 1920–1921, as did the more renowned figure Sulayman Murshid later on. But 'Alawite revolts reflected native tribal antagonism toward alien powers more than they sprouted as national liberation struggles. The French, rather than completely repress the rebels, co-opted them into the strategic framework of imperialist control.

This was a positive pattern of policy for the 'Alawites, but with a single though pertinent exception. The only feasible candidate to be a national leader of this minority, Sulayman Murshid (b. 1906), was exiled to the Euphrates area in 1925. Claiming a prophetic vision and founding a new Nusairi religious sect, Murshid would persist over the decades to rebel against central authority, be it French or Sunni-Syrian.

It is historically fascinating to recall the simultaneous national expressions among the Berbers, the Druzes, and the 'Alawites in the mid–1920s against French overseas rule. Yet in all cases the minorities suffered defeat and loss at the hands of a seemingly schizophrenic political authority, at times sympathetic, at times brutal. France's romantic sentimentality for exotic Mideastern groups stiffened into opposition when any move toward independence was attempted.

Building upon sectarian and regional consciousness, the French set about formalizing 'Alawite particularism in political and military forms. In 1922, an 'Alawite state was constituted, albeit in federation with Damascus and Aleppo, yet in 1925 it was separated and became an independent governmental entity. It had a local council with a majority of 'Alawite members, others being Christian, Sunni, and Ismaili. In the spirit of the times, Sunni tribunals were precluded from judging 'Alawite cases in their own state entity. While 'Alawite primacy was irrefutable in what was called L'État des Alaouites, the French nonetheless chose to modify its singular communal image. In 1930 the state was renamed le Government de Lattaquie. Meanwhile, Syrian Arab nationalism gained momentum in Damascus and other key urban centers, and its leadership aspired to reintegrate the outlying provinces of the Druzes and 'Alawites into the political fabric of national life.[12] In 1936, this was achieved with the annexation by Syria of the Lattakia entity, which, though subsequently reconstituted in 1939, disappeared wholly as a distinct political or administrative unit in 1942. When Syria became an independent state in 1946, nothing remained of the French devise of an 'Alawite *état* in the Jabal Ansariyya.

Military Professionalism, Political Pretensions

The military manifestation of 'Alawite particularity found vivid expression in widespread recruitment into the armed forces. From 1921 to 1945 three of eight infantry battalions in the *Troupes Spéciales* were 'Alawite units. Various minority peoples, like Druzes, Circassians, Kurds, Ismailis, and Assyrians served in the army of France. The majority Sunni Arabs were conspicuous by their absence. But in Lattakia and Antioch, in particular, some 90 percent of the soldiers were 'Alawites.[13] These excellent recruits, the pride of the 'Alawite community, chose the most expedient and natural path to escape endemic poverty and elevate their status in society. Later this cohesive minority would discover that the military profession could be a stepping-stone to political power. It was the policy of French imperialism, as the 'Alawite mercenary role merged with the cultivation of the 'Alawite *état* in the mountains, that shed light on the historical strategy of how a determined minority could penetrate the Syrian state establishment in future decades. The pursuit of *military* involvement and the attainment of *political* consolidation would later become a tried and tested 'Alawite formula for minority success.

The founding of modern Syria in the mid–1940s struck a blow at any semblance of 'Alawite autonomy or independence. No longer would this sectarian minority enjoy its own religious jurisdiction, nor would it maintain its parochial military units in the *Troupes Spéciales*. As part of Syria, surmised Albert Hourani, there was no justifiable reason why 'Alawite particularism should in any way "present an insoluble problem."[14] The idea of Syrian nationalism, in particular the Ba'thist ideological version, propagated the glorious myth of integrative Arab unity that would incorporate all Arabic speakers, presumably including 'Alawites.[15]

But the predominant force in political and economic terms was the urban-based, landowning elite. Living in the four key cities— Damascus, Homs, Hama, and Aleppo—the traditional Sunni class had historically dominated the peripheral rural-agricultural zones, relegating them to the margins of Syrian life. With independence, Syria would conceivably revert to urban Sunni overlordship as in the past, but now freed from foreign promotion of dissident minority groups. The 'Alawites numbered some 325,000 people, 10 percent of the Syrian population, though 20 percent of the army till 1946, and now seemed fated to oblivion, to lose whatever status they had enjoyed during the mandate regime. Nevertheless, the fact that 80 percent of the 'Alawites lived in their mountain refuge rather than in Sunni-dominated cities confirmed that minority survivability was linked to geographic isolation. It will be interesting to follow the historical course of this marginal Mideastern minority and how it transformed its mode of collective existence in just a few years' time.

The postindependence era in Syria was rocked with political turmoil and military coups d'états. The nearly 70 percent Muslim-Sunni majority was unable to establish a stable regime that could provide for economic wellbeing and national integration. As symptomatic within other Arab states, the army assumed the role of arbiter and organizer of power. But once again the convergence between the minorities and the military institution arose in Syria.

The non–Sunnis had predominated in the army during the French mandate period because of historical and political reasons. The minorities, such as 'Alawites, Druzes, Kurds, Circassians, and Ismailis, were considered born fighters and more trustworthy because of the role of Sunni-Arab sentiment against French control. Until 1946, less than half of the graduates from the Homs Military Academy were Sunnis. The 'Alawites might indeed be poor, undernourished, and illiterate in the Lattakia province, but the pursuit of the military career counterbalanced their inferiority and offered them an honorable way out of it.[16]

In the 1950s, the 'Alawites began to consolidate a strategy that combined upward mobility within the Syrian armed forces with membership in the politically radical Ba'th nationalist party. It was this fortuitous combination that would propel the disadvantaged peasants from Jabal al-Alawiyyin into the nexus of national affairs and ultimately to the heights of power. The path of 'Alawite separatism was clearly blocked. Sulayman Murshid's revolt in 1946 had ended in defeat, and the Syrians executed him. His son led an uprising in 1952, and he too was executed. Communal 'Alawite representation in the Syrian Parliament was terminated, and separate juridicial rights suffered a similar blow.[17] An alternative converse path to 'Alawite separation was 'Alawite integration by exploiting the army-Ba'th nexus for all it could provide this ambitious and capable minority community.

The permanent crisis in Syrian politics led to the formation of the United Arab Republic (UAR) by Syria and Egypt in 1958. This union, a temporary solvent for instability, symbolized national weakness under Egyptian hegemony. Opposition to the UAR was organized within the Ba'th Military Committee resident in Egypt, three of whose key members were 'Alawites. In 1961, the union dissolved with Syrian secession. But more to the point, it was this committee that decidedly planned and executed the subsequent Ba'th coup in early 1963 that signaled the ultimate takeover of power from the older and urban Sunni elite establishment.

Pivotal to this basic change in the power structure and to the ideological spirit of Syrian politics were the 'Alawites. They were strategically located in prominent military and party posts. Ba'thist officers, in particular 'Alawite and Druzes following the near wholesale purge of Sunnis after 1963, tightened their influence in and over the regime. From 1963 to 1966, the internal Syrian power struggle between 'Alawites and Druzes reduced the impact of the Sunnis and paved the way for the February 1966 coup, when the Ba'th Military Committee, particularly under the leadership of the 'Alawite general Salah Jadid, consolidated its control.[18]

The new Ba'th regime from 1966 to 1970 radicalized Syria's ideological orientation by engaging in the Palestinian Question and tightening ties with the Soviet Union. But underneath the political surface, Ba'thist officers acted out a minority scenario. Sectarian ambitions paraded about in an Arab nationalist setting, and while the official ideology opposed tribalism, that became the cornerstone of Syrian politics. With the removal of the historical civilian leadership of Michel Aflaq and Salah al-Bitar and the purging of Sunni and subsequently Druze officers, the optimal situation crystallized for an 'Alawite thrust to full power.

The stage was set for an 'Alawite protostate with its political headquarters not in Jabal Alawiyyin or Lattakia but in the capital city of Damascus. Herein lies the remarkable minority success: not a small separatist challenge on the periphery of an integrated existing state but a surgical operation aiming at the strategic heart of the entire body politic. The 'Alawites, who were incapable of establishing their own national entity in their own territorial homeland, went ahead and took over the already functioning Syrian entity. Manipulating it, managing its resources, maneuvering its divergent political, religious, and ethnic forces, and masterminding its collective internal and regional destiny—these were realizable tasks. Employing coercive power, not building constructive projects, fit the 'Alawite sense of things better.

The Assad Regime

On November 13, 1970, Hafiz al-Assad, former head of the Syrian Air Force and minister of defense since 1966, effectively led a successful coup d'état in Damascus. His loyalist troops took over the radio and the press, arrested opponents, occupied offices of the Ba'th party, and put Salah Jadid and President Atasi in custody. In February 1971, Assad became the first 'Alawite president of Syria following the consolidation of his coup and its culmination in a new regime.

The cohesive tribal community had now arrogated to itself a full-fledged state and began to pack its senior positions with its kin-group members. While some 'Alawite opponents were purged and even some 'Alawite leaders were assassinated, it was clear that Syria had basically come under the control of a small ethnic-religious minority from the northwestern part of the country. The periphery had captured the center, the peasants had revolted against the urbanites, the 'Alawite minority had overwhelmed the Arab-Sunni majority.

At the root of this extraordinary tale is a man and a process. The man is Assad, born of poor 'Alawite parents in 1928 from the small village of Qardahah in the Jabal Alawiyyin. His grandfather had fought the Turks, his father fought and then accommodated the French, and Hafiz, the son, would fight the Syrians—but later, with a crafty turn, become their leader.[19] He was the first 'Alawite to be accepted to the Homs Military Academy, trained as an air force officer, becoming its commander in 1964. From 1966 to 1970, Assad was part of the 'Alawite elite triumvirate with Salah Jadid and Muhammad Umran. During all these years, and indeed since the 1940s, Assad was an active Ba'th party member. His involvement in political and military affairs was the required tactical recipe to rise to the highest rung of power in 1970.

From that point on, Hafiz al-Assad solidified sectarian minority rule over a Sunni-Syrian population. The broad basis of the power system became 'Alawite kinship members. At least eighteen of twenty-five key military posts were held by 'Alawites in the 1970s.[20] 'Alawite representation in the Ba'th party soared after 1970; nearly 43 percent of the military members of the Syrian regional commands of the Ba'th party were from the 'Alawite community in Lattakia province.[21] It is important to remember that 'Alawites constituted only 11–12 percent of Syria's entire population; thus their predominance in the army and the party was astounding, testimony to ethnic solidarity of a high order.

In January 1980, the Regional Syrian Congress of the Ba'th party meeting in Damascus set up a central committee to study policy-making. Of the seventy-five members, no less than thirty were 'Alawites, most of them army officers.[22] A central pillar of the 'Alawite regime was the Defense Companies (Saraya al-Difaa), an 'Alawite praetorian unit headed by Rifaat al-Assad, the president's brother. This force, which numbered some fifty thousand soldiers until the early 1980s but was later reduced considerably, symbolized that true loyalty to the Ba'thist 'Alawite-based regime was ensured only by fellow 'Alawites.

The second more narrow and select basis of the power system related to Assad's tribe, al-Matawirah, and its members played a prominent role in regime stability. Ali Duba, the head of Military Intelligence; Ali Salih, the commander of Air Defense; Ali Aslan, deputy chief of staff; and Muhammad al-Khawli, the chief of Air Intelligence were major military figures from the president's tribe.[23] While this pattern strengthened cohesion in the more immediate circle of Assad's associates, it did imply that strict tribalism stood in tension with more all-encompassing 'Alawite ethnic and cultural solidarity. Indeed, after coming to power in November 1970, Assad ousted members of the Haddadun tribe from high office and replaced them with his own tribal elements. Inter-'Alawite rivalries actually erupted into battles in the Lattakia region in 1984. However, the general Sunni threat to the 'Alawite regime has helped to subdue outright hostility among the four 'Alawite tribes.

The third and most intimate basis of the power system touches on the family relatives of Assad. His brother Rifaat, both a vice president of Syria and commander of the elite Defense Companies, was close to the most sensitive nerve centers of regime existence. Rifaat's loyalty to Hafiz was never questioned, even though he caused considerable embarrassment through his ostentatious style of living, brutal corruption, and bravado manner. Four other brothers were in charge of elite military units in Damascus, responsible in particular for 'Alawite security as a sectarian imperative. A cousin, Adnan, commanded the Struggle Companies, and two nephews commanded key defense units. Nepotism would seem to come naturally to what is already a broad-based kinship regime.

Gerard Michaud was insightful to refer to the Ibn Khaldunian concept of *asabiyya*—a shared blood destiny—in explaining how a rural ethnic community penetrated the city and took it over.[24] But he was even more insightful in offering to answer the dilemma left dangling by Ibn Khaldun himself: How does the community that is compelled by the bonds of *asabiyya* maintain its virile nerve to rule for an extended period of time? The 'Alawites, Michaud argued, established a Mamluk-style regime based on a professional soldiery with the requisite budgets, authority, and resources. The 'Alawites do not just rule a state; they *are* the state in an enveloping process of having merged their minority fate with and within the Syrian state. *"L'état c'est moi"* is an appropriate formula that resounds with the personality cult that surrounds the person of Hafiz al-Assad and the policy strategy that secured the 'Alawites in power after 1970.

The 'Alawite "awakening stage" developed in conjunction with certain historical conditions, like French rule in Syria and unredeemable Sunni contempt for a heterodox deviation, but hardly from a modernizing ethos. The 'Alawites, though exposed to new technical skills within the military institution, remained for the most part a backward rural and peasant community. It took 'Alawite control of Damascus to catalyze 'Alawite development in the Jabal refuge. Exploiting their native talents, they moved to learn new skills and benefit from social progress that is typical of modernization. Drysdale demonstrated that significant advances in health care and education took place in Lattakia province in the 1970s. While Damascus remained the center of higher medical standards, rural areas like Jabal Alawiyyin began to receive a greater proportion of medical staff and services than in earlier years. A medical school was opened in 1975 at the new university, itself established in 1971 in Lattakia city. In the field of education, tremendous strides were registered in student enrollment in the 'Alawite region: While the 'Alawites constituted only 11 percent of the country's population, 18 percent of the country's students were in Lattakia province (admittedly, not all were 'Alawites). Female enrollment increased dramatically as did the opportunities for post–high school studies for the region's youth.[25]

The 'Alawite heartland has benefited from large government expenditures for regional development since Assad took power. Both national budget money and foreign aid, including that from the U.S. Agency for International Development,[26] were invested in irrigation, roads, ports, factories, and more. Particularly significant is the geographic and demographic outreach of the 'Alawites in recent years. The 'Alawite population increased by several tens of thousands in the northern Lebanese city of Tripoli, traditionally a Sunni stronghold, following Syrian military occupation of parts of that country. This northern Lebanese city is effectively becoming the southern defense line of an expanding 'Alawite entity.[27] The very establishment of a separate Lebanese political entity in 1920 was never recognized by Damascus. It is with impunity that Syria now exploits the weakness of its tiny western neighbor, as the 'Alawites slowly transform the very character of its human landscape.

A similar process is occurring east of Jabal Alawiyyin where Homs became an attractive urban alternative to traditional residence in the mountain villages. Accounting for the various development trends within the 'Alawite region and its southern and eastern fringes, it is clear that this historically isolated and cautious minority is now exuding new confidence and energy. 'Alawite city elites will likely arise from these modernizing processes and help consolidate, along with the rural-origin military elites, a surging 'Alawite society and political nationality.

The persistence of an 'Alawite-led Syrian state fixed the parameters for bitter conflict with the Sunni-Arab population. The religious and ethnic majority was stymied in its natural drive to assert control over this historic land of classical Islam and its imperial city, Damascus. Syrian human pluralism was twisted into a blasphemous political curse.

An Arab politician once related a conversation he had with President Assad during which various criticisms were raised against the 'Alawite regime. In the end Assad asked, "Why do you Arabs accuse me of ruling in the name of a minority? In which state in the Middle East does the majority hold power?"[28]

The idea that "tribal totalitarianism" is an Arab regional norm is an exaggeration, but only a small one. The Hashemite throne in Jordan, the Saud crown in Arabia, the Sabah dynasty in Kuwait, and the Takriti Sunni-Arab regime in Iraq are four political examples of minority rule that compare favorably with 'Alawite rule in Syria. But Yasir Arafat reportedly carried the charge of sectarian rule a step further when he accused the Assads, Rifaat in particular, of wanting to establish a union of minority groups—including the Jews—to challenge Sunni Muslim domination.[29] It was the anathema of non–Arab and/or non–Sunni rebellion, organized as minority states, that shed a greater light on the 'Alawite deviancy in the eyes of the majority population in Syria and across the region. Sadat had also labeled Syria at one point an "'Alawite-Ba'thi" state.

The mechanisms for conflict resolution have been only partially effective since the rise of Assad to power. Not unexpectedly, his rule aggravated confessional and ethnic conflicts in Syria. Most obvious as an ideological formula for coexistence is Ba'thist Arab nationalism in which the 'Alawites would be considered full-fledged Arabs. Certainly Assad's policies have been weighted heavily in the direction of Arab purism and primacy. Rhetorical, diplomatic, and military support for the PLO, brute antagonism to Israel, and calls for pan–Arab solidarity have colored the political and ideological tenor of Syrian life since 1970. As an Arab, Assad fights Israel, and as an Arab, he rejects making peace with Zionism. Arabism, however, is not a fully convincing slogan or strategy when, for example, the Syrian army entered Lebanon in 1976 to fight the Palestinians rather than assist them or when Syria supported Iran against fellow Arab Iraq in the Gulf War beginning in 1980. The 'Alawites speak Arabic and sing the virtues of Arab nationalism, but the Sunni Muslims have reason to doubt the authenticity of the 'Alawites' Arab identity and commitment. The credibility gap was symbolized by the July 1980 assassination in Paris of Al-Bitar, a founder of the Ba'th party. His dream of Arab nationalism was snuffed out by an 'Alawite bullet.

Islam as an integrating ethos has been manipulated for 'Alawite purposes of legitimizing their rule. Nagging questions of 'Alawite religious orthodoxy have never been truly resolved. Initially Assad tried to fashion a secular spirit and offered, for example, the following formula as a presidential oath: "I swear on my faith and honor." A popular uproar forced him to include the Islamic idiom of "I swear by Allah

Akbar" in good Muslim fashion. The 1973 draft constitution ignored Islam, but this too was remedied. At a certain point, the Syrian Sunni *ulema* declared Assad a Muslim, and the Lebanese Shia *ulema,* specifically Musa al-Sadr, declared 'Alawites to be Shiite Muslims. In 1974, Assad went on the *hajj* to Mecca and attended prayer services in Damascene mosques on occasion. He appointed Sunnis to senior governmental positions and sought to deflect ever-present suspicions that 'Alawites were inveterately hostile to Muslims and that they were themselves non–Muslims. It seems that the 'Alawites did not really adopt Shiite practices.

The Sunni majority in Syria remained unconvinced. In their eyes, the 'Alawites were ruthless usurpers of power, untrustworthy in their motives and worthy of punishment for the obscenity of minority tyranny. Islamic fundamentalist groups, in particular the Muslim Brotherhood, turned their repulsion into reprisal. In June 1979, they attacked the Aleppo artillery school, murdering thirty-two and wounding another fifty-four (other sources claimed sixty had been killed) — most of whom were 'Alawites. In the same year, riots broke out between Sunnis and 'Alawites in Lattakia.[30] In 1980, 'Alawite military units under General Ali Haydar, himself an 'Alawite, acted to quell violent demonstrations in Aleppo. The Muslim Brotherhood was outlawed as unrest continued into 1981.

In February 1982, the greatest confrontation took place when Islamic insurrection was confronted by the Defense Companies commanded by Rifaat Assad. Reports and rumors indicated that part of old Hama had been destroyed and anywhere from 10,000 to 30,000 Sunni residents killed by the security forces. But the Sunnis seemed not to give up. They were intermittently successful in assassinating key officials and close friends of Assad, like the rector of Damascus University and the director of police. Assassination attempts were made on Assad's life as well, in June 1980, for example. In January 1982, Sunni officers were allegedly implicated in a coup effort against the regime.[31] It was this episode that forced the issue and brought Rifaat Assad to Hama a month later. The results were costly for the Muslim Sunnis, and the 'Alawites stayed in power. By 1987, the Muslim Brotherhood was severely divided into different factions and forced out of Syria, dispersed to West Germany, Iraq, Jordan, and Saudi Arabia. The movement seemed to be in eclipse, distraught to the point that it chose to negotiate with the Syrian regime after unsuccessfully trying to fight it.[32]

An Uncertain Gamble

Churning out 'Alawite-Sunni brotherhood from these circumstances was not very feasible. Not only was the Sunni community deadly opposed to 'Alawite dominance in Syria, but there was a suspicious slant to its regional Shiite role. Four Mideastern states highlighted a new and revolutionary Shiite axis in the region. Khomeini's Iran, the 60 percent Shiite majority in Iraq, Assad's heterodox 'Alawite regime in Syria, and the radicalized Shiite numerical plurality in Lebanon. Together they constituted a profound historical challenge to Sunni hegemony throughout the Muslim Middle East.

Assad, who sent students to learn at the Shiite theological center in Qom and supported the 'Amal Shiite militia in Lebanon, was a vital part of this political alignment that brought together the classically underprivileged Muslims. Noteworthy in Assad's strategy was collaboration with Shiite Iran against Sunni-led Iraq in particular during the initial stages of their prolonged war. Islam, in the view of Syria's Sunni community, was a banner of *jihad* against the 'Alawites rather than a tie of brotherhood with them.

Policies based on civilian integrative mechanisms and institutional adjustments only partially overcame sectarian conflict within the polyglot Syrian republic. Certainly notions of Arab nationalism, socialism, and modernization reflected a mobilizing sense of a collective national mission. Assad had become the contemporary fabricator of Syrian stability and a most dedicated promoter of the anti–Zionist campaign. In these and other ways, the 'Alawites spread their rhetorical and political net very wide, seeking safe consensus issues, avoiding divisive ones as much as possible. Exercising Syrian hegemony over vulnerable Lebanon to the west and declaring greater ideological Ba'thist purity than a competing Ba'thi party regime in Iraq to the east stood as pillars of Assad's unifying strategies. Co-opting Sunnis into senior positions, like Abdel-Halim Khaddam as a vice president and foreign minister, was part of the subtle manner to lend legitimacy to an otherwise illegitimate minority political blasphemy.

Damascus, once the noble imperial capital of Sunni-Arab Islam, became under Hafiz al-Assad a city occupied by the heterodox 'Alawites. Unable to build their own state or secure one under and after the French, the 'Alawites took over an existing state. They never let numbers get in their way; an 11 percent ethnic-religious community just subdued all others. In order to preserve their own autonomy, they understood that it might be necessary to subvert the independence and authority of the Sunni-Arab majority. Ruling others became the prescription to ensure that no one would rule them and that they would rule themselves. By working within the system, the 'Alawites succeeded in exploiting it for their own group ambitions.

The development of the 'Alawite regional homeland followed naturally from the control exercised over Syria as a whole. The once marginal Jabal assumed national importance. Its traditionally backward society began to experience the birthpangs of modernity and progress. From being ethnically distinct and religiously parochial, the 'Alawites advanced along the road toward consolidating their political nationality. People consciousness slowly transcended minority consciousness as ideological, socioeconomic, military, and political strides were made. 'Alawite nationalism, supported in a fashion by the Soviet Union and based on tight Syrian-Russian ties, seemed to be the final political product of this maturation process.

This minority regime had crossed the threshold to face a momentous dilemma: continued control of Syria, or retreat and entrenchment in the Jabal? Many analysts believed that 'Alawite investment in the mountains was preparation for the time when Sunni-Arabs recover the Syrian state for themselves. At that junction the 'Alawites would seek refuge in their own geographic hearth.[33]

But the possibility of 'Alawite secession from Syria may not be easily achieved. Under circumstances of threat and repression created by a vengeful Sunni restoration in Damascus, 'Alawite separation may be a desperate decision—not only to maintain communal independence but also to assure collective survival.

Yet successful secession is highly problematic. As Mahmud Faksh put it, the process of political readjustment in Syria under the Sunnis "is likely to be untidy and disruptive."[34] History may eventually demonstrate that the 'Alawite victory in arrogating state power in Syria beginning in the 1960s, culminating in Assad's rise to power in 1970, set into motion their own future defeat and disaster. The Sunni-Muslim Arabs may never forget this outrage and conceivably may never forgive it. Assad, known for "his 'Alawite cunning," may have bitten off more than he and his kinship group can chew.[35] Meanwhile, strong and confident in the Lattakia region and its outlying areas, the 'Alawites decided to dig in their heels and face the crunch when it comes.

Part III
Christian Minorities

CHAPTER 7

Copts: A Precarious Community

Close to two thousand years of Christian history in the Middle East are encapsuled in the tenacious survival of the orthodox Copts in the Nile Valley. Living a closed communal existence, they assumed international noteworthiness in 1977 when Pope Shenouda III, their 117th spiritual leader, visited President Carter in Washington. Then, in 1981, President Sadat of Egypt imprisoned the distinguished pope and exiled him to a desert monastery. In 1983, President Mubarak of Egypt, in testimony to a joint meeting of the two Foreign Relations Committees in the U.S. Congress, denied any antagonism to the pope and promised his quick release.

These circumstances highlighted that the fate of an ancient segment of oriental Christianity was no longer just a domestic Egyptian issue. It had become an issue of global significance, for the Copts themselves but perhaps also for American-Egyptian relations. It remained to be seen whether a new activist strategy of communal behavior would solicit support or, on the contrary, aggravate an already delicate and dangerous minority condition within Egypt.

The ethnic continuity of the Copts, particularly in a country like Egypt that has known waves of immigration and conquest, is a remarkable testimony to group identity and cohesion. Laying claim to descent from pre–Christian ancient Egyptian peoples and linked to the Nilotic pharaonic peasant population, the Kibt (apparently the name of a small town in Upper Egypt, meaning "the land of black soil") was the European form of the later name, Copts. This is the Greek etymology for the name of Egypt (*Agyptos*) itself.

As the native inhabitants of Egypt, they preserved the proud title of indigenous uniqueness. Facing Europe and Byzantium, Bedouins and Kurds, Sunnis and Shiites, the Copts entrenched themselves in a situation of grave adversity. Holding tightly to their orthodox faith, they refused intermarriage with Muslims. As people of the land, they tended to reject migration or emigration as solutions to domestic threat. There is no denying the fact that following the Arab-Muslim invasion of Egypt in 640, much of the then 90 percent Christian population converted en masse, tempted by economic incentives and compelled by the sword, while some fled and some were expelled. But as a distinct community, the Copts survived.

Their racial line may not be as pure as Professor Sayce once argued,[1] though it has been resistant to alien admixture over the ages. Overall, the majority of the *fellahin* peasant-based population is native Egyptian Coptic, hugging the Nile Valley and resident in the villages and towns of the land. Arab-Oriental types, Turkish groups, Nubian and Ethiopian branches, constitute but a small minority in the ethnic distribution of Egypt's population.[2] This ethnic profile is explainable because the Islamic conquest of the seventh century did not bring in its wake a mass Arab influx. As a result, native peasant-Copt stock predominates in Egypt. It is tribally unaffiliated, as befits non–Arabs in the Middle East.

Religious Roots

While pagan art forms and religious notions did not fully disappear with the introduction of Christianity into Egypt, Copt culture is still overwhelmingly a product of its Christianity. In the year 64, St. Mark, martyred for the faith in 68, came to North Africa with a theology adaptable to the local sensibility. The pharaonic notion of man's being divine, expressed in the oneness of the leader and related to the cult of Isis, was a congenial background for faith in Jesus as a deified human. The idea of resurrection was also consistent with ancient Egyptian beliefs.[3] The establishment of Christianity in Egypt, centered in Alexandria, was a rapid development. Pagan temples were turned into churches. The seeds of former monastic practices provided the spiritual soil out of which a life of Christian solitude became a pillar of the Coptic church in Egypt. During the early centuries, Copt missionaries penetrated Africa, Arabia, and Europe in search of converts.[4] Until 381, with the Council of Constantinople, Alexandria was the focus of the universal Christian church before Rome and Jerusalem, and its pope was the doyen of its clergy, notably Popes Athanasios, Cyril, and Dioscoros.

The particularity of the Egyptian Copts was bound up with their independent theology. They ultimately constituted a national church with the Council of Chalcedon in 451, at which point the Monophysite doctrine positing the single nature of Jesus, as divine, was now a fixed principle. Until 311, the Egyptian Copts faced the onslaught of pagan

Rome; thereafter they faced the enmity of the Byzantine church and its Melkite branch. After Chalcedon, the Copts set out to purge all Greek influence from their literature and liturgy. Ancient Bohairic Coptic became the language of religious prayer and ritual as vestiges of Greek were swept aside. Until today, notwithstanding the arrival of Arabic in Egypt in the seventh century and its total adoption by the fourteenth century at the latest, the Coptic language persists as the unique cultural mark of the national church. It was not until the sixteenth century that all of the canon of Holy Scripture was finally translated by the Copts into Arabic. In the seventeenth century, Arabic Bibles appeared.[5] It is important to add that efforts have been undertaken to resurrect the Coptic tongue as a spoken language, a project of the Institute of Coptic Studies in Cairo. The language was being taught in Sunday schools and adult educational programs, and some small successes were recorded in its active revitalization.

Coptic culture has always been primarily a religious, though also a nationalist matter since the coming of Christianity to Egypt. The cross is the symbol of a martyr's experience characterized by suffering and persecution. Sunday mass is the day of community and communion. The tattooed cross on the right hand is the sign of faith. Family gatherings, in which Copt women appear more visibly than their Muslim counterparts, forge collective solidarity. Certain names (Ghali and Hanna), though Arabic, continue to identify the Copts.[6]

The higher level of secular culture among Copts has always exemplified their social station in opposition to the Muslim population of Egypt. As scribes and accountants in the service of diverse Islamic regimes and conquerors through the nineteenth century, Coptic Christians maintained an economic edge over Muslims. Richard Burton noted this fact during his sojourn in Egypt in the 1850s,[7] but Edward William Lane, a fellow Englishman, castigated what he called Copt "presumption and intrigue."[8] While he admitted Coptic skills as tradesmen and civil servants, Lane upbraided their ethnic inwardness and social haughtiness.

At the turn of the twentieth century, another Englishman, Lord Cromer, who administered Egypt in the name of the British Empire, mentioned the Copts' skills as surveyors, scribes, and clerks. Cromer recognized Lane's prejudice against Copts and his being "a strong Mohammedan sympathizer," but thought the Copts in no fashion morally superior to the Muslims of Egypt. Indeed, he found them similar to the majority population, having assimilated its Muslim language, customs, and manners over the centuries.[9] He added somewhat unfairly that a long history of Muslim repression had led the Copts to cultivate "remarkable powers of intrigue."

Traditionally the vulnerability of Copts forced them to hire Muslim protectors. Better educated but nonviolent did little to ensure physical well-being.[10] Based upon a cohesive religious way of life, and bolstered by a tradition of occupational professionalism, the Copts maintained a positive self-image notwithstanding Muslim (and Arab) predominance in Egypt extending over a thousand years.

The Monophysite doctrine was a spiritual divide from much of Christendom, and monastic practices illustrated a move toward physical isolationism. The administrative custom of a Copt bishop's securing his diocese for life, itself a manifestation of the spiritual community of faith binding individual Christians to their ecclesiastical leader, also captured the inward and closed organization of Copt society.[11]

The geographic hearth of Copt settlement in Upper Egypt was also a major element in their distinct peoplehood. Although Copts are found in Cairo and Alexandria and constitute about 20 percent of the population in these major cities, their particular settlement map extends from Minya to Girgeh, and even farther south, with Asyut the key zone. In these administrative districts the Copts are slightly less than 30 percent of the total population, surrounded by the remnants of age-old churches and monasteries, maintaining a Christian life among a Muslim majority. Hourani reported that Christians (mainly of the Orthodox Coptic church) were about 25 percent of Asyut province in the 1940s, at a time when they constituted some 13 percent of Egypt's total population.[12] These figures were conceivably underestimated at the time and may be for the more recent period.

Sectarian rioting led by Islamic fundamentalist groups erupted into violence and harassment in 1980 against the Copt community in Minya and Asyut,[13] perhaps because of their minority predominance in that part of the country. The Copts were targets of Muslim attacks in Cairo and Alexandria as well.

The center of Egypt is in the North, dominated by Cairo and the Nile Delta, which extended its authority throughout history into the South. Making Egypt a united country was, in part, an imperial necessity combined with a hydrological imperative. But the centralization of power was a constant discriminatory scourge for the weaker South. Leonard Binder illustrated this (though without ever mentioning the Copt factor) when he noted the existence of a higher percentage of university graduates from the North, better health services in the North, and lower levels of industrialization and provincial budgets in the South.[14] Upper Egypt, a significant Copt geographic zone, was in many respects an economic periphery of the North. This stunted the prospects for collective Copt development and encouraged migration to the larger Northern cities. However, even in the large urban conglomerations, Copt identity did not diminish and, perhaps not surprisingly, was accentuated in the last few decades especially. But the notion of a geographic hearth in Upper Egypt, with Asyut as the Copt capital, resounded with national Christian pride.

Excommunicated by the universal Church and subdued by the Islamic-Arab power, the Copts have a history of long suffering and vibrant persistence. The Council of Ephesus denounced the Copt theologic heresy in 431, and the Pact of Umar, following Muhammad, castigated the Christian *dhimmis* as inferior social beings. Significantly though not exclusively concentrated in the Egyptian interior, and alienated from the wider Christian world community, the Copts were fated to a history of defiant self-reliance as veritable aliens in their own land.

The Islamic conquest of Egypt from 640 to 641 inaugurated the decline of Christianity in the Nile Valley. There were one hundred bishoprics in the year 600, but only seventy by 700; in the year 1300, only forty remained.[15] While some Copts joined the Arab governmental apparatus as accountants and translators, others engaged in revolt to secure Christian self-expression. Over time, the burden of *dhimmi* taxation compelled thousands to accept Islam. The surge to revolt, like the insurrections from 725 to 773, persisted intermittently until 830 at least, but to no avail. Copts were dragged off to Baghdad as slaves. By the tenth century, the spoken Coptic language had all but died, replaced by Arabic. The caprice of changing rulers would arbitrarily affect the Copts' condition. It is said that Saladin, suspecting Copt collusion with the Crusaders, punished them sternly. The overall Christian population, formerly some 90 percent of Egypt, dwindled incessantly to some 10 percent.

The extreme fragility of Copt existence was rooted in the superiority of Muslims exercised through the *dhimma* doctrine. Islamic primacy often degenerated into brutal repression. A Maghrebian visitor to Cairo in 1301 witnessed the degradation of the Christians: None could ride a horse or hold public office; churches were closed; and Christians had to wear a distinguishable colored turban different from that of the Muslims.[16] Violence against Copts and their ecclesiastical establishment was a central theme in the sectarian relationship. Muslim mobs, based on the rule of Islam, ransacked Copt neighborhoods and massacred their inhabitants, as in Cairo in 1343.[17]

This situation led continually to mass conversions from the Cross to the Crescent. Islamic legal opinion developed a harsh attitude toward churches, as both Ibn Taimiyya in the fourteenth century and Shaykh Ahmad al-Damanhuri in the eighteenth century condoned the destruction of churches.[18] Sixty churches were destroyed in 1321. With the Copt religion victimized, the Copt language fading, and the Copt community straining under heavy *jizya* and *kharaj* tribute, Copt history was burdened with minority-status bitterness under Islam for more than a thousand years.

During the French and British Years

Flashes of good fortune and bright hopes rose in the Copt skies from time to time. Even during the Mamluk period, individual Copts attained high government position, such as chief of the mint. But it was the coming of Napoleon to Egypt in 1798, establishing Christian European power in Cairo itself, that became a historic opening for the Copts. Muallim Ya'qub Tadras, a Copt born in 1745 in Upper Egypt who had risen to a high position in the previous neo–Mamluk regime, was then appointed by Napoleon in charge of finances in his home area. Ya'qub then joined the French army commanded by Desaix and fought against the Mamluks in Upper Egypt.

It was during 1799 that the idea of a Copt entity was canvassed, with Ya'qub destined to be its leader. He began to organize a Copt legion in the service of the French. The entire project was fated to dissolve, and Copt liberation from Islamic oppression faded like a dream.[19] However, other Copts besides General Ya'qub advanced impressively during the French occupation of Egypt. Girgis al-Gawhari was minister of finance, and Elias Buqtur from Asyut was Napoleon's private secretary and the official interpreter for the Egyptian Army.[20] This brief episode from 1798 to 1801 demonstrated that foreign sponsorship within the country could transform Copt weakness into a newfound vitality. Yet when the French withdrew, the Turks killed the Copts for having collaborated with the enemy from Europe.

The Muhammad 'Ali regime established in 1805 was another stroke of Copt good luck. The entire period until the British conquest of Egypt in 1882 was generally characterized by official tolerance and opportunity. Edward Lane did not fail to note that Muslim children learned "to hate the Christians" at an early age, and even the slaves in Egypt impudently insulted the Christians. But this popular antipathy to the *dhimmis* was in the nineteenth century offset by Muhammad 'Ali's liberalism. The Copts were widely employed in government service as clerks and superintendents, though this would further aggravate conflicts with the Muslims. The public authority of the *kafir* (infidel) in conducting the tax registers contravened the holy tenets of the Pact of Umar. But the Copts advanced nonetheless, strengthening their native community simultaneously with greater participation throughout Egyptian society.

During Muhammad 'Ali's rule, which lasted until 1849, the Copts could ring church bells and carry the cross in public. His successors were no less accommodating. In the 1850s, Copt schools opened, and the first girls' school in Egypt, which was Coptic, began to function in 1853. The debilitating *jizya* was abolished in 1855, and the Copts awakened to the prospects of full equality with the Muslims.[21] Christians were generally to be seen riding horses, symbolic of prestige and security. Cultural activity further developed with the establishment of a Copt printing press. In 1873, community councils were inaugurated, part of the consolidation of Copt minority autonomy. In 1874 the Coptic al-Majlis al-Milli was set up to run national Copt affairs throughout the country. While this development enabled popular participation in community affairs, it also engendered tensions with the holy synod of the Coptic Orthodox church. In 1875, a Coptic Theological School opened in Cairo, and the collective self-confidence of the Christians whirled through the century with a flourish of activity. The era was, however, marred by some dark moments like the apparent assassination of Pope Cyril IV by poisoning.

The integration of Copts on the broader national plane was not less significant. Muhammad 'Ali himself appointed a Copt, Mu'allim Ghali, as his financial adviser, though he later had him killed (perhaps to mollify Muslim grievances at the rise of the Christians). During Khedive Isma'il's rule, the Copts entered the Assembly and filled the civil service, and by the 1880s, perhaps as many as 90 percent of state employees were Copts. They could now join the army (though many preferred not to) and were recruited to fight in the Sudan in 1885. In this liberal atmosphere, a Copt established a newspaper, *al-Watan (The Homeland)* in 1877, both the name and the action expressive of Christian legitimacy and activism as Egyptians, not merely as tolerated but benign *dhimmis* in a Muslim land. A bold note of collective confidence was struck when *al-Watan* wrote in 1908 that "the Copts are the true Egyptians" and the "real masters of the country." All others, they added, were invaders.[22] It was in this spirit that the nineteenth century served as a period of national awakening for the Copts. The unanswered question was how all this would affect the place of the Copts in relation to the Muslims and what goals could realistically guide Copt efforts in the modern era of nationalist consciousness and struggle.

From the invasion of 1882 until the Free Officers' revolution of 1952, the British period in Egypt was mixed in its opportunities and results. The operative Copt strategies included integration within the wider Egyptian society, standing with Muslims against alien rule once the nationalist campaign for independence began, but also local group consolidation in the face of Arab and Islamic challenges. These years were also known for major Copt advances, individually and collectively, in spite of the objective disadvantages of minority status.

The new era opened with the not unfamiliar chant of "death to the dogs of Christianity," directed specifically to the Armenian prime minister Nubar Pasha in 1879. The Urabi mutiny of 1881 instilled fear in the hearts of the Copts and culminated in the massacre of some fifty Europeans in June 1882 in Alexandria. Thousands of Christian

Europeans fled the country, but the native Copts remained. They sought security in the interior and hoped that the coming of the British would ensure Christian well-being, perhaps even preferential treatment.

But this was not to be the case, though individual Copts advanced in filling high offices in the Egyptian administration. Butrus Ghali Pasha successfully organized the judicial system, became minister of finance in 1893 and minister for foreign affairs in 1894, and ultimately prime minister in 1908. However, he was murdered in 1910 at the hands of a Muslim fanatic, Ibrahim El-Wardani, following the decision of a judicial tribunal presided over by Ghali that sentenced Muslim villagers to death for their role in the Denshawai incident of 1906.[23] Other important individual Copt successes included Marqus Hanna Pasha, who became the minister for public works in 1923; Nagib Iskander, the minister for public health; and Nagib Ghali Pasha, son of Butrus, who was the under secretary in the ministry for foreign affairs.[24]

Facing Islam, Arabism, and Egypt

The pivotal Copt figure of Makram Ebeid Pasha (1888–1961) highlighted their participation and integration within twentieth-century Egyptian political society. He was born in Qena in Upper Egypt, studied at Oxford, and returned home to work in the Ministry of Justice in 1913. During this time, the National party tried to bring Muslims and Copts together to express the distinctive Egyptian personality. But of greater historical moment was the Wafd, led by Sa'ad Zaghlul and formed in 1919. It was this party that fostered the Copts' active involvement in the independence movement. Ebeid, Sinout Hanna, and other Copts became credible Egyptian patriots, rallying around the emblem that interlocked the cross within a crescent.[25] Ebeid, the Wafd leader following Zaghlul's death in 1927 and a senior minister in various Egyptian governments, was relentless in aspiring to full Copt integration. He would sprinkle Koranic verses in speeches and unashamedly declared in 1936: "I am a Christian, it is true, by religion, but through my country I am a Muslim."[26] Just two years later, Mustafa el-Maraghi, the rector of Al-Azhar and a former tutor to King Farouk, called the Copts "foxes."[27] This rhetoric was designed to discredit the Wafd party and the public role of the Christians, and expressed the tight linkage between religion and politics. Egypt, as an Islamic land and a Muslim society, would not countenance an equal and public role for Christians. The efforts and sacrifices of Ebeid and other Copts, like Wisa Wasif and the Ghalis, withered in the wake of a cold rejectionism.

The age-old hunger for acceptance was a painful self-exposure for the Copts. Seeking legitimacy in Egyptian political life compelled them to admit the primacy of Islam. Salama Musa, Christian author and Arab socialist, opposed the Copts' being a separate faction in Parliament. He glossed over religious distinctions in proclaiming that "Islam is the religion of my country," and it therefore became his duty to defend it. Yet anti–Copt feelings never disappeared from Egypt. The minority syndrome, reflected in Copt grasping for legitimacy, proved a political path fraught with dangerous pitfalls at every turn. The dream of a secular society in Muslim Egypt was more a Copt wish than an attainable political goal.

When the *millet* principle was abandoned with the 1923 Egyptian Constitution, the Copts were thrust into the national waters with no institutional raft. By 1937, as Muslims rose continuously in all areas of public life, only 9 percent of government employees were Copts.[28] The struggle for an egalitarian pluralistic polity had been a Wafd ideal but not an Egyptian reality. Helping move Egypt toward full independence failed to bring in its wake the necessary conditions for collective Copt viability. Joining with the majority group had also threatened to undermine the cohesive solidity of the minority group in the age of Egyptian nationalism.

The alternative Copt strategy was based on group separation, striving for collective entrenchment in the older forms of religious organization and communal consciousness. Entrenchment within, however, could lead to exacerbation of conflicts without. Central to Copt thinking was counting on the British to stand up for their oriental Christian brothers. Yet this proved to be an unfounded wish. In March 1910, more than 1,150 delegates attended the Coptic Congress at Asyut, the headquarters of the entire community, to lay before the British authorities long-standing grievances. In the name of justice, the Copts demanded an end to job discrimination and unequal educational opportunities, and demanded greater representation in provincial councils and exemption from Sunday labor.

The *al-umma al-qibtiyya* (Coptic nation), numbering some 700,000 in all of Egypt, confronted British obduracy and hostility. Instead of considering Copt complaints, the British agent, Sir Eldon Gorst, organized a Muslim counterdemonstration to invalidate Christian demands. In April, a large Muslim Congress gathered in Cairo, calling for recognition of Islam as the country's official religion and rejecting all Copt demands outright. Sir Eldon dismissed what he termed "Coptic chauvinism" and the "Coptic agitators." He reminded everyone that 92 percent of the Egyptian population was Muslim.

Throughout these months, the recollection of the murder of PM Butrus Ghali was fresh. Fearful and indignant, the Copts sought to sway the public atmosphere in their favor. But Kyriakos Mikhail clarified the situation with great insight:

Boutrous Pasha belonged to a people under tribute, and a conscientious Mohammedan is bound to look upon assassination as a light punishment for the tributary Christian who dares to assume semi-independent rule over a Mohammedan population.[29]

As Sir Eldon ignored Copt requests and the Muslims rose in fury against Christian initiatives, the drive for minority rights was destined to fail. In spite of opposition to Egyptian independence and the proclamation of the protectorate in 1914, the British had clearly manifested their preference for Muslims over Christians. At the most, the Copts might endure in the classic mold of the "protected people." Any greater and more assertive minority disposition would be foiled by the British from abroad and the Muslims at home. The talented Copts — still holding at this time 69 percent of the posts in the Ministry of Interior and 40 percent in the Ministry of Finance — lacked collective political power. Their personal ability, but without a sizable demographic base and political clout, was a weak weapon in the sectarian competition.

The interwar period seemed to seal the fate on the Copt community. The establishment of the Muslim Brethren (Al-Ikhwan Al-Muslimin) in 1928 under Hassan al-Banna raised the specter of Islam as a pointed threat against the Christians in Egypt.[30] Symptomatic of the era was a 1934 law that prohibited the construction of a church in the vicinity of a mosque. The question of Palestine and the rise of German nazism radicalized political currents of thought in Egypt, as the Copts were caught between an alienating British regime and a growing Islamized public atmosphere.

The secular vision of the Wafd, rooted in territorial nationalism of a local variety, was dissolving as the 1940s arrived. Egyptian gestures to Arab nationalism further complicated the delicate relationship between Muslims and Christians. The Copt minority, uneasy without being at all separatist, could turn nowhere for political salvation.[31] The die was cast: the ideological turmoil and political instability culminated eventually in a military coup on July 23, 1952.

This soon led to the elimination of Egyptian political parties, primarily the Wafd through which Muslims and Christians had tried to consolidate interreligious cooperation. Now the Copts were completely on the outside. The takeover of power by the Free Officers Club was a purely Muslim enterprise. No Copt was part of this conspirational clique. In the army as a whole only one Christian was found among ninety officers of the rank of brigadier and above, and he was a major general in the Medical Corps.[32] The initial winds blowing from the 1952 revolution did not portend happy days for the Copts of Egypt.

The Copts — possessing tight ethnic cohesion, rooted in a traditional religious culture, drawn to the geographic hearth in Upper Egypt, and enjoying a unique national history—never abandoned their distinct identity and role over the centuries. But the revolution of 1952 inaugurated a fundamental change in the Egyptian (and Mideastern) political environment. Nasserism and Arab nationalism, socialism and nationalization, agrarian reform and etatism, military dictatorship and a unidimensional radicalized mass society, all cut to the core of Coptic survival. New challenges surfaced to confront an old people. It was ultimately the steady resurgence of Islam during the reign of Gamal-Abdel Nasser and his successor Anwar al-Sadat that threatened perilously to erode the viability of the *al-umma al-qibtiyya* in the land of the Nile.

During the following decades the Copt community tried vainly to cope with the rising tide of Arabism and Islam in Egypt. Nasser opposed the Copts in an abusive fashion. Permits to build churches were delayed, and Christian religious courts were closed. The nationalization policies of the regime confiscated land from the Copts, then distributed it to the Muslims. Church land was seized by the Ministry of Islamic Affairs. University grants to study abroad were sparsely accorded to Copts. After the Suez debacle in 1956, European Christians left Egypt, a telling indication of the political and religious insecurity felt by non–Muslims (or non–Arabs). Nasser traditionally appointed one or two Coptic ministers to the cabinet, a political crumb with no concomitant power.[33]

The overall situation of the Copts, perhaps at least 15 percent of Egypt's population, witnessed a steady dissolution of any role in national life. Before 1952, the Copts composed a significant part of the Egyptian diplomatic service and educational and economic elite. After the revolution, their public station decayed immediately. There was some saving grace during Nasser's regime because of his trepidation about the Muslim Brethren. But the Islamic religious aspect spread, as in the public schools, while Copt deliverance was not a priority on the president's agenda. Nonetheless, an independent weekly *Watani* appeared in 1958, edited by the great names of the Coptic middle class and intelligentsia. Nasser even permitted the construction of a new cathedral in Cairo in 1964.

Perhaps in reaction to the assertion of Arab socialism and the growth of the Muslim Brethren in spite of Nasser's persecution of them, the Copts looked for ways to strengthen the binds of religious faith within. In the early 1950s, an Institute of Coptic Studies was established and headed by Professor Aziz Atiya, a distinguished Oriental and Coptic scholar; and in 1957 a rural community program was initiated to distribute literature and provide teachers to outlying Christian areas. Likewise, the Orthodox Coptic church encouraged the study of the ancient Coptic language.

But the predominant experience was of discrimination and hardship. As a result of dire economic and educational circumstances, tens of thousands of Copts emigrated to Canada, Australia, and the United States from 1965 on. Toward the end of Nasser's life, the Copts knew few good days. In April–May 1968, the Christians (and indeed Muslims) of Egypt reported "the apparition of the Holy Virgin" in the Cairo suburb of Zeitun. For a fleeting moment, the Copts were invigorated in their ancient faith. Yet Nasser's famed "three circles" and their claims to identity and power—the Arab circle, the African circle, and the Muslim circle—precluded participation by the native Copts of Egypt. Islam was the state religion of Egypt, and Arabism was its ideological leitmotif.

The gap between the successful *embourgeoisement* of the Copts and their political impotence remained at the heart of their condition. They boasted a higher literacy rate than the Muslims and had a proven record of educational attainments. In Cairo, some three-quarters of the pharmacists and about a third of the doctors were Copts in the 1970s. Yet in official Egypt the Copts were hardly represented. No Christian was a college dean, a university president, a police commissioner, a city manager, or a provincial governor. Out of the 127 ambassadors, just 1 (in Nepal) was a Copt. In the Ministry of Foreign Affairs only 2.5 percent of the employees were Copts.[34] Of 360 heads of state-owned companies, a mere 10 were Copts.

Since the revolution, the state apparatus had arrogated wide-ranging interventionist powers throughout Egyptian society. As Christians subject to debilitating *dhimmi* inferiority, the Copts found themselves abandoned to their own meager resources and self-reliance. A revealing personal instance of the general state of affairs was the role of Dr. Boutrous Ghali. He was the grandson of the murdered prime minister from 1910 and a successful academic and political personality.[35] President Sadat appointed him minister of state for foreign affairs in 1977, but not *the* minister for foreign affairs. Ghali, a native Copt from a distinguished family, could achieve public prominence, though only on condition that Islamic discrimination against Christians apply to him as well.

At the core of the new Islamic era in Egypt was the controversial figure of Anwar Sadat. Many considered him a traditional Muslim who would, upon becoming president in 1970, support the forces of religious fundamentalism. Others saw him as mesmerized by the technological modernity of the West and attracted by the institutions of political freedom—a staunch proponent of moving Egypt into the twentieth century. Yet others recognized in Sadat an "Egyptian-first" orientation that would facilitate the full integration of the Copts in a political society less susceptible than in the past to the stridence of Arab nationalism.

On May 20, 1971, just six months after taking office, Sadat addressed the National Assembly concerning the adoption of a permanent constitution for Egypt.

> I would like to say that our constitution must be derived from our true nature, and from this land of ours.... We have our traditions ... and we have, above all else and before all else, our mission of faith.[36]

In this categorical statement Sadat proudly waved the banner of Islam. Something new was afoot in Egypt. No longer would the Ikhwan conspire against the president, as characterized the Nasser era. Now the president himself legitimized the rhetoric and reform that the forces of Islam wanted to introduce into the country.

Indeed, the new constitution passed by the National Assembly on September 5, 1971, not only declared Islam the religion of the state, but the Islamic *shari'a* was defined as "a principal source of legislation." Within another decade, on April 30, 1980, the People's Assembly amended the text to read that the *shari'a* is *the* principal source of legislation. Turning Egypt into an *Islamic state*, not just a *state of Muslims*, was the next logical step. When Sadat tried to stem the roaring religious tide—which surely would have personally delegitimized him, his wife, his policies, and his very way of life—he confronted fundamentalism head-on. In September 1981, he arrested hundreds of Islamic militants, but this failed to secure him. The next month, on October 6, members of the al-Jihad society murdered President Sadat as he celebrated the eighth anniversary of the Ramadan War in 1973. The genie had overwhelmed its liberator.

Insecurity and Abandonment

From the 1970s, coincident with the presidency of Sadat and the rise of Islam as a vital force in Egyptian politics, the Copts experienced a new bout of problems. Numbering close to 8 million, though perhaps more, of a population approximately 50 million, they were not a negligible minority group.[37] Nonetheless, developments in official Egypt and in the popular domain shortened the rope on Christian existence. Discrimination from the top and violence from the bottom converged to victimize the Copts. They had fought with the Muslims for Egyptian independence in 1919 but found that independence culminated in the sovereignty of Islam.[38] In such circumstances, it would be problematic for a minority to cultivate successfully its political nationality and advance toward an "awakening stage" in its collective life.

The modes of disfavor directed against the Copts were diverse and demeaning. From about 1980, no presidential permits were issued to authorize the construction of new churches or the repair of older ones. Examples included a number of church sites in Alexandria and in Sohag. The government repeatedly confiscated Coptic trust lands and schools, which were then handed over to the Ministry for Islamic Affairs. The official Copt weekly magazine, *Al-Keraza (Sermon)*, with a circulation of 400,000 copies, was ostensibly banned in September 1981.[39] In 1988, the Copt lobby in the United States and Canada continued to address requests to the Egyptian authorities that the ban be lifted.[40] Discrimination against Copts in education was blatant as Muslims were accepted for university studies at Al-Azhar (which offers both secular and religious disciplines) with lower grades than their Christian counterparts. The authorities refused to allow the Christians to construct their own university, even if privately financed.[41]

The proposed utilization of the *shari'a* as the basis for Egyptian law was a formidable issue even before or without its full and immediate codification. The People's Assembly, called upon to pass new Islamic legislation in 1977, did not include one elected Christian member. The draft law included provisions to administer *shari'a* punishments for criminal offenses, like forty lashs for drinking alcohol or death by stoning for an adulteress. The death penalty was the appropriate Islamic measure for an act of apostasy, and it was this particular reform that mobilized the Copts to protest.

In order to carry out a divorce, which the Orthodox church forbids, Copts were known to convert temporarily to Islam. They then execute the divorce proceedings only to return to the Christian faith thereafter. The recommended law on apostasy was a dire threat to Copt communal integrity. On April 8, 1980, the Administrative Court of Egypt decided that a former Christian who converted to Islam did not have the right to denounce Islam and readopt Christianity. This judgment was a denial of freedom of religion based on the higher principle of Islam's authority in Egyptian law. In a related case, four converts to Christianity between 1976 and 1978 were forced to hide their actions, later arrested, and then accused of "despising Islam."[42] From the court's viewpoint, a Muslim who adopts another religion is legally dead.

In the early 1980s, Islamic reform was a major public issue in Egyptian life. Parliamentary discussion and press coverage dealt intensely with religious penetration in all realms of society. The speaker of the People's Assembly, Dr. Soufi Abu Taleb, demanded the introduction of training courses for lawyers to study the new proposed Islamic legislation.[43] The grand sheikh of Islam at Al-Azhar stated that "Islam is a nationality," thus effectively depriving Christians of their Egyptian identity. In 1986, a parliamentary committee finalized the draft law that would make defamation of the Islamic religion a full crime.[44] Coincident with the increasing sensitivity to the sanctity of Islam was an official policy to appoint only Muslims to senior state posts. For example, eleven vice presidents and sixteen deputies were appointed to the Administrative Court in 1984, but not a single one was a Christian.[45]

Either in immediate confrontation with Islamic fundamentalism in Upper Egypt itself or exposed to its wrath as new rural migrants in Cairo, the Copts had little wherewithal but for Christian faith to refurbish their sense of an integrated existence.[46] By the mid–1970s, Islam was a popular force, itself beyond even government control. Few of the 70,000 mosques in Egypt by the mid–1980s were under government control.[47] It was this kind of atmosphere that was conducive to an alternative ethos opposed to the pluralistic, liberal, and secular Egyptian polity, now toward a monolithic Islamic polity according to the *shari'a*. Indeed, as long as the state would not yet completely be transformed into a full Islamic polity, the Muslim groups (the Ikhwan and the al-Jama'at al-Islamiyya) moved to construct a parallel infrastructure of educational and religious services.[48] From medical clinics to nursery schools, the private religious societies fashioned a subculture with a political message not lost on the authorities, or on the Christians.

Violent sectarian clashes became part of the new social reality as Muslims carried their struggle to the streets. Beginning in 1972, Muslim groups attacked Copt citizens and set fire to their church at Khanqa, north of Cairo. In August 1978, two Copts, Emad Hanna and Boushra Barbary, were brutally murdered in Menshat Damallo, also north of the capital. In September, Father Gabriel, Coptic priest of Tawfikia village near Samalout in Upper Egypt, was killed with an ax by Muslims. In April 1980, sectarian clashes raged again. In 1981, Jama'at extremists pounded away at Christians in the Cairo suburb of al-Zawiya al-Hamra, and left 100 dead, 112 wounded, and 270 homeless. Five churches were burned down, as were Christian shops and businesses.

On May 14, 1980, President Sadat had addressed the interreligious problem in a major speech in the People's Assembly, the tenor of his remarks drawing from classic Islamic themes. He offered security to the Christians under his Muslim wings. But he warned them to maintain a low public profile and against carrying the domestic problem to international forums. He offered the Copts physical protection in Egypt but resented bitterly the Coptic notion that global Christian protestations could help them. Sadat left no room for doubt as he proclaimed: "I am a Muslim president in an Islamic state." The clear implication was that he assumed responsibility to watch over the Copts and allow them free religious worship within Egypt. But religious freedom, he emphasized, could not be exploited as a lever to cause sectarian crises and religious disturbances. The moment the Copts internationalized the internal tensions, demonstrating in Washington and at the United Nations headquarters in New York, Sadat heavy-handedly conveyed his determination to repress "my sons, the Copts."

Muslim violence against Christians persisted relentlessly nonetheless. Sadat might cow the Copts, but he failed to intimidate the Islamic fervor. Fanatical Muslim gangs continued to attack Christians and their property. In February 1987, Muslim fundamentalists burned churches, houses, and shops belonging to the Copts. Muslims demonstrated in Asyut, Sohag, Qena, Luxor, Aswan, and elsewhere in Upper Egypt. The same Muslims claimed they were responding to the burning of a mosque.[49] In April, the Ikhwan became the major opposition force in the People's Assembly following national elections. In September, Muslim groups set up unofficial religious courts in Minya, the prime targets being the Copts. It was in this atmosphere that Adley Mousa was fatally wounded by knife-wielding Muslims; the arrested suspects later mysteriously escaped from prison.[50] Other Copts, in Asyut for example, were also beaten in the months thereafter, and again the wheels of Islamic justice failed to turn for the Christian minority in Egypt.[51] Later, in November 1988, a 32-year-old Coptic priest was shot and killed upon leaving his church located south of Asyut. The gunmen were suspected to be Muslim fundamentalists. In March 1990, Muslim militants attacked Copts in Abu Qurqas, some 250 kilometers south of Cairo, as the struggle went on.

The Copt response was basically a rhetorical and symbolic one, as befits the parameters of their restrictive condition in the country. Pope Shenouda III, the Coptic patriarch of Egypt, demonstrated inner strength and Christian dignity. He reacted to events by deciding on noncooperation with the authorities. For example, the pope canceled Easter holiday celebrations in April 1980 in light of ongoing Coptic persecution. He encouraged his Christian flock to bolster their faith and learning. He traveled abroad to arouse the conscience of an indifferent world. Coptic church conferences assembled to declare their commitment to "the ministry of the apostle Mark and the sacrifices of its holy martyrs over the centuries." At the same time, the Copts proclaimed loyalty to the motherland of Egypt in which, they recalled, they "represent the most ancient and pure descendants of Egyptians."

When the pope was arrested in September 1981 along with numerous bishops and priests, the church protested vehemently. The deposition of Pope Shenouda III was an insulting slap in the Christians' face, but they did not turn the other cheek. Christian spokesmen and organizations rejected governmental interference in church affairs. In 1985, President Mubarak allowed the pope to return to Cairo from his exile in Wadi al-Natrun, but he was still restricted in his ability to assume normal work. The activist church leader, practicing a kind of "liberation theology" since becoming the patriarch of 1971, had been politically incapacitated.

A revealing note touching on the situation of the Copts came from the city of Asyut. The Copts constituted at least 25 percent of the population there. It is the historical capital of the Copts but also a hotbed of Islamic passion. The governor of the city was M. Osman Ismail, a member of the Muslim Brethren, who declared publicly that "Egypt has but three enemies: communists, Christians, and Jews."[52] The lack of symmetry was obvious — the Muslims permitted with impunity to say and do almost anything they chose while the Copts were oppressed by a regime and a populace that refused to accord respect and freedom to fellow citizens of Egypt.

In this century the tenacious and talented Copt community maintained its deep roots in the soil of Egypt, emigrated in only relatively small numbers, and cultivated high levels of education and urbanization. The church elite, in particular under Pope Shenouda III, was highly reliable. While the monastic life was a religious ideal, it could also be seen as political isolationism. Yet it has fortified a threatened people and injected a constant dose of determination over the ages. The official policies of discrimination and deprivation denied access to national resources but did not seemingly undermine the spiritual poise of the Copts. Indeed, official repression and popular antagonism probably strengthened their collective fiber.

In turning to the world for sympathy and support, Copt expectations could not have been excessive. There was no history of external assistance for the Copts. In November 1979, a delegation of Copts approached the governing board of the National Council of Churches. They requested international help, but the Council did not even let the delegation address the session. On various occasions, Copts in America demonstrated in the streets of Washington against Egyptian policies. A congressional resolution on November 29, 1982, made reference to the denial of human rights in the case of the Copts, but this awareness of religious persecution never affected America's strategic effort to enlist Egypt as a bulwark for stability and moderacy in the Arab Middle East. The Copts continually issued pleas for help, ads appeared in major American newspapers, and Amnesty International did at times adopt the claims of the Copts as legitimate and warranting consideration.

But the overall impact of Copt endeavors to enlist global action was negligable. Throughout, the Copts demonstrated their energy within Egypt and a sophistication in the world, but Muslim predominance at home and international indifference abroad determined the Coptic condition in the land of the Nile. A noteworthy departure nonetheless was reference to Copt disabilities and discrimination in the U.S. State Department's 1987 report on human rights. Meanwhile, the American and Canadian Coptic Association and the Rassemblement Copt, the latter centered in Europe, organized Copt communities and endeavored to preserve a collective coherence on foreign soil.

Within the bireligious reality of Egyptian society, mechanisms for conflict resolution have met with but partial success. The ideology of Arabism in Egypt has been suffused with an Islamic idiom for a long time, and this was so even during the Nasserite period. Some had proposed in the ongoing debate about Egypt's self-image that the country's priority was to disconnect from the wider Arab world and proclaim a position of neutrality. This was advanced by Tawfiq al-Hakim, also by the Copt writer Lewis Awad.[53] Were Egypt to reject outright the ideas of Arab nationalism and pan–Islam and look to its purely domestic tasks of national construction, then Muslim-Copt linkage could perhaps flourish. As it was, however, Egypt never did withdraw from the Arab world, in spite of its peace treaty with Israel in 1979. By 1987, the Arabs were coaxing the Egyptians to reassume their mantle of leadership over the distraught Arab world.

No semantic acrobatics would convincingly turn Islam into a vehicle of sectarian cooperation in strife-filled Egypt. Fouad Ajami, analyzing the rise of fundamentalist forces, concluded with an unchallengeable message: a believing Islamic political order has no way to accommodate the millions of Egyptians who are Christian Copts.[54] Such a theological truth would tear Egypt asunder and inevitably demote non–Muslims to a base status under Muslims. The formal reimposition of the *jizya*, based on *shari'a* principles, would institutionalize intolerance and block any path to Copt dignity or freedom.

Even without this step, Islam already controlled the moral and ideological high ground in Egyptian life, wresting from the Copts any opportunity to play a role in national society.[55] It was interesting in particular that Sadat had said the commander of the first infantry brigade to cross the Suez Canal in the 1973 war was a Copt, Major-General Fuad Ghali, the "token Christian" in a Muslim war.

The development of civil politics that would overlook communal religious identities appeared a lost vision in Egypt. Attempts to resuscitate the Wafd began especially in 1976, after the outlawing of political parties in 1953. Yet the Wafd's association with the Copts served to limits its effectiveness.[56] Even though the Wafd ran candidates in subsequent elections in Egypt, it was unlikely to capture the enthusiasm and support of wide sections of the population. It did, however, receive sufficient votes to pass the electoral threshold in 1984 and 1987. It later actually associated with Islamic forces.

It is quite unlikely that a doctrine of pluralism based on equal ethnic rights could penetrate the public consciousness or political system. Advocated by Sa'ad El-Din Ibrahim, this plea remained a voice without public force. Meanwhile, the idea of formal confessional policies, à la the *millet* in whatever form, was abandoned with the 1923 Constitution. The zeitgeist in Egypt is uncongenial to such a restorative reform.

The Copts faced the twentieth century hoping to enjoy full integration and equality. The historic wager failed, though nondiscrimination was the official program of most or all Egyptian parties, even the Muslim Brotherhood. The overwhelming input of new ideological themes — Islam, Arabism, and socialism and statism — smothered the minority Copts and ensured, by implication, the deepening of sectarian tension. As difficult as earlier centuries were in the Copt experience, it is the twentieth century that became the most threatening to the original and ancient sons and daughters of the Nile Valley. Even though they served the country with great talent and in absolute loyalty, the Copts were never truly accepted as equal and legitimate citizens of Egypt.

It is within the parameters of this objective situation that Copt peoplehood must contend in history. Allegiance to their own community and church, maintaining collective distinctiveness and pride, are elements for a status quo existence. Any progress toward ethnic autonomy, minority equality, or territorial independence is unlikely. Sadat accused the Copts of wanting to establish a Copt state in Upper Egypt; however, anything on the order of secession is far beyond Copt capacity. A profound disruption within the Egyptian body politic — perhaps based on intra–Muslim conflict between fundamentalists and "secularists" — could provide the opportunity for Coptic self-assertion. Alternatively, a major Arab-Israeli war leading to a devastating Egyptian loss might also constitute an opening for the Copts. But as long as the old Egyptian territorial state survives and functions, as it has over the millennia, the Christians seem barred from exploring new ways to preserve and cultivate their unique collective survival.

CHAPTER 8

Armenians: Talent, Tragedy, and Territorial Loss

Xenophon, a classical Greek historian, passed through Armenia, with its "plains and gently sloping hills," in 400 B.C. but was unaware of the country's identity.[1] The Armenian boys in their pagan dress made a negligible impression on the sophisticated Athenian.

More than 2,400 years later, the same Armenian people, long Christianized, were trying to impress their existence upon the world community following the genocide and expulsion they suffered in the twentieth century. In 1965, on the fiftieth anniversary of the massacre in Turkey, an Armenian national revival arose. In 1975 a resolution by the U.S. House of Representatives recognized their bitter loss. But in 1978, the final document on minorities issued by the UN Human Rights Commission ignored the Armenian Question completely.[2] During the same decade, Armenian terrorist groups formed, chief among them the Armenian Secret Army for the Liberation of Armenia (ASALA), dedicated to preserve the memory of this ancient people's homeland and their loss and persecution in modern times particularly. Then in 1990, as domestic dissolution weakened the fibers of the Soviet Union within, an Armenian National Army formed to contend with neighboring Azerbaijan. Yet Armenian independence remained a political long shot. When Xenophon traveled through Armenia, he had to be apprised of what country it was. Over two millennia later, because of the overwhelming transformation of life there, it was again necessary to recall that the country is historically called Armenia.

Existing as a distinct community at least from the eighth century B.C., the Armenians are descendants of ancient tribes in eastern Anatolia. Allegedly of Semitic stock or perhaps of Indo-European descent, they were forced to engage in warfare against Assyrians and

Persians, later falling under Greek rule with the coming of Alexander the Great to Asia. Caught between and ruled by more powerful imperial forces, the small Armenian community survived throughout centuries of changing circumstances. Alternating between Rome and Parthia was Armenia's fate in the years just before, and then following, the establishment of Christianity. In spite of obscure origins, Armenian ethnicity always differentiated this people from all others about them.[3] Often described as short and stocky, Armenians were testimony to endogamy and tight familial preservation, notwithstanding the movement of many peoples, including Greeks, Romans, Persians, and Turks, though Armenia over the ages.

Christianity and National Character

The cultural traits of Armenians were historically not unique. Their language, though specific to them, was a derivative from the Indo-European branch and lacked its own alphabet for many centuries, until 404 in fact. Their religious affiliation was apparently with Zoroastrianism, linking them to Persia, with the insignia of the sun symbolic of this historical tie. Introduced into the country by Bartholomew in the first century, it was the adoption of Christianity as a national religion in 301, following the conversion of the pagan sovereign Tiridates III by St. Gregory, that imprinted the people with their most recognizable feature. Indeed the Armenians claim to be the first people in history collectively and officially to adopt Christianity as their national religion. This event would seem central to the strength of the new faith in Asia or the Middle East in its early development. Rome adopted Christianity in 313, slightly later, after which it began to spread throughout Europe.

The Armenian national orthodox church, with its chief ecclesiastical see at Echmiadzin north of Mount Ararat, became Monophysite in doctrine. Its condemnation at Chalcedon in 431 served to consolidate the Armenian Christians as a separate national community. Later, in 506, the Armenian church fully broke with Constantinople, the official home of the Eastern church. The liturgy was translated from Syriac to Armenian as the national language became a vehicle for sacredness at the same time that the community strengthened its spiritual seclusion. Between Diophysite Byzantium and Zoroastrian Persia, the Armenians cultivated a native Christian myth that extolled martyrdom as the path of Jesus elevated to a historical national fate.[4] The faith spread throughout Armenia, where a city like Ani was picturesquely described as dotted with a thousand and one churches. The coming of the Crusaders into Asia Minor, passing through Cilicia ("Little Armenia") where Tarsus, the birthplace of St. Paul, is located, strengthened the community generally and catalyzed a closer association with the church of Rome.[5]

But the predominant thrust was fortifying the national foundations of the Armenian Apostolic church. An Armenian patriarchate was established in Istanbul in 1461 but with a separate catholicate in Sis, situated in Cilicia, and separate patriarchates in Jerusalem in addition to the holy see in Echmiadzin. In 1701, a Mekhitarist congregation was founded in Venice, and its monks were active in the revival of the community's language and liturgy. But it was only in 1863 that constitutional reforms within the Ottoman Empire served to recognize the patriarch of Constantinople as the sole representative of the entire Armenian population of the realm.[6] This development of the Christian *millet* highlighted the religious definition of the Armenian people, a fact of cultural life now consolidated in political form. The church could rightfully assume its leadership role, having been the historical bearer of the community's soul.

The broader cultural features of Armenian society related to its high educational standards and the prominent positions filled by this old Mideastern people. In the early days of Islam, the Egyptian caliphs appointed Armenians to administrative offices.[7] In the Middle Ages, Armenians were doctors in the Kiev kingdom.[8] At the new Lycée of Galatasaray founded by the Ottomans in 1868, an Armenian became its second director.[9] Throughout, one encounters a Christian community with impressive gains that reflect their talents and aspirations. Often success was temporary, a never-failing comment on the fragility of the *dhimmi* condition. Count Loris-Melikov, chief minister to the Czarist court, found himself dismissed in 1881 when political troubles surfaced and the regime took steps against the Armenian minority.

Armenian economic advances were inevitably associated with an astute capacity for diligent endeavors. In the sixteenth and seventeenth centuries, they basically monopolized the Persian silk-trade industry. In the eighteenth century, Armenians, taking advantage of the opening of the Black Sea to Russian trade, developed commercial contacts from Trebizond overland to Persia. In the nineteenth century, members of the affluent Amira Armenian class in Constantinople were pivotal figures in Ottoman economic affairs. Many were bankers; others predominated in the jewelry business. The Dadian family was famous for its industrial activities, and the Balian family played a central role in architectural developments.[10] Sir Edwin Pears provided a succinct and complimentary description of Armenians:

> Throughout the Empire they are a sober, thrifty and intelligent people. Wherever they exist they are noted for their industry, their aptitude for business, and a certain obstinacy of character. . . .

In modern times they have been the pioneers of commerce and industry in the near East, and have occupied high positions in Turkey,
Russia, Persia, and Egypt.[11]

By way of further example, Nubar Pasha became prime minister in
Egypt, and in Turkey Dadian Effendi served as under secretary of state
for foreign affairs toward the end of the nineteenth century. Perhaps
part of the secret of Armenian successes was captured by the insightful
remark that "being an Armenian is equated with performing better than
others."[12] Travelers in the areas of Armenian settlement never failed to
comment on the high standards of family living and cultural sophistication. The opinionated Mark Twain, visiting Smyrna (Izmir) in Asia
Minor, praised their clean houses and their sociable women, judging
the latter "a shade better than American girls."[13]

The area of Armenia called Hayastan constituted a particular geographic zone for this distinct people over the ages. Between the
Mediterranean and Black seas and lodged between central Anatolia and
Azerbaijan almost to the Caspian sea and Persia, Armenia lay astride an
international crossroad throughout its history. Never an imperial power
center itself, it was surrounded by imperial or national powers always.
As a consequence, Armenia was often partitioned—between Byzantium
and Persia in 387, between Russia and the Ottomans in 1827, and again
following Russia's capture of Kars in the Crimean War. The divisions
separating Armenians within different contiguous states was a national
liability that specific successes in Constantinople, Cilicia, Anatolia, and
the Caucasus could not deny. With no salient natural borders, Armenia
was more of a popular geographic image for an ancient people than a
definitive political territory in sharp spatial terms.

In itself, Armenia generally appeared as a land mass covering over
100,000 square miles, from the source waters of the Tigris and
Euphrates southward to Lake Van. Its terrain was predominantly plains
but equally noteworthy as a large mountainous massif. Within this
plateaulike topography fertile valleys were scattered, a kind of overall
natural fortress that served as a corridor for armies, a battlefield and not
only a caravan trade route. Yet the movement of conquerors and the
longevity of history left few marks on the indigenous Armenian people
and its culture. The country might appear "desolate" and the epitome
of "Asian poverty," in the words of Alexander Pushkin during his
journey to Erzerum in 1829;[14] nonetheless, its important mineral
resources and flowing rivers, exploited for communal welfare by the
talented native people, certainly had the potential to make Armenia a
focus of civilization rather than a peripheral sideshow.

The core of national settlement lay in what was called "the six
Armenian provinces" of the Ottoman Empire. These referred to

Erzerum, Bitlis, Van, Diyarbekir, Kharput, and Sivas (generally ex-
cluding Trebizond in the North and Cilicia in the Southwest). Across
this plateau region Armenian peasants, artisans, and tradesmen earned
a meager livelihood and endured the rapacity of Kurdish brigands and
Turkish officials. In 1890, the Armenians, it should be emphasized, were
not a majority in any *vilayet* (province)—indeed just 25 percent of the
variegated population, even in Erzerum.[15]

The link between a problematic geography and an inferior demography suggested military weakness. The link too between Christian submissiveness under Islam and peasant vulnerability from raiding plun-
derers affixed the Armenians as a victimized minority. It appeared that
unlike most neighboring groups, the Armenians were passive and
cowardly, which might better be recognized as the path of prudence.
Servility was the tested prescription for peace, yet always a precarious
one. There was, it is true, a legend of mountaineering daring and
warlike proclivities among certain Armenians, in particular those in
Zeitun in Cilicia. During the proceedings of the post–World War I San
Remo Conference, where the idea of Armenian statehood was discussed, Boghos Nubar Pasha argued that no one "could question their
[the Armenians'] military valour." In fact Prime Minister M. Veniselos
of Greece described them as a "warlike people."[16] But it was undeniable
that the martial tradition in Armenian culture was markedly underdeveloped in comparison with that in Turkish or Kurdish cultures (both
Muslim peoples). And when Armenians manned armies, it was often in
the service of foreign powers. Over the centuries, indeed, Armenian
soldiers fought in the Byzantine, Fatimid, and Crusader forces.

In Tiflis in Russia, Constantinople in Turkey, New Julfa in Persia—
and in overseas Armenian colonies like those in Italy and India—the intellectual and commercial skills of the Armenians were well known and
often admired. Cognizant of the situation within Armenia itself and
among Armenians beyond its borders, nothing suggested that in a contest of arms the Armenians could win. The brutal historical fact is that
over the centuries the Turks successfully conquered and colonized the
bulk of the Armenian homeland, ultimately to empty it of its native
Armenian population.

In addition to ethnic cohesion, a culture defined by specific linguistic and religious particularity, and an ancient geographic heartland, the
Armenians were in possession of a long national history. It reached far
back to the kingdom of Urartu, or Ararat, whence the Armenians allegedly descend. In the area of Lake Van, between the Caspian and the
Euphrates, an independent national life under King Aram existed nine
centuries before Christianity.[17] The Assyrians and the Medes were constant regional protagonists, but the Armenian entity never fully succumbed to foreign conquest. The most heroic period in classical

Armenian history revolves around Tigrane II, who ruled from 95 to 55 B.C., fought the Parthians in the East and the Romans in the West, eventually compelled to submit to Pompey in 66 B.C. The Armenian empire that included greater Armenia, Mesopotamia, Cilicia, and Syria, fell under Roman hegemony. Notwithstanding, a distinct Armenian homeland remained.[18] But it became a geographic buffer and a theater of war between more powerful neighbors, Rome and Persia in ancient times, between East and West as a fixed condition in history.

The coming of Christianity to Armenia did not alter the geostrategic bind endemic to the country. Caught between Byzantium and Persia, Armenia persevered in developing its new religious faith. National unity, however, often suffered within because of the rivalry between dynastic rulers and church bishops. Then, with the Islamic-Arab invasion of 716–717, Armenia was devastated. Soon thereafter, the Christian Armenians found themselves surrounded by Muslims in the Caucasus to the north, Azerbaijan and Persia to the east, and Syria and Mesopotamia to the south. The encirclement was completed by the arrival of the Seljuk Turks in 1064, who proceeded westward toward central Anatolia and Cilicia, ultimately conquering all Asia Minor.

Yet even then all was not lost. Native rulers continued to exercise authority in areas of Armenian settlement. The Bagratids made their capital at Ani in the eighth century, while Ashot the Great held court over Georgia and Armenia during the ninth century. The constant spread of the Turkish tribes and the Islamic religion pushed some Armenians westward where in the late eleventh century Ruben the Great established his kingdom in Cilicia, or Little Armenia.

The coming of the European Crusaders in 1097 gave hope and strength to the Armenians, and cooperation developed between the occidental and oriental Christians. In the thirteenth century, some Armenian bishops actually recognized papal supremacy, but the Orthodox Apostolic Armenian church as a national ecclesiastical body did not abandon its primacy or independence. Thereafter, in 1375, Mamluk forces penetrated the Armenian kingdom and eliminated its separate existence. Surrounded and subdued by Turks, Mamluks, and Persians, the Armenians fell into a state of national impotence for the next few centuries. Later, Israel Ori in central Armenia, trying his hand at international statesmanship in the 1680s, and David Bek from Karabagh in Azerbaijan, trying his hand at warfare in the 1720s, tried to elevate the Armenians to military struggle and national independence.[19] In the mid–eighteenth century, Joseph Emin spoke to Edmund Burke concerning Armenian liberation and even turned to the king of Georgia for assistance. But these efforts yielded no solid political fruit, and it was not until the nineteenth century that formidable circumstances and opportunities arose for a pervasive "awakening stage" in modern Armenian history.

Toward Independence in Armenia

Progressing from a religious identity to a nationalist movement typified Armenian affairs during the entire nineteenth century. The catalyzing context of Russian wars and Ottoman reforms invited this old minority to advance toward a more articulate collective self-expression. American missionaries and British consular officials augmented Armenian self-confidence, notwithstanding the permanent risks involved in trying to change the status quo with the majority Turkish population and power. But bearing in mind these circumstances, it would be surprising if a talented community like the Armenians did not aspire to national success in some political form.

Internal developments touched on various areas of Armenian life. The wealthy Amira class in Constantinople, while decidedly self-centered, nonetheless provided funds for Armenian schools and secular Armenian education. In the native Armenian provinces themselves, such as Diyarbekir and Erzerum, Armenian businessmen and merchants were predominant in the economy, notwithstanding their minority presence there.[20] In Van, including the city and surrounding villages, the Armenians were feasibly the majority group. Opportunities to pursue a public role in Ottoman society were legitimized by the 1839 Tanzimat reform decree, followed by another in 1856, which together granted formal minority equality and official integration within state institutions. The underlying Ottoman strategy, while intended to appease European liberal expectations abroad, was also a way to generate a modicum of social cohesion throughout the land.[21]

The increasing consolidation of the Armenian community in the empire and beyond, assumed varied forms and arose in various places. In Venice, Armenians learned their classical tongue and wrote about national liberation. Books in Armenian appeared with greater frequency in Tiflis in Russia and as far away as the Armenian dispersion in India. In Constantinople, an Armenian college was established in 1871. The following year, after the promulgation of an Armenian Constitution to regulate communal affairs in an autonomous *millet* fashion, the call was heard for substantive reforms in the six Armenian provinces in the interior of the country. But this demand could seem to threaten undermining Muslim supremacy in the Turkish-led empire.

In 1876, Sultan Abdul Hamid II issued a liberal constitution for the Ottoman realm that included the promise of autonomy for the non–Muslim provinces. A year later, the National Assembly was inaugurated, but very soon thereafter, the sultan prorogued it. The constitution was abolished, and the emperor sent the Kurds out to massacre the Armenians in the East.[22] The emperor feared that Anatolia, the very birthplace of the Ottoman Empire, might be wrested from his hands by the Armenian minority working in collusion with the not-too-distant Russian Army. Turkish nationalism had earlier lost ground in contests with European challengers and indeed was continuing to do so in the Balkans.

All this served to sharpen the Turanian spirit that dressed in Islamic and Ottoman colors.[23] At root was a growing and tense confrontation between two national peoples—Turks and Armenians—during the last third of the nineteenth century.

Armenian nationalist agitation was the fruit of educational advances and revolutionary ideas current within the homeland and beyond. Some examples illustrate the feverish spirit of the times. In 1853, Melikian Hovagin came from Constantinople to Zeitun in Cilicia and proceeded to Russia to collect arms for a rebellion. On his way back, however, he was caught and hung by the Turks. In 1854, an Armenian students' literary club was organized in Moscow. In the 1860s, a Young Armenia Movement functioned. In 1860, Zeitunis resisted a Turkish force sent to collect higher taxes. In 1861, an Armenian revolutionary actually presented a petition to Napoleon III in solicitation of French support for Cilician independence. Then, in 1862, Van rebelled against Turkish rule and Kurdish rapacity under the banner of an underground group, the Union of Salvation. Not far from the Russian border, the Armenians hoped for fellow–Christian intervention. In 1863, Armenians rose against the Muslim Kurds in Erzerum.

In all of these places the message was that the springtime of Armenian freedom had arrived. As Rafael Patkouian (1830–1892) wrote during the Russo-Turkish War of 1877–1878: "Awake! The happy fortune of Armenia has begun."[24] There was reason to believe that at last the Armenian cultural revival that had begun in the eighteenth century was turning into a vibrant political movement. An energy of cultural activity was providing the catalyzing power for nationalist action: secondary schools in Armenia itself; Armenian books published in Europe; foreign colleges for Armenians in Constantinople, Tarsus, and Kharput; Armenian university studies in Russia, Venice, and Paris; and a plethora of Armenian magazines and newspapers that appeared after 1820.[25] The unresolved question was whether reform and democratization of the Ottoman Empire, assuming they were authentic, would satisfy Armenian expectations. A separatist struggle was the obvious alternative avenue of national ambition.

Yet this internal renaissance required an external boost to give credibility to the national struggle. This came in the form of the war between Russia and Turkey in 1877, as the Czar's army crossed into Armenia up to Kars and Erzerum. Just as the Russians helped liberate the Greeks in 1829 and were indispensable in liberating the Bulgarians in 1877, it seemed reasonable for Armenians to expect to be the next fortunate beneficiaries of Russian military intervention against the Ottomans.

This formula for national success seemed warranted by the Treaty of San Stefano, of 1878, in which Article XVI referred to the need for reforms and security in the interest of the Armenian minority in eastern Turkey. Hopes for autonomy, perhaps as a step toward ultimate independence, were now openly discussed. But in the subsequent Treaty of Berlin in July, arranged at the congress attended by an Armenian delegation, few concrete gains were achieved. In Article LXI the Sublime Porte assumed to initiate reforms and provide security, but nothing in the spirit of Armenian autonomy or self-government, or the appointment of a Christian governor-general, was broached. The British, who wanted Turkey intact as a barrier to further Russian expansionism, won the day. The Armenians were drawn to conclude that military passivity and unobtrusive cultural sophistication were not the ingredients to earn a political victory. A spirit of revolution then surfaced with greater urgency at the top of the Armenian national agenda.

In 1878, the Black Cross Society formed in Van. In 1880–1881, another group, Protectors of the Fatherland, organized surreptitiously in Erzerum, its motto "Liberty or Death." But in 1882, the Turks discovered the group's existence, and forty members were found guilty in 1883. Yet the more significant national venture in this period was the formation of the Armenakan party in Van in 1885. It called explicitly for revolution, began weapons training, killed some Turks, and established branches in other parts of Turkey and beyond. Two years later, the socialist Hunchak party was constituted in Geneva, a city of Armenian dispersion. In 1890, the Dashnak party (the Armenian Revolutionary Federation) arose in Tiflis in Russian Georgia, distinguishable as a nationalist group dedicated to a people's war against the Ottoman Empire.

The Armenian enterprise spread and proliferated in and beyond Turkish Armenia itself. It sought to ignite a revolutionary campaign and enlist foreign support. It raised the flag of Armenian honor in modern times and turned to the 1890s in a spirit of defiant determination. Under an educated young leadership that was dissatisfied with mere minority representation in a Turkish-dominated empire, Armenians set their national sights on revolution, not reform. They sought to bring the Armenian Question to the fore, not unlike the Greeks, Serbs, Bulgarians, Romanians, Arabs, and Kurds in their quests for national self-expression. It was an hour of historic drama dazzling with the idea of liberation.

Raffi, the Armenian novelist, struck a popular chord when he denounced national resignation and the deadening influence of the clergy. Fortresses were more important than convents, he said, arms more valuable than sacred vases, and the smoke of powder more agreeable than incense.[26] The drums of secular nationalism pounded heavily across the Armenian homeland, and in Russia, Switzerland, France, and England, where Armenian writers and agitators dreamed of nothing less than complete Armenian national independence at last.

Yet reality struck with an immediacy and a viciousness that should have left no doubt about Armenian miscalculations. Of Abdul Hamid it was said, "He had come to hate the very name of Armenia."[27] Of the Europeans and Russians it could be said that their empty moral rhetoric and narrow political interests hardly coincided with Armenian expectations for foreign assistance. Of the revolutionaries it might be argued, in the fashion of historian William Langer, that their confrontational tactics toward the Ottoman regime, generating military ventures without adequate preparation, could not fail but induce fatal reprisals.

When they came, during 1895–1896 in particular, some 300,000 Armenians were dead. Europe and Russia stood on the sidelines as the Armenians had failed to gain anything. Provoking the Turks, whatever the inherent justice of the national claim, was a catastrophic error. Armenians were butchered in Trebizond, Urfa, Sivas, Erzerum, Bitlis, Marash, Zeitun, and elsewhere. In Birijik some Armenians converted to Islam to stay alive. In August 1896, Armenian revolutionaries attacked the Ottoman Bank in Constantinople, providing the Turks with another pretext to kill more Armenians.

At the dawn of the twentieth century, the Armenians had awakened to the awesome task of making their own national history. But they were also compelled to awaken to the grave dangers in pursuing such a struggle. Ottoman oppression clarified Armenian particularity and exposed Armenian impotence. Foreign assistance was highly abstract and notably thin in material substance. A revolutionary elite existed, but it remains unclear to what extent it mobilized the mass of Armenian peasants in the homeland. Trying to tear off a piece of the empire in the name of a separate Armenian state elicited fierce Turkish opposition. The problem did not lie in any fundamental Armenian disability. The problem was more decisively in consequence of the geopolitical landscape and the incompatibility between an Armenian secessionist drive in the land that Turks had ruled, one way or another, for some 1,000 years. Two peoples claiming the same land made for a bitter zero-sum conflict, to be resolved, if at all, only by raw force. It was unreasonable to assume that the Turks would lose in such a confrontation. The whole Armenian effort, suggested Elie Kedourie, was fanciful and irresponsible, hoping for things that could never be.[28]

A brief historical interlude of twenty years separated the massacre of 1895 and the genocide of 1915. In Russia, the czarist regime confiscated Armenian church property and even deported Armenians, as in 1912, to Siberia. In Turkey, the Armenians participated in the Committee for Union and Progress (CUP) and its successful revolution in 1908. Yet the ethos of Turkification led ineluctably to a further onslaught on the Armenians a year later, when thirty thousand people were killed in the Adana area. The Sultan was ousted, but the arrival of the Young Turks was hardly a blessing for the Armenians. Abdul Hamid was gone, but hatred of the "infidels" was as visceral as ever. Troubles in the Balkans in 1912 did not promote a spirit of Turkish-Armenian rapprochement, nor did the presence of British advisers in the Armenian *vilayets* provide the security so lacking there. The Turks were still committed, as far as their power would permit, to retaining all parts of their crumbling empire; and the British were still committed, as far as their influence would permit, to employing the Ottomans as a bulwark against Russian aggression.[29] And yet the capacity for self-delusion had not been exhausted. On the verge of the 1914 war and the greatest tragedy in their national history, Armenians still hoped for Turkish reform or a Russian protectorate.

The First Genocide of the Twentieth Century

The singular experience of mass murder in 1915–1916 will remain the most indelible and dark memory in the modern history of the Armenian people. With a painful legacy of persecution over the millennia, the suffering of this century finalized the inherent vulnerability of Christian minority existence in the Muslim Middle East.

On April 24, 1915, Turkish policemen in Constantinople were sent to arrest Armenian leaders, the opening shot in the roundup, destruction, and expulsion of the old Armenian people from their homeland. The Committee of Union and Progress (Ittihad), intending to forestall the presentation of the Armenian Question as a political and international issue after the war, offered three reasons for the deportation plans: Armenian voluntary forces serving in enemy armies; Armenian parties in the interior organized against the army; and firearms and war materiel discovered and confiscated everywhere in the country.[30]

By explaining Ottoman policy as a necessary self-defense precaution against an insurrectionary people, the Turks tried to revoke from the record a long history of Turkish racism and Muslim revulsion against a small Christian minority. For in truth, as Geoffrey Wigoder argued, "What happened in 1915 was the climax" of an ineluctable process whose genocidal dimension "began already in 1894."[31]

In the view of Christopher Walker and Yves Ternon, the extermination of the Armenians was premeditated and prepared. In the space of a few months, 1.5 million Armenians were dead. They perished under an outright massacre, as in the *vilayets* of Van and Bitlis. They perished from exhaustion, sickness, and starvation, as in the case of those expelled from Cilicia. They perished by drowning, their corpses subsequently mutilated after floating down the Euphrates River. Armenian girls were abducted from the convoys; others jumped into wells and died rather than fall into Turkish hands. Some children ended up in Muslim families and survived.

Kerop Bedoukian, a child survivor from Sivas, later told the tale of misery, whippings, and rape, but also one of Christian determination. In martyrlike fashion, his father had said to his mother: "You will go and die on one mountain and I will go and die on another, but we shall not deny our Christ."[32] Bedoukian himself survived and later emigrated in 1926 to Canada. Yet he was an exception. Most Armenians did not survive. Even those who made it southward to apparent safety in Aleppo and Deir-ez-Zor suffered from Turkish blows, held as cattle in forced encampments. The American Committee for Armenian and Syrian Relief reported the Armenians' condition as one of no clothing and no food, tortured and enfeebled. Mounds of dead covered the road from Meskene to Deir-ez-Zor.[33]

An alternative interpretation of events, by Robert Melson and Gwynne Dyer, understands Turkish behavior without justifying it. Labeling Armenians in the empire traitors and nationalist agitators, the Turks moved to take revenge on the insubordinate Armenian *millet.* They were outraged by Christian *rayahs* seeking a status above their traditional *dhimmi* station. Whether the Armenians were actually a threat, they appeared to be one in Turkish eyes. This "provocation thesis," related to the minority's educational and economic successes, offered the Turks an excuse.[34] Armenians had formed revolutionary political movements in the interior and had formed volunteer corps in the Russian Army. They appeared deadly opposed to Ottoman rule in Armenia and committed to exploit the war as an opportunity to reach for the reins of freedom.

Minister of Interior Talat and Minister of War Enver were, concludes Gwynne Dyer, desperate, not evil.[35] In a conversation with American Ambassador Henry Morgenthau, Talat had indeed claimed that "the Government was acting in self-defence." Kerim Kevenk argued that the Armenians had had a long history of terrorism against the Turkish nation.[36] The Armenian genocide of 1915 was, in his view, an invention and a distortion of the truth. Armenians killed Turks, were not only killed by them. In this Turkish-oriented analysis of the horrific massacre of more than half of the Armenians in the empire, the murderers were perfidiously transformed into the victims.

The ultimate collapse of the Ottoman Empire in 1918, while no compensation for the unspeakable Armenian loss, opened a door to a new and better future. Many Armenians had fled to Russia, and there, in Yerevan province in particular, a national home began to develop. To the north in Georgia, in the capital of Tiflis, Armenians organized a congress that spoke of an independent Armenia. For a moment, the idea of a transcaucasus government that would include Georgians, Armenians, Tatars, and Azerbaijanis appeared the appropriate political formula for multiethnic coexistence.

Meanwhile, in Turkish Armenia, on the Erzerum–Sivas highway, the Russian army's invasion and conquest offered an alternative though related opportunity for Armenian rebirth. During 1917–1918, the dream of Armenian independence from the Euphrates to Karabagh aroused hopes. For a moment, the conquering Russians edged toward finally assuming the historic task of liberating the Armenians.[37]

But it soon became vividly clear that as in the past, the Armenians lacked the power and the numbers to realize their national ambitions. The Russians withdrew from Kars as the Turks under Mustafa Kemal, the famous Ataturk, recovered their momentum and drove eastward. In September 1918, Turkish forces reached Baku, and soon thereafter a massacre of Armenians was carried out on Russian territory. In Karabagh, part of Azerbaijan, the British forces were unhelpful in protecting Armenians from further suffering. Neighboring Muslims, Azeris in particular, cornered the Armenians from the east as did the Turks from the west. At the same time, the Communists penetrated Armenian Yerevan to undermine any modicum of national autonomy. Meanwhile, in Anatolia the Turks fought incessantly against the Greeks and their fellow Christians, the Armenians.[38]

Lacking the wherewithal on the military front, the Armenians turned to the diplomatic front for national salvation. Again their destiny was in the hands of others whose concerns and considerations would not necessarily match those of the ancient Armenian people. In January 1918, Prime Minister Lloyd George of Britain had affirmed that Armenia was "entitled to a recognition of its separate national condition." The French agreed, as did President Wilson, whose famous Point 12 called for "autonomous development" of the nationalities under Turkish rule.[39]

Thus, when the Paris Peace Conference convened in January 1919, the devastated Armenians had reason to expect the revitalization of their historic aspirations. The massacre of Armenians at Shushi in the Caucasus, the existence of the Yerevan Republic, the U.S. Harbord Commission report that favored an American mandate over Armenia, and the profound distaste for Turks in European and American eyes — all provided the context for a breakthrough in 1919. At the peace conference itself, two distinguished Armenian spokesmen advocated Armenian national rights: Avetis Aharonian, author and statesman, represented the Yerevan republic; and Boghos Nubar Pasha, son of an elite political family in Egypt, represented the Armenian dispersion and explained that an Armenian homeland must include not just the Caucasus but Erzerum and Cilicia as integral parts of an Armenian state. All in all, 1919 was a year of international grace, an interlude of hope.

In 1920, the signs for Armenian recovery were mixed. In the Asian theatre, the Armenians were being crushed between the Russian Bolsheviks, the Muslims of the Caucasus, and the Turkish nationalists. Dashnak resistance to the USSR was unsuccessful, and Russian Armenia was smothered within the confederated Caucasus republic that joined it with Georgia and Azerbaijan. At the San Remo Conference in April, Boghos Nubar Pasha told the Allies that Armenian soldiers fighting the Turks had no munitions, and Avetis Aharonian asked for Allied military equipment as he pressed for a territorially solvent Armenia — with Erzerum and Trebizond — in the final settlement.[40]

But little help was forthcoming. The French were in retreat from Cilicia, and the British were withdrawing from the Caucasus. And the Americans, notwithstanding Wilson's sentimental support for an independent Armenia, were floundering ignominiously in diplomatic retreat. Beyond formal recognition granted Armenia (in Turkey) on April 23, 1920, and the knowledge that without an active American role all would be lost, the United States still failed to translate moral rhetoric into political involvement.[41] While Woodrow Wilson wanted a Greater Armenia as a strategic imperative, the U.S. Congress overrode the president and decided that America would not assume a mandatory responsibility for an Armenian state. Later, it is said, Wilson had a portrait of an Armenian refugee girl hung over the living-room mantel of his private Washington residence.[42]

Nonetheless, the Allies persisted in the fabrication of a political illusion. In the Treaty of Sèvres of August 10, 1920, Turkey was brought to the point of recognizing "Armenia as a free and independent state." But this treaty was never implemented as Ataturk thundered through Cilicia. Hadjun, an Armenian town with 30,000 inhabitants in 1914, was no longer on the map in 1920. In the East, Turkish forces took Kars with the typical attendant cruelties. Again the Allies did nothing to stay the hands of the Turks from bloodletting. And yet the diplomatic farce continued into November as President Wilson awarded Armenia its exclusive and extensive boundaries. In the same month, the Bolsheviks helped finish off the dream by invading Yerevan. Armenian revolts lasted until February 1921.

The ultimate finishing touch to the drama and destruction of these years came with the Treaty of Lausanne on July 24, 1923. Now there was no mention of an independent Armenia, as the military realities had fatally foreclosed this option. The six "Armenian vilayets" became a security zone in eastern Turkey, and the Yerevan Armenian republic, part of the Soviet Union, dissolved in the Transcaucasus Federated Republic. The historical Armenian Question seemed now irrevocably laid to rest through the uneasy balance, so long endemic to the Armenian predicament, between two strong and determined neighboring powers to the east and west.

A summary of the period from 1914 until 1923 suggests that the significance of an impressive Armenian national awakening became a source for unrealistic goals. The deep envy Muslim Turks felt toward Armenian Christians left the latter committed to a reckless campaign for separatism in the Anatolian heartland of the Ottoman Empire. The Young Turk successors proved themselves even more fanatically committed to an ethnically homogeneous country than Emperor Abdul Hamid. The Greeks were transferred out, the Kurds were repressed and removed, and the Armenians were massacred and expelled.[43] While Armenian national consolidation was forged in the crucible of conflict, and notwithstanding foreign assistance of certain kinds, the basic objective parameters of the Armenian condition still precluded any realization of political freedom. A thousand years of Turkish predominance had become the major and preemptive fact that clouded any Armenian liberation struggle.

Subsequent decades in the twentieth century provided Armenians with few opportunities. Taking revenge against Turkish murderers, however, was another matter. The Dashnak network (Nemesis) killed some CUP leaders and officials; Talat was eliminated in Berlin in 1921; and in 1922 Djemal Azmi, "the butcher of Trebizond," was murdered. In the same year, Enver Pasha was also killed, probably by an Armenian.

Dispersion and Continuity

The Armenian people had become highly dispersed, the majority living in the Soviet Union. There 3.5 million Armenians focused their efforts in the Armenian Socialist Soviet Republic, with its capital at Yerevan. In that city alone approximately 1 million Armenians were resident in the beginning of the 1980s. It is true that Communist policy in the 1920s had already set out to undermine Armenian society, destroy traditional elites, and nationalize all private land.[44] The kolkhoz was intended to replace the church as the focus of organized Armenian life and faith. Yet resistance arose as peasants tried to avoid military service and taxes. Communist ideology nonetheless appeared to overwhelm the Armenians through the years as the Sovietization of Armenia proceeded apace. Never, however, did ethnic resilience fade. The development of the Armenian republic itself strengthened national pride. Yerevan was referred to as the Paris of Asia, a beautiful city, modern and elegant in its physical ambience, with a reputable university. Symptomatic of Armenian diligence and advance within the Soviet Union was the figure of Anastas Mikoyan (1895–1978), a native Armenian who was a member of the Politburo of the Communist party of the USSR and chairman of the presidium of the Supreme Soviet during 1964–1965. The relative attractiveness of the USSR as an Armenian option was demonstrated when 100,000 people "repatriated" to the remaining Armenian entity there in 1945–1946.

In October 1968, Armenians in the Soviet Union celebrated the 2,750th anniversary of Yerevan's founding. This orderly but joyous demonstration of national pride was recast two decades later when, in massive and angry demonstrations in February 1988, Armenians in Yerevan demanded nationalist recognition for an alteration of the republic's boundaries. The initial focus of Armenian unrest arose in the nearby Karabagh province (part of Shiite Azerbaijan), 85 percent of whose inhabitants were fellow Armenians.[45] Reports indicated hundreds dead in ethnic riots whose spark was Azeri reforms to forbid the teaching of Armenian history.

Armenians in the Yerevan republic became agitated over the ethnic-political anomaly of fellow Armenians subject to Muslim Azeri dominancy nearby. This entire episode attested to the vibrancy of Armenian identity and its trials and tribulations in the Soviet Union. It was czarist Russian policy, as it is Communist Soviet policy, to utilize the Armenians to the point where they become a disturbing minority problem that must be contained. The Armenians are caught in the complex maze of sectarian-minority diversity within the USSR. In fact, violent confrontations between Armenians and Azeris, and Armenians and the Soviet security forces, continued throughout 1988–1990. In the Azerbaijani city of Sumgait, Muslims carried out atrocities against Armenian women in a maternity hospital in February and March 1988. But Armenians may nonetheless be a useful lever outside the USSR to advance Soviet goals in the region.

In addition to the Armenians' presence in Communist Russia, smaller communities dotted the extended dispersion. Some 200,000 Armenians resided in Lebanon, slightly fewer in Syria, while yet another traditional location of Armenians was Iran where they played a role in the Communist Tudeh party in the 1950s, perhaps thereafter as well. A larger number lived in France, perhaps some 300,000, of which 100,000 resided in Paris. In the United States, somewhat less than a million Armenians are to be found, particularly in Boston, New York City, and California. It was in Fresno that the famous Armenian author William Saroyan, whose father was born in Bitlis, lived and wrote. His son was named Aram.[46] Still smaller Armenian communities lived in Canada and Egypt. One estimate of the total Armenian population in the world in the 1980s was approximately 7 million, though this might be slightly high.

All in all, some two hundred publications appeared in the Armenian language as the people cultivated its cultural particularity, its national church, and the memory of a long history.[47] The genocide of 1915 is the cornerstone of all commemorative nostalgia. Having lost their territory and their mountain-warrior tradition, Armenians cling to the essentials of a unique experience. Ambition and competency as minority traits alternate at times with disorientation and anxiety as minority deficiencies.[48] But a compulsive determination to persevere dominates all other community characteristics.

Meanwhile, the Armenian population in Turkey has dwindled drastically. About 250,000 remained in Turkey by 1925, while a Turkish census from 1960 reported just 52,756 Armenian speakers.[49] A state policy that prevents religious and educational freedom for Armenians, in addition to the institution of special taxes for non–Muslims, would inevitably dilute the Armenian Christian population and undermine its linguistic viability. In 1974 it was reported that the Turkish authorities prevent the repair of churches and act with resolve to Turkify Armenian schools. In 1985, an estimated 50,000 Armenians, perhaps slightly more, continued to live in Turkey. Bedoukian reported in his autobiography that an earlier turn-of-the-century Armenian population of some 30,000 in Sivas had been reduced by the 1960s to just eighty families. Tarik Soner, the president of Ankara University, contended in 1983 that no discrimination against the Armenians existed in the country.[50] Perhaps it was now no longer necessary since the Turks had brutally solved the minority problem in a decisive fashion some years ago.

Revenge, Not Revolution

However, in the 1970s Armenians underwent a radical revival as they adopted the tools of terrorism to convey a collective anger and determination. It all began with a personal outburst by an 84-year-old Armenian, Gourgen M. Yanikian, who killed the Turkish consul-general and vice consul in Los Angeles on January 27, 1983. This act from the depths of long-repressed frustration turned a history of Armenian suffering into the language of modern terrorist warfare. The neglected

Armenian Question had surfaced far from the homeland, perhaps inevitably so.

Two years later, in 1975, from the quagmire of violence in troubled Lebanon, the sons of Armenian refugee families took up the gun. Under the leadership of Iraqi-born Hagop Hagopian, who grew up in Lebanon though allegedly educated in the Soviet Union, young Armenians formed the Armenian Secret Army for the Liberation of Armenia (ASALA). Specifically in Beirut, with approximately 100,000 Armenians, the Lebanese national contingent lived a vibrant communal life. They boasted some twenty to thirty newspapers and magazines, a school system, and confessional representation in the Parliament. ASALA soon became a flamboyant and deadly symbol of national revival, abandoning the Christian myth of martyrdom in favor of a secularized struggle for political liberation.

Three basic goals dominated the overall vision of ASALA: revenge, reparations, and return. Initially, however, it was the notoriety of terrorism against Turkish and international targets that the media purveyed to a generally uninformed and bewildered global audience. Linked to the Soviet anti–Western network, ASALA developed in the PLO-Palestinian environment of Lebanese terrorism, studying its techniques, adopting its ideology, training in its guerrilla camps, and maybe collaborating in its campaign of murder.[51]

In ten years, from 1975 to 1985, ASALA eliminated some thirty Turkish diplomats around the world. The targets, located in Beirut, Zurich, Athens, Vienna, Madrid, Lyons, Rome, Geneva, Copenhagen, Ottowa, Los Angeles, and Ankara, were all seen as contemporary accessories of Turkey's evil past. ASALA gunmen stalked through airports and consulates, infringing on states' sovereignty in the name of a higher principle. These Armenian nationalists, small in number but bound by tight organizational discipline, sought publicity from an indifferent world. Thirty-three attacks in 1980, forty-nine in 1981, and twenty-four in 1982 were sufficient to instill fear and disgust in the Turks. The fact that victims were often innocent bystanders caught in the web of Turkish-Armenian warfare demonstrated the unrelenting commitment of ASALA to continue its murderous policy. Raising the Armenian Question on the international agenda was the unqualified goal.

The pro–Soviet and pro–Palestinian connection of ASALA was a function of geographic considerations in two senses.[52] One factor was that a framework for collective Armenian life still existed within the USSR just a few miles from Turkish Armenia. Another was the Beirut-based PLO phenomenon of the 1970s, an inspiration for Armenian youth in the Bourj el-Hamud district. An intermediary link became the Syrians as ASALA fighters were reported training in Kamishli with the PFLP faction of the PLO and in the Bekaa Valley of Lebanon under

Syrian control. Further reports indicated that Soviet instructors had trained Armenian terrorists in Syrian camps, at Tadmor, for example, in the early 1980s. The Soviet role, never exactly proven yet highly credible, brought together seemingly disparate groups — PLO, Iranian Mujahedeen, the German Baader-Meinhof, the Italian Red Brigades, the Japanese Red Army, ASALA, and others — in a radical network that was orchestrated by Moscow.[53] It was not irrelevant that ASALA's terrorist campaign was directed against the West, in Europe, Canada, and the United States. Soviet involvement would of course ensure that.

The symbolic significance of ASALA was that its strident message, put somewhat simplistically, was no longer just for Armenians to "love Jesus" but to "hate the Turk." It followed that once typified as a profoundly Christian religious community, Armenians would now exploit the language and idiom of a nationalist struggle. Collaborating with the devil, in this case atheistic Russia, was legitimate if the Armenians could thereby develop a viable struggle against the alien Turks. Meanwhile, the Russians could simultaneously support and suspect ASALA's rhetoric against *Turkish occupation* of the Armenian homeland.[54] This line of thought could under certain circumstances be turned against *Soviet occupation* of parts of the Armenian homeland in the USSR.

As beneficiaries of U.S. Marshall Plan assistance in 1948, and valuable to the "northern tier" on Russia's southern boundaries, the Turks were quickly brought into the post–World War II NATO military alliance. In the eastern Mediterranean and across the Zagros Mountain line, Turkey was perhaps the most vital element in Western strategy to arrest Soviet aggression into the Mideast heartland.[55] Turkey provided invaluable services to the United States, which in addition to placing Jupiter missiles on Turkish soil, utilized Turkey for monitoring radar and for base purposes vis-à-vis the USSR. After the Iraqi revolution in 1958, the fall of the shah of Iran in 1979, and the Communist takeover in Afghanistan leading to the Soviet invasion in 1980, Turkey's strategic importance for the West skyrocketed.

But America's relationship with Turkey experienced very tense times. In 1964, the United States warned Turkey not to use its weapons against Cyprus, and in 1967 Turkey refused to let American planes refuel during the days of the Arab-Israeli Six-Day War. When Turkey occupied Cyprus in 1974, Washington imposed an arms embargo upon its Asian ally. A year later, Turkey reciprocated by suspending U.S. operations at military installations in Turkey. Tension between the two countries continued when Turkey turned part of Cyprus into a self-proclaimed independent "Turkish-Muslim" entity. But U.S. assistance to Turkey continued, as when economic aid totaling $100 million was agreed upon by America in late 1985.[56]

Central to Soviet strategy is to cultivate Turkish friendship while undermining Turkish integrity for broad regional and global interests. Soviet penetration of Turkey has been diverse and perhaps perverse and profound. The Russians have supported certain underground terrorist groups, one being the Kurdish Workers' party that opposes the Turkish regime. In this context, Soviet Armenia can be seen strategically as ASALA's "Hanoi," a bridgehead toward Van and Erzerum. The exploitation of Armenian terrorism against Western targets globally may arouse Western sympathy by the paradoxical twist of expiating Western guilt for allowing the Armenian genocide of 1915. Yet all along, the Soviets courted the Turks; in 1978, for example, Turkey received more Soviet aid than any Third World country.[57] With a carrot and a stick, Moscow pursued a pernicious policy designed to soften Turkish national resistance. The fall of Turkey would open up the Armenian plateau for a Communist military thrust toward the Persian Gulf. Along the way, Soviet forces could easily pass through Arab allies, Syria and Iraq.

The historical role of Turkey as a barrier to Russian expansion southward would — at last — be terminated. Playing the Armenian card against Turkey therefore fits this grand strategy concocted centuries ago. And yet it bears emphasis that ASALA did not in effect change anything fundamental in Armenian community life. It arose outside the national party system and attracted relatively little active or direct Armenian participation. It was a Mideastern phenomenon at a time when the focus of Armenian life was elsewhere, in Europe and America in particular. Indeed by 1983–1984, the organization was going downhill, its hatred of the Turks an insufficient and nonideological basis for a national and political Armenian renaissance.

In addition to ASALA, the Dashnak movement gave rise to its own terrorist arm, the Justice Commandos of the Armenian Genocide (JCAG). It was a conservative-rightist political force identified with the phalangist Maronite forces in Lebanon and sympathetic with a pro–Western orientation on the global stage. The JCAG, from Beirut and exported to North America, carried out attacks against Turkish targets and personnel. They killed the Turkish consul-general and his bodyguard in Sydney in December 1980 and the Turkish consul-general in Los Angeles in January 1982. Unlike ASALA, the Justice Commandos limited their violence to Turks and left non–Turks out of the bitter arena of war.

In seeking revenge against Turkey, some Armenians coined a new modern and effective political axiom: The Armenian victims became killers, and *revenge* has been taken. The goal of Turkish *reparations*, which the 1983 Armenian National Congress mentioned, is not a very feasible goal. The Turks have never assumed responsibility for the events of 1915 and are not likely to do so. Yet the June 1987 resolution of the European Parliament, which recognized the Armenian genocide as a historical fact, contains a message of Turkish guilt that may become politically significant over time.

But for now, another goal, that of Armenian *return*, would appear all but impossible in the normal state of affairs. Michael Gunter has written that chances to "carve an independent Armenian homeland out of eastern Turkey at this late date would seem nil."[58] The very effort to do so, in reliance upon terrorism against Turkey and various Western targets, may turn the effort into a veritable act of suicide. The West will lose all remaining sympathy for the Armenians, and the Turks will ruthlessly repress them wherever possible. Terrorism as a psychological outlet may be functional, but as a political strategy, it looks irrational and hopeless. It has probably warmed some Armenian hearts and melded national sentiment. But this alone does not measure up to the prescription required for a national liberation struggle.

It remains to comment on methods for conflict resolution within Turkey. Certainly the Turkish-Turanian ethnic spirit cannot and will not smoothly absorb Christian Armenians as equal and legitimate members of the national community. Islam, definitely on the rise in what was touted as a secular republic since the 1920s, will definitely harden Turkish attitudes toward those obstreperous *dhimmis* who chose the path of terrorist warfare. No semblance of a Turkish civil political ethos, with or without the army generals, can fashion coexistence with the Armenians, who in any case are but a small inconsequential minority in the country today. Alleged Armenian-Kurdish collaboration against the common Turkish enemy can elicit greater repression rather than a policy of integration. There is, in addition, no institutional mechanism for accommodating the Armenians, for the modern Turks have been bitterly opposed to any compromise of Ankara's central authority, exercised at times through civil or martial law. And lastly, the option of secession for the Armenians—perhaps attempted prior to and at the start of the twentieth century—is no longer a discussable item.

The Armenians have become a miniscule minority since 1915, and turning the clock of history back to the brighter days of Armenian national life in its native soil is a monumental, near impossible task. It could come about were Turkey to disintegrate as a viable nation-state because of pathological domestic instability and pervasive minority insurrection of a high order. Were this to develop in conjunction with massive Soviet intervention of a conventional and/or terrorist variety, perhaps Turkey would indeed collapse.

In the event of an Islamic takeover in Turkey with a deleterious impact on Muslim restiveness in nearby Soviet Union, the Russians could consider invasion of Turkey (the Afghanistan model). In justification, a doctrine of Soviet self-defense would be argued. The precedent of Iran, if it is to be one, points to ignoble American abandonment of an ally when the full weight of internal opposition becomes unbearable. In this kind of multifaceted scenario, the Armenians could recover their historical homeland or minimally earn the right to return to it.

Turkey remains the last link of what once was the West's "northern tier" in the Middle East. At a time when superpower detente may weaken the strategic springs of U.S. protection of Western Europe, NATO's southern flank could also become enfeebled in a further deterioration of American-Turkish relations. Nonetheless, Turkey was a staunch ally of the U.S. in early 1991 in the Gulf War against Iraq during the Kuwaiti crisis. Much will depend on the long-term tenacity and outreach of U.S. foreign policy and the ability of the USSR to continue striving for a revision of the status quo regarding Turkey. The rise and fall of the Armenian Question will ultimately be, as always, contingent upon factors and actors beyond the influence of the Armenians themselves.

Meanwhile, Armenian life, more secularized over time, continues with a linguistic, cultural, and artistic vitality on three continents — Asia (including the Middle East and the Soviet Union), Europe (France especially), and America. Armenian identity is solid and independent of extraneous circumstances, including the ASALA phenomenon. And all along, remembering the genocide and propagandizing against the Turks fill the Armenians with unforgettable pain and unbounded purpose.

CHAPTER 9

Assyrians: An Ancient
People, a Perennial Struggle

Ancient Assyria, the rod of God's anger against a sinful Israel in the words of the prophet Isaiah (10:5–11), was itself destined to fall for excessive pride in its power. Assyrians created an advanced civilization of imperial proportions, conquering far and wide, and developing arts and agriculture of legendary fame. In antiquity, their kings occupied the throne of Ashur, their sculptors and architecture a remnant of human creativity. Their empire fell in 612 B.C., but their national descendants linger on in Iraq in the land of origin, as well as in America and elsewhere.

At times called Chaldeans and noted for their classic astronomical expertise and later Catholic turn, also known as Nestorians based on their adoption of the religion of the apostles, called Jacobites or Syrians too, the claim of historical continuity back to the power of Assyria on the Upper Tigris lives on.[1] The ambiguity of defining this old Eastern community may be considered resolved if we accept their view, which says, "We were Assyrians long before we were Christians."[2] It is in fact this interpretation that offers to transcend the linguistic and denominational confusion in trying to name this people.

In recent years the name Assyrian has been revived and given greater prominence in the diaspora communities, those in America particularly. Assyrian national consciousness was the catalyst for establishing the Bet-Nahrain Democratic party in 1976 that called for an autonomous state for Assyrians in northern Iraq. Gone, undoubtedly, was the famed hubris of ancient Assyria, for now only a small candle is burning to rekindle hopes of renewal. Ancient Assyria fell to the Medes and Persians. Today its lands fall within the states of Turkey, Iraq, and Iran. The restoration of Assyria would seem to require a divine miracle on the scale of biblical miracles related long ago.

Although Assyrian origins are less than scientifically demonstrable through archaeological findings, ethnic cohesion characterizes this Middle Eastern Semitic community. Of the various sects in the Mosul plain, where their villages dot the region, Nestorian–Chaldean Assyrians were and are one among many diverse peoples. Henry Charles Luke was able to identify them in the early part of the twentieth century,[3] just as a more recent sociological study described Assyrian village life in the far north of Iraq, bordering Turkey. The patriarchal ideal was the social norm in the family unit.[4] Further north in the Hakkiari Mountains, tribal formations remained the grid of communal life. These units did not prevent joint action and the cultivation of national unity but still relegated that achievement to days of threatening trouble. Ethnic solidarity, as doctor-missionary Asahel Grant reported in the nineteenth century, assured no intermarriage between the Nestorian-Assyrians and other Christians.[5] Intermarriage with Muslims was unheard of. These basic features were appropriate signposts for a traditional people factionalized within but tenacious without.

Facing Antiquity, Christianity, and Islam

The cultural particularity of Assyrians is riveted to two fundamental sources through their extended and convoluted trek through history. There is the legacy of ancient Assyria to which they lay claim as direct descendants. This turns on the ruins of Nineveh, excavated in the 1840s, and the link with Jonah the prophet's message of doom. It relates to the memory of powerful monarchs like Ashurbanipal, an Assyrian king in the seventh century B.C. who boasted a famed library. The Assyrian heritage rests too on the Code of Hammurabi, while various cultural artifacts adorn major museums of the world, as in London, Berlin, and Chicago. The continuous usage of old Assyrian names such as Sargon, Ramsen, and Ninos in their family life until today illustrates Assyrian continuity over the ages.

The Chaldean study of the stars culturally epitomized intellectual curiosity and scientific advance. Recording their history upon stone and generally the art of writing illustrated a sense of the transmission of life's experiences to succeeding generations. Most important has been the linguistic continuity of Syriac, or Semitic Aramaic, which was the Assyrians' national tongue from pre–Christian days into the twentieth century. It remained a spoken vernacular even after Turkish, Persian, and Arabic spread in the areas of Assyrian settlement, not only persisting in the liturgy of the Nestorian church. The fact that Syriac continued as a minority spoken language based on 75 percent pure Aramaic was an impressive index of in-group particularity.

The place of women in ancient Assyria, while not exalted, did suggest a dignity not always attained in the East. The daughter of Sargon the Accadian was a chief priestess in Ur, a poetess of renown, and a mistress of a large household that she administered. Queen Samooramat (or Semiramis) actually governed the country of Ashur following the king's death while her son was not yet of an age to rule.[6] In more recent times, Nestorian women were known to be treated with respect, veritable companions to their husbands and open participants in social gatherings. In the modern era, Assyrian-Christian women of Iraq were apparently more literate than Muslim men.[7] Family hierarchy nonetheless assured male predominance as the leading motif of husband-wife relations.

Besides ancient Assyria as an orienting cultural feature is the adoption of Christianity in highlighting this old people's collective identity. The gospel of Jesus appeared in the language the Assyrians spoke and transmitted a message of salvation that appealed to the Assyrian seers, or magi.[8] The new religion quickly reached the pagan Assyrians who had then been practicing the Zoroastrian faith. St. Thomas taught the gospel, and a church stood in Urmiya (present Reziyah) in the second century.

But it was the personality of Nestorius, patriarch of Constantinople, that provided the national Assyrians with the *raison d'être*, or perhaps excuse, for a national church. His views on the human nature of Christ elicited condemnation at the Council of Ephesus in 431, and it was this decision that in effect gave birth to the new Nestorian church in Mesopotamia. Followers of Nestorius fled Syria toward Persia to turn his hereticism into a legitimate doctrine. In 451, the Council of Chalcedon again declared that the errors of Nestorius must be repudiated, but to no avail.[9] Born in persecution as a kind of seminal Protestant deviation, these Nestorian Christians in the Kurdistan mountains would preserve their Assyrian identity, Syriac language, and now their sectarian Christianity in a state of extended autonomy for long centuries.

A last group feature worth noting is the Assyrian martial tradition and a remarkable native pugnacity in the face of neighboring marauders, Kurds in particular. In the period following World War I, Assyrian recruits to British military forces in Iraq were praised for their innate battle readiness and fighting qualities.[10] This portrayal of Christian warlike capacities has not gone unchallenged. Habib Ishow argued that the Assyrian Chaldeans of the Mosul plain were markedly pacific in contrast to the attacks perpetrated by groups, Muslim obviously, for whom the language of force was commonplace.[11] The apparent divergence in interpretation is resolved if we identify Assyrian bravery and militarism in particular with those Nestorians in the Hakkiari Mountains, exempting their proximate brothers in the Urmiya plain to the east and the Mosul plain to the south. Even this dichotomy cannot be considered absolute and valid for all times and places.

The geographic hearth of Assyria was traditionally located in the north Tigris highlands, north of Babylon or Mesopotamia, yet south of Armenia, below Lake Van. In classical times, Persia and Byzantium boxed in the mountain Assyrians. Later, they found themselves between Turks and Persians, Kurds and Arabs. Once Islam made its tremendous appearance, the Assyrians were the target of converging Sunni forces from the south and the north, and Shiite forces from the east. It therefore became of the utmost security importance to seek collective well-being in the wild and rocky Hakkiari Mountains, an area of rural village life that served as a natural military fastness. Always threatened, the Assyrian tribes in this rugged region were compelled to face seminomadic Kurds within and Turks, Arabs, and Persians on the geographic margins. The Great Zab River flowed through the country, and numerous Nestorian villages hugged its banks. To the south (in what is today northern Iraq), many singular or mixed Assyrian-Chaldean villages stretched across the Sapna Valley north of Mosul in a potentially rich agricultural zone. To the east (in what is today Iran), near the western shore of Lake Urmiya, other Assyrian communities dwelled. Overall, the Assyrians lived in a relatively contiguous and compact territory whose disability was, beyond internal tribal and topographic differences, the problem of boundary discontinuity among three states — Turkey, Iraq, and Iran — in the twentieth century. Nonetheless, the presence of ancient Assyrians and their modern Nestorian-Chaldean descendants in the same national homeland was a clear sign of a specific collective and vigorous experience.

The Church, Facing East and West

The history of this community derives naturally from its singular ethnic, linguistic, religious, and geographic features across a broad canvas of national history. Central to the consciousness of Assyrians is the feeling of continuity joining the ancient imperial legacy with the Christian religious era. Nestorian monuments are analyzed in terms of their earlier Assyrian forms. When the Nestorian church fathers organized the "Chaldean or Assyrian Church" at the Council of Seleucia in 498, they meant to convey the ethnic roots of the people in its pre–Christian period. They were not outwardly ashamed of their pagan ancestors but elevated them to a pedestal of national inspiration. According to certain sources, the Assyrian city of Urhay (Urfa in southern Turkey, or the Chaldean town Ur) was allegedly the first kingdom to adopt the Christian religion officially. Eusebius the Assyrian left a written record of the evangelization of Urhay and the initial establishment there of the Assyrian church (Church of the East), and how it later spread eastward with enormous missionary zeal. In these instances the connection between Assyrian antiquity with later Christian developments becomes clear. The history of this people incorporates a national and religious character that transcends time and circumstance imprinted on the people's life.

The indomitable Christian aspect of Assyrian history is indeed the organizing principle of an impressive chapter in Eastern history. Counterpoised to the role of the monastery as a guidepost to spiritual entrenchment, like the one at Mar Gewargis (Saint George) north of Mosul, was the role of the missionary reaching out to distant lands to propagate the faith. Already by the fifth century, Nestorian missionaries had traveled across Persia to India and China. Between the years 636–781, some seventy of them had been in China.[12] This evangelical work, which became legendary as a Christian breakthrough, led to the conversion of some Tartars and Mongols in Asia. While no massive conversion ever took place, the Nestorian church in the East lasted until the fifteenth century for approximately one thousand years. Missionaries were present in the courts of rulers and openly practiced their Christian religion, trying to impress its validity on their open-minded Chinese hosts. Besides Asia, Nestorian missionaries reached into Arabia in the ninth century as well as to Europe. For a small people, this was a far-flung and extravagant religious campaign, even though it yielded only partial concrete results.

The appearance of Islam constituted a grave danger to the Assyrian Christians but also opened up new and exciting opportunities. In the 640s, some defected or were forcibly converted and joined the banner of Muhammad in the area of Persia. The conversion of the Kurds to Islam would inevitably complicate the situation. At the same time, the native Christians in the vicinity of the Abbasid Empire, with its capital at Baghdad, participated in the intellectual efflorescence of the age.

The transmission of Greek thought and works to the Muslims was processed by the Assyrians in translating texts from Syriac to Arabic. Yuhanna ibn Masawayh (d. 857) was an eminent Assyrian physician who headed the Bayt al-Hikmah, established as a translation center in 832. The vigorous role played by Assyrian-Nestorian pedants served as a civilizational bridge between the East and the West, the Muslim Orient and the Christian Occident. The minority as a cultural middleman seemed an optimal situation for the talented Assyrian-stock people. And while much or at least part of Syria, Iraq, and Khurasan (Persia) were still Nestorian Christian until the eleventh century, political independence was beyond the realm of possibilities once the dawn of Muslim ascendancy arrived.

Assyrian national history developed into an internal struggle between the native Nestorian church and the spiritual inroads brought about by Catholicism in the East. In the sixteenth century, following earlier initiatives, Roman efforts to inaugurate Uniate churches began to bear fruit. This development coincided historically with the Nestorians' failure to convert the Turks or to persevere in their oriental missionary campaign. At the same time, Nestorian clergy traveled to Rome, and a union was formed in 1552. This was the origin for the Chaldean Catholic church, though it took another full century for the rites to conform to the Roman model. In 1683, the Chaldean church fully recognized papal authority. Known as the patriarch of Babylon seated in Baghdad, the head of this Nestorian branch symbolized oriental Christian subservience to the European orthodox leadership.[13]

In the nineteenth century, the Chaldean Catholics were prospering while the older Nestorian Church, under its patriarchal leadership, was growing weaker. Assistance from Protestant communities in the United States and Britain was forthcoming. The American Board of Commissioners for Foreign Missions in the state of New York sent emissaries to the Nestorian community in Persia in the 1830s, as did St. Andrew's Church in Philadelphia. The archbishop of Canterbury's mission reached them in the 1880s. Together, the English and the Armenians opened schools, particularly for Assyrian girls; provided medical care; operated a printing press; and tried to learn Syriac in order to converse in the native tongue.[14] The missionaries suffered terribly from ill health and nostalgia for home in their rough-and-tumble environment. Problems were so daunting that the Sisters of Bethany were unable to provide replacements in 1898.

The conflict between the competing churches — native Nestorian and Chaldean Catholic — invited external involvement from abroad and while exacerbating division within the total Assyrian community, stimulated hopes for national advancement. Professing the religion of the West had advantages and disadvantages. French and papal support for Eastern Catholic churches offered both spiritual sustenance and political leverage. The Ottoman Empire in the beginning of the Tanzimat period created a Catholic Nestorian, that is, Chaldean, *millet* in 1844. The more independent Nestorian mountaineers in Hakkiari also enjoyed a de facto autonomy, paying tribute really to no one. Russia's invasion of Persian Azerbaijan in 1828 also encouraged Assyrian fellow Christians to believe that a historic opening was at hand. Liberation from Islamic rule appeared possible in the bright new era of the nineteenth century. Yet when Hakkiari Kurds set out to massacre the hopeful Nestorians in the 1840s, no European intervention was there to save the day.[15]

The very tie to the Christian West became an inevitable source of intercommunal and interreligious aggravation, though optimism rose on the Assyrian horizon. Missionaries played a role in creating a uniform Syriac written language based on the Urmiya dialect in Persia. Some Nestorians looked for protection to Russia as the 1880s dawned and nationalist stirrings and growing communal dignity, inspired by European influences, spread across the Middle East. Under British pressure, Christian testimony was now to be heard in a Muslim court in Persia, a similar development having occurred slightly earlier in the Turkish Ottoman Empire. Rising British interest, via diplomacy, archaeology, and religion, induced Nestorians to write Queen Victoria in 1863. These desiderata turned ultimately on Russian-British competition in patronizing the Nestorians, but also on local Muslim-Christian hostility that resulted at times in the pillaging of Christian villages. Collaborating with the West and occidental Christianity threatened to arouse a fury of unrelenting Eastern opposition against the Nestorian community.

Toward Assyrian Independence and Failure

By the end of the nineteenth century, the Assyrians were on the verge of a "national awakening." Their national history, notwithstanding sharp twists and turns since Assyrian antiquity, was a consolidated corpus of communal identity. Foreign involvement had served to mobilize national thinking, increase literacy, standardize Syriac, and offer encouragement that even the traditional religious leadership, in particular under Mar Shimon, could exploit for political possibilities. In addition, unabated local conflict with the Kurds, and a life of marginality and deprivation within the Turkish and Persian empires, contributed to sharpening Assyrian consciousness. Prior to the First World War and up to its beginning, further contacts were made with the Russians. Some Nestorians even considered uniting with the Russian Orthodox church. A religious upsurge, they might have inferred, could catalyze the political struggle for freedom.[16]

The war, when it came, was a watershed for the Assyrians as for other Mideastern peoples. The rise and decline of their fortunes engendered optimism when the Russians entered Turkish territory but culminated in despair when the Turks recovered. In June 1915, both Turks and Kurds attacked the Assyrians "for the simple reason that they were Christians," commented Arnold Toynbee.[17] The massacre led to a panicky flight from the Hakkiari Mountains eastward to the plain of Salmas and Urmiya in Persia. Some eighty thousand destitute people arrived there, most of them Assyrian refugees. Nestorian military assistance for, and political and religious identification with, the Russian advance led the Turks to seize the opportunity to square an old score with this Christian community. This was transparently in the spirit of Turkish behavior toward the Armenians and the Greeks, other Christians targeted for repression, destruction, and expulsion.

Meanwhile, the Kurds continued to play their part in the developing Assyrian tragedy. Simko, their leader in Persia, had invited Mar Shimon for a conference in Urmiya, kissed him—and then treacherously murdered the Nestorian patriarch and his men. By 1918, the Assyrians were in full flight out of Turkey and Persia, heading toward British lines in northern Iraq. Once again, reliance on the West became a choice compelled by necessity.

The problem of physical security was linked to an amorphous effort for political independence. Subjection to the rule of others had proven its undesirability over time. In 1918, the Anglo-French Declaration referred to indigenous government for the Assyrians as part of postwar principles of settlement. In 1919, Assyrian representatives in Paris laid claim to a state from Diyarbekir in Turkey to Mesopotamia in Iraq. Others called for a British protectorate from the Jezirah (in Syria) to Mosul (in Iraq), ending in Urmiya (in Persia). Appearing before the King-Crane Commission in August 1919, the Chaldean patriarch requested a European-protected state for Chaldeans, Nestorians, and Syrian-Jacobites in the area of Mesopotamia and the Jezira. However, the British showed no enthusiasm for this proposal. Some British spokesmen actually raised the idea of repatriating the Assyrians to Canada rather than fantasizing about a return to the Hakkiari Mountains. The remaining Nestorians in the historical mountain zone, where the patriarch's seat in Julamerk was located, seemed heading for disaster should the British be unsuccessful in incorporating Nestorian areas of settlement in the Iraqi state.

Meanwhile, in 1920, an Assyrian military leader, Agha Patrus, failed to recover ancestral villages in Hakkiari. The Persians opposed Nestorian repatriation to Urmiya, and the Kurds and Turks opposed their repatriation to Hakkiari. In 1924, the Turks actually invaded Hakkiari, and 8,000 Assyrians were again driven south. A League of Nations recommendation to establish Assyrian autonomy in British-mandated Iraq, with the Mosul *vilayet* part of this new state, seemed the last line of Assyrian defense in this trying and complicated tale.[18] But while the 1924 Iraqi Constitution guaranteed religious representation in the legislature, no political provision would be foolproof in the new Muslim state in the land of the Tigris and Euphrates rivers. In 1930, an idea was actually canvassed to settle the Assyrians in South America.

A related but unique development was the formation of the

Assyrian Levies under British officers on loan from the Royal Air Force. Originating in 1915, they were formally constituted in 1919. They became a central instrument to ensure internal security in the chronically volatile Iraqi state. Their loyalty to the British and their fighting prowess became legendary among all who knew or heard of them. The Assyrian Levies distinguished themselves, for example, in the fighting to overcome the Rashid Ali revolt of May 1941. The force thereafter grew and survived until the final British military withdrawal from Iraq in 1955, when they too were disbanded at Habbaniya west of Baghdad. Yet the Assyrians' military role alongside the British brought with it no political gains whatsoever; in fact, Assyrian trust in the British because they too were Christian seems to have been misplaced. British manipulation of them fit the broad strategy of "divide and rule" in colonial terms and conformed to the historical British thrust in the Middle East to cultivate the Sunni Muslims, as in Egypt so in Iraq, against all other communities, Christian ones included.

In 1932, the British mandate in Iraq was terminated. Simultaneously with this, the Nestorian patriarch wrote the Permanent Mandates Commission to guarantee local Assyrian autonomy. Fear was in the hearts of this old people. Iraqi Arab leaders made it clear that they opposed a single Assyrian settlement zone in the country; they also chafed from the fact that many resident Assyrians were refugees from the Hakkiari Mountains in Turkey. The British responded to this developing tension by suggesting that the Assyrians migrate to French-controlled Syria to the west. Assyrian apprehension grew drastically when Iraqi officials invited the patriarch, Mar Eshai Shimun, to Baghdad in May 1933 and immediately placed him in detention.[19]

The fateful year of 1933 in modern Assyrian history demonstrated the fragility of minority Christian life in the Islam-dominated East. In May, Mosul was the scene of deteriorating Arab-Assyrian relations. One consequence was that Assyrians in the police force were transferred to the South of Iraq. Thereafter, certain Assyrian leaders who disapproved of the Iraqi settlement plan to disperse the community rather than allow it to enjoy geographic compactness decided to leave for Syria. Upon their innocent return in August, the Iraqi army opened fire and killed six hundred Assyrians in the vicinity of Simel, a large Assyrian village not far from Mosul. The Iraqis accused the Assyrians of rebellion; the Assyrians accused the Iraqis (Arabs and Kurds) of cold-blooded murder. The former spoke of unproven intentions, the latter of an unadulterated fact. When the massacre was over, after priests were tortured and some Christians were forcibly converted to Islam, some sixty-five of ninety-five Assyrian villages in northern Iraq had been ransacked, destroyed, or burned to the ground. Assyrians from Dohuk had been removed from the town, and one hundred were machine-gunned to death.[20] In the course of these days, the British Royal Air Force took the patriarch to Cyprus for safety. Many Nestorians in the North fled to the Jezira in Syria, though most Chaldean Catholics in central Iraq remained.

Past Assyrian service for the British, against rebellious Arabs and Kurds in 1919–1920 particularly, had been all but forgotten. In 1934, the idea of resettling the Assyrians outside Iraq was again raised by the League of Nations. Neither Christian affinity nor military service were sufficient to assure Western support for the distraught and damaged Assyrians. A British brigadier general and a League of Nations high commissioner for refugees actually went on a mission to Brazil in 1934 to examine settlement possibilities there. Assyrian clansmen were deserving of a better life than Iraq had offered them, but the emissaries considered a better life within Iraq beyond their ability or Britain's political capacity to ensure. The cutting edge of modern Middle Eastern statehood was a cruel portent for certain minority peoples, specifically Christian ones like Armenians in Turkey and Assyrians in Iraq. The Western notion of "the tyranny of the majority" was not just a liberal fear for minority freedom in democratic systems but in the East a formula for repression and human loss on a grand scale.

Dispersion and Revitalization

In a sense, Assyrian history stopped in 1933. It was more the finality of the event, not so much its numerical proportions, that conveyed the dissolution of a modern dream for security, perhaps independence and dignity. The flight from Hakkiari in 1915 and the massacre near Mosul in 1933 set the chronological parameters for collective defeat in the first third of the twentieth century. From then on, Assyrian existence was confounded by dispersion and disunity, weakness and despair.

In the Middle East, small communities have nonetheless succeeded in transmitting their communal identity in times of stress. Most Christians remaining in Iraq are Chaldean Catholic Assyrians, numbering approximately 750,000 people, estimated at about 4 percent of the total population. Nestorians have joined the Communist party of Iraq and even served in governments. In fact, Yusuf Salman, one of the founders of the ICP, was an Assyrian. Their ideological impetus is rooted in opposition to Arab nationalism and its pan–Arab stress that is uncongenial to minority communities. The Mosul massacres of 1959–1960 found the Assyrians, particularly in Tall Kayf, loyal to Kassem in his struggle against Nasserite insurrection. But the Ba'thist coup in 1963 forced many Christians to flee the North of Iraq. From then on, the Assyrians were known to support, or to be sympathetic with, the Kurdish struggle. Indeed the bishop of Zakho called for cooperation with the Kurds in March 1974.[21]

The situation of the Assyrians has not been sanguine, notwithstanding formal recognition of Assyro-Chaldean cultural and linguistic rights by the Iraqi government in 1972. Little was done to give concrete significance to this declaration (probably designed primarily to erode Assyrian sympathies for the Kurds). Many migrated to the cities, particularly Baghdad, leaving unfulfilled the hope for agricultural development and undermining the natural tie between the people and their land. Their religious leader, in the person of Mar Shimon, left Iraq in 1939 for the United States, whose two major Assyrian centers are Chicago and California, with a third concentration of Chaldeans in Detroit.

Within Iraq, the Assyrians have in fact been denied basic communal rights. The end of the *millet* has not been replaced by minority status secured by law. Some Assyrians have been executed by a regime that suspects and oppresses with arbitrary willfulness. Three Assyrian nationalists (among others) were put to death in February 1985: Youkhana Shemoun, Yousip Toma Hormiz, and Youbert Benyamin Shlemon. Other Assyrians have been forced to flee Iraq because of their religious faith. As followers of the Chaldean rite, many chose to become refugees in Rome in 1983.[22] Ba'thist party policy has denied them Christian schools and work opportunities. Cultural repression is basically an Arabization campaign that defines Assyrians as "Arabs" in the Iraqi government census, forbids Assyrian schools, seizes churches, and compels Assyrian social organizations to be renamed with Iraqi Arab names. Most poignant in recent years has been the large number of Assyrian soldiers unwillingly serving in the Iraqi Army, some forty thousand of whom have been killed, wounded, imprisoned in Iran, or missing in action after the Gulf War erupted in 1980.[23] Solving the "Assyrian problem" on the Iran-Iraq front is a sinister development in the Assyrian determination for survival.

In other countries in the region such as Lebanon, Syria, and Persia, the Chaldean church and Assyrian communities continue to exist. In Arab countries they have adopted the Arabic language and live on the margins of society. The historical trend of abandoning Iraq for other Mideastern countries denies the Assyrians their territorial base for engaging in a full-scale nationalist struggle.

In the United States, the most active Assyrian diaspora has been the carrier of an ardent collective revitalization. The Bet-Nahrain Democratic party (BNDP) bears a name reflecting the land of the Tigris and Euphrates rivers. From a geographic perspective, this could legitimately incorporate areas in Turkey and Iraq. It appeared in 1976 as the first Assyrian political party committed to aspiring, as the literary organ of the BNDP stated, "to regain independence and dignity for our people."[24] While the specific ideological orientation of the party was not explicitly central to its credo, an exposé on the American arms deal to Iran in 1986 was discussed in the BNDP newspaper in a vindictive anti–United States tone.

This national Assyrian movement has directed its attention to all Assyrian elements, regardless of religious affiliation, and has pointedly dedicated itself to addressing the fundamental problem of persecution in Iraq. Reports of deportation to Turkey and Iran conveyed the dismal situation of Assyrians in the "homeland" that their American conationals raised for discussion and action in America. Various communal organizations—like the Assyrian American National Federation and the Assyrian National Council, both with their headquarters in California—propounded national questions in addition to sponsoring a variety of cultural activities in Assyrian communities. Preserving ethnic ties and cultivating social relations have become important in diaspora Assyrian circles. In Chicago, for example, a vibrant Assyrian-American cultural life reflected the vitality of communal cohesion. The churches are now complemented by clubs, a political purpose now galvanizing a people whose roots were traditionally nourished by the planting of a stable cultural diet in the hearts and minds of the Assyrian people.[25] Assyrians have acquired modern skills as engineers and teachers in the United States. But individual achievement cannot in any way ensure collective strength. This is as true in America as it is in Iraq.

Activities have developed in other parts of the world in a variety of ways. In 1984, the Nestorian patriarch Mar Denka IV visited Pope John Paul II in Rome. In Lebanon, different Assyrian parties joined together under the aegis of the BNDP. In the Soviet Union, where a small Assyrian population resides, sentiments of solidarity have been expressed for the condition of their brethren in Iraq. In Wiesbaden, (West) Germany, an Assyrian Nineveh Club began publishing its own magazine in three languages—Assyrian, Arabic, and German.

The Assyrian struggle from within is one toward renaissance and unity. These goals still require much work prior to contending more effectively with the ultimately visionary goals of return and independence. For now, the rallying cry is in the spirit of early stages of national regeneration, captured in the poem by Elisha Oushana:

Wake up Assyria . . .
From thine everlasting slumber
The time has come to heed the call
Of thine determined men and women
From across the seas and oceans,

From beyond the valleys and mountains
And the distant corners of the world![26]

An internal awakening can energize an old people that in spite of
geographic dispersion, still persistently maintains its ethnic, linguistic,
cultural, and historical identity. Yet how long and how strong these
forces of cohesion will persist it is too early to know. John Joseph argued
that in earlier decades of the twentieth century it was "difficult to speak
with confidence of a national sentiment among the Nestorians."[27] It will
inevitably become more problematic to develop and strengthen national Assyrian sentiment in the conditions of dispersion in a modern
world as the century draws to a close.

The question of conflict resolution in the Assyrian case has been
all but foreclosed in history. Arabism in Iraq and Turanian ethnicity in
Turkey precluded the smooth integration of the Christian Assyrians.
The rise of Shiite Islamic fury in Iran makes impossible any quest for
equality there. Autonomy for a Christian *dhimmi* is no longer a
legitimate element in Mideastern political calculations. The *millet* is
dead and minority inferiority or persecution now highly entrenched and
legitimized in the ways of contemporary regime performance.

No obvious mechanism for integrative civil ideologies or institutions exists in Iraq, though recollections of ancient Babylonian civilization, Hummarabi and all, can help arouse a memory of ancient Assyrian
civilization. Yet even there, Arab-Assyrian confrontation today may
become more strident in the light of history's old wars and struggles in
the land of the two rivers. The rejection by Iraq of full Kurdish
autonomy, let alone independence, augurs ill for the Assyrians, weaker
and smaller than the Kurdish minority in the country. Lastly, the halting
moves — or minimally, hopes — in the direction of secession during
World War I led to a heavy national Assyrian loss. How the remnant in
the land could today do better is an unanswerable question.

External and internal agents for radical change in Iraq could theoretically provide the requisite elements in a scenario of future Assyrian
achievement. A Kurdish victory against the Ba'thists of Baghdad would
open the way to the dissolution of pan–Iraqi territorial integrity but
would not necessarily overcome long-standing tensions between Assyrians and Kurds in the Mosul area. Still, a Baghdad defeat could be exploited by all embittered oppositionists — Kurds, Shiites, and Assyrians — to try to redefine the political and territorial configuration of the
Iraqi state. The fact that it is a relatively modern fabrication from 1920
can arouse fantasies for a radical transformation. Yet the staying power
of the Arab Muslims and the Ba'thist regime cannot be ignored. Only
a dramatic and unqualified Iranian military victory over Saddam Hussein in Baghdad, which did not occur, linked to a Kurdish recovery in

the North after setbacks in winter 1988, could realter the facts of political life.

Alternatively, the Iraqi invasion of Kuwait in August 1990 aroused the specter of a major war, as the United States and various allied powers sent military forces to confront and repel further Iraqi aggression. All-out warfare could conceivably culminate in a formidable blow to Iraq. The collapse of the Saddam regime and a new political order could then prepare the way for an Assyrian opportunity.

Meanwhile, Iraq hounded Assyrian elements in the United States who symbolize opposition to the Baghdad regime. An editor of an Assyrian newspaper in Detroit was murdered in 1983. In April 1990, the U.S. Justice Department indicted a former employee of the Iraqi mission at the United Nations who had been accused of planning to assassinate Sargon Dadesho, an Iraqi-born American citizen who heads the Assyrian National Congress and produces media broadcasts in southern California on Assyrian affairs. Intervention from the outside and upheaval within Iraq could enhance the chances for Assyrian self-determination. But until then, the bitter Assyrian experiences of the twentieth century will continue to constitute a stark lesson for this old Mideastern community.

CHAPTER 10

Maronites: Sophistication and Opportunity

In the land of Lebanon, the ancient Phoenicians looked outward to commerce and wealth, intrigue, and pleasure while setting the stage for a daring human experiment on the Syrian coast. Later, a similar people, now of the Christian spirit, drew upon Greek and Hellenic civilization and called Euclid of Sidon their son. With Christianity as their religious calling and a European linking as their armor in a Muslim region, the Maronites not only survived but flourished as a small Mideastern people.

But in the modern era, savagery and violence, not uncommon in Lebanon, threatened to destroy the fabric of secure Christian life. The civil war beginning in 1975 culminated by the late 1980s in the near demise of one of the most viable Christian communities in the Middle East. The West and the papacy looked on as the multiple forces of Islam raged through Lebanon. "I wrote to the Pope but never got an answer," recalled Sa'ad Haddad, the military commander of predominantly Maronite forces in southern Lebanon in 1980.[1] Time will tell if this recent episode erupting in the 1970s is just another chapter in a long succession of conflicts in the land of the cedars or the last chapter in a long Maronite struggle to survive.

Central to the consciousness of a collective Maronite ethnic identity is a reaction to the equation of Arabism with Islam. Their corollary equation identifies Lebanon with Christianity, thereby denying that speaking the Arabic language makes one an Arab. As such, the Maronites claim that their origin is from greater Syria and not the Arabian peninsula. Descending from native Phoenician stock and/or Mardaites who moved south from northern Syria,[2] the Maronites always sharply differentiated themselves from Arabian-stock groups, the Arabs among them. Never tribalized, Maronite society was also more than a large clan conglomeration. It was an identifiable ethnic community bound by tight kinship ties, traditionally closed to marriage with other Christian denominations. The family unit was key to identity and group solidarity. Indeed, political action was a direct derivative of kinship commitment for Maronites as for other Lebanese communities.[3] But the Christian Maronite people was primarily captivated always with the sense of being the true Lebanese people. Being neither Arab nor Muslim confirmed this national equation.

The classic roots of Maronite culture, while providing a flavor of worldly savvy, were based firmly in oriental Semitic features. Syriac, an Aramaic dialect, was the spoken tongue for long centuries, only to be replaced with Arabic by the fifteenth century at the latest. Yet Syriac remained as the language of liturgy in the Maronite church, whose origins on the banks of the Orontes River in the person of Maron the priest is the most vital aspect of the people's particular culture. Volney reported that Jean le Maronite lived in the sixth century near Antioch and was buried near Hama,[4] though others date him in the fifth century.[5] Another theory, a distinct minority view, claims that Jean-Maroun lived in Lebanon in 1070.[6] His followers, called Mardaites and later Maronites, established their home in Mount Lebanon. It was soon dotted with monasteries, convents, and churches. Fending off the Islamic challenge, the Maronites were a distinctively religious people, though considered heretical by other Christians.

Lebanon's European Connection

In the twelfth century, having experienced contact with the Crusaders in the East, the Maronites turned in communion to the orthodox Catholic church. They travelled to Rome in the fifteenth century, took priestly orders, studied Latin, and preached the papal faith.[7] Yet Maronite religious particularism was nonetheless maintained. Not only did Syriac continue as the liturgical tongue, but an indigenous patriarch headed the community from his seat in Bekerki, north of Beirut overlooking Jouniya. While a Maronite college was founded in Rome in 1584, the church within the homeland always remained close to the people.[8] Although the clergy was often divided, the Maronite people as a whole deferred to the patriarchs and prelates in the resolution of local community conflicts. Foreign visitors to Lebanon, like the Frenchmen Volney and Lamartine, were impressed by the religiosity of the people. The church acted to consolidate and unite a small, often threatened, Christian group, and the establishment of the National Seminary in Ain-Warkah in 1789 symbolized the native strength of the faith at home. The secularism of revolutionary France, while not completely alien to the Maronites, contrasted with the religious entrenchment of traditional Lebanon.

Maronite distinctiveness celebrated a tie to Europe with unabashed publicity over the centuries. Of special moment was the adoption of the French language as a cultural tool for acquiring the essentials of occidental civilization. Jesuit missions and studies in Paris were primary means of immersion into the language, which beyond its intrinsic educational value, acted to differentiate the Maronites from other Christian and Muslim denominations. From 1655 to 1858, for example, France employed Maronites from the Khazin family as consuls in Beirut.[9] The French language became a veritable spoken second tongue for the Maronites, who conducted conversation in it with facility and demonstrated their broader cultural horizons than those of the Muslims of the region.

In North Africa, French colonialism imposed its language on the native society, but in Lebanon the native Maronite society chose to adopt the French language. The Eddé and Jemayel families were choice products of French Mediterranean culture, lodging Lebanon as part of the West more than the Arab world. The poet Sa'id Aql actually called for replacing Arabic by French in Lebanese education. All the while, Maronites sprinkled their Arabic with French words and expressions.

The style of Maronite life, particularly among the educated and economically solvent elite, also reflected a European-inspired ethos. A viable agricultural vocation in the mountain and commercial vitality in Beirut particularly lent an energy and prosperity to Maronite society. Business in Constantinople and connections with French manufacturing, like the silk industrialists in Lyon, widened Maronite economic activities. A bourgeoisie sprouted and contrasted sharply with the endemic poverty of Druzes and Shiites in the country. Money was available to build villas and afford foreign education. In modern times, money was also available for hiring maids, traveling to Europe, playing at the casino, and purchasing the fashions of Paris and the cars of Germany.[10] The Maronite sophisticates did not have to be blatantly ostentatious to arouse Muslim envy. Resentment arose naturally against the superior successes of the Christian *dhimmis.*

A long legacy of threat from Arabs, Turks, and other assorted protagonists over the centuries not surprisingly generated a warrior tradition among the Maronites. Mardaite raids in the vicinity of Damascus in the late seventh century, confronting the Mamluks under Baybars in the thirteenth century, and the battles of Bashir II facing local Druzes and rebellious Arabs in Palestine and Syria in the nineteenth century were some highlights of Maronite warfare. They could raise some 40,000 armed men if necessary and this martial readiness impressed those near and far. A kind of feudal mentality of allowing the traditional *zu'ama*, or leaders, to call the men to arms became an accepted Maronite norm. The establishment of the Kata'ib (phalangist) militia by Pierre Jemayel in 1936 and the "Tigers" of Camille Chamoun were twentieth-century expressions of that old Maronite urge to organize independently for communal security. In the 1970s the Kata'ib alone allegedly included some 60,000 members, of which 30,000 were active fighters, dominated by the Maronites but with other minority participation.[11]

Traditionally opposed to foreign military conscription, as during Ottoman and Egyptian periods of rule in Mount Lebanon, Maronites nevertheless asserted their willingness to fight if based on local need and organized under native auspices. The military forces of Fakhr al-Din in the early seventeenth century and those of Bashir II in the early nineteenth century were apparently dominated by Maronites. This dimension in Maronite culture was not restrained by Islamic superiority feelings, as a vulnerable Christian society successfully adapted to the requirements of survival in a permanently threatening environment.

The territorial hearth of the Maronites in Mount Lebanon has been their home for about 1,500 years. It is there and there alone that this people has built a national life, in the northern regions of Bsharra and Batroun down to the central regions of Kesraoun and the Shouf, indeed farther south yet to the area of Jezzine and Marja'youn. The personal origins of Maron on the Orontes River never played a major role in the establishment and entrenchment of the community. Maronite history, as Robert Haddad wrote, "was almost wholly centered in the rugged terrain of the Mountain,"[12] hardly at all in the Bekaa Valley to the east and until recent centuries not on the coast, including Beirut. In the mountain, Maronites sought and found refuge, for example in 1660 when the Ottoman Army chased them to their natural fortress. There a Maronite majority predominated others, Druzes and various Christian sects in particular.

In the last few centuries, Maronites moved from northern Lebanon southward to the heart of Mount Lebanon, the area east of Jebail and Jouniya. There they constituted the largest single community: 77,589 of a total population of 110,000 in the 1830s, 176,248 Maronites in 1944, while the next largest confessional group were the Druzes, numbering 59,303.[13] In the far north of the country, the Sunnis predominated, and in the far south, the Shiites. But in the center, astride Beirut and to the east and northeast, the Maronites enjoyed hegemonic preponderance.

The mountain was not a peripheral zone appended to a distant central core zone. It *was* Lebanon, between the Mediterranean coast and the Anti-Lebanon Mountains to the east, a home and a refuge, a land of extraordinary natural beauty. Even the trend of moving down from the mountain to Beirut, noticeable in the nineteenth century, never superseded the primacy of the mountain. This was so for Maronite families who purchased a winter home in the city but dwelt in their village during the summer. Most significant was the physical security provided by the mountain itself. In September 1903, sectarian fighting between Muslims and Christians in Beirut compelled thousands of Maronites to seek refuge in the mountain.[14] With a total Maronite population numbering some 377,000 in 1951 and established at 837,000 in 1976,[15] the largest portion has always chosen the Lebanon Mountain as their one and singular national geographic hearth. It is there that they organized their collective existence, and without it they would be, like the Greek Orthodox perhaps, merely a dispersed Christian denomination across the region, not a compact territorially rooted Maronite people.

Beyond a distinct ethnicity, culture, and geographic abode, the contours of Maronite history are naturally cut from the cloth of their national church. Seeking refuge from religious persecution, initially spearheaded by orthodox Byzantium and later by conquering Islam, these Eastern Christians were forced to pay tribute to these foreign powers. Arab invasions toward Mount Lebanon in the seventh and eighth centuries aroused native resistance. Into the tenth century Arab predators destroyed monasteries in the mountain.[16] Yet during these years a veritable independent Mardaite (Maronite) state existed in northern Lebanon, while an Arab area in the South and the Bekaa Valley was linked to the Abbasid Empire.

The mountain nation was later strengthened by Europe in the form of the Crusader warriors coming to the Orient. Soon thereafter, the Mamluks of Egypt and Syria succeeded in overwhelming the Christians in Kesraoun, and Lebanese independence ended there in 1305. The disabilities of Maronite history were somewhat compensated for in the cultural and spiritual domain by European sustenance in the form of Vatican training. In the fifteenth century, a Maronite from the mountain, Jibrail Ibn Al-Qila'i, actually preached Roman Catholicism and then became a Franciscan.[17]

The involvement of France offered protection and prosperity in various ways. The Capitulations of 1535, subsequently reaffirmed and strengthened over the centuries, guaranteed French support for the Uniate Maronites swimming like a ready catch in a Muslim sea. Louis XIV issued a statute to the Maronites in 1649, which was received by Patriarch Jean Sefraoui, that confirmed France's commitment to oriental Christians. They could duly turn for assistance to French consuls in Lebanon and to the French ambassador in Istanbul. A dramatic initiative was voiced by the Capuchin Order in 1657 to purchase the government of Mount Lebanon as a Christian Maronite state.[18] Instead,

Louis XIV issued a new Capitulation document in 1673 for the protection of the Latins, somewhat soothing assurance to the compact Maronite Uniates.

Ottoman Days, Maronite Nights

The Ottoman period of rule, beginning in 1517, once formally inaugurated and Islamic in spirit, aroused a permanent Maronite effort for independence. Notorious Turkish methods of deceit and treachery kept Christians attuned to the necessity for alertness and courage. It was the political institution of Shihabi emirs that basically ruled Mount Lebanon from 1697 to 1841 that consolidated the Maronite struggle, though the earlier period of the Ma'anid dynasty already provided an environment for Maronite welfare. That regime was allegedly Druze-led but highly tolerant of religious diversity, and the Maronites had coexisted tolerably in the area.

The increasing stability and confidence in Maronite life was reflected in the conversion of Shihab rulers to Christianity in 1756 and again in 1770. The Shihabis strove to maintain Lebanese autonomy from a rapacious Ottoman regime. At other times, Shihabi forces fought with Ottoman forces against external enemies—for example, Russia in 1770 and rebellious pashas off and on. The period until the beginning of the nineteenth century was generally one of religious consolidation and political welfare. The opening of a new era, with the French Revolution in Europe and Napoleon's invasion of Egypt and the Levant, would have far-reaching implications for Maronite society and hopes for the future.

The opportunity for Lebanese independence arose from the Egyptian campaign of 1831 against the integrity of the Ottoman Empire as a whole. Bashir II, emir of the mountain, had demonstrated the military capacity of his Maronite troops in various actions in the 1820s. In now joining Ibrahim Pasha's assault, Bashir assisted in the conquest of Homs in the summer of 1832 and pacified the area of Tsfat (Safed) two years later. His son went on to scorch the earth in the Nusairi Mountains and subdue the Hauran.[19] But thereafter Muhammad 'Ali, the viceroy of Egypt, decided to institute forced conscription for the freeborn Lebanese. Efforts to disarm the native Druzes and Maronites (who had otherwise benefited from a "freeing of the *dhimmis*") followed suit.

The ultimate settlement of Lebanese matters turned upon British and other European countries' intervention—bombing Beirut in 1840, for example—and then the collapse of the Egyptian offensive in the Levant specifically and the Fertile Crescent generally. Bashir's gamble for full independence was now exposed as an imprudent decision. The Ottoman Empire reestablished its authority, and the Shihabi regime was to end its legacy of autonomy on the Lebanese mount. In truth, that autonomy had already been compromised by an alliance with the Egyptians that became, in part, a cruel trap. The minority predicament surfaces with poignancy when the temptation for greater freedom entails simultaneously the danger of greater subjugation. Bashir was subsequently exiled and died in Istanbul in 1850.

During the period of the double governerate *(kaymakamat)* inaugurated in Mount Lebanon in 1842 and lasting until 1861, Maronite weakness became a function not only of European abandonment but also of Muslim recovery. The Ottoman regime granted the Druzes administrative equality with the Maronites and insidiously goaded them to revenge the Tanzimat benefits earlier granted the Christians. Anarchy followed the end of the emirate as the Druzes exploded into action after (as the story goes) a Maronite had killed a partridge on Druze property. This seemingly innocuous event catalyzed Druze attacks against the Maronites and other Christians.

The Christians were momentarily not averse to strong Ottoman order. The Sublime Porte exploited the new situation, and eighteen battalions arrived in September 1845 to restore tranquility in the tense confessional atmosphere. The Maronites were largely disarmed as the Ottoman authorities stressed the need for visible and demonstrable central power in order, as a circular from July had already pointed out, that "the deployment of the intimidating force will persuade the inhabitants of the Mountain of the necessity of returning within the bounds of obedience."[20] The restriction of European consular intervention in Lebanese affairs and the reassertion of direct Ottoman rule brought the Maronites to ignoble submission, the pride of former autonomy tarnished badly. The failure of Maronite feudal leadership against various adversaries from without also probably contributed to peasant opposition that surfaced against the landowners and clergy. Overall, the turn of events was highly deleterious for an 85 percent Maronite majority in the mountain, now divided and disintegrating in communal power.[21]

The civil war of 1859–1860 and the audacity of Druze violence against the Maronites was the culmination of unrestrained Turkish-Muslim rule over a vulnerable Christian minority people. Confessional hostilities in the summer of 1859 mobilized the Druzes to take the offensive against the Maronites in Jabal Duruz, the Shouf area in the southern part of the mountain. The following year, Druze forces, assisted by kin from the Hauran, attacked the Christians. Sixty Christian villages were destroyed in the Matn area. In June, the Druzes fell upon Dayr al-Kamar and Jezeen, and murdered ruthlessly. Brandishing words of comfort and reconciliation, the Druzes first psychologically disarmed the Christians before suddenly pouncing on them. In Hasbaya, bodies were mutilated; in Zachle, Christian heads were poised on the points of Druze spears; and in Dayr al-Kamar Christian blood "rose above the ankles, flowed along the gutters, gushed out of the water spouts, and gingled through the streets," as Colonel Churchill later described the infernal scene.[22] When it was over, some 11,000 Christians were dead in Lebanon. Thousands of other Christians in Damascus were victims of the Muslim massacre, while in Palestine still other Christians embraced Islam to stay alive.

The plight of the Maronites in 1860 lay in the inefficacy of European, specifically French, protection. Only when it was all over did France land soldiers under General Beaufort in late June. But they toured the beautiful land more than they acted to punish the criminals or redress the grievances of the victims. Yet more vital as an explanation of the disaster was Christian disunity in the mountain when, for example, 15,000 armed Maronites within six hours of Zachle, a predominantly Greek Catholic town, did not come to defend their brethren. Pure Maronite districts in the North were not targets of the onslaught, but neither were they prepared to come to the rescue of those in the South who were. Localism and stratification pervaded the Maronite nation, a wry instance of factionalism, even when grave danger struck with savagery. Christian peasants who had raised the banner of a social struggle against Druze overlords were perhaps not worth defending in the eyes of Christian landlords elsewhere in the mountain. Narrow economic and social interests could erect a wall of alienation between different Christian groups, even in the heat of ravaging religious-ethnic warfare.

The immediate political impact of the civil war turned out to be radically different from its immediate military results. Although the Maronites lost badly, foreign intervention salvaged them from complete physical annihilation and communal dissolution. It was the lingering "Eastern Question" between the Europeans and the Ottomans converging with the status and integrity of oriental minority Christian groups, which now became the hinge upon which to fasten the Maronites' rescue. An 1861 Règlement Organique created Mount Lebanon as an autonomous *sanjak*, with its own Christian governor and administrative council. This was a curt denial of Ottoman authority. In 1864, these new arrangements were formalized in the mountain *mutasarrifiya*, Christian-dominated and French-protected, providing the Maronites an unearned opportunity to recoup their predominant position.[23] Although only four of twelve members of the council were Maronites, though seven altogether were Christian, the French patron was close at hand as never before. This historical juncture awaited the Maronite response: Would the community slink back to minority introversion or exploit the opportunity for a national awakening?

Toward Independence in Lebanon

The period from 1864 until 1920 offered a mixed response, though one increasingly forthright by the time of World War I. A unified Lebanon under both local and foreign Christian domination provided a native administration that offered positions to qualified Maronites. Yet this opportunity served the tendency for political manipulation more than national construction. Central to Maronite feelings was a dissatisfaction with the *mutasarrifiya* as it was. It lacked economic foundations, cut off from the commerce of Beirut and the agriculture of the Bekaa. It lacked political legitimacy because it was subject to non–Maronite governors, the first being Daud Pasha, an Armenian Catholic. The residual and ever-present Ottoman Empire was a lingering sore spot leading to Maronite agitation. Maronite rebellion in Batroun and Kesrouan, led by Yusuf Karam Bey in 1866, was a brief victory. Karam was exiled to Algeria, and the Lebanese administration was then extended to the North, no longer challenged.

Maronite alienation was profound, and its clergy gave voice to it as well. Mutasarrif overlordship and Ottoman repression were overbearing and veritably unbearable.[24] As a result of multiple pressures in the economic domain — the weakening of the Lebanese silk industry, the role of the Suez Canal as an alternative transport route for Europe, and tax burdens — a large-scale emigration from the mountain transpired. Fleeing the uncomfortableness due as well to the influx of Muslims entering all of greater Syria, Christian Lebanese looked out to the Americas, and well over 100,000 settled there.[25] Maronites in the United States were not always graciously received, but they could enjoy minimal physical security and economic opportunity the likes of which Mount Lebanon could no longer guarantee. The sinews of resolve were weakening for an old oriental Christian people in its native homeland. Rather than trying to take hold of the administrative regime in the mountain, giving it energy as a tool of communal development, the Maronites chose in part to keep their distance. Neither the political vocation nor the military one was a sufficiently attractive pursuit; instead, private welfare and a passion to be free from others' authority typified their outlook.

At the same time, however, a cultural resurgence involving the natural talents of the Maronites progressed in the latter half of the nineteenth century. Along with Melkites, Maronites provided an elite in the fields of journalism and poetry, as well as government service for foreign consulates. Butrus Bustani (d. 1882), admittedly a curious case because of his conversion to Protestantism, was a leader in cultivating the modern Arabic vernacular and propagating the enlightenment ideas of Western learning and political consciousness. Beirut was a focus of

Arab nationalist stirrings, and Bustani became the secretary of the Society of Arts and Sciences established there in 1847. Bustani worked on an Arabic translation of the Bible and an Arabic encyclopaedia. The Syrian Scientific Society that arose in 1857 included one of his sons. It was in the bosom of foreign ecclesiastical missions sponsored by the Jesuits and the Americans that Maronites, and indeed other Christian denominations, studied and wrote, and planted the intellectual seeds for political change.[26] The epitome of educational developments was the Syrian Protestant College, founded in 1866, and St. Joseph University in 1875. It was in particular the latter, Catholic-inspired and teaching the French language, that became a home for the new Maronite intelligentsia in Lebanon. Fenced in politically but flourishing educationally, the ground was sown for a potential Maronite national breakthrough. Its intellectuals were dispersed in Beirut, Paris, and Cairo, but their primary focus was toward the mountain and Lebanon as a whole.

For a time, and indeed until the days of the First World War, Maronite personalities were campaigning for two different though potentially intertwining possibilities: pan–Arab national independence from Ottoman rule and local Christian Lebanese independence. Having themselves played a major part in advocating the role of the Arabic language, Maronites supported the rights of the region's Arabs, who numbered 11 of 22 million inhabitants of the empire yet were just four of forty-five Ottoman senators and 65 of 240 deputies. In attendance at the famous Arab Conference in Paris in June 1913 was an equal representation of Muslims and Christians. Earlier in the same year, a Beirut Reform Committee convened; one signer of a memorandum it subsequently submitted to the French Foreign Ministry, Youssef Hani, a Maronite, was later hung by the Turks in Beirut in 1916. Arab nationalism was a commitment, not just a slogan, in those days. Another example was Iskander Ammoun, who favored Lebanon becoming part of a larger Arab entity. He served as minister of justice in King Faisal's government in Damascus from 1919 to 1920.[27]

But the more native sentiment among Maronites was the idea of constituting Lebanon as a national home for the Christians. Processes of urbanization (Beirut and Jouniya) and educational mobilization (church missions and the universities) were indicators of social change in Maronite society. The political appetite developed as a natural consequence. Products of both Arab and French culture, the Maronites wanted more than just participation in someone else's political production, be it Ottoman or pan–Arab. In 1877, Ibrahim Thabit called for an enlarged autonomous Lebanon under a native Maronite prince.[28]

In 1902, a Maronite lawyer drew up a plan to expand Lebanon's boundaries to the coast, where French investment in the harbor and railroads in the area of Beirut were exactly the kinds of developments so vital and attractive for the inland mountain. The geographical smallness of the mountain alone and its mere administrative autonomy were insufficient and cramping. In 1905, Patriarch Huwayik visited Paris to enlist greater French involvement in the interests of the Maronite community. Soon after, in 1912, the demand for restoring Lebanon to its "natural frontiers"—to include the coast in particular—was articulated by a Lebanese Committee in Paris. This was another way of advocating Lebanese independence.

In the drive for freedom, Maronites maintained a traditional hostility to military service in the Ottoman Army. They preferred to pay the exemption tax *(badal askari)*. Yet the obligation to heed the conscription summons, for decades kept in abeyance, was reinstituted with the Young Turk revolution of 1908 and the revitalization of the 1876 constitution. But when the military draft was inaugurated for Christians in Beirut (not the mountain), many Maronites chose to emigrate from Lebanon. This suggested that achieving political power would, if ever won, derive from foreign intervention on their behalf rather than by independent mobilization. The Maronites wanted to be left alone but not left out of the future settlement of the "Eastern Question" as it pertained to their Lebanese homeland. For these urban sophisticates and literary adepts, the military vocation was not their forte or apparently their preferred vocation.

The ultimate collapse of the Ottoman Empire in 1918 and the establishment of French rule in the Levant set the historical stage for Maronite political success. Daoud Ammoun, born in Dayr el-Kamar in 1867 of a distinguished family with a record of high education and government service, assumed the leadership of the first Lebanese delegation to the Paris Peace Conference in February 1919. He demanded an independent Lebanon that would include the coastal cities (Tripoli, Beirut, Sidon, and Tyre) and the Bekaa Valley. For this to come to fruition, he openly admitted, French assistance was required.[29] It was the French who had basically watched passively when the Druzes massacred the Christians in 1860 and again when the Turks had imposed a famine across Lebanon and starved hundreds of thousands to death in 1915–1917. Yet there was no feasible alternative to French involvement. Although the Turks were now beyond the pale, the Muslim Arabs were the immediate challengers at the gate. To stop their charge—Sharifian from Damascus and with British aid—the Maronites reached out for French salvation.

This time the call was answered, a kind of Crusader replay across the centuries. French troops under General Gouraud took Damascus in July 1920, cleared out King Faisal, eliminated the Syrian option, and then went on to proclaim an independent Greater Lebanon (Le Grand Liban) on September 1. The Maronites had experienced an awakening stage in modern times, though Lebanese independence came not so much from internal change and political achievement as from a new constellation of regional factors and direct foreign help. The Maronites were a religious-cultural community and also the nexus of an economic society. Now, with the aid of the French, they moved to become a political nationality in their own state. When the opportunity knocked, they were ostensibly ready to answer it.

While the small territory of Mount Lebanon contained a largely homogeneous and predominating Christian majority, the larger boundaries of Greater Lebanon reduced the Christians to a very narrow majority. Various Christian groups, like L'Alliance Libanais and Le Parti National Libanais in Cairo and the Lebanese League of Progress in America, had campaigned for an economically solvent Lebanon. This meant that the urban commerce, banking, and port facilities of the coast be available to the new state. In addition, the Christians feared fusion with Syria, which could make Lebanese political independence impossible. The Muslims, who desired union with Damascus, saw Lebanon as an integral part of the Arab world and its Islamic civilization. The Christians, who rejected union with Damascus, saw Lebanon as a historical enclave of oriental Christianity and an outpost of Western civilization. With the help of the French, the Christian Maronites won the day.

Between Statehood and Sectarianism

Yet the price of victory was heavy, even prohibitive from a certain perspective. The 1920 map of Greater Lebanon included the Sunni-dominated cities on the coast, from Tripoli to Sidon, and the Shiite-dominated Bekaa Valley to the east. These new boundaries offered a semblance of geostrategic and economic viability, yet left the Christians with only a bare majority. The Maronites remained the largest single community in the country but only slightly ahead of the Sunnis. Yet they clearly expected French assistance and assumed Christian dominance.

When the Lebanese republic was constituted in 1926, a Greek Orthodox Christian, Charles Dabbas, became its first president. This in itself implied that Maronite wishes would not be fully accommodated. The Greek Orthodox (Melkite) community was traditionally immersed in Arab culture and political identity, less particularist than the Maronites. Yet the pattern was set whereby only Christians would be presidents of Lebanon. In fact, when a Muslim, al-Jisr, wanted to be president in 1932, the French high commissioner demurred; the constitution was suspended, and the chamber was dissolved. It was thus affirmed that only Christians were to be presidents in Lebanon.

The distinguished Karami family of Tripoli might dream of an Arab empire based in Syria and including Lebanon, but it seemed an empty Sunni wish.[30]

In 1932, a Lebanese census found that the Christians constituted slightly more than half of the population. Eleven years later, in 1943, a National Pact (al-Mithaq al-Watani) was worked out among Lebanon's confessional groups. It was based on the 1932 census and strove to freeze the political distribution of power in accord with it. No provision was made for amending this pact were demographic changes to justify reform. Christian supremacy was intended to be a permanent feature of the Lebanese polity. The ratio of assembly representatives was determined as 6:5 in favor of the Christians. This would mean, in 1960 for example, fifty-three Christian deputies and forty-five Muslim deputies (with one Jew).[31] More specifically, the pact provided that the president be a Christian Maronite, the prime minister a Sunni, and the speaker of the House a Shiite.

In this confessional spirit, senior military and administrative posts were also to be distributed among the communities. The political system was provided a democratic exterior by the French but a sectarian interior by the Lebanese. Its Christian-Maronite raison d'être was only one of two types of collective ethos, for the competing one was a delicately balanced pluralistic entity. Without any obvious foundation for unifying Lebanese nationalism, the country would be compelled to choose between singular Maronite rule or a regime hamstrung by incompatible diversities but committed to tolerant coexistence. Would Ibn-Khaldunian *asabiyya* guide the Lebanese polity or Actonian liberalism?

Symbolic of the predominant orientation in Maronite circles was the establishment of the Kata'ib (phalangists) by Pierre Jemayel in 1936. Its ultimate vision was Maronite dominance of Greater Lebanon and against Muslim Arab pretensions. It strove to develop and maintain ties with Maronites abroad, enlist their material support, and even have them considered Lebanese citizens with active voting rights. Based on a philosophical outlook rooted in Western humanism and a national outlook that defined Lebanon as an ancient and integral national unit, Jemayel explicitly equated patriotism with Maronitism.[32] Those who opposed union with Syria or with a pan–Arab political framework were necessarily Lebanese patriots, but this patriotic position came naturally to the Maronite Christians, who had always spearheaded the struggle against Lebanon's absorption, indeed strangulation, by any comprehensive larger system.

From the Maronites' perspective, the phalangists were designed as a paramilitary force to defend Lebanese independence. Yet Christian security was uppermost and it contained the political kernel of the

Maronite strategy, whose profound implications help illuminate the Maronite future in Lebanon. From the start, the confessional configuration of the country was always its most striking social, ethnic, and ultimately political characteristic.[33] Religious diversity, geographical distribution, and parochial styles of leadership ensured the confessional basis and reinforced it, even after the establishment of what was to be a secular democratic republic.

Each distinct group in the Lebanese confessional mosaic maintained its own communal solidarity and institutional networks. These inevitably extended to the establishment of armed forces to protect the group in a society without a Leviathan guardian. This set of circumstances limited the role and authority of the national army of Lebanon, which never acquired the size and importance required to impose central rule effectively over the entire land. It was the outbreak of the 1958 civil war that demonstrated the precarious situation, as competing militias, primarily Christian-Maronite versus Sunni-Druze, confronted each other in street fighting. As pro–Nasser pan–Arab forces squared off against pro–Lebanese forces, the army under General Shihab remained neutral.[34] The small armed forces of the state were a feeble instrument to control the violent situation.

Sectarian discord was a bane to Lebanese unity. And while communal cleavages did not permanently prevent some overlapping of interests that did produce cooperative efforts transcending confessional distinctions — for example, during election competitions — the hallmark of Lebanon was the absence of an integrating national sentiment. Or if that sentiment existed in some hearts, the institutional or regulating forces did not exist to turn it into a unifying political reality.

It is with this set of conditions in mind that the Maronite strategy can best be examined. The formal state arrangements confirmed in the 1943 pact recognized Maronite predominance, a situation that had its origins in the mutasarrifiya of 1864 and serving as the legitimizing spirit for Le Grand Liban of 1920. In addition to these governmental facts were impressive Maronite credentials in the domain of economics and education whereby this community enjoyed a superior position. Thus, rather than limiting Maronite goals to survival and group welfare alone, and this within the ambiguity and anarchy that interlaced the body politic, a strategy of building state power as a Maronite minority prerogative was an alternative option. The Sunnis were stymied in their aspiration for Syrian union, the Druzes had much earlier (1861) witnessed the collapse of their influence, and the Shiites were still a weak and passive community. This left the Maronites in a decidedly optimal position in the confessional mix.

But certain choices were made that illustrated the Maronite decision to choose freedom *from* the state, not power *over* the state.

Maronite particularity and insularity guided the communal strategy distinctly from state power instead of building those communal features into state power. Rather than taking over the state and thereby cultivating it for their minority purposes, they let it lie fallow. When this became transparently obvious during the 1975 civil war, the failure of earlier Maronite strategy was clear. When the state fell, so too did the Maronites. Remaining alone as a separate group without turning the state instrument to their private advantage abandoned the Maronites to a world of savagery that would threaten to undo centuries of primordial perseverance in the land of the cedars.

By comparison, the 'Alawite case is striking in its bold and determined strategy. Just some 10 percent of Syria's population, this rural and underprivileged minority utilized the army as a stepping-stone to communal power, beginning at a time when the French mandatory authorities were congenially oriented to this martial group. Later, the 'Alawites penetrated another nationwide institution, the Ba'th party, and ingeniously exploited it for their goals and interests. The Maronites, some 30 percent of Lebanon's population when the state was founded, chose privacy rather than power, preferring group isolation out of a sense of historical self-indulgent communal confidence. In 1982, President Assad of Syria, an 'Alawite, orchestrated the assassination of President-elect Bashir Jemayel of Lebanon, a Maronite. The Syrian 'Alawites controlled a state; the Lebanese Maronites had squandered the opportunity to build one for themselves.

Two choices were central in the fruitless Maronite strategy: the establishment of a specifically Maronite phalangist militia in 1936, and the stance of solidarity with all Lebanese groups against the French in 1943 specifically. The first choice was based on the seemingly valid premise that self-defense was the necessary requirement in the whirlpool of confessional tension. But this choice sharpened the tension and encouraged a further escalation. In 1937, the Sunnis established the Najjada militia in response. Rather than building the national army into a veritable Christian militia, the Maronites built a Christian militia on their own. This inevitably enfeebled the state instrument at a time when Maronite predominance in the state had already been legitimized as a recognized political norm.

The second choice dealt with Maronite opposition to the continuation of the French mandatory presence in Lebanon. While it is true that advocating an opposite position would have led to the charge of collaboration with imperialists, a public stance against the French denied the Maronites a benefit cooperation would have provided. In 1943, the French arrested President Bishara Khoury, who had called for the end of French privileges in Lebanon. When the French arrested him, all Lebanese—including the Jemayel clan—united in demonstrative support of Khoury's position. Certainly Khoury's "pro–Arab orientation" did little to strengthen the Maronite particularist option. And yet the Maronites stood against the French, their historic patron for centuries. So here, too, the Maronites failed to utilize a favorable opportunity and contributed to the exit of the French, officially in 1946, and were therefore left to fend for themselves. Without a state apparatus in their hands and without foreign support at hand, the fate of the Maronites had been sealed.

A historical corrollary of this was President Franjieh's collaboration in letting the Syrians penetrate Lebanon in the late 1960s. The eventual clash between Syria and the Maronites in the 1970s and 1980s was a further demonstration of poor political judgment by Maronite leaders.

The breaking point in Maronite political history is linked to the PLO-Palestinian presence in Lebanon and the disruption of the delicate relationships among the country's indigenous confessional communities. There were, it is true, other factors. The banking crisis in 1966, the underdevelopment of the Shiite South, the endemic multiplicity of parties, and the rapidity of cabinet changes (forty-five from 1943 to 1972) all contributed to the collapse of national confidence and political stability.[35] The absence of lower-class elements in the Parliament and the debilitating phenomenon of bribery as the "grease of government" undermined the system as a whole. In the 1968 elections, for example, all of these aspects of decline were apparent.[36] Always pervasive was the unresolved ideological incompatibility between Maronite conservatism and Joumblatt socialism, between Sunni Arabism and Christian Lebanonism. And all the while the localist Za'im-led cast to the country's politics inhibited the consolidation of a unified national elite.[37] Getting not giving was as always the Lebanese norm.

Maronite Decline and the Lebanese Civil War

Yet it was the "Palestinian problem" in the Lebanese context that catalyzed the downfall of the system, and the fall of the Maronites with it. A large Palestinian refugee population from 1948, then over 100,000, but increasing to about 300,000 by 1975, provided the national justification for the PLO's role. The geographic contiguity of Lebanon with Israel provided the strategic justification for the PLO's presence. The latter point was basically a post–1967 development as infiltration across Israel's northern border became a major PLO priority. Palestinian attacks led to Israeli retaliation, like the raid against the Beirut airport in late December 1968. A pattern appeared of Sunni prime ministers resigning in protest of Lebanese military weakness and phalange opposition to the PLO's very presence.[38] The level of instability rose; the gate to anarchy was jarred open. In the breach, the Maronites were exposed and vulnerable.

In 1969, the Cairo Agreement established what the realities already suggested — that is, the PLO was to enjoy extra-territorial rights in Lebanon, particularly in the fifteen Palestinian refugee camps. Southern Lebanon was becoming a PLO guerrilla focus; this "Fatah-land" exposed the decay of governmental authority. After the civil war in Jordan in 1970, including its finishing touches applied by Hussein's loyal army against PLO forces in 1971, the guerrilla presence in Lebanon increased. The PLO fled to its sanctuary in the Kharoub region near Mount Hermon. Fatahland received new blood, and the PLO became more boldly independent. In May 1973, President Franjieh tried to approach PLO leader, Yasir Arafat, with a request for restraint.[39] But by then the die was cast as PLO units traveled freely in Beirut itself. The "state within a state" was truly more like a "state within a nonstate."

The outbreak of Christian-Palestinian fighting in April 1975 constituted the beginning of the civil war whose initial period lasted into the summer of 1976, with the fall of the Tel el-Zaater refugee camp in Beirut. The noninvolvement of the Lebanese Army in 1975 turned into its dissolution in 1976. The initial confrontation between the Maronite phalangists and the radical PLO factions, the Popular Front for the Liberation of Palestine (PFLP) and the Democratic Front (PDFLP), soon included the Fatah faction as well. The loss of life reached beyond sixty thousand people in the human carnage that racked Beirut specifically but extended to the north and south of it as well during 1975–1976. Damour, a Christian town south of the capital, was all but emptied of its inhabitants. Nabatiya, in southern Lebanon, suffered a like fate.

During the course of events from 1975 until 1982, three groups were visibly increasing their military strength, hoping to translate it into a political transformation of the Lebanese system of government and distribution of communal power: (1) The growing Shiite religious group, numbering some 900,000 people, was the single most dramatic new element. Following the creation of the Higher Shiite Council, headed by Imam Musa Sadr, as well as the Mahrumin (disinherited) movement among its impoverished masses, the Amal military arm appeared in 1975. The Iranian Islamic Revolution catalyzed a further sharpening of Shiite consciousness based on their numbers and strength. Nabih Beeri, Amal's leader, began to challenge the regime's authority. At the same time, Hizballah (party of God) was created, this in the spirit of Khomeini's ideology and militant in the spirit of the PLO. It called for the overthrow of the Christian-led Lebanese regime and its replacement by an Islamic republic. (2) The entrenchment of the PLO in Lebanon expressed the rise of the Palestinians from a weak and alien community in 1948 to a new force in the country. Beirut was significantly a PLO headquarters, a global terrorist center, and the locus of the Palestinian revolution against the conservative (Christian) forces in Lebanon. It was the PLO that helped further polarize the Lebanese confessional equilibrium, adding to Muslim self-confidence and leading to the breakdown of any workable government in the country. (3) The relatively small Druze community, led by Kamal Joumblatt, later by his son Walid, and represented by his Progressive Socialist party, challenged the legitimacy of the political system. They called for greater Druze participation in national affairs, yet at the same time advocated the secularization of the polity to make it a more purely democratic system. The radical socioeconomic program of Joumblatt was directed, in particular, against the Christian upper middle class and bourgeois elite.

Therefore, the weakened and threatened position of the Maronites was a direct result of the strengthening of the Shiite, Palestinian, and Druze communities. When the Syrians recommended constitutional reform with a fully shared Christian-Muslim governmental balance, thereby overcoming the 6:5 Christian primacy, the Maronites felt the flow of the tide. Presidents Franjieh and Sarkis already symbolized the Syrian hand in the Lebanese political deck. They recognized the role of Damascus in coordinating the politics of Beirut by alliance building and client-patron relationships that rested upon, most obviously, the presence of the Syrian Army in Lebanon as of 1976. The destruction and bankruptcy of five hundred commercial firms and the flight of some 300,000 people during 1975 alone were specifically damaging to the Christians, whose welfare was wedded to the stability of the entire economic and social environment.[40] The port of Beirut unloaded 3,412,000 tons of merchandise in 1974, but considerably less beginning in 1975.[41] The permanent disorder that marked life in the capital turned the financial image of Lebanon being "the Switzerland of the Middle East" into a transparent delusion.

The years from 1975 to 1982 did not witness the requisite dose of Christian unity, specifically Maronite solidarity, to face the new and dangerous situation. While the Jemayel family utilized the phalangists as the nucleus of the Christian Lebanese Front, disunity continued to prevail. Raymond Eddé led the National Bloc party, and Camille Chamoun had his National Liberal party. Bashir Jemayel commanded the united Lebanese Front from 1976, yet division persisted. Eddé's turn to the Muslims aroused phalangist charges that he was a traitor, and they tried to kill him. Suleiman Franjieh's flirtation with the Syrians led the phalangists to murder his son Tony, as well as his wife and daughter.

Another indication of division was the rift between the Lebanese Front and the forces of Sa'ad Haddad in southern Lebanon. This lone army major from Marj'ayoun led his Christian-dominated militia against the PLO and its "reign of terror"; yet he lost the support of the military command in Beirut, which charged him with desertion at the same time that he gained Israeli assistance. In 1979, he proclaimed the "Republic of Southern Lebanon," a kind of liberated zone. Until 1982, when Israel invaded southern Lebanon in its war against the PLO, and indeed until Haddad's death in January 1984, Israeli support through weapons, military training, finances, and moral encouragement helped keep alive the hope of Christian independence across Israel's northern border. And yet the rift between Bashir Jemayel and Sa'ad Haddad persisted until the end.

Thus the variety of parties and militias in the Maronite community, the geographic factionalism and strategic divergences (pro–Syrian and pro–Israel), and the endemic clannishness of Lebanese society precluded the unity so desperately needed. The civil war was a Maronite tragedy and also an incentive to join forces. But only partial unity was achieved. Meanwhile, Israel's invasion of June 1982 offered to salvage the sinking Maronite political ship. Bashir Jemayel met with Defense Minister Sharon, and common strategies were discussed. When the initial attack succeeded, Israel had hoped this would facilitate Bashir's assault on the office of the presidency. When he was elected in late August 1982, the plan seemed consummated and destined to fulfil the expectations of both the Israelis and the Maronites. Then, in a moment, the gamble went up in smoke: In September, Bashir Jemayel was assassinated in Beirut, a Syrian plot that canceled out the Israeli wager.

In spite of the formidable benefit that Israel's war against the PLO in Lebanon seemed to offer the Christians, its impact was brief and disappointing. The so-called Republic of Jouniya in the northern mountain was an outgrowth of various circumstances, but more a "last stand" than a step forward. De facto Maronite autonomy therein was a result of the cantonization of Lebanon on the practical plane of confessional confrontation. As indicated, the effort to alter the intersectarian system, as the Maronites hoped, did not come to pass. Instead they lost further ground in ongoing battles.

In what became known as the war of the Shouf, some fourteen hundred Christian civilians were massacred by Druze warriors in Autumn 1983. Fady Frem, commander of the phalangist militia, added that in fifty-six villages the Christians suffered Druze superiority.[42] Cruel instances of massacre took place in Bhamdun and in Kafr Matta; and in Dayr el-Kamar—the scene of a Christian massacre in 1859–1860—the Druzes laid siege and surrounded the town. Only Israeli intervention prevented what would have become a repeat barbaric scene. Meanwhile, throughout 1984 and 1985, Christians were the targets and victims of kidnappings, as in Tripoli; attacks against the Southern

Lebanese Army, headed by General Antoine Lahad; shellings of Christian residential areas like Beit Mery and Broumana; and Druze bombings in Iklim el-Kharoub.

Syria and its proxies—Palestinians, Druzes, Shiites, and Sunnis—had succeeded in sowing anarchy and destruction in Lebanon and dictating a reevaluation of relations between Lebanon and Israel. In fact, the May 17, 1983, agreement between the two countries was subsequently nullified by Beirut under compulsion from Damascus. A Syrian protectorate over Lebanon was the old sought-after goal, and it seemed to have been won.

Different reasons converge to explain the Maronite failure, and that of Christians generally, to preserve their position as "a political majority" in the polity.[43] Maronite divisions were never resolved. In the spirit of localism, a Maronite would be willing to fight for his home and family or village, but it was not as obvious that his obligation extended to all Maronites throughout Lebanon. Clannishness undermined the consolidation of peoplehood and certainly that of a cohesive political nationality. When Maronites fought, one wondered if they acted always as altruistic freedom fighters or, as in the case of the Israeli-funded Southern Lebanese Army, self-interested mercenaries. However, of course, the southern Christian inhabitants were defending their homes and villages from the PLO and the Shiites. They were not defending Lebanon, the country.

The urban mentality of Maronite culture made them bourgeois merchants and antirevolutionary conservatives. This converged with their Christian mission in the East, a historical holding operation, a last fortress against the fire of Islam ablaze across the region. But the city, while it symbolized Maronite success economically, stood in contrast, for example, with Druze success militarily in the mountain. And it was the Druzes who got the better of the Maronites in the Shouf battles in 1983. Ibn Khaldun's warning that the city breeds complaisance and erodes manly vitality seemed to become a dark Maronite truth. For money and leisure, Maronites not only left the mountain for the city but left Lebanon for the West. Joie de vivre replaced *asabiyya* as the ethos of the day. Or as John Sykes wrote, the Maronites "were completely like West Europeans."[44] (Yet, it must be noted that in certain instances urban life confronted the Maronites with Sunni militancy and pushed them into the ranks of the phalangists as a natural response.)

Looking out to Europe historically, to the United States and Israel in recent years, proved to be a precarious policy at best. Emigration—to America, Brazil, West Germany, and elsewhere—reduced Maronite manpower at home, though it perhaps served to activate aid in such countries. Seeking foreign assistance had proved its value in the past, admittedly only at certain times, but the fundamental lesson was indeed

just that: Christian Maronite success came *only* when foreign intervention was available. Left to themselves, as in 1859–1860, 1915–1918, and
since the civil war beginning 1975, the Maronites were unable to
achieve basic communal goals. This deus-ex-machina explanation suggests that no continuous, organic, communal growth process occurred
among the Maronites in the modern era. The fall after 1975 becomes,
then, a historical prognosis and not a precipitous event.

Notwithstanding the Maronite failure to secure the feasibility of a
Christian state in Lebanon, the success of communal survival is still
striking. Multiple group competition in Lebanon, without a single
dominating power, alleviated minority suffering by allowing it to endure as minority particularism. The mountain homeland of the Maronites still offered a semblance of security and a spirit of struggle.
Fighting readiness had not been direly eroded, only compromised in
the modernity of the Levant. Ties to foreign actors, Israel particularly,
and with Iraq after the ending of the Gulf War in 1988, provided military
support and encouragement in troubled times. It is true that Israeli aid
was motivated by an anti–Palestinian purpose and that Iraqi aid was
motivated by an anti–Syrian calculation. Nonetheless, the Maronites
did not demand pure idealism as the guiding motive. The Maronites
have not gone the way of some other Christian peoples such as the
Armenians and Assyrians. They still dwell in their land and can dream
of better days.

Conflict resolution in Lebanon, which would solidify Maronite life,
appears a fragile political matter. Arabism and Islam are powerful
alienating principles and forces unable or unwilling to integrate other
elements. Etienne Saqr, leader of the Guardians of the Cedars, a right-
wing Christian militia, commented on the community's Aramaic linguistic roots and added that "the Lebanese are not Arabs."[45] He went
on to define the Palestinians as foreigners in Lebanon; his solution was
to force them to go eastward to Syria as they had "killed 120,000 of our
people and displaced 500,000." Such feelings reveal the vast gulf between different communities and the consequent inability of any comprehensive ideology—like Arabism or Islam—to accommodate the
competing goals and visions of all sides.

Civil politics as a mechanism of conflict resolution contravenes the
confessional feature of the Lebanese state. The Lebanese are not
citizens of a state but blood brothers living in separate communities.
Group diversity has not produced Actonian freedom but has fulfilled
Hobbes's anarchic apprehensions. The Joumblatt idea of a secular
democratic Lebanon can be a rhetorical device for Druze legitimation
in revolutionary circles, yet it goes against the conventional confessional grain in the *millet*-style structure of Lebanese political and social
life.[46]

In late 1989, a Lebanese conference for political reform was convened in Taif, Saudi Arabia, under the aegis of the Arab League. It decided on communal Christian-Muslim parliamentary balance and restricted presidential powers, while a Christian Maronite would continue to man the office. Meanwhile, Major General Michel Aoun, ensconced in the Baabda presidential palace southeast of Beirut, rejected the Taif scheme outright and considered it a suicidal plan for the Lebanese Christians. The upshot of these developments was rapid. The election on November 5, of a new president, René Moawad, who advocated close ties with Syria, ended with his assassination less than three weeks later, allegedly by Aoun's forces. The Maronite community was sharply divided — part supporting the official institutions of state and part loyal to General Aoun. A new president, Elias Hraoui, was thereafter elected, but disunity continued to mar Maronite affairs. General Aoun soon found his authority challenged not just by the Lebanese president, who demanded he leave the palace, but by Samir Geagea, the head of the Lebanese forces. Intra-Maronite warfare in Beirut left hundreds dead in January–February 1990. Disunited within and threatened without, the Maronite future looked tragically dim.

On October 13, the end came. Syrian military bombardment forced Michel Aoun to abandon the presidential palace. His forces were routed, and Aoun sought political asylum in France. A week later, Danny Chamoun, son of former Lebanese President Camille Chamoun, was murdered in his home, along with his wife and two children. He had been a supporter of Aoun and Christian predominance. Toward the end of 1990, Maronite stakes had drastically fallen. A painful symptom of this was the tragedy and loss suffered over the years to its three prominent families — Jemayel, Chamoun, and Franjieh. An era was over in modern Lebanese history.

Institutional adjustments can offer interesting theoretical solutions. A pact of regions, cantonization or confederalism, would permit local autonomy for the different peoples and jettison the idea of a Christian-dominated Lebanon.[47] In this scenario Mount Lebanon would be a Maronite canton, a replay of the *mutasarrifiya* from 1864. A quite different approach would be the formal recognition of Syrian hegemony with the imposition of an overarching single authority to impose stability in Lebanon. This is, in part, the situation that developed from 1976 on, particularly in the light of Israel's major military withdrawal from Lebanon in 1985. A particular ideological twist of this idea is the notion of a Greater Syria as advanced by the Syrian Social Nationalist party, founded in the 1930s by Lebanese Christians and supported by some Maronites. The Greater Syria notion in itself — and not the SSNP version, which denied the notions of Arabism and Islam — has been a fearsome alternative for the native Maronites of Lebanon.

The temptation of Christian separatism as a Maronite doctrine has sometimes arisen when Christian power was strong, sometimes when it was weak. Islam's opposition to a secular state, especially since the marked military strengthening and religious zeal of the Shiites, puts pressure on the Christians to take a stand. Under certain circumstances, the Maronites, in the judgment of some authors, "could call for a separate Christian state."[48] However, internal and external opposition to such a move would appear inevitable and effective. Fighting to remain in Lebanon rather than fighting to control all or even part of Lebanon is the stage at which the Maronites have arrived toward the beginning of the last decade of the twentieth century. They traveled with dignity through Lebanese history and experienced notable advances in modern times. But all this was insufficient to allow them to become a "minority state" in the Middle East.

CHAPTER 11

Sudanese Christians: Tribulations in Black Africa

In the Arab-Muslim country of Sudan, in the heart of Africa, a small Christian community is engaged in a struggle for survival. A bitter civil war beginning in 1955 has raged across the jungles and forests of southern Sudan, leaving an estimated 500,000–800,000 dead.[1] But it is the Christian dimension that intrigues. It is one of the major symbols of the war and an instance of the fate of Christianity as a whole throughout the continent.

The Biafran secessionist attempt in Nigeria from 1966 to 1970 was in part a Christian fight; so too the historical attempt to secure Christian communities from Egypt and Nubia through Sudan and Abyssinia, modern Ethiopia. Facing the forces of Muslims and Marxists, the challenge to the welfare of Christians in Africa is enormous. In the Sudan, "the Bible in the bush" may be a quaint image, but it is also the target of Islamization, whose intense threat arouses painful memories of southern enslavement by Arab marauders from the North. Extracting slaves and ivory from southern Sudan in the past underlies the war against Christianity in the twentieth century.

Meanwhile, the persistent conflict in the southern provinces of Sudan interlocks with superpower machinations—American policy maneuvering and Soviet interventionist strategies. In fact, some have considered the eventual detachment of southern Sudan and its alliance with Ethiopia, under Marxist control since the mid–1970s, part of a grand imperial design by Moscow to overlord Africa as a whole.[2] The Christian leaders of the Sudan People's Liberation Army (SPLA) in the South have taken up a fight whose historical, civilizational, and political significance extends far beyond the banks of the Nile River that flows through their land.

Christianity in the Jungle

The question of Christian survival in southern Sudan is intertwined with the ethnic individuality among the Nilotic tribes who are a majority of the Sudanese population. Just 39 percent of Sudan's people were Arabs in the official census in 1956. Among the Dinka, Nuer, Shilluk, and smaller tribes, the non–Arab identity is a distinct ethnic divergence from the Arabs in the North of the country. Chief Pogwot Deng of the dominant Dinkas stated categorically, "We are not part of the Arabs."[3] Kinship marriage patterns traditionally preserve group particularity, though marriage between a Dinka and a Nuer is hardly considered to be an exogamous union.[4]

Sudanic tribes, being essentially Nilotic and Nilo-Hamitic, organized their lineage in a segmentary, not hierarchical, fashion. As such, tribal formations are significantly acephalous in social organization, though chiefs are known to regulate some basic communal affairs.[5] The proud Dinka have always tried to prevent others from lording over them. As the largest single group in the South, numbering 1.5 million members of a total Southern population of 5 million people in the mid–1980s, though divided into twenty-five tribes, the Dinkas set the tone for rejecting alien penetration. Altogether some two hundred separate Southern tribes constituted the human bedrock of black non–Arab ethnic particularity. It was indeed the black African feature, different from the Arab Semitic aspect, that provided southern Sudan with its prominent ethnic identity.[6] Widespread tribal atomization was partially transcended by the pervasive sentiment of black identity—and the Dinkas are the blackest of them all.

It is the Christian dimension of Southern culture that is central to our concerns, though it is one component of a wider cultural landscape. Within and notwithstanding the animist-paganist religious universe of southern Sudan, Christianity had to contend with Islam as its major external challenger. Within tribal society, animal sacrifices, rainmakers, and magical curses and blessings typified the spiritual parameters of life. Among the Azande, witchcraft prevailed;[7] among the Dinka, a world of spirits organized the tribes' beliefs. And yet even without formal conversion to Christianity, the influence of Christian cosmology was apparent among the Dinka. Myths of the Garden of Eden and the personality of Issu (Jesus) entered into the collective consciousness.[8] Francis Mading Deng has gone so far as to suggest that the very notion of rectitude in the Dinka family derives from the religious influence of Christianity.[9] The penetration of Christianity, either from the North many centuries ago or the coming of missionaries in the nineteenth century, was a pole of attraction for Southern tribes to deflect Islam's expansion.

Although the proportion of Christians within Sudan is only about 4 percent of the total population, numbering from 200,000 to 500,000 of 22 million people in the 1980s, the Southern elite is particularly a Christian vanguard. Their higher educational standards derived from missionary-school education, which offered religious instruction, the English language, and a worldly outlook. Though less than 10 percent of the South's inhabitants, the Christians have led its struggle since the 1950s against the Muslim-Arab North.[10] Churches in the jungle coexisted with old native cultural forms, such as African dance rhythms and mythological tales of the origin of man.

Southern Subjugation and Slavery

A few additional features capture the contours of life in the southern Sudan. It is a traditional cattle economy organized around a pastoral existence. Villages are situated near water resources, while a nomadic pattern characterizes the Nilotes in Bahr el-Ghazal. Without permanent settlement forms, few permanent institutions administered communal living. But also because of the nomadic form, the tribes were inevitably "prone to fighting,"[11] intertribal wars not being uncommon and physical violence itself an assertive masculine quality in native culture. Division based on tribal affiliation, underscored by the diversity of languages numbering anywhere from fifty to eighty in the South alone,[12] gives vitality to native pugnacity throughout society. Added to the endemic disabilities of a poor economy and social anarchy was a traditionally low literacy level.

An interesting aspect of Southern life was a markedly active role for the women—in Dinka life, for example, where they played a part in work and trade. In fact, matrilineal authority has its roots in tribal life, and symptomatic of this is a woman's agnatic kin's having enjoyed an influence over her children. This pattern diverges from the norm in Arab-Muslim society.

The three southern provinces of Sudan—Bahr el-Ghazal, Upper Nile, and Equatoria—are the geographic locus of the Christian population. This region is historically unattached to the northern part of the country, rather a target of conquest and exploitation in order to unify a land that lacks natural borders. It is the *sudd,* a marsh of floating vegetation, that serves as a topographical barrier between North and South in Sudan. Savannah, jungle, and forests characterize the land to the south, a rainy zone in comparison with the dry northern area. A subsistence economy based on fish, tea, coffee, and cotton—in addition to the primacy of cattle—has provided a livelihood for the Southern tribes.

Yet the relative inferiority of the South to the North in social development and economic standards is a permanent reality. In the late 1970s, for example, there were nine secondary schools for girls in the North, but not one in the South.[13] There was no large urban center in the South; Juba, the most important town, did not compare or compete with the primacy of Khartoum, the capital in the North. The discovery of oil at Bentiu in the Upper Nile province and the intention of the central government to build a refinery at Kosti in the northern Blue Nile province illustrated the peripheral status of the South in national life. The South is conceived to be a colonial dependency for the extraction of raw materials by an exploitative superior North. The overlapping of geographic and economic dichotomies sharpened North-South divisions and catalyzed a specific Southern self-consciousness beyond the level of the tribe toward the level of a geoeconomic society. Still, this was a far cry from the articulation of peoplehood, even though the territorial grid for this development is available in the Sudanese South.

The history of Sudan revolves around the triple contraries of Arabism versus Negroism, Islam versus Christianity, and free men versus slaves. In Blad as-Sudan (literally, the land of the blacks) Arab racial superiority was always considered a normative status vis-à-vis the animist blacks to the South. Its most significant expression was the institution of slavery, itself an African phenomenon from the Maghreb in the west across the Saharan desert, in Libya and Egypt, and southward in the Sudan, Somalia, and Zanzibar.[14] The practice of slavery in Arab countries—Arabia, Oman, and elsewhere—was dependent on the extraction of slaves from Africa. The Sudan was par excellence a source of slaves from the ninth century until the twentieth century.

Men, women, and children were hauled away from their homes. Many would die enroute to a distant destination; others would arrive at Egypt and Turkey to the north or the Arabian Peninsula and the Persian Gulf to the east, ultimately uprooted from their native culture and subsequently Islamized. The household economy of Khartoum was itself dependent on the slave trade as black Africans in Bahr el-Ghazal were seized by Arab slave traders like Rahman Zobeir, also known as Az-Zubair Rahman Mansur, who operated in the South.[15] Older survivors in the twentieth century were able to transmit orally gruesome tales of massive suffering in the 1870s as tribal chiefs were slain, people massacred, cattle seized, and houses destroyed—along with wives and children dragged away during Arab-Dinka wars that inevitably ended with Arabs turning free Africans into slaves.[16]

Christianity along the Nile River is a great historical venture in the African continent. In Upper Egypt from Aswan and Nubia and into northern Sudan, in Dongola and Darfur, down to Abyssinia or Ethiopia, Christians already inhabited these lands in the fourth century.[17] The entire Nile Valley was significantly Christian in faith by the sixth century. Dongola, north of Khartoum, was a veritable Christian kingdom until approximately the fourteenth century. However, it was the consolidation of Egypt as a Muslim entity, particularly with the crushing of the Copts in the ninth century, that portended a change of the religious tide in the Nile Valley.[18]

Mamluk rule in Egypt, beginning with Baybars in the mid–thirteenth century, led to the full subjugation of the Christians. Egyptian forces penetrated Dongola and eliminated its last Christian king in 1311. Arabs from Mesopotamia and Egypt poured into Sudan, Dongola, and Darfur especially; thereafter, in the sixteenth and seventeenth centuries, Fung Muslims from Nubia to Abyssinian defeated the Christians in battle.[19] Churches were destroyed, and Christians and animists were converted by the sword of Muhammad to Islam. And yet while Christianity was losing ground in the Nile Valley, southern Sudan specifically remained largely isolated from the religious struggles conducted to the north and the east. Black Sudan below the *sudd* was an unknown and difficult terrain for spiritual conversion, though it was historically always a lucrative source of slaves.

In the nineteenth century, the forces of Arab-Islam in the North organized for a concerted effort to rule the peoples of the South. Following the establishment of Muhammad 'Ali's power in Egypt and his dynasty's persistent efforts to extend authority southward toward the sources of the Nile River, a sixty-year period of Egyptian-Turkish rule (Turkiya) consolidated in the Sudan. The slave trade assumed a dynamic momentum in Bahr el-Ghazal and Equatoria. The subsequent rise of Mahdism under Muhammad Ahmad in the early 1880s offered a hope of salvation for the black South. Fighting the *jihad* in the name of messianic Islam, the Mahdists were able to defeat an Egyptian army of ten thousand under Hicks Pasha in September 1883. In 1885, Khartoum fell to the Mahdists, and British General Gordon was killed.

The end of British-Egyptian hegemony in Sudan served Southern interests. But the Mahdists then penetrated the South and treated the black animists ruthlessly as the latter found themselves having exchanged one alien ruler for another. Arab superiority feelings toward Africans led to efforts to impose Islam on the Southern tribes in the late 1880s, a new chapter in an old tale of Muslim expansionism in the Nile Valley.[20] Until September 1898, with the fall of the Khalifa's army at the hands of an Egyptian army headed by Kitchener, life in the South was hellish. But the elimination of the Mahdist state was a liberation for the tribes.

The British-Egyptian condominium over Sudan from 1899 restricted the slave trade and legitimized the spread of Christianity among the Southern population. As the British stopped the French and the Belgians from sharing the benefits of the Mahdist defeat, the way was opened for Southern freedom in the "land of the blacks."[21]

Christianity had first reached south of Khartoum in the middle of the nineteenth century when Roman Catholic missionaries-adventurers descended dangerously into the African jungles.[22] The major push was initiated by Italian churchmen who linked religious outreach with Italian imperialism into Africa. In the early twentieth century, British policy-making regarding the spread of Christianity in the southern Sudan was a focus of disagreement: One approach, that advocated by Reginald Wingate in Khartoum, favored missionary efforts; a different view, represented by Lord Cromer in Cairo, was committed to avoiding any antagonism with the Muslims of the Nile Valley. Nonetheless, Christian missions spread southward, to Wau, the capital of Bahr el-Ghazal, where, it is told, black missionary boys were stoned.[23]

Traditional Muslim hostility to *dhimmis* converged with ingrained Islamic prejudice against black-skinned peoples in Africa. Ibn Khaldun had basically considered blacks of Sudan naturally submissive, proximate "to the animal stage."[24] Having enslaved blacks from Darfur and Bahr-el-Ghazal in the nineteenth century, Egypt had mixed feelings about the spread of Christianity on the one hand and the steady abolition of slavery in Egypt and the Sudan on the other.

British Rule: Toward Southern Freedom and Back

From the Anglo-Egyptian condominium over Sudan in 1899 until the Sudan Administration Conference of 1947 in Khartoum, the cornerstone of British policy was to develop the South as a distinct, separate, and Christianized territory. A strategy of divide and rule, linked to the utilization of native tribal elites as domestic leaders, combined to stress Southern particularity. Tribal courts were established, and Africans rather than Arabs were brought into administrative positions.

The linguistic policy adopted was based on English as the sole official tongue, along with the preservation of local vernaculars. Arabic was excluded, this with the obvious corollary of rejecting Islamization as well. Missionary groups were responsible for educational activity in the South: Presbyterians in the Upper Nile, Rome Catholics and Anglicans in Bahr el-Ghazal and Equatoria.[25] Christian education in missionary schools, now supported by the British authorities, was of a piece with fixing in 1919 the official day of rest in the South on Sunday (not the Muslim Friday). Africans assumed Christian names, and Catholic conversions in particular spread rapidly. By 1960, a hundred missionary stations covered southern Sudan, which boasted a Christian population of over 200,000 people. Islam's historic conquering stamina was arrested from at least this part of the Nile Valley.

The formation of the Equatoria Corps in December 1917 provided the South with its own military garrison until 1955. An English-language force composed of animists and Christians would naturally be alienated from the spirit of Arabic-language Sudanese nationalism in the North. The corps offered the tribes a legitimate military arm of their own, a source of regional pride and a confirmation of native fighting talent. Additional measures taken by the British included the 1922 closed-districts policy to preclude non–African Sudanese from penetrating the southern provinces. This measure was decidedly an anti–Islamic prescription, intended to inhibit Arab traders from traveling freely among the pagan/Christian population. This Southern strategy, the effective division of Sudan into two separate parts, was laid out in the 1920 Milner Report and later strengthened by the 1930 Memorandum.

With the South sufficiently pacified, the full co-optation of the local elites proceeded apace. The British acted to resettle Southern tribes away from Arab ones. At the same time, some Dinka elements in the North were invited to return to the South. Tribal chiefs were told to abandon Arab dress and names. In 1936–1937, certain administrative measures were designed to organize a single regional government for the South with its headquarters at Juba in Equatoria province.[26]

The Southern policy, Christian in spirit and anti–Arab and anti–Islamic in orientation, brought together an old tribal world with vivid European confidence to imprint a new face upon Black Africa.[27] The Stack Memorial School at Wau in 1926 testified to Britain's commitment to this imperial project. A South loyal to the British could serve to consolidate the Nile Valley, from Uganda and Kenya to Sudan and Egypt, as a secure possession for the Crown. The Christian community in the Sudan shared the ultimate goals of the British, and the latter's permanence in this part of Africa coincided with the separate existence and welfare of the southern provinces.

Various elements to induce a collective awakening were present in a nascent form by the 1940s. The rise of a literate Christian elite was developing beside the general progress of educational standards. In 1932, there were 189 village schools, yet by 1938 the number had increased to 585.[28] This dimension in popular mobilization within the South was coincident with historical feelings of repression and deprivation due to forced ties with the North. Enjoying British foreign assistance in a direct and substantive fashion provided the needed catalyst to consolidate Southern identity. In sum, this interwar era from 1917 until 1945 turned on the blessings of territorial partition and local kinship allegiances as the route toward autonomy, if not independence.

Yet this rather sanguine vision endured for a relatively brief period.

Post–Second World War England was in a withdrawalist mood, and its imperial possessions were soon earmarked for national freedom. A new Southern policy was deliberated as early as 1945, and integration of North and South became the essence of British thinking and a clear abandonment of the earlier approach. Association with the Arab-Muslim North would deny the South self-determination and put a brake on the processes of local particularism. The imposition of alien Northern features (Arabic language and Islam) would assure that.

In April 1946, the British civil secretary announced the union of the two Sudanese regions at the Administration Conference held in Khartoum. No Southerners were present to voice their views on this change. In June 1947, a conference held at Juba in Equatoria provided an opportunity for Southern fears to be expressed, but the official British position, while declaring safeguards to be appropriate for the southern provinces, was determined to avoid as much as possible the divisiveness of regionalism in a united Sudan.

The 1948 Legislative Assembly Ordinance brought an end to the previous Southern policy: Arabic was to become the language of the South, and Christian missionary activities were to be curtailed. In subsequent planning for Sudan's independence, the governor-general convened a commission in 1951 that rejected the establishment of a Ministry for Southern Affairs. In the following year, Egyptian overtures for the "unity of the Nile Valley," a political euphemism for the incorporation of Sudan within a single Egyptian state, further aggravated the tense atmosphere. Subjection to Khartoum would be at the least a severe Southern challenge, but Sudanese envelopment within Egypt would deny the South any possibility for preserving its cultural-regional distinctiveness within one large Arab-Muslim entity.

However, this fear was not actualized, as the Sudan was ultimately to become an independent and unified state in January 1956. By that time, the British had authorized a policy of Sudanization of the civil service, the generation of economic projects overwhelmingly in the North, and the cultivation of Northern political elites. Sudan's independence was an Arab-Muslim national démarche, as the 30 percent southern region found itself in a decidedly inferior position. When a National Constitutional Committee assembled in September 1956, only three of forty-six members were Southerners. The committee not surprisingly rejected any federal solution to the North-South problem and called for a centralized regime with its capital at Khartoum.

Sudanese Independence and Southern Rebellion

The definition of Sudan as an Arab-Muslim state was a rejection of its African, black, and Christian features. In December 1954, the

Southern Anti-Imperialist Front tried to preempt the flow of events and called for three separate states in the South—Malakal in Upper Nile, Wau in Bahr el-Ghazal, and Juba in Equatoria. In July 1955, workers' riots broke out against Northern factory managers at Nzara; eight people were killed in the altercations. But the most important event, and the moment for triggering the Southern revolt, occurred on August 18, 1955, when a military mutiny at Torit in Equatoria released the accumulated fears and hatreds Southerners had felt all along.

Apprehensive that Southern troops were to be sent north and that Northern troops would be sent south, troops at the Torit garrison broke ranks and killed 261 Northerners. The British reacted by ordering their troops to leave the South and by airlifting 8,000 Arab troops to the South. They burned villages and murdered randomly; schools were closed, and anarchy spread throughout the region. From the mutiny in 1955 until the peace agreement of 1972, a vicious civil war was fought in the southern Sudan whose significance was whether force could keep a divided country together, a compelling mechanism to turn diversity into a tolerable situation.[29] Always, the Christian side of these questions was never negligible.

Independent Sudan became the political embodiment of a repressive regime, in particular after the military coup by General Abboud in 1958 and especially directed against the South and its Christians. The Islamic groups and the Northern traders *(jellaba)* were strong advocates of an Arabization policy that included the primacy of the Arabic language and the spread of Islam. English was officially replaced in the educational system, though it partially remained, along with tribal vernaculars. In 1958, the Southern Federal party called in vain for Christianity to be recognized as a state religion in addition to Islam, with equity between the Arabic and English languages. The two issues clearly intersected because, from the fundamentalist Ansariya perspective, the sacredness of Arabic made the linguistic question a religious matter.

The homogenization of Sudan was a national imperative that Khartoum would not relinquish. In 1960, Friday replaced Sunday as the day of rest, and the Muslim governor of Equatoria, Ali Baldo, told the tribal chiefs to take Muslim names. During the 1960s, the spirit of *jihad* in the South was visible. While the building of a mosque in Juba was still a source of controversy in 1946,[30] the Department of Religious Affairs preemptorially built many mosques and established many Islamic schools throughout the South in the 1960s. Christian students at Rumbek and Juba were agitated over the pro–Islamic and anti–Christian measures, but centralized policy-making from the North would not yield. The 1962 Missionary Societies Act imposed strict government controls that led, in effect, to the nationalization of mission schools. Two years later, missionaries were actually expelled from the South as government policy hardened markedly. Sadiq el-Mahdi, the president of the Umma party, had declared in 1966 that his mission was to convert Africa to Islam—beginning with southern Sudan.[31] He became prime minister of Sudan in 1985.

The Southern struggle against the North was a rebellion more than a revolution, a tenacious and determined fight that ultimately led to a kind of Pyrrhic victory. In the military domain, guerrilla warfare best exploited the topographical terrain of jungles and forests, based on a rural population base, to attack army posts, destroy bridges, block roads, cut phone lines, and then hide in the bush. The Anya Nya (poison snake) rebels, tribally diverse, not fully united as a cohesive military force until the 1970s, became the embodiment and continuation of the Torit mutiny in 1955.

Founded in 1960 in the rural areas, the Anya Nya began with few weapons, literally with just bows and arrows. They trained in neighboring Zaire, later in Ethiopian camps. Thereafter, the political headquarters was in Uganda, and weapons were procured from the Congo. Many were ex-soldiers from the disbanded Equatorial Corps that successfully carved out some "liberated zones" in the South. Over time, the Anya Nya put together the rudiments of a civilian administration, provided courts of justice, set up schools, and developed medical services. Weapons procurement progressed in the mid–1960s from bows and arrows to rifles, grenades, and land mines.[32] After 1967, Israeli arms filtered into the South.

Recruitment of guerrillas went well, and a Sudanese Army numbering more than 8,000 soldiers in 1964 had been unable to defeat the Anya Nya, numbering about 5,000 men. The "Land Freedom Army" of the South had defied the Northern goal of a united Arab-Muslim Sudan. By 1967, about a half a million Africans had been killed, but the war went on.

The Sudanese national army, basically a Northern force, fought relentlessly to repress the Southern rebels. Destroying villages and murdering their inhabitants was the order of the day throughout the 1960s. But a particular significance was directed against the Christian aspect of the Southerners' life. Government troops leveled churches, as many as half of the Southern churches according to O'Ballance. In July 1965, Northern soldiers opened fire at Wau on worshipers leaving a cathedral. In July 1970, soldiers burst into a Christian community at prayer in Bakerole Church in Banja. They set fire to the church with the worshipers still inside, and fifty died.[33] Symbolic of the Southern struggle was that Christians in the Anya Nya took their oath on the Bible.

The political organization of the Southern struggle underwent

numerous changes. An early voice for the deep grievances that catalyzed the struggle was the Southern Federal party. Later, a Southern
bloc formed in the National Assembly and was led by a priest. In 1962,
the Sudan African Closed Districts National Union declared the Southern goal to be nothing less than independence. This was followed by the
Sudan African National Union (SANU), led by Agrey Jadeen and William Deng. Its public position was ambiguously divided between two
factions at cross-purposes, one for autonomy, another for independence.

In 1966, a breakaway movement formed under the name of the
Azania Liberation Front (ALF). During the same period, SANU absorbed ALF, prior to the impressive effort at political self-representa-
tion in August 1967 when a Southern Sudan Provisional Government
(SSPG) was declared, adorned with flag and all. Its key achievements
were to augment cooperation between the military and political wings
of the struggle and to unite leading personalities working in the Sudan
with others propagating it outside the country (in Uganda, Ethiopia, and
Europe). In 1969, a further instance of fractionalization led to the formation of the Nile Provisional Government (NPG) representing the idea
of a "Nile State," against Arab domination and in the spirit of a
geographic node of Sudanese life. All of these organizational efforts
reflected an incipient national maturity and a drive toward Southern
political articulation. Spokesmen and politicians worked with the
fighters in the bush for a common cause as the war went on.

The peak of these developments was the establishment of the
Southern Sudan Liberation Movement (SSLM), led by Colonel Joseph
Lagu, in the summer of 1970. Northern repression and brutality had not
dampened the spirit of Southerners to persevere. The bloodbaths at
Juba and Wau in July 1965 had if anything tightened the Southern
nerve. Moreover, inherent divisions within the struggle had not para-
lyzed the movement but energized it through internal conflict. Thus,
when Lagu took charge of the SSLM in 1970, the struggle had already
been through the fire. It now consolidated under Lagu in an impressive
display of unity. At the helm of the overall movement from the beginning were leaders mainly of the Christian faith. Many were mission-
educated. Lagu himself was a Protestant (b. 1932), son of a lay teacher
in an Anglican mission. Joseph Oduho, a central actor in the struggle
from the early 1960s, was a Catholic. Other leading personalities included Lawrence Wol Wol, a Catholic, and Fredrick Maggott, a Protestant. Among the Dinka, who provided the main body of Anya Nya
fighters, were a number of chiefs who had earlier converted to Christianity. Chief Stephen Thongkol of the Atuot Dinka in Bahr el-Ghazal
was one of them; so too were two Catholic converts, tribal chiefs from
the Twic and Malual Dinkas.[34]

According to Cecil Eprile, the civil war from 1955 on was not a religious war but concerned Southern life and not Southern souls. However, this is a facile distinction because there could be no Christian souls if there was no possibility to conduct Southern life freely. It would be more correct to suggest that the civil war was not just a religious civil war. Its roots and reasons extended beyond the rivalry between Islam and Christianity. However, a historical Christian aspect was present, the issue of Christianity in the southern Sudan remained a burning political issue, and quite significantly, the elite Southern leaders came from the Christian-educated populace. After all this is recognized, it may be added that the conflict did incorporate other dichotomies, ranging from racial and economic divisions to political competition and linguistic tensions.

The cease-fire agreed upon in March 1972 was made possible by three specific developments. One was the tenacity of the Southern struggle itself, and this in spite of tribal divisiveness, a lack of fighting and monetary resources, and global indifference. Over 150,000 refugees languishing in Uganda, the Congo (Zaire), the Central African Republic, and Ethiopia was a heavy price to pay. But this, plus burned villages and human massacres, was not able to squash Southern determination.

A second development was the coming to power in May 1969 of Jaafar Numeiry, a Sudanese officer who was committed to ending the civil war. He announced his support for Southern regional autonomy and arose as a credible Northern leader. Without Numeiry, no reconciliation would have been feasible.

A third development concerned the role of third parties in mediating a cease-fire settlement. They included, in particular, Haile Selassie of Ethiopia, who stopped giving arms to the Southern forces, and the vital intervention of the World Council of Churches, which helped bring the North and South to negotiations. In Addis Ababa, an agreement was ratified on March 27, 1972, that brought the civil war to an end. In providing for Southern regional autonomy based on a local government apparatus, the path to reconciliation through compromise and unity seemed to fulfill both sides' aspirations.

The postsettlement problems were enormous, and much good will, political wisdom, and economic resources were essential to cope effectively. Refugee repatriation on the order of more than a million Southerners was a critical priority. Various Christian organizations—particularly the World Council of Churches, its Sudanese branch, and other church groups—along with the United Nations high commissioner for refugees, participated actively in providing medical, educational, and agricultural assistance to the South.[35] By 1973, approximately 1 million refugees were back in Sudan, and Juba particularly experienced urban demographic growth.

A regional government headed by Abel Alier was instituted in the three southern provinces. Alier and other prominent government members were former pupils at the Church Missionary Society educational complex at Loka in Equatoria. The 1972 settlement invigorated the Southern churches, now strengthened by the active involvement of foreign churches in the development of Sudan's battered war zone. President Numeiry was accommodating to Southern sensitivities, and the future looked bright. Regional autonomy within a united Sudan constituted a formula for local individuality and national consolidation. Religious freedom and recognition of Christianity were guaranteed in the 1973 constitution, while recognition of English as "the principal language in the southern region" mollified past grievances. Yet stressing English limited the opportunities Southerners could enjoy in all of Sudan, which was in principle an Arabic-speaking country.

War: Religious, Regional, and Russian Factors

But for various reasons the 1972 settlement failed to satisfy expectations, and the South once again took the path of a liberation war. The economic rehabilitation planned for the South was slow and ineffective; government institutions there were beset with internal political struggles and tensions with Khartoum in the North; and the discovery of oil at Bentiu, with the decision to build a refinery at Kosti in the North, revived the historical complaint of the North's treating the South as an "internal colony." SANU became exceedingly hostile to the North by 1978. Fears of Sudanese integration with Egypt in 1982 further raised Southern apprehensions.

And again, recalling Torit in 1955, the signal for rebellion came from black military garrisons in the South that were allegedly to be sent north.[36] In January 1983, the Southern army, which included thousands of Anya Nya who were absorbed into the military after the 1972 agreement, revolted in Bahr and Upper Nile provinces. The tone of the confrontation was sharpened considerably when in late 1983 the Numeiry regime promulgated the *shari'a* as the law of Sudan. Administering its penal code, in the words of Archbishop Gabriel Zubeir Wako of Khartoum, necessarily "entails the suppression of Christians or the curtailing of their freedom of worship." A French priest, Father Pierre Conon, who had been forced to leave Sudan after criticizing the regime, said, "An Islamic constitution makes it impossible for Muslims and Christians to live together. It forces upon Christians *dhimmi* or second-class citizen status."[37] The civil struggle in the 1980s was still tied to its religious aspect.

Various guerrilla groups, known as Anya Nya II, reappeared in the three southern provinces.[38] The declared goal was Southern independence, though the immediate result was economic chaos and massive human suffering. At the head of the struggle was the Sudanese People's Liberation Army (SPLA) led by American-educated Colonel John Garang. Supported from Ethiopia and engaged in global contacts to enlist assistance, the SPLA was the military arm of the Sudanese People's Liberation Movement. The North pounded away at the South, massacring thousands of Dinka tribesmen who constituted the main body of SPLA, yet the fighting continued.[39]

In March 1984, John Garang, a Protestant, declared in his call to the Sudanese people that the goal of the Southern war was national unity, not Southern secession. This statement was compatible with a position announced by Sadiq al-Mahdi, who took power after the coup against Numeiry in April 1985. He was willing to attenuate the Islamic character of Sudan in favor of a secular state.[40] Yet this appeasing rhetoric was not a Northern Muslim consensus. The Umma party (and perhaps el-Mahdi himself), along with other Islamic forces, still hoped for the entrenchment of the *shari'a*. Offering the South autonomy, as el-Mahdi did, failed to resolve the conflict. Ethiopian aid in the form of arms, military training, and the locale of SPLA's political headquarters, gave the war needed sustenance.[41]

SPLA control of the South's rural countryside, itself a major strategic achievement, later included the capture in 1987–1988 of Kapoeta in Equatoria and Karmuk and Geissan in the Blue Nile province.[42] Government forces later recovered, but the daring SPLA tactics broadcast a clear message. SPLA capacity was demonstrated in the shooting down of two civilian aircraft in August 1986 and May 1987. The seminal point was SPLA's success in tying down large Sudanese military forces and denying them sovereign authority over the South; in enjoying some regional African support (Ethiopian in particular) in spite of continental opposition to secessionist movements; and in persisting in the war in spite of tribal divisions, within the Dinka in particular, and notwithstanding some tribes lining up with the government and against the SPLA.[43]

The African and global contexts of the Southern struggle changed over the years. The role of neighboring Ethiopia ranged from prop for the South to peacemaker, then reverting back to prop in the 1980s. Khartoum's support for Eritrean rebels in Ethiopia was balanced by Addis Ababa's support for Southern rebels in Sudan. Uganda, a vital ally of the South in the late 1960s in particular, became alienated from the Southern struggle under Idi Amin's radicalized politics in 1972. Libyan relations with Khartoum were unstable as Qaddafi adjusted his policy in tune with personal vagaries and strategic considerations relating to Chad and Sudanese water resources that Libya coveted.

The role of the Soviet Union in the Sudanese equation has also been a tale of strategic reevaluations. In the 1960s, the Soviets supported Khartoum and acted as a military supplier unto active participation in Sudanese Army actions against the South. Later, the USSR collaborated with the Marxist regime in Ethiopia, following the disposal of Haile Selassie in 1974, to plan a new political map for the Horn of Africa, if not all of Africa. Soviet strategy in the mid–1980s could utilize a Libyan-Ethiopian axis to move toward control of the Nile waters, bringing enormous pressure to bear on American-oriented Egypt. This axis could be extended to southern Sudan and thus include this vital geographic chip. From that base of radical territorial continuity, the road to Zaire and into southern Africa—relying on Angola and Mozambique—would be open. In this scenario, rumors of John Garang's communist convictions merit attention. Certainly both the Russian and the Christian Sudanese would share fears of fundamentalist Islam spreading in the area. In like fashion, American support for the Cairo-Khartoum Arab axis put Moscow on the side of Southern liberation as part of the global network of Soviet-backed insurrections.

The challenge of conflict resolution in Sudan has been a demanding enterprise since 1955 in particular. The ethos of Arabism can only partially provide a solution. National integration via the adoption of the Arabic language as the statewide educational tongue has progressed in southern urban centers; in Juba a local creole, *juba-arabic*, has appeared and is related to but different from northern Arabic. SPLA leader Garang has said that Arabic should be the national language of Sudan but without Sudan's being an Arab country.[44]

This is the crux of the question: Can linguistic assimilation avoid serving as the socioeconomic and educational vehicle for national assimilation? A country that is ethnically both black and Arab cannot overcome this division without coercive methods for homogenizing a diverse population. Arabism carries with it an inevitable strain of ethnic superiority toward "inferior" non–Arabs and raises a demand for Northern primacy that affixes Southern inferiority as a condition for a political settlement in Sudan. So long as Southern allegiances are bound by ethnicity, religion, and geography, no dosage of Arabism can overcome Southern apprehension and, apparently, Southern resistance.

Islam as a way to solve the North-South problem is a political nonstarter. Mohamed Omer Beshir concluded that Sudanese nationalism had an important Islamic dimension, and it is this basic fact that alienated the Southerners, Christians and animists. Nullifying the 1984 Shari'a Law would seem a prerequisite to make reconciliation appear credible. In March 1986 in fact, the SPLA came to an agreement with the Alliance for National Salvation based on canceling the Shari'a Law. But the Sudanese forces in favor of *shari'a* will not easily concede.

Certainly a group like the National Islamic Front is staunchly committed to consolidating Sudan as an Islamic state for a majority Muslim
population based on Islamic law. Indeed steps were taken in this direction in the fall of 1988. The implication for the Christians is clear:
dhimmi status awaits them; indeed it arrived long ago.

Conflict resolution based on civil integrative strategies can rely on
nationwide ideologies or educational programs. Yet a common sense of
Sudanness, above local tribalism and yet below the religious demarca-
tions separating Islam and Christianity, has yet to surface. It is feasible
that centralized policy in the area of culture, language, and education—but not religion—would strengthen a pan–Sudanese identity for
Southerners as well as Northerners. Diluting the potency of Arabism
and Islam would be a condition to move in this direction of cultivating
emotional bonds among all Sudanese population groups.

Institutional adjustments in the Sudanese polity have always
seemed the most realistic path of reform and reconciliation. Dunstan
Wai and Bona Malwal have advocated a federal regime resting upon the
twin principles of decentralization and regionalism. The dispersion of
power could be, as the 1972 Addis Ababa settlement proposed, the most
reasonable and equitable resolution of the conflict. A new national pact
would justly distribute power between a *hukuma merkaziya* (central
government) and a *hukima iklimiya* (regional government), not as a
Khartoum ruse but as an authentic regulation of affairs between competing and distinct poles of authority.[45]

A variation of this Khartoum-Juba dichotomy is the division of
Sudan into four regions—North and South, East and West—based on
signs of additional regional agitation beyond that in the southern provinces. For example, a General Union of Nuba appeared that called for
western Sudanese autonomy, and its proponents contacted the Southerners as part of a joint strategy against Khartoum. Interestingly enough,
Numeiry considered the idea of dividing Sudan into four regions in
1979. This kind of institutional adjustment would take the political sting
out of Southern unrest by spreading the problem of regional disaffection
across the country as a whole. General Omar al-Bashir, ruling since
1989, voiced his opposition to any federal solution to Sudan's problems,
arguing that a multiplicity of governments would hamper national planning and impede national unity. The South, he added, had historically
always been part of another, larger political unit.

The idea of Southern secession has been fought tooth and nail by
the government at Khartoum, before independence in 1956 and certainly thereafter. The number of dead and the number of refugees attest
to Northern determination against any concession of the sort that might
open the way toward splitting Sudan into two separate countries. In
1987 there were reports that some mainstream Sudanese were willing

to consider letting southern Sudan secede. But neither this rumor nor alleged peace talks in London at the time led to any concrete results. Colonel Mengistu in Marxist Ethiopia and Colonel Garang in Sudan, allegedly sharing a common ideological orientation, may try with Soviet orchestration to bring about the partition of Sudan. The Sudanese People's Liberation Movement conceivably favors Southern independence, even though it might willingly or unwillingly turn the new state into a proxy base for quite broader strategic aims. The very possibility of Southern secession is, to the extent it is at all realistic, a function of outside forces that transcend the power base of the SPLM itself.

A multitude of groups, parties, and movements exist to express Southern aspirations, like the People's National party, the Southern Sudan Political Association, the Sudan National Union, and the Sudan African Congress. In October 1987, these and three other parties formed a political bloc called the Sudanese African Parties, based on a written set of principles formulated as a shared covenant. Two points were of great moment: the emphasis on Africanness as a cultural and political dimension in the South and the desire for an equitable and complete peace throughout Sudan.[46]

It is abundantly clear that the South had awakened to the opportunity of educational advancement and urbanization, received certain levels and kinds of foreign aid, and sharpened its collective consciousness because of Northern policies of repression and deprivation. Vivid expressions of this consciousness were in the realm of persistent military struggle and expanded political articulation. And yet the Southerners did not rise to the level of a single united nationality, for tribal conflict was not overcome. The ties of long struggle were packed into a modern legend that the world ignored but Southern peoples felt. And yet turning this experience into a concrete political gain remained the awesome problem, as Islamization remained the official policy of Khartoum.

Part IV
Jews, Israel, and
Other Middle Eastern Minorities

CHAPTER 12

Jews: Zionist Achievement, Lingering Question

The establishment of Israel in 1948 as a Jewish state, or state of the Jews, provided a unique case of a historical Mideast minority people becoming a majority sovereign community in the modern era. In this *dhimmi* rebellion, a veritable slave revolt according to Islam by a submissive and inferior group, Muslim superiority and pride were challenged in the most ominous way. Jewish political equality with Muslims and Arabs signaled the potential end of the religiously grounded and historically confirmed primacy of the Middle East's dominant Arab-Muslim peoples.

And yet the instability of the Arab-Israeli conflict, particularly in the wake of the 1973 war, the oil weapon, and the rise of the PLO, raised questions about Israel's long-term viability. Also, the growth of a large Arab minority within the Jewish state seemed an imminent and perhaps fatal threat to even a Jewish majority population.

Butrus Ghali, noted Egyptian academic and minister of state for foreign affairs under Presidents Sadat and Mubarak, had echoed Arab thinking regarding Israel's very existence in a revealing set of statements in June 1975. He seemed outraged at the very idea of Israel's maintaining its Jewish character based on the notion of self-determination. Moreover, he added, "assuming that Israel takes this very stiff attitude, defending its sovereignty according to this very radical way of thinking, I think you can have no peace in this region."[1] Arab rejection of Jewish statehood, adumbrated in Ghali's remarks, is of a piece with classic minority demotion throughout the Middle East. Israel's ability to withstand and contend with such rejectionism is nothing less than a historic test of the first order.

But beyond Israel's being a distinct Jewish national venture in contemporary Middle Eastern political history, it can also illuminate the broader question of minority status and opportunities throughout the region. The Jewish case, it is true, is unique because it is a non–Muslim and non–Christian example, and its lessons may therefore be unique. The ultimate resolution or clarification of the Jewish people's effort, though, may reverberate in significance across the East and the world as a whole.

Judaism: A Religion and a Nationality

The elemental ethnic distinctiveness of the Jews derived from the biblical portrayal of the first Hebrew, Abraham, and the family that he established distinct from all surrounding peoples. His own commitment to a new and particular peoplehood demanded a careful choice of the right spouse for his son Isaac, a practice based on a principle that is repeated in subsequent family inbreeding. This established Abraham's seed as the biological root of a new nation bound by both a new spiritual mission and unique bloodline.

While conversion was always a legitimate and accepted form of entry into the people's ranks, the sharp wall of separation from others made endogamy the strongest of Jewish social norms. Marriage with a non–Jew was a national betrayal and a religious violation. It was this tight ethnicity that elicited charges of racial superiority by the enemies of the Jews. The bottom line of all this, as one historian wrote, was anti–Semitism defining the crime of being Jewish as the Jews' guilt.[2] Being Jewish meant inevitably close endogamic practice in marrying one's own kind alone.

Formative Jewish life persisted in the tribal pattern from the period of the patriarchs until after the conquest by Joshua. Tribal divisions of land constituted the basis of Hebrew settlement, and this older familial segmentation continued after the period of the kings, only disappearing with the destruction of the kingdom of Israel in 722 B.C. But tribal divisions did not hinder a common ethnic identity that was born of a shared origin from the three primeval forefathers. Pan-tribalism converged with national cohesion as time passed.[3] War and statehood were the crucible for centralized political organization as the biblical period advanced. This phenomenon has been elucidated as an anthropological principle reflective of the unity at the root of heavenly rule and reality. From the existence of clans and the role of judges, the Hebrew tribes consolidated as an Israelite nation under kings.[4]

The subsequent loss of ten tribes and their dispersion in 722 B.C. became a problematic oddity of Jewish history. Legends of their geographic location — beyond the Sambation River — entered into folklore but had no detrimental impact on the perenially valid notion of Jewish peoplehood itself. The distinct Jewish ethnic line runs through the length of Jewish history until modernity and in spite of assimilationist developments during the nineteenth and twentieth centuries. Beyond this, communal fissures surfaced among European-based Ashkenazi groups and Middle Eastern–based Sephardic-oriental groups. But even this consequence of dispersion did not erode the commonality of Jewish existence throughout the lands of Jewry. In contemporary Israel the communal gap between Ashkenazi and Sephardi groups is giving way to the cohesive forces of "ethnic intermarriage" and an inevitable "melting pot" phenomenon that integrates the various communities homeward bound from the four corners of the world.

At the core of particular Jewish culture is the monotheistic faith of Abraham and the Sinaitic jurisprudence of Moses. The religion of Israel, its special battle cry and universal mission, is a tale of determined opposition to paganism and idolatry.[5] The distinctive character of the Old Testament relates to God's separateness, holiness, and righteousness.[6] But it is the acceptance of God that opens the spiritual door to acceptance of his law, a radical development in the ancient East, which becomes the definitive order of Jewish collective existence after the exodus from Egypt.[7]

Jewish legal literature — Mishna, Talmud, rabbinic exegesis over the ages — articulated the formal ritual, intellectual, and behavioral parameters of individual and communal Jewish life. When alien ideas confused Jewish minds, great rabbinic leaders arose to withstand the challenges and formulate the distinctive response of Judaism in the appropriate idiom. Such was the task of Maimonides in the twelfth century or of Samson Raphael Hirsch in the nineteenth century.[8] It is this unswerving commitment to the Torah, Judaism in its own language, that made the Jews different from the "nations of the world" and made them what they could not be without the Torah. Integration and assimilation always lurked cunningly when the Jews took steps toward abandoning their Torah and their God.

Jewish culture was always served by the vehicle of the Hebrew language, both sacred and vernacular for much of Jewish national history. Basically, only Jews spoke, read, and wrote Hebrew; their linguistic particularity was absolute, their collective separation from others a natural concommitant of this fact. Yet the Hellenization of the East prior to Christianity penetrated the borders of Eretz-Israel and made Greek a native tongue in Judea.[9] However, Hebrew was never eliminated from the Jewish intellectual landscape. Later, Jews in Arab lands either wrote in Hebrew or wrote in Arabic using Hebrew characters. Hebrew legal tracts and poetic works revealed a vital and indigenous cultural life in the Middle Ages,[10] and it was only the Age of

Enlightenment (and assimilation) that threatened to erode familiarity with the people's national tongue. It remained for the Maskilim, Jewish Hebrew-writing intellectuals, to revive the language—even though, it must be noted, Hebrew always retained its singular status as the vehicle of prayer, learning, and literature.

Yet the adoption of foreign languages in the Jews' "host centuries" of residence undermined widespread and popular knowledge of Hebrew. It was this danger—and in the Jewish homeland too—that catalyzed Eliezer Ben-Yehuda (1858–1923) to dedicate his life to making Hebrew the spoken language of modern Zionism. In 1880 he wrote that "today we may be speaking alien tongues, but tomorrow we shall speak Hebrew."[11] The holy tongue of the Jewish people, unique to them in ancient days, was again uniquely to mark their national renaissance in modern times. The essential element of language, along with religion, was an external label of collective identification throughout the ages and wherever Jews "lived their culture," which is, of course, the only way culture can mean anything at all.

Distinctive Jewish customs abounded in the rich tapestry of a comprehensive Jewish life. Much of traditional custom evolved from Jewish law; other strands of culture were interwoven with the ways of lands in which Jews dwelt. The Hassidic frock and fur hat, and the colorful ceremony for Yemenite brides prior to the wedding, are examples of distinct Jewish customs that arose through the diaspora millennia. Noteworthy aspects of traditional Jewish life were the modesty of Jewish "women of valor," who exercized not irrelevant influence on family affairs, and the reverence accorded *talmedei chachamim*, rabbinic scholars, in a culture that always elevated human wisdom to the highest of personal virtues for Jewish individual aspiration. The rhythms of Jewish life—so deep, varied, and enduring, so pervasive over time and territory across the generations—demonstrated the vitality of native Jewish culture. And this in spite of minority status and physical dispersion, obviously lacking national power but with enormous willpower to act out a distinct cultural script.

The Everlasting Homeland

Of paramount significance in Jewish peoplehood is the Land of Israel (Eretz-Israel) as the locus of spiritual fulfillment and political freedom, if not always in practice, then in redemptionist dreams. The land was promised to Abraham and his descendants; it was the territorial goal of the liberation from slavery in Egypt, the target of conquest by Joshua, and it became the scene of military struggles under the judges and kings.

Subsequent defeat and expulsion, the loss of both Temples, turned a thriving national homeland into an abandoned homeland. Bar-Kochba's revolt that ended in A.D. 135 signaled the end of Jewish political hopes. Yet Eretz-Israel, particularly the areas of Judea and Galilee, resonated throughout the centuries with ancient Hebrew memories: synagogues and cemeteries, place-names and artifacts. The village of Betar, where Bar-Kochba's last stand was made, became Batir under Arab rule thereafter, but even then, a vestige of historical truth resonated at Khirbet al-Yahud (the ruins of the Jews) as a section of Betar was called.[12]

With Eretz-Israel so central to Jewish memory, ingrained in the Hebrew calendar holiday cycle, in the prayer book, and in rabbinic dicta, the Promised Land was never uprooted from Jewish consciousness, even though the Jews were uprooted from the land. As James Parkes understood, spiritually the Jews had never really left Eretz-Israel.[13] King David the psalmist had captured the point when he pined, "If I forget thee, O Jerusalem."

Indeed Jerusalem, set atop the mountains of Judea, symbolized the physical heights and spiritual quality of the land as a whole. Set between the Mediterranean Sea to the west and the desert, the valley, and the Jordan River to the east, the country as a whole was both austere and fertile, a mixture of plains and mountains. Of Jerusalem George Adam Smith had written, "The desert creeps close to the city gates."[14] Lacking a natural water supply and sitting on the edge of Arabian desolation, Jerusalem was a formidable challenge to human ingenuity and persistence.

However, it was there on the mountain spine of the country that earth and heaven met in the imagination of the Jews, as it did for many other peoples. Never an imperial capital worthy of the name, Jerusalem was still a magical attraction throughout history. So too the land as a whole. But only when modern Zionism made it again the target of Jewish national aspirations did others—Arabs in particular—identify it as their goal as well.

The Zionist organization finalized its political quest focused on Eretz-Israel in 1903 when the Uganda proposal was exposed as a spiritually vacuous option. Territorialism was to become a political nonstarter in Zionism, for only the Land of Israel could elicit the latent energies of Jews to resettle and reconquer the only country they ever claimed as their own. When they chose to resolve the territorial question in their own mind, the mountain element in the geographic equation might have been recalled with benefit. In point of historical fact, entrenchment in the central heights, from the Galilee in the north, through Samaria, and crossing into Judea in the south, alone could assure strategic control of the country as a whole. This was a military lesson of the first order for thousands of years.

And yet modern Zionism largely ignored this when the Jewish Return commenced in the late nineteenth century, only to be confronted with the opportunity and dilemma of controlling the mountain area in the wake of Israel's military victory in the 1967 Six-Day War. Beyond the elemental purpose of security afforded by the mountain range of the land, its topography bearing down on the plains to the west and the valleys to the east, the value of the area lay in its historical cultivation with good soil and an ample supply of rain. Josephus had remarked at the time of the Jewish revolt in A.D. 66 that Galilee and Judea were particularly productive—final proof of which was "the swarming population of both countries."[15] Zionism's orientation toward the mountains of Judea and Samaria in the era of modern Israel therefore touched on military and historical themes of great national significance.

With such salient and identifiable elements as ethnicity, culture, and geography uppermost in Jewish peoplehood, the historical panorama rising from the chronicles of this "special people" may now be delineated. The eras of the patriarchs, judges, kings, and prophets were all concentrated, more or less, in the homeland, resting upon a greater or lesser degree of political sovereignty. The personality of King David and the centrality of the Temple in Jerusalem became elements of national pride and memory never superseded or forgotten. A popular Jewish musical refrain continued to sing that "David, King of Israel, lives on." A seminal Jewish belief for the last two thousand years was that the Temple (Beit Hamikdash)—the third one—would be rebuilt again in the Holy City. Holidays and prayers served as exceptional vehicles of cultural retention and transmission of ancient milestones in the history of the Jewish people.

Great visions and gnawing vicissitudes mark the life of the Jews from their collective appearance in history until today. Taking account of the externally defined contexts in which Jews lived, we can identify three basic chapters in their record of experiences. Organizing Jewish history in this way demonstrates the perennial vulnerability that was the people's fate for so long.

The Jews, a small Eastern people, were confronted by powerful military neighbors from all sides, some of whom challenged the cultural integrity and not only the physical survival of this old community. In particular, *Hellenism* as a combined military-spiritual civilizational threat invaded the Promised Land with a universalist and pagan mission. Decrees against the Jewish religion, not only against Jewish sovereignty, exemplified the problem. The gymnasium replaced the Temple, Greek names pushed aside Hebrew ones, idolatrous cults were introduced, and Jewish observances (like the Sabbath and male circumcision) were prohibited. Antiochus, the Greek king, claimed divine status in his egomaniacal frenzy. Jewish Torah study and prayer were forbidden. And then, in 167 B.C., the Hasmoneans began to lead the Jews to revolt against the Greek-Syrian power. Guerrilla warfare from the Judean and Samarian mountains bore fruit: In 164 B.C. the Jews liberated Jerusalem and purified the Temple.[16] This act of religious rededication inaugurated the holiday of Hanukkah, recalling the Hasmonean-Maccabean victory over an alien occupier of Eretz-Israel.[17]

But the political fruits of victory proved temporary. Rome imposed its rule over the land, and its paganistic religion and imperialist designs led to violent confrontation with the Jews resident in their land and elsewhere in the empire. Cicero, rhetorician and legal expert, demeaned the Jews and their religion from his political platform in Rome. Meanwhile, Rome subdued the Jews and their struggle for independence in Eretz-Israel. A revolt broke out in Galilee in A.D. 66, but hopes for renewed independence were quashed by Titus's conquest and repression by A.D. 70. Hellenism as a cultural-spiritual threat and Rome as a politicomilitary adversary effectively undid Jewish sovereignty in its own land.

Survival Despite Dispersion

A long era of Galut (exile) began. The Jews lost not only political independence but also their very physical presence in the country. The rabbinic sages preserved the people's way of life and religious faith. The synagogue replaced the Temple, prayer replaced sacrifices, but dispersion came in the place of homeland.[18] After the failed rebellion in A.D. 135, the idea of the end of Jewish history surfaced.

The Romans eliminated the names Jerusalem and Judea from the map of Eretz-Israel. The land was now called Palestine, and the task of perpetuating national existence without national territory became the Jews' preoccupation for two dark millennia around the world. The horrors of the siege of Jerusalem in A.D. 70, the famine and the misery, and the inestimable Jewish dead at Betar in 135 seemed to be the zenith of suffering in Jewish history. From 66 to 70 more than 1 million Jews were killed, and close to 1 million were taken into captivity.[19] The pagan world had developed a doctrine of anti–Semitism and had carried out a brutal policy of oppression and destruction against the Jews of the East. Was this to be the beginning of the end of Jewish history?

A second context of Jewish history was the *Christian world,* which made a triumphant entry into Western and Eastern civilizations after initial stages of persecution. Hatred of Jews was awkwardly combined in early Christianity with respect for "the firstborn" of God. The New Testament criticized Jewish Pharisees (rabbinic observers) as men who cared for the externals but not for the spirit.[20] Even when Christians were admonished to love Jews, it usually reflected a missionary purpose toward the people who had rejected Jesus as a Jewish messiah. Yet there were Christians, like Pope Gregory the Great, who opposed religious compulsion to bring Jews to the baptismal font.

By the fifth century, doctrine and disposition had formalized Christianity's position of deep hostility to Jewry. Synagogues could not be built, and existing ones were attacked; Jews could not enter military service; Jews were barred from law courts; at times, Jews were reviled as sorcerers and heretics. Pope Stephanus IV in the eighth century taught that Jews must suffer for crucifying Jesus. Pope Leo VII in the tenth century called Jews pigs. A slew of violent anti–Jewish incidents revealed the precarious condition of Jewish life within the realm of Christianity in Europe. The Talmud was burned in Paris in 1242. In 1290, the Jews were banished from England. In 1348, a whole town of Jews in southern France was burned.[21]

During the Middle Ages, the Jew assumed demonic proportions in the Christian mind. Jews were alleged to have horns, drink Christian blood, poison wells; they caused the Black Plague and desecrated the ritual Host.[22] Luther railed against the Jews who refused to convert and called for burning their synagogues. The Cossacks under Chmielnicki massacred them in 1648 and thereafter. The ghetto became the enclosed home of persecuted Jews. The yellow badge became a sign of Jewish degradation. The Crusades and the Inquisition served as the inferno of Jewish hell in the name of the Christian cross.

Later, modern European history became a human and political laboratory for a philosophy of universal and equal rights that Jews too were invited to enjoy. Jewish emancipation from the ghetto opened the door to two developments: (1) the Haskalah movement for a Hebrew and Yiddish cultural renaissance with a linkage to national renewal focused on Eretz-Israel;[23] (2) the assimilationist-integrationist movement for Jewish participation in the life of the "host countries" as a way to bridge the barriers between Jews and non–Jews. Modern Jewish history has been a stage for a tenacious contest between these two polar alternatives: the nationalist versus the internationalist choice. The Zionist movement itself combined elements from the two strands and has tried to unite them in the fabric of the Israeli state and society. Zionism, indeed, is the consequence of both Jewish sources and gentile influences, the relative potency of each still unclear in the continuous process of clarifying the quality and identity of Israel today.

Yet from within the confines of Christianity and Europe, Jewry found itself caught between opportunity and crisis. Between the Damascus Blood Libel of 1840 and the Dreyfus trial of 1895—and Jewish civic equality and political participation. Between the Kishinev pogrom[24] and the Beilis trial—and the personal successes of Foreign Minister Walter Rathenau in Weimer Germany, Premier Leon Blum in interwar France, and Louis Brandeis and Henry Morgenthau in twentieth-century America. Between the Holocaust and Jewish highbrow status in the modern history of Western countries. Between the new anti–Semitism and Catholic-Jewish ecumenism.[25]

The third context of Jewish existence has been the *Muslim world* since the foundation of Islam in the seventh century. Like Christianity, Islam hoped to absorb the Jews by persuading them that the new faith was a continuation of the older Judaic one and related in many ways to it. The legal framework, prayer and charity, pilgrimage and the central pillar of monotheism—all provided a semblance of "Jewish-Muslim" cultural symbiosis for Islamic proselytising purposes.[26] The fact that Jews were defined as People of the Book elevated them to spiritual legitimacy, while various tales in the Koran were grafted from materials in the Bible. According to Torrey, Islam was little more than "Arabian Judaism" that Muhammad put together based on discussions he held with Jews.[27] The overall notion of Jewish-Arab coexistence, a social reality representing fourteen centuries of interaction across the region, then becomes a credible idea.[28] Cultural interchange and linguistic affinity served as the touchstone of civilizational linkages that would inspire hopes for political accommodation in the Zionist age. Instead, war and conflict have characterized the relationship between Jews and Arabs prior to and since the establishment of Israel.

The historical record was not a one-sided ledger of idyllic Jewish-Arab coexistence, notwithstanding aspects and instances of this. The darker side began with early Muslim military victories, leading to Jewish loss and suffering. In Yathrib (Medina) and Khaibar, Jews were expelled and massacred by victorious Arab-Muslim forces.[29] During the medieval period Muslim polemics focused on the unacceptability of Jews' rising above their lowly *dhimmi* status. A classic and noteworthy case was the attack by Ibn Hazm (994–1064), a famous poet in Muslim Spain, who railed against Samuel the Nagid, a successful Jew in Grenada. The blistering revulsion against the Torah and its alleged discrepancies was coupled with a brutal denunciation of Jewish immorality.[30] This was but one instance of a Muslim diatribe directed at Jews whenever the latter attained positions of power in Muslim lands. Other instances were Lady Esther Kayra in Turkey, a woman of great influence in the politics of Constantinople who knew state secrets but met a cruel death in 1600, and Yehezkel Gabbai, a well-known Baghdadi banker brought by the Ottoman sultan to serve the empire in the capital; false charges were brought against him, and in 1856 he was decapitated. These tales demonstrate the vulnerability of successful Jews in Muslim lands and the general precariousness of Jewish existence under Islam.

The normative discriminations had to be upheld. Jews were forbidden to carry weapons or raise a hand against a Muslim, on pain of death. They had to live in separate quarters (*mellah* in North Africa) and keep their religious practices private and innocuous. They were expected to accept insults and defer to Muslims with absolute submissiveness. Popular fanaticism against Jews was not uncommon — including massacres in Baghdad in 1941 and in Aden and Libya after the Second World War. The practice of throwing rocks at Jews was widespread, as William Shaler, the American consul to Algiers, reported in the 1820s. In Tunisia, Jews would fall to their knees if they passed a mosque. Paying the *jizya* tax was for the *dhimmi* a moment of financial exploitation and religious disgrace. Even the great Maimonides, the twelfth-century Jewish sage, philosopher, and doctor, was forced to endure the indignities of Jewish life under Muslim rule.[31] During his lifetime some 100,000 Jews in Fez and 120,000 in Marrakesh were reportedly killed. Maimonides himself served the Sultan but could ride only a lowly ass, not a noble horse.

The decline and fall of Mideastern Jewry in the twentieth century became interwoven with European withdrawal and Arab nationalism.[32] Any signs of Jewish-Muslim symbiosis ended in modern times, and the persecution of Jews in Syria and Iran in the 1980s were two persistent cases of Jewish vulnerability that did not pass. Jewish minority life under Islam was without dignity and short on security. Nonetheless, a long history of Jewish peoplehood from Morocco to Afghanistan, based on the rich and always problematic encounter with Islam, remained compact and coherent, for more than a thousand years.

It is no small achievement that the Jews survived as a distinct people with their ethnic and cultural integrity in tact, peering toward their territorial homeland and with a continuous national history. Dreams of redemption alternated with bitter persecution. Jewish life was in a state of suspension: Living in the present, the Jews yearned for a better future. False messiahs failed them; and pangs of a physical return to Eretz-Israel proved abortive.[33] Galut (exile) was the operative archimedian point of Jewish alienation for 2,000 years until the rise of modern political Zionism.

Toward Jewish Independence in Eretz-Israel

The birth of Zionism as the Jewish liberation movement is the central motif of an "awakening stage" in the people's history. The geographic locus of Zionism across the European continent testified to the role of alien soil in the planting of the Zionist seeds. Zionism adopted secularism as an ideology, and nationalism, as opposed to religion, as a collective faith. The radical turn in modern Jewish life away from Judaism imitated the move in Western European history away from Christianity as a definitive orientation for man and society, as well as the moral ground for the political order itself.

Christian Europe, which had devastated Jewish existence for close to two thousand years, now contributed obliquely but vitally to the origins of Zionism. It was in Europe, its soil drenched with the blood of martyred Jews, that Zionism's great humanitarian hope—"to be a nation like all the nations"—blazed its message on the banner of the New Age.[34] In their iconoclastic fever, early Zionists daringly rejected "the Jew" in his traditional mold in a desperate attempt to liberate him from the chains of ghetto Judaism and its political passivity. Moving toward the future demanded a revolt against the past, Berdichevsky would argue (d. 1921). Brenner could not be more blatant in demanding that Zionism had to be atheistic so that the Jew could renew himself from the silence of national history.[35] Herzl, the founder of political Zionism in the 1890s, was basically an illiterate in Judaism. Nordau, his colleague, was apparently an atheist. Running through the spiritual sinews of secular Zionism was a veritable rejection of Judaism, a reaching out for the hands of the gentiles—ironically while Zionism sought relief from the rule of the gentiles. Universalism was stitched together with nationalism. Many Zionists hoped that the ultimate end product must and would be "a secular nation and not a sacred tribe."[36] And it was this new definition of the Jewish people that became a catalyst for a transformation in the Jews' mentality and capacity for mobilization of latent popular energies.

At the core of secular Zionism is a direct cultural assault on the Jewish family as well as on the Jewish religion as its inner spirit. Young men and women left their parents to become adventurous pioneers in the ancient homeland. Such was the character of the first *aliya* (immigration to Eretz Israel) in 1882. Deganiah, the first kibbutz, situated in the Jordan Valley near the Sea of Galilee in 1909, expressed in its social composition a rupture from traditional Jewish family life: Single men and women avoided marriage and when married nonetheless, shunned childbearing as interference with the collective tasks of building the new society. Later, in the 1920s, the labor brigades (*gedudei avoda*) made a compelling call for youth to leave their families and move about the country to work wherever the need demanded.

With no ties to any local residence, the family unit lost its moral legitimacy in the new Hebrew society (*yishuv*) of Eretz-Israel. The fanatical dedication of the early pioneers knew no bounds. The extraordinary story of a family in Hadera illustrated this when three children from a single family died from malaria. Despite this tragedy, related Ben-Gurion, both parents and family would not leave. It was this kind of national commitment, even at the personal sacrifice of family, that would mobilize national renewal of Jewish life.[37]

Zionist revival found heroic expression in fascinating personalities who pioneered the way to national development. A. D. Gordon (1856–1922) articulated a "religion of labor" that would symbolize the tie between the Jews and their land in an organic relationship of love. Gordon himself, arriving in the country from Russia at the age of forty-eight, abandoned white-collar work to become an agricultural laborer, reflecting a personal redemptive experience. Berl Katznelson (1887–1944) became a central figure in socialist Zionism as a voice of hope against despair in the difficult early days. He, with Ben-Gurion, was instrumental in developing the institutional apparatus for national construction. Medical, political, housing, intellectual, military, and other organizations were formed to build the collective strength of the Jewish community. A new Jewish elite formed to lead the Zionists toward national majority power in the land — against Arab opposition from the beginning — culminating with statehood in 1948.

Indeed, from the beginning of the Zionist period, there was major opposition that had to be overcome, or at least contended with. As Herzl recognized, European Christian anti–Semitism was the initial motive force of Zionism, though it was also a barrier to garnering foreign support for the Zionist answer to the "Jewish problem." The eventual triumph of Zionism was the Balfour Declaration in 1917, a British commitment to "view with favor the establishment in Palestine of a national home for the Jewish people." British moral support and solidarity with Jewish renaissance in Eretz-Israel assumed formal legal, political, and international dimensions.[38] The League of Nations in 1920–1922 certified that the Balfour Declaration commitment stood at the core of the British mandate over Palestine, and this assured basic foreign support for the building of the country as a Jewish homeland.

The first signs of a Jewish desire to return in an organized Zionist fashion had confronted Turkish opposition. The Ottoman Empire administered Palestine according to a patchwork of *sanjak-vilayet* district borderlines that denied the land any territorial unity.[39] Haifa, for example, was ruled from Damascus. The Ottoman authorities opposed Zionist immigration. In the early 1890s, this policy was proclaimed, and steps were taken to enforce it. During the First World War, repressive measures threatened the viability, perhaps even survival, of the Jewish *yishuv*. But the advance of the Allied forces, the subsequent Ottoman collapse, and the British victory removed the Turkish obstacle from the Zionist path.

The Arab presence in Palestine was a formidable problem. Historically, it is true, the Arab population was thin, lacking collective cohesion or national impetus. The myth of Palestinian-Arab rootedness and longevity in the country has little factual validity.[40] The poverty of the *fellahin* (peasant farmers) and the infertility of Palestine were legendary. The 250,000 Arabs in Palestine west of the Jordan River at the end of the nineteenth century were victims of backwardness and divisiveness, subject to absentee landlords and Ottoman rapacity.

Jews had begun to settle in Eretz-Israel over the centuries, even before the 1882 *aliya* and the Herzlian breakthrough in 1897. In the 1820s, some settled in Tsfat, others in Jerusalem.[41] The major increases in the Jewish population came later with the Zionist waves of immigration that were largely unimpeded by native Arab opposition and hostility. Jewish colonies like Rehovot and Gedera, Yesod Ha'maaleh and Metula, older Jewish presence in Shefaram and Pekiin in addition to Jerusalem, Hebron, Tzfat, and Tiberias, began to provide the outlines of an expanding Jewish *yishuv*.[42] Arab opposition assumed violent forms, beginning with the riots in Jerusalem in 1920, and a political struggle ensued to arrest Zionist growth. But Arab efforts were only partially successful. Palestinian rejectionism and absolutism backfired, and violence brought about British repressive methods in the 1936–1939 period in particular.

In spite of British waverings in the commitment to develop the Jewish national home, Zionism continued to move forward. Social changes and national mobilization from within, and repression and deprivation from without, helped inspire Jewish efforts. Foreign aid — British in particular, though international recognition in general — also contributed to energizing the Zionists to believe that the Return was feasible and a Jewish majority an inevitable reality. Just 10 percent of Palestine in 1920, the Jewish proportion rose to 33 percent in the late 1930s. When later established in May 1948, Israel included a 90 percent Jewish majority within the boundaries of the new Jewish state.

The sine qua non of Jewish nationalism was articulating Zionism's territorial focus, inaugurating a sizable immigration process, and building the country for the future Jewish state. Sentimental and symbolic ties to Eretz-Israel were for Zionism the nostalgic background required for substantive settlement and construction. The latter actions transformed the Jewish attitude into a functional purpose of strategically planning "the state-on-the-way."

The Zionist Organization memorandum submitted to the Supreme Allied Council at the Paris Peace Conference in February 1919 explained the movement's territorial conception:

> The fertile plains east of the Jordan, since the earliest Biblical times, have been linked economically and politically with the land west of the Jordan. . . . It could now serve admirably for colonisation on a large scale.[43]

The desired Zionist boundaries were also to incorporate the water resources north to the Litani River and the Hermon Mountains, and a harbor on the Gulf of Aqaba in the South. In 1949, Israel captured all of the Negev desert and made possible the establishment of Eilat as a southern port on the Gulf of Aqaba—for Israel, the Gulf of Eilat thereafter.

Unlike other minority movements in the Middle East, whose historical territory was their very place of residence, the Jews scattered around the world—in Europe, Africa, and the Middle East as well—faced the enormous task of returning to their historical territory. Eretz-Israel had been emptied of its Jews for millennia, except for small pockets that clung to the land, especially in Jerusalem the Holy City. Nonetheless, the Zionist Return won out against international indifference, severe regional hostility, and growing local Arab opposition. As Menachem Ussishkin, the head of the Jewish National Fund, said in 1939: the Jews need a homeland, not in Russia but in Eretz-Israel.[44] And so it came to be.

The elements of national political statehood were constituted in a few decades, from the period of the First World War until just after the Second World War upon the eve of Israel's founding. The Jewish population rose to over 650,000 by 1948 from a mere 25,000 in the land seventy years earlier. An economic infrastructure was established in agriculture, small industry, and electrical power. Lands were purchased and settled, particularly the coastal plain, the Jezreel Valley, the Jordan Valley, and the Galilee. Urban centers developed, Tel Aviv and Haifa in particular. Political articulation of the Zionist enterprise led to organizational-party multiplication, Mapai (the socialist movement) toward the Left and revisionism on the Zionist Right, with a variety of smaller parties. A Jewish "shadow state" was consolidated by the 1930s with its own institutional structure, like the Jewish Agency, the National Committee (Va'ad Leumi), and the People's Council (Minhelet Ha'am).

The Hebrew language was resuscitated as a spoken tongue throughout the country.[45] A vibrant cultural life developed in the press and in theater, and all in the ancient vernacular of the Jewish people. Universities were established, the Technion seminally in Haifa in 1913 and the Hebrew University in Jerusalem in 1925. An ideology of heroism and pioneering commitment was cultivated by arousing the myths and symbols of the Maccabees and recalling the purity of purpose at Masada, the last Jewish stronghold in the war against the Romans in 73 B.C. after the destruction of the Second Temple. The Zionists took an old Jewish dream and turned it remarkably into a new Jewish reality. This minority, a historically weak Mideastern people, became a majority in their own land.

The Key to Zionist Success

This success, in contrast to other Mideastern minority failures, enjoyed the advantage of an odd beginning. The European origins of modern Zionism provided a radical and revolutionary political environment for the nationalist and socialist principles that ideologically stimulated the movement. Its secularist spirit legitimized autonomous human action. It bypassed theological impediments to Jews' choosing to "make their own history," this in ostensible defiance of the Kingdom of Heaven mediated by cautious rabbinic leaders.

Various political and technical skills equipped the Jews to persuade foreigners of their rights and to demonstrate the land's productivity ("absorptive capacity," in the language of the Mandate) in contrast to Arab abuse and disuse of Palestine. And while the Zionist leadership elite was sharply divided on various types of ideological questions, Zionist spokesmen and activists were articulate and educated, versed in the ways of the world. They were also adept at mobilizing Jewish masses through political organization and its symbolic accoutrements. In the land, Zionism fabricated a dynamic society and the infrastructure of a seemingly viable economy. In addition to domestic productivity, they harnessed the capital resources of world Jewry for Zionist redemption.

Beyond growing British hostility to Zionism in the 1940s, the broad canvas of global politics was not at all uniformly antagonistic. Of the most historic significance was the support of both the United States and the Soviet Union for the United Nations Partition Resolution of November 29, 1947, which recommended the establishment of a Jewish state in part of Palestine, alongside an Arab state. This international support, even though it was not followed by direct military assistance by either superpower, gave political credibility to the Zionist drive toward statehood. The Jews, coming from afar, had made a miraculous reentry into Eretz-Israel. This minority people had advanced from the rung of ethnic community and cultural group all the way to the stage of political nationality and statehood.

The origins of Zionism among Ashkenazi Jews in Europe, rather than among oriental Jews in the Middle East, is therefore clarified as a historical necessity. Eastern Jews living under Muslim rule could never turn their *dhimmi* existence, or imagine they could, into the stuff of revolutionary politics and national liberation. In addition, Mideastern Jews, untouched by the impact of secularism and irreligion, were more attuned to awaiting direct divine intervention in history rather than haughtily assuming they could make it themselves. European Jews, largely unaware of the political dimensions inherent in Islam and Arabism, could imagine in their Enlightenment romanticism that any-

thing was possible. Ignorance became a springboard for a national venture of questionable practicality. But it succeeded because ignorance —
that is, unfamiliarity with all the facts — is sometimes a condition for
making history.

Ashkenazi Jews in Europe put aside their Judaism to liberate themselves for a break with the past as they struck a national trail in the East.
Secularism was a prerequiste, Judaism being for them an impediment.
They exploited the age-old "Jewish Question" lying deep in Christian-
European consciousness and advocated the radical Herzlian political
solution until its ultimate consummation in statehood. This Zionist
effort exemplified a unique convergence of mythology with modernity
that culminated in Israel's rebirth. At the core of this convergence — and
its most celebrated expression — was a Jewish military ethos. Zionist
militia and defense forces — like Hashomer, Haganah, Irgun, Palmach,
and Lehi — recaptured a fighting spirit that had waned during centuries
of dispersion. In Zionist dress, the Jewish soldier reappeared as a vital
requirement of national survival and strength.

The Dhimmi *Syndrome*

And yet the degree to which Zionism had actually inaugurated a
revolution in the heart of Jewish existence was not clear. It had created
a state and had turned the Jews into a majority in their own country.
But it is the psychological domain that is most critical as a test of liberation. Taking the Jews out of Galut (exile or diaspora) does not assure
that you have taken Galut out of the Jew. For Galut is a psychological
reality, a feebleness and a fear, a loss of dignity more than just a lack
of power, all derivative from centuries of persecution and homeless-
ness. It is shame of oneself and in front of others.

In particular, it is the *dhimmi* situation that must be overcome, and
the meek identity associated with it must be shattered. "Protected
Jews," be they in the West or the East, Europe or to the south, must
pass from Jewish history as a bad dream upon the new morning.[46]

A remarkable incident is related from Cairo in 1047 concerning the
assassination of a Jew who was a dealer in gems. He was exceedingly
wealthy, and the royal Muslim Fatimid house had complete confidence
in him.

> One day, the royal troops fell upon this Jew and killed him. . . . That
> murdered Jew was named Abu Sa'id. He left behind a son and a
> brother. . . . His brother (Abu Nasr) wrote a letter which he sent to be
> presented to the Ruler. In it, he offered to make an immediate gift of
> 200,000 Maghrebi dinars to the treasury, for he was very much afraid.

The Ruler sent back the letter and had it publicly torn up, saying: "You may consider yourself safe. Go back to your home, for no one has anything against you."[47]

The lesson regarding contemporary Jewish affairs can be elucidated with an eye to culturally constant variables. From the moment of its founding proclamation on May 14, 1948, Israel has been the target and victim of Arab aggression and warfare, military the most obvious mode, but political, ideological, psychological warfare also part of the Arab assault.

The Jews have at the same time often reached out for peace through concessions and territorial withdrawals. Gifts toward reconciliation and gestures of appeasement have been made by the victim, not the aggressor. Indeed, the Arabs have by and large multiplied their demands and maintained a bellicose posture toward Israel. This anomalous state of affairs persists notwithstanding more than forty years of bitter conflict. The Arab onslaught has been unrelenting and constantly seeks new opportunities; meanwhile, Israel desperately talks of peace. A gift of territory and oil to Egyptians, political autonomy or self-determination to Palestinians, may not have the exotic quality of 200,000 Maghrebi dinars. But such Israeli generosity recalls, as in the Cairo incident from 1047, the fear and self-deprecation of Jews in the face of Muslim power.

This strange scenario demands further commentary. Jewish victimology from the past conjures up the *dhimmi* image, the "protected Jew," and the Galut syndrome in the reconstituted Jewish state of Israel. Israeli diplomatic finesse, as exemplified in the Camp David Treaty, for example, carries with it a deeper significance. The Jews invariably reflect the spirit of a minority, even though they have become a majority in their homeland.

The Arabs of Palestine suffered defeat and dispersion in 1948, were reduced to a minority within Israel, and have been vainly struggling ever since to overturn the results of the 1948 and 1967 debacles. Yet, at the same time, the Arab self-image in Israel remained grounded in a belief in power and superiority. Loss of political and demographic predominancy did not erode the conviction in their cultural, psychological, and religious superiority.

One symbolic and vivid expression of this phenomenon in Judea, Samaria, and Gaza specifically is the Arab norm of throwing rocks at Jews. Historically this practice was widespread throughout the Muslim East.[48] Astounding as it may seem, this practice of rock throwing at Jews surfaced in Israel too. Arab youth have renewed this old aggressive practice during the 1970s and 1980s. Jews have been killed and many maimed by rocks. This Arab practice from Fez and Yemen is also practiced in Hebron, Ramallah, and the Tel-Aviv–Haifa highway—within Israel or Israeli-ruled areas.

The Arabs are weaker and a minority within a Jewish state but nonetheless assert their feelings of being in control. The Jews are objectively stronger and a statistical majority but allow inculcated inferiority to influence them. In the *mellah* ghettos of North Africa, Jews locked the gates at night, fearing Arab-Muslim attacks. In many Jewish settlements in Israel, the gates are locked, and fences encircle the perimeter; the fear here too is Arab-Muslim attacks.

Overall, then, the objective change that transpired in Jewish existence through Zionism and with Israel's establishment has not visibly or fundamentally altered the profound psychological realm of ingrained self-perceptions and other-oriented perceptions. Jewish liberation, for its part, awaits its true revolutionary moment. Arab adjustment to Israel, in its way, awaits its compelling realism.

Yet the political achievement of Zionism was a particular kind of Mideastern minority success. It arose outside the region yet succeeded ultimately in the region. It was a Jewish deviation in secularist form, but this constituted the requisite spirit for mobilization and change. It saw the country's territorial memory as an energizing mechanism, though the mountain heartland—Judea and Samaria—was beyond the borders of Israel in 1948 (and until 1967). Zionism was a different minority enterprise that worked.

Nonetheless, challenges to the integrity and survivability of Israel loom large. Arab bellicosity met this *dhimmi* rebellion. Arab demography threatens it from within. The requirements for initial success, up to 1948 at least, may not be sufficient or appropriate for ongoing success indefinitely. We shall return to this point in the last chapter.

The Problematics of Arab Opposition

The possible varieties of conflict resolution in Israel between Jews and Arabs, and between Israel and the Arab world in the Middle East, are not mere theoretical alternatives. They have been politically advocated and attempted in part. The notion of Arabism, veritably the Arabization of Israel and the reduction of Jews to a *dhimmi* condition, has been a program or plot since 1948. Arab nationalism and its Palestinian offshoot alike envision the subjugation of the Jews—in the classic Islamic mode—a just and necessary resolution of the conflict.

The incompatibility of this vision with permanent Israeli sovereignty makes this proposal nonnegotiable and, we may assume, unrealizable. Some, like Elie Kedourie, may recall nostalgically the small communities of the East that constituted a commonwealth of indigenous peoples living tolerably well under some paternalistic imperial authority, Ottoman until the twentieth century.[49] The European ways of nationalism were alien and infected the region with wild political dreams that wrought destruction on the dreamers and others.

But the Jews did not struggle for statehood just to issue their own postage stamps. Zionism was an authentic national idea rooted in history and bolstered by suffering and hope that became a heroic victory. The record suggests it can be a viable enterprise even when, or if, the period of heroism passes. Mere Jewish autonomy under Islamic rule, offered by Iraqi Prime Minister Nuri Sa'id and King Abdullah of Jordan in the 1940s, was consistently rejected. After decades of statehood, the Jews are unlikely ever to accept this diminutive *dhimmi* offer.

A more limited definition of Arab nationalism and its territorial aspirations could accommodate the reality of a Jewish Israel. Signs of this existed in the immediate aftermath of the Balfour Declaration. The written agreement of January 3, 1919, between Dr. Chaim Weizmann of the Zionist movement and Emir Feisal representing the Arab movement was a positive and explicit mutual acceptance. Other correspondence confirmed this readiness to restrict the broader purposes of Arab nationalism at the borders of Palestine. From there the Jewish-Zionist venture would reign supreme. Considering resurgent Islamic fundamentalism, modern Arab nationalism, and Palestinian political aspirations, it is undoubtedly more complex seventy years later to implement a program of this type than it seemed back in 1919. The possibility, however, should not be dismissed.

The notion of an integrating strategy of civil politics is in Israel's case primarily focused on the variety of Jewish communities in the country. Legitimizing the social order and the national ethos took on a secular and symbolic form. Older Jewish themes, like Passover liberation or the Masada myth, were reintroduced into Israel's culture by way of readaptation to fit the particular Zionist idiom. The Bible was studied, but not revered as a holy book.[50] Yet it is this very denaturalizing of the Jew via secularism and its related democratic and egalitarian principles that can theoretically accommodate the Arabs of Israel. In the 1980s, a campaign extolling the virtues of coexistence and tolerance was undertaken in earnest. State institutions in the areas of education and culture propagated these ideas as dogmatic values and the expression of political prudence. The fact that the Arabic language is official in Israel and that Arab education is a state-funded policy gave weight to the call for Jewish-Arab tolerance, if not full equality.[51]

Yet the simultaneous rise of Palestinian nationalist sentiment and PLO identification among the Arabs of Israel was a fly in the political ointment. Indeed, the very question of Arab loyalty to the state became a real problem as expressions of disloyalty in word and action increased. Time will tell whether an ideology of civil politics, with increasing Arab participation in the national body politic, Knesset members and all, can supersede and outweigh the tension and alienation that have grown in Jewish-Arab relations. Certainly the infusion of stronger doses of Palestinian nationalism and Islamic religion into the political consciousness of Arab Israelis will complicate any integrative effort. At the same time, Jewish nationalism at an increased ideological pitch will not welcome any program designed to integrate Arabs into the official strata of Israeli public life more equitably.

The Israeli case has not successfully applied institutional measures to resolve domestic Jewish-Arab conflict. The idea of confessional politics, in the form of Arab electoral lists tied to the Israeli Labor party, for example, was never really considered a legitimate mechanism for seriously resolving differences. Nonetheless, Arab members of the Knesset do, along with Jewish leftist members of the Knesset, represent Arab views and grievances. The cabinet system of government, or coalition government in itself, has not served as a vehicle for Jewish-Arab elite interaction and bargaining.

In addition, the autonomy plan for the Arabs of Judea, Samaria, and Gaza as part of the Camp David Accords of 1979 was rejected by the Arabs as politically insufficient. Little less than a complete Israeli pullback from all the territories and a Palestinian-PLO state would satisfy their aspirations, for the time being at least. It is this and more that force the matter of secession onto the political agenda. Certainly the Arab-Palestinian population in the areas taken by Israel in 1967, and even parts of the Arab population within Israel since 1948, continued to see separation from Israel as the best and only congenial solution.

Israel has, at most, been willing to consider a partial withdrawal from *some* of the post–1967 areas. Even this willingness is not at all a consensus view; indeed it is a minority view within the Jewish population. There is room for doubt, therefore, regarding the prognosis for Arab secession (otherwise known as Palestinian liberation). Israel, in spite of the domestic Arab demographic threat, cannot conceivably and without limits trade geography for a political settlement without at the same time undermining the strategic integrity of the state and eroding an image of national fortitude in the face of foreign pressure.

Conflict resolution between Jews and Arabs in Israel is a complicated path, burdened with historical and religious stereotypes and overladen with contemporary political and demographic complexities. From the Jewish point of view, the problem is a Mideastern paradox: Can a small minority *dhimmi* people assert indefinite superiority over the Arab-Muslims — "born to rule" as they are — and permanently withstand Arab internal and external challenges? The Jews broke the Covenant of Umar, the *dhimma* pact that fixed clear limitations on minority life, as an act of Jewish political blasphemy that aroused Arab rejectionism of Zionism's quest for freedom and dignity. This occurred as the Jews fulfilled, in whatever fashion, the Covenant of Abraham in which God promised the land of Canaan to the children of Israel. The land of Canaan indeed became the land of Israel. Israel's ultimate fate will reveal the potency of the two covenants and the conflict between them.

CHAPTER 13

Jews, Israel, and the Minorities

The establishment of Israel was not only a dramatic breakthrough in Jewish history for which political hyperbole was used with generosity in describing the grandeur of the event. The Jews are a Middle Eastern people whose presence in the region transcends the territorial ties to the specific Jewish homeland. In the 1948 breakthrough, one Mideastern people achieved independence and majority status as no other people had done.

Moreover, the Jews had always had contacts and relations with a wide variety of regional communities who, upon Israel's establishment, looked on with vicarious satisfaction, or at least derived from the event inspiration for their own future. The Jews had turned their historic Hebrew language into a living spoken tongue. Perhaps the Maronites or Copts might try to imitate this linguistic recovery. The Jews had built sufficient military strength to withstand Arab invading forces. Perhaps the Kurds could learn something from the Zionist success for their own undauntable, but unsuccessful, campaign against Turks, Iraqis, and Iranians. The Jews had adapted the knowledge and skills of modernity for a viable liberation movement in the relatively backward Middle East. Perhaps the Berbers or the Baluch could copy something of the Jews' capability and win their freedom too.

The Mideastern Minority Equation

The Zionist achievement was viewed as a historic opportunity to redefine the national character and political geography of the Middle East. Israel was not interested in converting the old communities of the area to Judaism but could perhaps infect them with the spirit of minority struggles against an Arab-Muslim world that if not defeated, had been stunned by Israel's military victory in 1948. In truth, the Arab loss in Palestine in 1948 symbolized more than just a military defeat on the battlefield against a more efficient and determined Jewish adversary. The loss in Palestine reflected as well a veritable civilizational crisis at the heart of Arab Islam. Zionism had exposed the feebleness of the Arab world in the modern age; Israel in May 1948 was the sparkling symbol of that age. The unsuccessful effort by Egypt, Syria, and Iraq in particular raised the possibility, at least in theory, of further Arab defeats in other parts of the region.

Some Israeli authors and activists advocated Israeli support for the formation of small Middle Eastern nation-states, Maronite and 'Alawite, for example.[1] The multiplicity of indigenous peoples in the region, subsumed clumsily under a net of Arab nomenclature, undermined the very notion of pan–Arab unity. Non-Muslim Druzes and non–Arab Kurds were two peoples that provided human diversity to what otherwise appeared to be a monolithic Sunni-Muslim–Arab Mideast. The core zone of the Fertile Crescent contained Jews, Maronites, 'Alawites, Druzes, and Kurds who had faced Arab imperialism and underdevelopment, according to A. G. Horon.[2] The liberation of these peoples would be a springboard to justice in the Mideast and the way for Israel and the Jews to overcome their isolation in the region. Without cooperating with the minorities, Israel will be a lonely island in an Arab sea.

But the Arab war against Zionism and Israel constituted a challenge to the possibility of further minority advances across the Mideast. If Israel were to fall, no other minority campaign would stand a chance of success. Were Israel to survive and strengthen, other minority campaigns might be encouraged to persevere toward majority status or political independence. The minorities' future seemed after 1948 inextricably tied to the Israeli experiment.

For some, this was an opportunity and responsibility to be pursued with diligence. Shimon Peres, later to become prime minister of Israel, had written about the cruel fate of national minorities such as Armenians and Assyrians in this century. He went on to add:

> For half the period of their existence, the Jewish people lived as a national minority, and it is natural that they should be particularly sympathetic towards other national minorities. Israel would like to help them but it is no simple matter, and she would not wish them to be under illusions. The struggle of these national minorities is worth aiding, politically, morally and materially.[3]

Israeli solidarity with Mideastern minorities rang with altruistic sentiments. But it also reflected strategic calculations to widen the sphere of Israel's integration and normalcy within the region as a whole.

Yitzhak Rabin, Israeli prime minister from 1974 to 1977, had envisioned support for the Christians in Lebanon as an element in this broad political orientation.[4] Fighting Muslim domination therefore necessitated Israeli collaboration with the victims of that domination.

"Ultra-Zionism" became a slogan to arouse the latent potential of Kurdish Zionism, Assyrian Zionism, Druze Zionism, Maronite Zionism, and other peoples' national struggles.[5] Each community would strive to imitate the pattern of national revival reflected in the Zionist movement. But the minority struggles could not hope to succeed without active Israeli assistance. What the Soviet Union and the Comintern constituted as legitimizing agents and ideological inspiration for communism around the world Israel and Zionism would be for the minority Middle Eastern peoples around the region.

Former Israeli ambassador to the United Nations, Benjamin Netanyahu, had written that "the Jews of Israel are the only non–Arab people to have successfully defied Arab domination and achieved independence."[6] He appropriately mentioned in this context numerous other peoples—like Berbers, Kurds, and Copts—who lived in the Mideast but remained politically under the hegemonic authority of the Arab Muslims. Implicit in his analysis was a hint at an Israeli role in aiding the minorities to follow the successful Jewish example.

For Lebanon, in particular, the notion of Israeli ties with the minorites had been a lively issue. Christian Maronites not only openly turned to Israel for assistance but also conceived of its role in a broad regional fashion. Roger Eddé, son of Raymond Eddé from the Lebanese National Bloc, perceived Israel's growing power as the step to "imposing its imperial leadership over minorities in the Middle East."[7] The commander of the phalange militia, Fady Frem, was known as distinctly pro–Israeli. He too widened the perspective when he advocated "an interrelation between all the minorities in the Middle East."[8] Pierre Yazbeck, Maronite spokesman in Jerusalem following the 1982 war, underscored the regional significance of Israeli-Lebanese ties. The minorities in general require an alliance with Israel whose very existence is "a vital factor for their survival and freedom." The long-term goal, Yazbeck added, is the minorities question: "The Christian issue, the Druze issue, the Kurdish issue, the Armenian issue and soon an 'Alawite issue."[9]

Within the purview of Israel's foreign policy since 1948 loomed a recognition of the importance, and apparently the viability, of relations with the geographically peripheral regional states. Widening Israel's strategic sphere to include such countries as Turkey, Iran, and Ethiopia was an attempt to break out from the alien inner regional core of the Arab state system. In December 1981, Defense Minister Ariel Sharon explicitly discussed this policy conception in an address at Tel Aviv

University.[10] While this strategic conception did not necessarily overlap fully with the minorities conception, the common thrust of Israel's leapfrogging to the periphery was singular. Islamization in Iran and perhaps Turkey, certainly in Pakistan, along with Marxism in Ethiopia, nevertheless turned the strategic conception into a weaker policy option than formerly, though later developments in both Iran and Ethiopia would offer new Israeli opportunities. The specific minorities conception, never proven, had not, however, been invalidated.

For some, the link between Israel and the minorities was marked by a diabolical effort to undermine Arab nationalism and "Balkanize" the Middle East. The Zionist virus could become a regional cancer if the minority germ was allowed to spread. Mohamed Sid-Ahmed, an Egyptian writer of socialist leanings, charged that Israel is interested in

> the creation of a constellation of mini–Israels around Israel as a buffer zone against the Islamic avalanche — that is, a Maronite state, and a Kurdish state, and a whatever. All sorts of states who would derive their legitimacy from opposing the Arab or Islamic identity, who would be linked to a revival of confessionalism.[11]

Destabilization of the Mideast, "ottomanizing" it back into small fragmented and discrete ethnic-religious communities, would serve Israel's interests first and foremost.[12] This argument by Noam Chomsky contributed inadvertently to the often-contested Israeli thesis that the Arab world is truly a fearsome and serious enemy of the Jews. Were this not the case, Israel would have no desire to balkanize the region into ministates.

For years, Israel has been suspected of scheming to divide the Mideast, rearrange its political geography, and foil Arab designs against Zionism. In 1978, a conference held at Princeton University was alluded to as revolving around this Israeli conspiracy.[13] In 1982, an article appearing in a Hebrew-language Israeli journal, subsidized by the World Zionist Organization, evoked a wave of interest and wrath. Oded Yinon, an Israeli author, analyzed the incipient divisions within the Arab world and then forecast its ultimate political dissolution into smaller ethnic entities.[14] The author's ostensible suggestion that Israel adopt such a forecast, as the basis for an active interventionist strategy, gave the appearance of a sinister Israeli regional offensive employing the minorities issue on the way to exercising hegemony across the Mideast.[15]

The international and regional outcry at this article was exaggerated and bordered on the incredulous. And yet the extent of public attention regarding an article written by a private person illustrated the great sensitivity felt in the Mideast, among Arabs in particular, to the question of minority claims toward and within a relatively tender state system built on imperial sands in the days after World War I. The Arab war against Zionism was meant to abort such claims and solidify the state system for good.

Mythology and Memorabilia

The long dispersion of Jews throughout the Middle East led to legendary tales of interaction and involvement with a variety of regional communities. It is difficult to separate scientific evidence from mythological suppositions regarding such interethnic contacts. Only circumstantial support could be provided to identify Jewish origins of, or influences on, the small Yezidi group in northern Iraq. The practice of male circumcision and the Passover holiday were reported amongst Yezidis, but these otherwise fascinating reports are not sufficient proof of Hebrew descent.[16]

The Bahais of Persia revere many prophets, among whom is Moses, and they have a history of contact with Eretz-Israel since Baha' Allah, the Bahai founder's successor, arrived in Acco in 1868. This is the Holy Land for the Bahais, and their world center is situated in Haifa. This shrine in Israel would seem to symbolize ties between the Jews and the Bahais, but the charge by Iranians that Bahaism derives from kabbalistic Judaism is unconvincing.

The Zoroastrians are an ancient religious community from Babylon, often resembling Jews in their literate and mercantile attributes. However, historical crossing of paths thousands of years ago, along with a like minority fate, do not add up to shared origins or intertwined existences. Some links with Samaritans in Samaria go back millennia and, with Circassians before 1948 and within Israel thereafter, are telling evidence of minority interaction but not the stuff for anything more politically significant. However, all these instances—Yezidis, Bahais, Samaritans, and Circassians—illustrate the historically and geographically far-flung links between Jews and other Mideastern groups. This is a comment on the Jews' being a central and vital element in the mosaic of Mideastern life.

The most intriguing mystery of Jewish ties with other minorities involves the Lost Ten Tribes of Israel. Particularly fascinating is the Pathan community, living primarily in Afghanistan, and partially in the Northwest province of Pakistan. Their area of settlement near the Khyber Pass strikes up a linguistic connection concerning Israelite exile in the eighth century before Christianity to Chavor, Hera, and the river Gozan.[17] Through the ages, Jewish travelers noticed Afghan tribes who bore a resemblance to Jews. From physiognomy to prayer shawls and sidelocks to menstrual purification customs, the Pathans actually seemed Jewish and maintained oral traditions of their Hebrew descent.[18] They reported of themselves that Pathan ancestry derives from the tribe of Benjamin and the seed of King Saul. Pathan tribal names even attested to a biblical origin. Customs like candle lighting for the Sabbath and hopes for messianic redemption coupled with returning to Eretz-Israel followed them through history.[19] Although outwardly Sunni-Muslims, the Pathans and other Afghanis never shirked their Jewish roots, even until the twentieth century.[20] Yet final judgment on the veracity of Jewish roots was a debated question. Fredrik Barth said that "the proof of such descent is patently spurious,"[21] while Itzhak Ben-Zvi, Israel's second president, referred to this legend as "an ancient tradition, and one not without some historical plausibility."[22]

British involvement in the Indian subcontinent and in trying to manage Afghanistan as a buffer against Russia, offered Rudyard Kipling an opportunity to examine the Pathan tribes. In one description he referred to Afghan prisoners as "these huge, black-haired, and scowling sons of the Beni-Israel" (sons of Israel). In "The Man Who Was," Kipling commented on "a few thousand gentlemen of Jewish extraction who lived across the border and answer to the name of Pathans."

The Soviet invasion of Afghanistan in December 1979 forced the Pathan question to the surface of international affairs. Afghani resistance fighters (Mujahedeen) were ostensibly Muslim freedom fighters conducting guerrilla warfare against the forces of alien communism. Soviet use of poison gas and cluster bombs — and a scorched-earth military campaign — created an enormous Pathan refugee problem across the border in Pakistan. Western aid to the Afghani liberation struggle was small, though American assistance was forthcoming.[23] Meanwhile, Trotsky's prophecy that "the revolution's road to Paris and London might lead through Kabul, Calcutta and Bombay" looked, with a stretch of the political imagination, almost credible in the early 1980s.

And with another stretch of the historical imagination, it seemed that Jews in Moscow and Leningrad, Israelis in Jerusalem and Tel Aviv, and Pathans (Jews) in Herat and Kabul were all bound by ancient ties in a common front for freedom against Soviet hostility and oppression. The Pathans number about 15 million people spread across Afghanistan and Pakistan. Their "Pushtunwali" military code and their native creed of male virility would undoubtedly add to the prowess of the Israeli Army should the Pathan *marranos* return home one day to Eretz-Israel. Another lost Israelite appendage from the tribe of Dan were the Falashas of Ethiopia. But unlike the Pathans, the Falashas have been returning to Zion since the 1970s.

Minority Connections

Kurds

The Assyrian conquest of the northern Hebrew kingdom of Israel, along with a determined policy of population transfer, led to a long exile of Jewish tribes in the mountains of Kurdistan. In villages like Zakho, Amadiya, and Dohuk, Jewish life was preserved in a Muslim-dominated environment for more than 2,500 years. Some few Kurdish Jews came on *aliya* to the Promised Land as early as 1812; by 1952, with Israel acting as a magnetic pull, no Jews were left in Kurdistan.

The relationship between the Jews and the Kurds was ambiguous. At times, Jews were veritable slaves to Kurdish chieftains, yet required protection against Arabs to preserve a semblance of security in an anarchic and dangerous land. The Kurds revealed a spiritual affinity with Judaism. Kurdish Muslims would visit the tombs of Jonah (Yona) the prophet and Daniel the seer near Nineveh outside of Mosul.[24] One Kurdish sect in Turkey, the Kizilbash, allegedly revered the Torah and venerated Moses, and above all respected the memory of King David.[25] Some Kurds actually claimed that they were once Jewish, giving voice not to Jewish influences but Jewish origins.[26] This would converge with the notion of the Kurds' being remnants of the Ten Lost Tribes who, upon the Islamic conquest of Kurdistan, adopted the religion of the Muslims.

When the Kurdish liberation struggle began in 1961, Israel offered to help this rugged mountain people in their war for freedom. Mustafa Barzani himself admitted to Arieh Lova Eliav, an official Israeli emissary who arrived in the summer of 1966, that in truth only the Jews cared about the Kurds.[27] In addition to providing medical assistance and putting together the apparatus for a field hospital, Israeli aid was basically military in form. Prime Minister Menachem Begin revealed in 1980 that from 1965 until 1975 Israel gave weapons and provided instruction for the Kurdish *pesh merga* fighters.[28] Israeli army officers, among them future cabinet ministers Rehavam Zeevi and Rafael Eitan; visited Kurdistan in the late 1960s. Moreover, during the years when America supported the Kurds against the pro–Soviet Iraqis, an Israeli agent allegedly traveled to the Kurds every month bringing a $50,000 check from the CIA.[29] It was not for nil that Barzani was quoted as saying, "We are brothers," underlining the intimate Kurdish-Jewish relationship and his gratitude that the war effort, though ultimately unsuccessful, was a brave assertion of minority steadfastness against a powerful Arab enemy. It appears that Mustapha Barzani himself, and his son Masroud Barzani actually visited Israel twice during the decade of intense contacts between the two.

Israeli support was not just of a moral or altruistic quality but also reflected very immediate national interests. Baghdad's preoccupation with a difficult internal mountain war would relieve Israel's eastern front from any likely Iraqi military participation. Worth recalling is that Iraq fought Israel in 1948 and sent military assistance to Arab armies in the 1967 and 1973 wars with Israel. In this Kurd-Jewish case, the minority nexus against a common Arab adversary was blatantly apparent. Israel also benefited from Kurdish assistance in evacuating Jews from distraught places in the Middle East on their way to freedom in Israel.[30] A shared worry about repression by a post–Khomeini Iran against Jews and Kurds could also bind the two peoples together.

At one stage in the Kurdish liberation struggle, Barzani offered the oil of Kurdistan to the United States if Washington would actively and consistently provide assistance. Certainly Israel, returning the Sinai oil fields to Egypt in 1975 and in the 1979 Camp David Accords, is always desperate to purchase oil. Any weakening of Iraq and strengthening of the Kurds, ultimately the latter's highly unlikely political independence, could possibly consolidate the Jews and the Kurds in a formidable strategic alliance. With oil and military variables uppermost in the calculation, Israel and the Kurds together would ensure their respective capacities for national welfare.

And yet darker pages continued to be written in the book of Kurdish suffering. Iraqi chemical warfare against Kurdistan in 1988 compelled thousands to flee to Turkey, near Diyarbekir, where they were housed in makeshift refugee camps. Kurdish leaders there hoped, perhaps incredulously, for Israeli assistance, and indeed Jerusalem offered to take a few hundred Kurdish children as a sign of cooperation. In discussions with Israeli visitors to Diyarbekir, Kurds recalled Jewish friends who lived with them before going to Israel. The gravity of Kurdish fate in early 1991 again elicited expressions of solidarity in Israel and medical assistance from the Jewish state.

Berbers

Jews lived in the Atlas Mountains of Morocco from the destruction of the First Temple in 586 B.C., some twelve centuries prior to Islam's appearance and later conquest of North Africa. There contact was inevitable between the Jews and the indigenous Berber population, whose origin may be Canaanite according to one legend. It is known that later, many Berbers, previously pagan and later Islamized, adopted Judaism. Indeed, Jews from Iberia called native Jews Berbericos. In some cases, like that of the famous warrior-priestess Kahena in the seventh century, Islam's ferocious threat induced some Berbers to turn toward a "religion of the Book." Kahena led tribal resistance against the Arab-Muslim invaders in 687. She actually ruled the Berbers in the Aurès Mountains and was recognized as queen of the Maghreb. After her defeat and death, many Berbers came to terms with Islam and converted to the new faith. Meanwhile other Berbers adopted Judaism, some as late as the sixteenth century, and perhaps even more recently.[31] Some Berber tribes, like the Baragwata in northwest Africa, claimed descent from the Israelite tribe of Simeon (Shimon).[32] The fanatical Almoravids destroyed the Baragwatas in 1030.

A symbiotic relationship between Berbers and Jews was rich and enduring over the centuries. Conversant in Berber dialects, Jews dressed like Berbers, practiced saint worship like them, and participated in each other's celebrations. It was reported in the eighteenth century that Jews and Berbers visited a certain Jew's grave near Fez; barren women would traditionally go pray there.[33] In order to be free from the Arabs, the Berbers preferred trading with the Jews.[34] But this preference was bound up with the imposition of inferiority on the Jewish *dhimmis*. For example, Jews required Berber protection in the valley of Drah in southern Morocco, and they were required to pay the *jizya*.[35] Jewish submission under the Berbers was demeaning *('ar)* but tolerable.

But overall, the relationship was beneficial for both sides, and instances of mutual assistance abounded. It was reported that Berbers were unhappy about the Jewish departure for Israel in the 1950s, as they would then be left alone to face the Arabs.[36] An interesting footnote is that Jewish artifacts with Hebrew writing were found in a Berber store in Fez as late as the 1980s when only a few thousand Jews remained in all of Morocco.[37]

Ties between Berbers and Jews were not only social and economic but were filled with ritual and religious similarities too. The Riffian Berbers in northern Morocco had a legend of possible Jewish origins and maintained many practices that are clearly Judaic in content. These included handwashing prior to eating, abandoning gleanings in the field for the poor, wedding feasts lasting seven days after marriage, and seven days for expressing condolences in mourning following death.[38] Coon's research on the Riffians found and presented a picture of a man upon whose garment was a patch of the Star of David, a particularly Jewish symbolic design.

The fact that Berbers in Morocco and Kabyles (Berbers) in Algeria have both had to contend with Arab nationalism, and at times Islamic fundamentalism, could establish common political ground with Israel. A Kabyle renaissance culturally and nationally would contribute to neutralizing the involvement of Algeria in pan–Arab politics and in the conflict against Zionism and Israel. Certainly the uranium found in Berber areas in Morocco could assist in Israel's nuclear-development efforts. In these ways cooperation among these Mideastern minorities contains the spirit of mythological lore but potentially also the substance of contemporary intersecting interests.

Baluch

The origins of the Baluch in northern Syria may point to contact with Jews rooted in ancient Mideastern history. Yet living a rather isolated existence across eastern Persia toward the foothills of Afghanistan left the Baluch without intense interaction with other peoples. Of particular interest nonetheless are certain customs that resemble Torah-based practices. The Baluch woman washes on the seventh day of her menstrual cycle, a vivid Biblical injunction; the idea of a mother after childbirth being in a state of uncleanliness also can be related to Judaic dicta. Jewish identification is implied in the woman's custom to embroider a skullcap for her lover.[39]

The Baluch insurrection in Pakistan could be construed as politically consistent with Israel's anxiety about Karachi's "Islamic bomb," about whose construction a flurry of rumors was reported in the 1980s. Both long-term Jewish welfare and short-term Baluch welfare were threatened by Pakistan's waving its strident Islamic banner. A Pakistani nuclear capability, perhaps initially designed to match that of India, portended transforming the Arab-Israeli conflict into a Muslim-Israeli conflict. This Islamic *jihad* in image and reality, linked also to the Iranian fundamentalist spirit, widened the perimeters of the conflict eastward past the Persian Gulf. Attempts to repress Baluch nationalism in Pakistan and Iran could turn Israel into a natural ally of the Baluch against common adversaries.

Druzes

The link between Jews and Druzes assumes mythological origins as the Druzes claim descent from the father of Moses, Jethro (Yitro) the Midianite or Kenaite. While rabbinic literature has a mixed view of Jethro, though the Bible is singularly praiseworthy of him,[40] the tie between the two men suggests legendary interaction as a historic motif for contemporary cooperation. Amel Nasser Al-Din, former Druze member of the Knesset in Israel, expressed the religious connection as follows: "We believe in the same Bible as the Jews. We believe that Isaac, not Ishmael [as Islam claims], was brought for sacrifice. Mohammad is not our prophet. We are the descendants of Jethro, Moses' father-in-law."[41] It is faith in the transmigration of souls that can rationalize Druze belief in the historically fantastic idea that the Druzes, who appear only in the eleventh century, descend from a Biblical personage approximately twenty-three centuries earlier.

The Jewish-Druze relationship assumed various modes of expression over time. The twelfth-century Jewish traveler Benjamin of Tudela encountered the Druzes in the Lebanese mountains, free and under no authority, with no perceptible religion that struck the visitor's eye. Benjamin commented in particular on the bravery of the Druzes and how "they loved the Jews."[42] For centuries, Jews lived comfortably with Druze populations in Shfaram, Pekiin, and Kfar Yasif in Eretz-Israel. In Lebanon, a Jew served Fakhr al-Din II in charge of finances for his mountain state.

In the twentieth century, the Druzes rather quickly identified Zionism as representing a minority struggle not unlike their own perennial effort for communal survival. Prior to 1948, during the Arab rebellion of 1936–1939, for example, the Druzes in Palestine refrained from joining the Arab campaign against the Jews. A Druze brigade arriving from Syria in the course of the 1948 war was rather quickly disabused of its participation in the conflict against Israel. Isma'el Kabalan, a soldier hailing from the "Druze mountain" in southern Syria, related how a meeting was arranged in April with Israeli officer Moshe Dayan, who explained the naturalness of two Mideastern minorities living in peace.[43] Soon thereafter, the Israel Defense Forces (IDF) inaugurated the "Minorities Unit" (primarily Druze, though including Circassian, Bedouin, and other elements), which distinguished itself as a highly capable and courageous element in the army of Israel.

Druze integration within Israel followed suit after the state's establishment and consolidation. In 1956, the Druzes accepted obligatory military conscription into the IDF. In 1957, the Druzes were recognized as a separate religious community, thus not subject to Muslim courts and *shari'a* law. Through the Ministry of Education and Culture the Druze population of Israel was able to cultivate its own separate confessional heritage distinct from Arab culture and disengaged from Islam. Druze local government councils also served to separate them from Arab local councils. When the latter called for striking on March 30, "Land Day," every year since 1976, the Druze councils refused to join in this Arab nationalist action.

While only some Druzes would actually consider themselves full-fledged Zionists, most came to see no contradiction between Israel defined as a Jewish state and the Druzes considered as a legitimate, separate, and participating minority community within that state. This Jewish-Druze partnership was often referred to as a "covenant of blood," in recognition of the common military yoke carried by the two peoples for the security of the country.

In certain Druze circles, however, expressions of anti–Israeli sentiment were audible. At Druze weddings in the Galilee, as at Palestinian celebrations, strident Arab nationalist songs were heard in the late 1980s.

Israeli involvement with the Druze people seemed to preempt the idea of Druze statehood or to conjure up possibilities of its realization.[44] Enjoying communal freedom and social development could reasonably satisfy the group's aspirations. Yet enjoying Israeli support could make the ethereal notion of statehood seem almost feasible and worth pursuing. In 1973, Israel's deputy prime minister, Yigal Allon, had actually declared himself in favor of a Druze entity in the Golan Heights, captured from Syria in 1967.[45] In the Yom Kippur War, Allon again considered playing the "Druze card": the IDF, he argued, should pass from the Golan to the Hauran and into Jabal Druze in southern Syria as the focus of an Israeli counterattack against Damascus.

By the 1970s, a Druze state, if it was ever to arise, could more naturally be located in Syria itself, as Israel consolidated its rule over the Golan Heights. The subsequent legal incorporation of the heights into Israel came about by a Knesset law in December 1981. Still, a separate Druze educational curriculum was inaugurated, as in other parts of the country, different from the Arab curriculum.

Israel's evident ties with the Druzes were a most obvious concretization of minority cooperation against a shared Arab-Muslim adversary. The Arab-Israeli conflict had juxtaposed the Druzes against the Arabs and on the side of the Jews. In spite of serious complexities, many signs of cooperation existed between Israel and the Druzes, even in Lebanon. No doubt, the common sensation of smallness and abandonment can generate the feeling of a shared fate in the Middle East. Certainly Lebanese Druzes are unsympathetic with the rhetoric of an Islamic *jihad* against the Jews, as the Shiite Hizballah would have it.

Within Syria, where the Druzes are a tiny but highly proficient group via their role in the military, no obvious ties between Israel and the Druzes were apparent. In the past—for example, the 1950s, certainly from the 1920s to the 1940s—Druze particularism weakened the effectiveness of the Syrian state. Any future impulse in the way of Druze particularism could help to neutralize the ability of Damascus to play an active and leading role in the war against Israel. But the willingness or capability of Syrian Druzes to assume such a neutralizing task is dubious at best. So it remains highly theoretical, though playfully imaginative, to foresee a Druze buffer entity separating Israel and Syria, from the Golan to the "Druze mountain" with its capital at Suwayda. However, the considerable links between Jews and Druzes in general, based in mythology, military camaraderie, and shared political interests, make for a very interesting relationship between two regional minorities.

'Alawites

In the northern part of Jabal Ansariyya, the mountain homeland of the 'Alawites, lies a village named Qalaat Beni Israel (Castle of the Children of Israel). It is listed as an abandoned Ismaili chateau by Weulersse.[46] A few features of 'Alawite religion are reminiscent of Judaism, like circumcision and fasting on the tenth of Muharram. But Dussaud, for one, considered the idea of Nusairis being deviant Jews a "fantasy."[47] The very fact that a Jewish-'Alawite connection had to be denied implied at a minimum that concocting one was somewhat tempting.

Beyond the mythological fog, a scenario for strategic cooperation between Israel and Syria, where 'Alawites took power fully in 1970, is mildly feasible though prima facie it appears bizarre. But these two minority peoples share a basic objective goal: preventing Arabism and Islam, in their onward rush to imprint a monolithic stamp on all Mideastern peoples, from smothering them. According to one rumor, Israeli Defense Minister Ariel Sharon actually met Rifaat Assad, the president's brother, prior to the IDF's invasion of Lebanon in June 1982. Perhaps Sharon even met Hafiz el-Assad, Syria's strongman himself.

The common political purpose would allude to opposition to the rising role of the PLO in Lebanese affairs. Later, when Israel was negotiating its troop withdrawal from Lebanon in 1984, the possibility of a meeting in Europe between Rifaat Assad and Israeli officials was again referred to.[48] Rifaat's known pro–West orientation could facilitate a meeting of minds with Israel. The interesting addendum is that Ariel Sharon actually divulged in an address to a Washington audience in 1987 that Israel "has ties, perhaps even discussions, with the 'Alawites of Syria."[49]

The fact that Syria under Assad had assumed a forthright Arab nationalist ideological posture against Zionism and Israel cannot be overlooked. Nor can Syria's aspiring to strategic parity with Israel be dismissed. It is only that underneath this public veneer of audacious warmongering is the otherwise precarious position of the 'Alawite minority in a Sunni-Arab country and region. The assertion of minority 'Alawite power in Syria is as outrageous to the Muslims as the assertion of Jewish power in Palestine. The Islamic theologian from the fourteenth century, Ibn Taimiyah, judged the 'Alawites more infidel than even the Jews in his derogation of Nusairi deviancy. So, in an interesting way, the Jews and the 'Alawites are in a similarly problematic situation, historically and in contemporary Middle Eastern political life. It is not impossible, aside from the rhetoric of animosity gushing from Damascus against Israel, that the compelling reality of a common condition can awaken the possibility of Jewish-'Alawite cooperation. Perhaps this

will become true not in the present situation but when the 'Alawites fall
from power and return to their classic minority vulnerability as in the
past.

Copts

Any serious relationship between the Copts and the Jews would
focus on Israel's contribution to alleviating the Christians' condition.
Within Jerusalem, Coptic grievances regarding the Deir El-Sultan
monastery in the Old City tried to elicit Israeli intervention against
competing claims for religious primacy raised by the Ethiopian church.
Yet Israel's delicate relationship with the Ethiopians, particularly in
light of the precarious position of Jewish Falashas in their country, complicated satisfying Copt demands.[50] The Camp David Treaty between
Israel and Egypt, however, could assist the Copts in their struggle in
Jerusalem as Israeli sensitivity to good ties with the Egyptians redounds
to the benefit of the Copts.

However, Israel's linkage with the Copts can assume a much larger
strategic purpose. It is presumed that the Copts hoped Israel would not
only defeat Egypt in the 1967 and 1973 wars but enter Egypt and "liberate the Copts." But this was not to be. Squeezed between irreducible
Arabism and fundamentalist Islam, the Copts might still see their interests supported by Israel. Any strengthening of the Copt community
or solidarity with it minimally by Israel's highlighting minority mistreat-
ment at the hands of the Egyptian Muslims could undermine Cairo's international status and somewhat divert its attention from the Arab-
Israeli conflict. It was hoped that the Camp David Treaty would remove
Egypt, at least partially, from its pivotal role in that conflict. A more
ideologically sedate Egypt, one more preoccupied with domestic Egyptian affairs, might offer a more congenial environment for the Copts. In
this regard, the normalization of Israeli-Egyptian relations could help
ease the Christians' condition in their ancient land.

Armenians

The home of Abraham the patriarch in Ur, in the vicinity of the
Euphrates River in upper Mesopotamia, could indicate a relationship
between the ancient Hebrew people and the ancient Armenian people.
Jews were living in Armenia itself, probably from the time of the Ten
Lost Tribes, certainly from the era of Tigranes' reign in Armenia. Jewish
origins for certain Armenian groups has been suggested. The Bagratid
dynasty at Ani claimed descent from Kings David and Solomon of
Israel.[51] Some Armenian feudal families from the fifth century have also
been considered of Jewish origin.[52]

This kind of possible ethnic mixing can explain some fascinating phenomena. One point is the physiognomic similarity suggested between Jews and Armenians, as when Cairo dispatched an Egyptian spy of Armenian origin to Israel in the guise of an immigrant Jew.[53] Another point is the widespread use of Hebrew names among Armenians, like Israel Ori (Israel my light), the sixteenth-century self-styled liberator of the Armenian people. An Armenian merchant in Trebizon in the eighteenth century was named Nigoghos Israelian.[54]

The modern connection between the two peoples is rooted in their hopes and tragedies of the twentieth century. Both peoples suffered terrible losses in modern times: the Armenian genocide in 1915–1916 and the Jewish Holocaust during the Second World War. Statelessness and weakness could have led to disappearance. The Jews bounced back, as it were, and established Israel. The Armenians survived but were unable to found a state or even remain in their historical homeland. Gideon Rafael, a former Israeli ambassador, had visited the Armenian Soviet Republic in 1967 and in Erevan felt himself moved by "the bonds of spirit and tragic experience" in Jewish and Armenian national history.[55] It was symptomatic of these bonds that Israel rushed medical and technical assistance to Soviet Armenia after the catastrophic damage caused by the earthquake there in December 1988.

The rise of Armenian terrorism against Turkey in the 1970s intimated a recollection from recent Zionist history. Some Jews would not have appreciated the analogy, but in the view of Kevork Donabedian, editor of the *Armenian Weekly* in Boston, the comparison was a compliment. As he said, "Maybe the terrorism will work. It worked for the Jews. They have Israel."[56] The Zionist tale of return and struggle could only be a great source of inspiration and admiration in Armenian eyes. Archbishop Shahe Ajamian in the Old City of Jerusalem considered Israel a sign of hope that one day the Armenians too would return to their land.[57] Of all the churches in East Jerusalem following Israel's incorporation of the city in June 1967, only the Armenian Orthodox church instituted Hebrew lessons and showed signs of accommodation with the new situation.[58]

Yet no sign of high-level strategic interaction was apparent in the contemporary Israeli-Armenian relationship. Renewing an ancient alliance, like that between King Asa of Judea and his Armenian counterpart, still awaits more propitious historical circumstances. The fact that Turkey maintained diplomatic ties with Israel prevented explicit Jewish identification with the Armenian cause. A moral conscience solicited sympathy for the Armenians, yet a realpolitik Israeli calculus demanded cultivation of a rare opportunity for normalcy with a Muslim state.

Any deterioration in Israeli-Turkish ties, however, could awaken interest in endeavoring to consolidate ties between Israel and the

Armenians. A similar image of human enterprise and literacy, of national tragedy and resilience, could build a relationship between the Jewish people and the Armenian people facing an Islamic-dominated Middle East.

Assyrians

The land of the Chaldeans, or Assyrians, was the birthplace of Abraham the patriarch at the beginning of Hebrew history, and Israel and Assyria (Ashur) are combined in a prophetic vision of unity for the end of history.[59] In the interim, Jewish-Assyrian relations were mixed and changing. Shalmanesser, the king of Assyria, conquered Samaria, the northern Israelite kingdom in 722 B.C., exiled its Hebrew inhabitants, and peopled the country with Samaritans instead. Ten tribes were brought to northern Mesopotamia, destined to return to Eretz-Israel from Assyria at the time of the final Jewish redemption.[60]

The similarity between the Hebrew language and the Aramaic (or Syriac) language of the Assyrians is an important link between the two Semitic peoples. The alleged origin of the Nestorians from the Ten Lost Tribes is also an intriguing tie between them. Biblical names, claims of Jewish ancestry, abhorrence of idolatry, and additional signs attest to a substantive legend of Jewish origins.[61] Conversion to Christianity according to this theory was not a flight from Jewish identity, only an abandonment of Jewish observance.

The Assyrian population in Iraq is subject to discrimination under the Arab-Muslim Baghdad regime. Any Israeli-Assyrian cooperation against the common adversary would be consistent with their respective objective interests. In Iraq both Kurds and Assyrians are natural partners to support any Israeli strategy focused on weakening the regime's ability to play an active role in the Arab-Israeli conflict.

Maronites

The biblical alliance between King Solomon of Israel and Hiram, king of Tyre (Tzur), is the historical precedent for friendship between the Jewish people and the people of Lebanon.[62] The fact that a spiritual purpose — the building of the Temple in Jerusalem — was the ostensible motive for cooperation conjures up the idea that a strategic Israeli-Lebanese partnership is not, and need not be, a result of shared national interests alone. A touch of intimacy and trust informs this relationship on the eastern Mediterranean coast from the days of old until the twentieth century.

By the First World War at the latest, Maronite Christians in Lebanon looked to Zionism as an inspiring model for national rejuvenation and for assistance.[63] In March 1920, Yehoshua Hankin, representing the Zionist Organization, signed a pact with some Maronite activists. In 1937, Dr. Chaim Weizmann met with President Emile Eddé in Paris, and they congratulated each other on their respective efforts to secure independence for small minority Mideastern peoples against the forces of Arab Islam. This meeting had been preceded by Jewish-Maronite contacts, deliberations on Zionist economic assistance to Lebanon, plans for Jewish tourism, and an agreement for joint security measures against extreme Palestinian Arab elements. During his conversation with Weizmann, Eddé did not refrain from expressing the hope that the future Jewish state's "first international friendship treaty be with its good neighbor, Lebanon!"[64]

Ben-Gurion recognized a shared fate for the Lebanese and the Jews in the region and spoke of the benefit that a Jewish state would bring to the Christians in Lebanon.[65] Archbishop Ignatz Mubarak of Beirut gave pro–Zionist testimony before the Anglo-American Commission of Inquiry in 1946. He later explicitly advocated an alliance with the Jewish state when he testified before the UNSCOP commission that examined the political future of Palestine in 1947. The outlines of Israeli-Lebanese friendship seemed mutually attractive and feasible well before the May 1948 founding of the Jewish state.

The manipulation of Lebanon's weakness and uniqueness became a key strategic calculation in Israeli foreign-policy thinking. Mordechai Ben-Tov, a leader of the Mapam socialist party, actually suggested in late 1948 that the IDF go up to Beirut, establish a Maronite-Christian government, and make peace with it.[66] Ben-Gurion, both prime minister and defense minister during the early years of Israel's history, was the driving force in favor of an interventionist policy toward Lebanon. Ties with non–Arab Mideastern groups and countries were in general Ben-Gurion's approach to regional alliance building. Specifically, he believed, as opposed to the orientation of Foreign Minister Moshe Sharett, that a minorities strategy could pay greater political dividends than a futile search for peace with the Arab Muslims.

In early 1954, Ben-Gurion advocated awakening the Maronites to proclaim Lebanon a Christian state. Sharett, then prime minister, considered this idea "a vain dream."[67] The following year, Ben-Gurion returned to the same subject, believing that an Iraqi threat poised against Syria necessitated Israeli action into Lebanon. Israel's army chief of staff, Moshe Dayan, supported Ben-Gurion, adding that a loyalist Lebanese military officer with IDF assistance would be adequate to bring about the crystallization of the Christian-Maronite element in the Lebanese entity.[68] When the Nasserite insurrection in Lebanon in 1958 verged on the radical Arabization of the country and the loss of its unique Christian and Western character, President Camille

Chamoun sought ties with Israel as a political and strategic counter-balance.

Noteworthy throughout this historical period was the close relationship maintained between the small Jewish community in Beirut and the Maronite population in Lebanon. Business ties and social intercourse characterized this relationship. The Maccabee Jewish youth organization joined with the Kata'ib (phalangist) forces to provide paramilitary training for its members.[69] In this fashion too, local Jews served as liaison between the Israelis and the Maronite Christians.

Israeli ties with the Christian population, both the phalangists in the heart of Lebanon and the forces of Major Sa'ad Haddad in the south of Lebanon, intensified considerably in the 1970s. From the start of the Lebanese civil war particularly and until 1982, Israel developed a multifaceted aid policy to the Christians. Military equipment and training; the "good fence" border that offered medical, agricultural, and employment services; the deepening of personal encounters between the Christians in the South and Israel, were all part of a de facto alliance between the two sides. Israel's role was significant to offset and partially neutralize the impact of PLO and Syrian activities within the country.

The Maronite-led phalangist militia most expressed the Lebanese desire for close ties with Israel. Pierre Jemayel, its founder, was pro–Israel in his personal sentiments. His son Bashir, who headed the phalangists and was later elected president of Lebanon, was known for his intimate association with Israel. The "war for peace in the Galilee" in June 1982 was welcomed (and encouraged) by Bashir, seen by him as a prelude to turning Lebanon into a more singular Christian entity. Fady Frem, who succeeded Bashir as commander of the phalangists (known more broadly as the Lebanese Forces), was explicit in calling for normal relations with Israel that could neutralize Syrian pressure on Lebanon.[70] Samir Geagea and Eli Hubeikah were two other key phalangist figures who advocated working closely together with Israel. They had a hand in fostering the relationship during the 1970s and early 1980s. Without Israeli assistance, the Maronites felt abandoned and unable to contend in the radically new Lebanese situation that formed in the late 1960s with the PLO's entry into the country and Syria's growing entrenchment within it.

The May 17, 1983, Israel-Lebanese Agreement appeared to fulfill at least part of Emile Eddé's wish expressed in 1937. This agreement, though not a friendship treaty as such, elevated the level of intended cooperation between the two countries. However the test of the agreement was not in its formulation but its execution. Syria was determined to prevent its effective implementation and compellingly prevailed upon the Lebanese Parliament to abrogate the agreement soon after it was signed.

Israel's basis of involvement in Lebanese affairs thereafter remained in support extended to the Southern Lebanese Army (SLA), a small military force working in coordination with the IDF to secure southern Lebanese territory from terrorist incursion by PLO and Shiite forces. The SLA could also be seen as a symbolic Lebanese barrier between Israeli military units in the South and Syrian units in the Bekaa Valley to the northeast.

The dream of consolidating a comprehensive Maronite-Jewish alliance in this century foundered on the shifting political sands of Lebanese politics and on the divisions and dilemmas that have hampered a forthright Israeli foreign policy. Shared sentiments were insufficient to unite the two sides so long as the requisite strategic wherewithal and political will were lacking. Certainly this most sanguine of Israel's minority relationships does not (considering its results, perhaps its denouement) augur success for long-term Jewish efforts in this direction.

Sudanese Christians

A mythological Jewish presence to the north of Sudan in Nubia and to the east in Ethiopia does not indicate any notion of interaction with the Christians in the South. A historical reference to a King David of Nubia in the thirteenth century, even with a Star of David emblem represented on the royal Nubian crown,[71] does not at all prove Jewish involvement. Likewise, the Ethiopian monarchy's claim to be based on the Solomonic dynasty, while derived from a legend with a biblical source, can only be judged circumstantial evidence of a direct Jewish role.

A more substantiated link relates to Israeli military assistance for the Anya Nya guerrilla forces, apparently beginning in or around 1967 and continuing into the 1970s at the very least. Using bases in neighboring countries, Uganda for a while and probably Ethiopia too, Israeli officers allegedly advised and helped train the Christian-led army of resistance. Heavy machine guns and old mines were sent to southern Sudan to fight the central government, whose involvement in the Arab-Israeli conflict had increased after the Six-Day War.[72] The Arab summit meeting in Khartoum in August 1967 enunciated the famous Three No's, in opposition to negotiations, recognition, and peace with Israel. Sudanese military units joined Egyptian forces on the post–1967 line along the Suez Canal facing the Israeli Army.

Thereby, Israel's aid to the southern Sudanese Anya Nya fighters fits the old Mideastern rationale of "the enemy of my enemy is my friend." Certainly the path of the Nile River through southern Sudan on its way to Egypt can make for fascinating scenarios of Israeli-Christian collaboration to disrupt or manipulate the flow of water to Egypt. A state of war between Israel and Egypt, unlike the peace inaugurated by the Camp David Accords, could catalyze Israel's role in the southern Sudanese struggle and make it a most critical dimension for the Arab-Israeli conflict and for the future of Sudan.

In any case, reports emanating from the National Islamic Front of Sudan in late 1988 spoke of Israeli weapons being transported to the SPLA forces in southern Sudan. A further report from December in *The Middle East Insider* related both Israeli and British assistance to the rebels, indeed the role of the Israeli Mossad security services and the death of one of its agents in southern Sudan. Israeli Foreign Minister Moshe Arens was reported to have met secretly with John Garang on the Sudanese-Ethiopian border in January 1989, additional evidence of strategic ties between the SPLA and the Jews. Yet a year later Prime Minister Yitzhak Shamir denied that Israel was providing weaponry to the Christians in southern Sudan.

Since 1977, Falasha Jews from the Ethiopian region of Gondar have traveled through Sudan en route to freedom in Israel. Apparently the Numeiri regime in Khartoum played a helpful role in assisting this "Operation Moses."[73] It would be interesting to conjecture that Sudanese Christians also contributed to the Jewish rescue mission in gratitude for Israel's contribution to the Christian-led liberation war in the South.

Conclusion

The pivotal place of the Jews and Israel in relation to the minority peoples is a testament of political significance and strategic potential. Most of all, this theme elevates Zionism to a broader plane of regional and historical significance. The Jewish Return is a national event but also a development of "international" importance. The Jews stand in relation to other minorities as possible genetic forebears, as spiritual guides, political mentors, and military allies. Thus far, however, any semblance of a minority strategy in Israeli regional policy-making has not proven very fruitful; in the case of cooperation with the Kurds and the Maronites, visions of success for all concerned receded before the formidable realities of Iraqi and Syrian perseverance, respectively.

Meanwhile, the minorities in relation to the Jews and Israel offer a welcome ethnic diversification of the Middle East and the Arab world, presenting a human mosaic of peoples among whom Jews can enjoy normalcy and acceptability. They can also induce Israel to reflect on reconceptualizing its basic foreign-policy orientation, away from singular peace with the Arabs toward diversified collaboration with the minorities. Perhaps neither choice is exceptionally feasible, which is but another way of formulating a dilemma while recognizing an opportunity.

CHAPTER 14

Conclusions

Arnold Toynbee, writing in 1925, believed that "apart from the Zionist experiment in Palestine, the general tendency in the Islamic World at this time was for minorities to disappear."[1] States certainly had the upper hand against tribes, political organization and authoritarian centralization being the modern stuff for assuring ethnic repression and minority defeat.

Blacks in Sudan and 'Alawites in Syria had historically known conditions of slavery. The Berbers had been maligned as primitive, and Jews were likened to dogs. Kabyle Berbers were targets of Arabization in the twentieth century, the Copts victims of harsh discriminatory measures. Through the decades, the Armenians were massacred, the Kurds expelled, the Assyrians butchered, the Maronites intimidated, and the Jews subjugated to intense and permanent warfare. All Christian minorities suffered defeats in the Middle East and Africa in modern times. It was in fact a marvel that Eastern Christians since the Islamic conquests "should have survived at all," D. S. Margoliouth concluded in 1914.[2]

However, by the end of the twentieth century, it was not obvious that the marvel had continued through the century or would last for much longer. Processes of deportation and dilution portended ill for Christian and for Muslim minorities, for as Toynbee accurately commented, "The general tendency in the Islamic World . . . was for minorities to disappear." It might be said that Kurds were most decidedly more of a distinct people than the Kuwaitis, yet Kuwait existed as a state, but Kurdistan did not.

Yet the very survival of the minorities over the ages is proof of earthy vitality and adjustment to debilitating circumstances. Many found roles to play, often to the benefit of the majority Muslim power. Ninth-century Kurds in Baghdad served as mercenaries for the Arab

254

caliph, while Kurd tribesmen defended the Abbasid caliphate against the Khwarizmshah threat in 1217.[3] Meanwhile, Berbers defended the Fatimid dynasty in Cairo in the eleventh century. Maronite Christians played a critical function in fostering the literary and political beginnings for modern Arab nationalism; Baluch soldiers offered their military skills to the Omani regime, as did the Berbers to the Moroccan throne.

While the minorities generally failed to establish their own native states, they were pivotal in the foundation of many Arab countries during bitter struggles for political freedom. History records the role of the Druzes for Syrian independence, Maronites for Lebanese independence, Kabyles for Algerian independence, and Copts for Egyptian independence. This record itself suggests how minority skills were exploited by Arab Muslim political campaigns for the freedom that the minorities would not enjoy. In this spirit, the Arabs would probably not be offended if Jews functioned as an economic elite in the region in return for dismantling the state of Israel. The Mideast minorities had a long history of contributing to Arab Muslim society in the past without deranging normative relations of power.

This particular minority role is an instance of a broader minority experience. Almost by definition, a minority lives a marginal existence in opposition to the fullness, or potential fullness, of the life of a majority people. Unable to achieve all its aspirations because of a deficiency of resources and opportunities, the minority lives in a world of discontinuous experiences. Success in one area cannot be repeated in other areas; the minority must find its niche, an opening to exploit, but not the gateway toward completeness. In this fractured reality alternative avenues must be reckoned and difficult choices made. Not everything can be done or won. The minority suffers from incoherence, extracting its victories and yet accommodating to deprivation that cannot be totally eliminated.

In the Middle East, minority survival was never equivalent to minority power holding. Elemental existence was ensured by the exertion of collective will to preserve the ethnic, cultural, and historic specificity of each minority group. Primitive strength, inwardness, and separateness were key ingredients always. Political horizons were limited, but tactical agility was impressive.

The mountain hearth, so prevalent a factor in our comparative survey of Mideastern minorities, was definitely a central component in their survival kit. Hisham Sharabi wrote:

> The rugged highlands and mountain regions — the Rif and High and Middle Atlas in Morocco, the Aurès and Kabyle in Algeria, the Lebanon and Anti–Lebanon in Lebanon and Syria, the Jabal al-Druze in

Syria, the Kurdish mountains in Iraq . . . are the home of linguistic, religious, or ethnic minorities.[4]

The historical pattern of mountain settlement smacked of a compelling Middle Eastern rationale in light of Ibn Khaldun's characterization of Arab (Bedouin) warfare: "Tribes that are protected against [the Arabs] by inaccessible mountains," he wrote, "are safe from their mischief and destructiveness. The Arabs would not cross hills or undergo hardship and danger in order to get to them."[5] Ibn Khaldun added that flat territory falls victim to Arab attack because it is indeed easily accessible to them.[6] Montesquieu adopted the same theme in affirming that mountain districts preserve liberty; they are attacked only with severe difficulty. Mountain peoples, in fact, enjoy no more valuable possession than their liberty.[7] Montesquieu's environmental explanation of human and political characteristics and behavior is a fitting commentary on the old Mideastern peoples, lodged in mountains and warriorlike, committed to a military ethos and convinced that lacking one is a recipe for defeat or destruction.

Israel might prudently reflect on the mountain factor in considering policy toward Judea and Samaria. The Levantine flavor of life in the Tel Aviv metropolis is in sharp contrast to the organic hardiness of life in the mountains to the east. The obvious topographic dimensions of Judea and Samaria require study, on the model of Druze, 'Alawite, Berber, or Maronite mountain fastnesses as relatively secure settlement zones, and the spirit of mountain life as a molder of primitive national strength and educator of patriotic sentiments should also be borne in mind. Without the mountains, Israel may lose touch with its historical past and lose the territorial integrity necessary for its contemporary strategic welfare.

The Elusiveness of Political Rule: A Comparison

The typical structure of minority societies was conducive to radical libertinism that boarded on anarchy, failing often to provide the spring for cohesive unity in feeling and action. It has been shown that segmentation and fragmentation denote group organizational patterns from the Berbers in the West to the Baluch in the East. Tribalism was a principle of localism and traditionalism, antagonistic to national consolidation. Disunited tribal society among 'Alawites and Kurds, among other minorities, illustrated that the very notion of political rule was markedly absent.

The twin principles of rule and hierarchy have, in contrast, characterized mainstream orthodox Islam from its beginnings. While the idea of equality was intended to foster fraternity among all Muslim believers, true equality was never achieved.[8] Authoritarianism predominated, in particular exercised by Arabs over non–Arabs in Islam's early history. Moreover, hierarchical structures have been paramount throughout Arab society—in the family, in male-female relations, and most clearly in the political arena between rulers and the ruled.[9] This may explain the plethora of dictatorial and tyrannical Arab regimes in modern Mideastern politics.

And yet these kinds of regimes, resting on the widespread principle of hierarchical relationships in Islam and Arab society, are the quintessence of the standard of rule. Ruling comes naturally to the Arabs, veritably "born to power" D. G. Hogarth once wrote. Relegating equality to the anthropological plane of mankind's oneness under God, the Arabs then get on with the political business of exercising authority over others.

Primitive tribalistic strength among the minorities did little to generate national consolidation for more extensive political endeavors. Historically, the Jewish people went from tribalism to nationalism; in modern times, too, they succeeded in transcending the plurality of pseudo-ethnic differences due to dispersion and consolidated unity in Israel. Others, like the Baluch, Berbers, and 'Alawites, still struggle with the impediment of segmented tribalism. Nationalism is still an elusive goal on the march to an effective political struggle for independent statehood.

However, even in the Israeli case, the Jews convey an uncomfortable posture toward the vocation of ruling. The Zionist approach to relations with the Arabs of Palestine was that of "nondomination" alongside the drive toward Jewish statehood. This orientation continued after 1948 when the Israeli authorities permitted Arab citizens to cultivate their own collective identity with relative freedom. It was the democratic regime in Israel, of course, that most pertinently highlighted the egalitarian principle.

Indeed, democratic regimes are not based on hierarchical rule but on principles of individual and group freedom, as well as sharing power. Perhaps most demonstrative of Israel's mind-set was Prime Minister Begin's offer of Arab autonomy for Judea, Samaria, and Gaza, a formula that made explicit a political philosophy of nonrule in Jewish-Arab relations. This approach was consistent with labor socialism and liberal egalitarianism—the two major ideological banners of Left and Right from Zionist days.

Nietzsche had considered all forms and expressions of nonrule merely as a cover for exhaustion and a loss of will. The real ill, he declared, is "the most decided conviction that the lust to rule is the greatest vice."[10] In Israel, ruling as such, certainly any lusting for it, is politically out of bounds, a sin against the democratic ethos and a tainting of secular Zionism's moralistic self-image.

The normative principle and practice of ruling in orthodox Islam has been an imposition on minority freedom and dignity. But even when minorities attain predominant power in their lands, they refuse to exercise rule or do so awkwardly, even shamefacedly. Examples are striking regarding the Jews of Israel and the Maronites in Lebanon. Neither people demonstrated a willingness or capacity to deal with Muslims in its country according to a clear-cut ruler-ruled relationship. Each country adopted democratic institutions, and remarkable is the fact that the only two democratic countries in the Middle East were the two non–Muslim political regimes in Israel and Lebanon.

Democracy fosters notions of equality and tolerance, pluralism and liberty. The fact that democracy sprouted in Israel and Lebanon in particular, headed by a Jewish and a Christian people, respectively, says much about nonruling as normative for the historical regional minorities. For the Muslim Arabs, to rule is natural, and to be ruled is unnatural, but ruling for these minorities is unnatural, while being ruled, it seems, is natural. Israel's Labor Party leader Shimon Peres was wont to state that it would be satisfactory that Jews live under Arab rule, were Israel to withdraw from Judea and Samaria.

If the democratic spirit of segmentation hinders unified forthright national self-rule, then ruling others will certainly be a political nonstarter. This endemic feature is a veritable minority syndrome that even Jewish and Christian independence in the twentieth century did not overcome. So while minorities may survive, they do not easily exercise authoritative power in general and over Muslims in particular. This may put into doubt their long-term ability to survive, minimally their ability to maintain statehood in the Mideast.

Note, in contrast, the 'Alawite-led regime in Syria where the ruling principle was practiced by a minority people. But the 'Alawites are pseudo–Muslims, not politically alien to the notion of rule as are Jews and Christians. It was the 'Alawites, since 1970 especially, who demonstrated a determination and capacity to rule Sunni Muslims and even brutally repress them. Being closer to Islam and Arab political culture, 'Alawites succeeded where Jews and Maronites appeared on the verge of failure.

Arab dissatisfaction in Israel became widespread and violent during the 1980s; any thought of an Israeli policy of repression was problematic in light of its fundamentally liberal and legalistic democratic system. Muslim dissatisfaction in Lebanon likewise became widespread and violent during the 1970s and 1980s. The Maronites had cultivated a confessional political balance since the country's inception. Not having ruled in the past, the Maronites were then unable to handle the massive

Islamic and Palestinian upsurge challenging Christian predominance and the country's stability.

The Jewish and Christian democratic regimes were under extreme pressure, while the 'Alawite authoritarian regime held its ground against its domestic opponents. Ruling was apparently the answer, but the Jews and the Christians proved neither particularly comfortable with the idea of it nor adept in applying it. Liberty was a fundamental value in their societies, but without rule, it can be lost.

Minority Mobilization and the Crusader Case

Beyond the questions of minority survival and power lay the question of nationalist mobilization for independence as such. The appropriate formula for liberty seemed to be a combination of rural rootedness, with all it contributes to group strength, and urban modernism, with its apparatus of skills and resources. Why some peoples engaged at all in an awakening stage and endeavored to achieve independence is based on the presence or absence of this combination. Collectives like the Berbers and the Baluch, the Druzes and the Kurds, remained primarily rural-based agricultural communities. The catalyzing life of the city, with its economic enticements, educational opportunities, and cultural amenities, was significantly foreign to them. Their lives took the form of cyclical organic experiences, based on the seasons and the working of the land. The qualitative jump to recognizing their freedom to change history was beyond them. The world was a static and closed system. They could survive but could not do more than that.

However, minorities whose lives interacted with the modern urban nexus came alive with an energizing awareness of history's possibilities. The Jews in Europe learned of other peoples' independence movements. The Maronites were familiar with the ideas of liberty, and France was their model and mentor. Even the 'Alawites at a certain point began to leave the mountain and experience city life, in Lattakia, Damascus, or elsewhere. The same was true for the Kabyles of Algeria.

In these cases political consciousness riveted to nationalist stirrings was apparent. The political passivity often associated with farmers and peasants was joined here to the self-consciousness of workers, entrepreneurs, and intellectuals. This combination was the secret to Zionism and explains why it succeeded. Kibbutz idealism coalesced with urban sophistication—a Yitzhak Tabenkin and a Moshe Sharett—to help form an effective independence movement. One without the other is a recipe for failure. But the two ingredients together offer a basis for minority struggle in the modern era. The rugged mountain hinterland producing primitive fighting strength is not sufficient on its own. Neither are the city environment and modern bourgeois skills, as in the case of the Copts, a sufficient foundation for minority political freedom. Optimal circumstances call for the two factors working in tandem.

It is noteworthy that commercial civilizations in themselves cannot necessarily contend effectively against warlike civilizations in conflict situations. The finesse of the commercial domain tends to dissolve the hard virtues required for physical endeavors. At the same time, a martial ethos does not easily cohere with a political talent for negotiating a liberation struggle toward nationalist victory. The two basic modern minority successes, that of the Jews and the Maronites, combined rural military virtues with urban political sophistication. No other regional minority was able to put this kind of national game plan into operation.

The interesting historical case of the Christian Crusaders, one that Arab propaganda believes to be a precedent for Jewish Zionism, is worth recalling here. The Latin Kingdom was, to begin with, more a religiously motivated crusade than a national liberation movement. Most of its primary strategic bases were on the coast of Palestine and Syria, from Gaza to Tripoli. But the Christians failed to expand eastward into the mountains of the country, even though they did prove to be a conquering minority power in an alien land.

Truly effective Crusader rule occurred nonetheless only on the coast. Acco (Acre) for a time was its capital and its last stronghold, falling in 1291. Christian military orders and a doctrine of chivalry were important ingredients in Crusader success, but a weak demographic base and few roots in the countryside were the Achilles' heel of the entire enterprise. As an appendage of Europe in the East, the Crusader kingdom could not survive.[11] Whatever else explains its demise, its disinterest in actually ruling the Muslims is a stark factor. The Italians were interested in commerce, and the Crusaders generally were interested in religion, honor, and leisure. Farming was anathema to these European nobles. They fared well for a time in implanting a Christian population in a distant land but without ever truly ruling the land and its hostile population.

The Arabs introduce the image of Israel as a European colonial implantation in Palestine to imply its eventual collapse and destruction. Interestingly, the Crusader case is highly consistent with our findings regarding Middle Eastern minorities. The lack of a firm mountain base for the Latin Kingdom was an unresolved impediment to strategic integrity. We have noted that the mountain variable is critical for minority survival. The absence of a hierarchical ruling principle in the Latin Kingdom weakened the Christian hold over Palestine. We have suggested that the development of formidable Arab-Palestinian internal opposition to Zionism is consistent with the absence of a fixed hierarchical ruling principle in Israel. The Crusader tale was a dramatic adventure without ever really becoming an entrenched political project. The ultimate destiny of the Jewish state will provide insight into the extent to which the Crusader case is a precedent for modern Israel.

Commenting on Crusader history invites reflection on the possibility for Christian rejuvenation in the Middle East. Signs of strength and renewal are few, though the variety and persistence of Christian minorities is still an impressive fact, indigenous, as in the Assyrian, Copt, and Maronite cases, and provides the modern Christian efforts with stronger roots than their European cohorts centuries ago.

Minority Particularity and the Israeli Case

Minority survival has often required separateness rather than integration as a way of realistically facing the Islamic or Arab challenge. Fostering particularity derived from a religious culture that led the minority to refrain from intense contact or geographic proximity with the larger Arab-Muslim community. Yet hopes for a national awakening are linked to interaction with other groups and usually in urban settings. There, a leveling and homogenizing ethos enwraps all peoples in a tight socioeconomic, sometimes linguistic, grid of intense contact. Particularity can be eroded, though it can be enhanced through the very contact newly experienced. It is the very breakdown of native group structures and norms — like family, religion, perhaps language — that can lead to secularism and eventually loss of particularist identity. Assimilation is the danger at the end of the modernist path minorities often travel.

The Zionist case is especially pertinent regarding the tension between modernism and traditionalism. For it was the veritable crushing of traditional values like religion and family that paved the way to erecting new social structures for national rebirth on secular foundations. Yet a virtue excessively applied can become a vice. Zionism's remarkable success can prepare the way for its ultimate failure. Older minority particularism, with the rhythms of the past resonating through the soul and society, cannot be compensated for by modern integration. At most, the modern urge to overcome separateness by embracing contact with other groups can supplement the resources and raise the horizon of an old community. But embracing others at the price of self-alienation may be a formula for losing the poise of autonomous group existence. In other words, pure *existence* without unique *essence* is not a prudent prescription for long-term survival.

Israel, representing one minority victory, will have to reflect not only on the reasons for its success in 1948 but also on the requirements for continuing success in the future. Identifying the correct balance between modernism and traditionalism will therefore be high on the Jews' national agenda. Integration within the Arab-Muslim Mideast may seem a glittering political plum for the Zionist pariah. But it would be foolhardy to believe that it can be achieved without paying a formidable cultural price. Jewish particularity should be understood as the bedrock of Israel's survival and place in the Middle East rather than the last obstacle to be removed to ensure its survival and place in the region.[12]

With this in mind, we might appreciate the remarkable record of minority survival across the region, admittedly without independence and power yet demonstrating stubborn entrenchment. Particularism in all its manifestations remains the root of minority existence in the Muslim-Arab Mideast. Minorities have survived without having their own states, yet Israel, following a veritable assimilationist-integrationist orientation, may—in a political paradox—threaten its own Jewish survival in its own state.

Peoples and States Across the Region

Only some of the small regional peoples experienced what Deutsch called "the growth of nations" process. The Jews, Maronites, Kurds to a degree, perhaps the 'Alawites, certainly the Armenians historically, did pass through stages of collective consolidation and political maturation. In some cases, the signpost of tribalism was replaced by communalism (Berbers, Baluch), even to nationalism or pseudonationalism (Kurds, Armenians). Others were free of tribalism from the start, like Maronites, Copts, and Druzes, and this facilitated group cohesion and common political action of some kind.

It is clear that the Christian group had a notable historical headstart in developing their collective capacity, but subsequent events impeded their efficacy. The general phenomenon of fluidity in minority fate is striking, though the general improvement in minority cohesion is a slow line of progress through most of history. One basic conclusion, however, is that the Mideast is not visibly on the threshold of imminent political dissolution with an array of small peoples' states waiting in the wings.

It is ironic that many states in the world have a decidedly much briefer history and considerably inferior group credentials for political independence than many of the region's peoples. Andorra and Lichtenstein as partial sovereignties, the Seychelles and Western Samoa as tiny countries, nonetheless dot the international map. Kalat is not the capital of a Free Baluchistan, nor is Juba the capital of a Free Christian Nile

State. Suwayda is not the capital of a Druze state, nor is Lattakia, for that matter, a capital of an independent 'Alawite entity. Sulaimaniyah is not the capital of a Free Kurdistan, nor is Asyut the capital of a Christian Copt state.

The paramount realities across the Middle East are those of Islam and Arabism, and they hinder minority statehood as permanent obstacles in the political arena. But beyond these external dimensions, internal dimensions also explain the minority predicament over time. The "growth of nations" is a challenge far different from, though connected with, the elemental challenge of physical survival.

As such, multiethnic states are the political norm throughout the region. Such a situation is highly problematic for internal unity; pluralism and diversity in the realm of religion, as in Egypt, or ethnicity, as in Iraq, are the root of grievous conflicts and tensions among different communities. Actonian liberal hopes for intercommunal symbiosis and cross-cultural fertilization are only dimly recognized. In most countries a permanent confrontation persists between the pole of group allegiance and the pole of territorial loyalty. The dilemma is often resolved by state coercion and intimidation at the expense of the vulnerable minorities. Minority unrest, as by Armenians in Turkey and Baluch in Pakistan, unleashed the sword of repression by the majority ruling people.

No sign exists for basic changes in this regard across the Middle East. Aristotle formulated the problem in *The Politics* when he wrote about causes for strife:

> Then there is difference of race or nation, which remains a source of dissension until such times as the two groups learn to live together. This may be a long process . . . civil strife is exceedingly common when the population includes an extraneous element. . . .

And meanwhile, repression and assimilation are offered as remedies, while equitable measures for integration, or secession, are nonexistent options that lie beyond the ken of feasible political alternatives.

While *majority-minority* relations are marred by tension and often by confrontation, *minority-minority* relations have no fixed pattern. There have been numerous instances where small Mideastern peoples conflicted rather than cooperated for common ends. Jews and Christians were in a state of mutual hostility in the early period of Christianity. Copts fulfilled the function of castrating blacks from the Sudan in the nineteenth century in preparing eunuchs to become slaves in Egypt, Syria, and Turkey. Kurds, either on their own volition or exploited by the Ottoman Empire for the purpose, were known to plunder and murder helpless Armenians. Kurds did much the same against

Assyrians. There were known periods of Maronite-Druze warfare, as in 1859–1860. On the surface, the following description does not seem exaggerated:

> The Druzes, the 'Alawites, the Metawalis [Shiites in Lebanon], the Armenians, the Shi'as, the various cultural divisions of the Sunnis— these groups tend to despise one another.[13]

But underneath all this typical Mideastern baggage of suspicion, even hatred, is a quiet minority feeling that a common disability of smallness and vulnerability should create a relationship of camaraderie and intimacy. In 1910, when the Kurds were being threatened by the Turks, the Shaikh of Barzan and his family took refuge with the Assyrians. Collaboration between the 'Alawite regime in Damascus with the Druzes in Lebanon is also an example of minority-minority ties. And Israel has served as a unifying force among some regional minority groups. Much in this regard depends upon whether a political conception will be articulated to juxtapose all the minorities against Arab-Muslim power generally, as well as Shiite-Persian power in Iran and Sunni-Muslim power in Turkey and Pakistan. This minority formulation could offer a working definition to organize the weak against the strong, the few against the many, the historic minority peoples against the Middle East state system. Even then, however, an effective degree of permanent minority-minority trust and cooperation would be required, and this has arisen only during passing episodes throughout the long history of the region.

The Middle East and the World

The role of foreign involvement in the minority issue reveals much about the connection between regional and global politics. Oriental Christian communities were generally highly interested in attracting European support to offset Muslim power in the East, even though missionaries were often equated with imperialism by the resident Muslims. Local minority communities found themselves awkwardly caught in a civilizational confrontation between Christianity and Islam, Europe against the Orient. It was in this same spirit that modern Arab nationalism perceived Zionism as an offshoot of European colonialism focused on Palestine. But the local Christians, like Maronites and Armenians, feared for their welfare if no foreign European assistance was available. In Egypt, where foreign support for Christians was nonexistent, Copt conversions to Islam were widespread for centuries.

Two sets of foreign powers can be identified and their respective roles delineated in the minority equation. The French had a historical proclivity to cultivate small esoteric peoples and did so rather diligently and often generously. Beneficiaries of the *mission civilisatrice* included Berbers, Druzes, 'Alawites, Copts, and Maronites. A curiosity with alien cultures and a desire to cultivate allegedly small "republican" peoples explained some of French policy.

But the English were largely antagonistic to Mideastern minorities. Examples include supporting Iraq in its repression of Kurdish and Assyrian struggles, and abandoning the Copts to Muslim hegemony in Egypt. There were instances of a contrary orientation, as when the British aided the Druzes in Lebanon and fostered Christianity in southern Sudan. But by and large, London allied with Sunni-Arab forces, hoping to establish a strategic alliance with them for British imperial purposes. The Arab Revolt phenomenon in 1916 is a famous case in point. The British turn away from Zionism early in the mandate period coincided with elevating Muslim Palestinian Arabs against the Jews. Hostility to Zionism from the 1920s was a link in a regional chain as the British tried to achieve their goals in concert with the dominant Muslim-Arab elements, not in opposition to them. The initiation of an Arab League in the 1940s was symptomatic of this orientation. Minorities were expendable in this broad strategic vision.

The United States became the political heir of British policy in the Middle East. Aside from transient support for minorities like the Kurds (early 1970s) and the Maronites (in 1958 and partially during the early 1980s), America has sought to develop regional influence via the existing regimes. Early in the twentieth century, U.S. policy went with the Turks and against the Armenians; late in the century, it went with Pakistan and, by implication, against the Baluch. Copt grievances did not gain a serious hearing from the American foreign-policy establishment, as fostering uncomplicated ties with Egypt was the uppermost priority. Even the American military campaign against Iraq in 1991 did nothing to elevate the victimized Kurds in the view of the Bush administration. Though American support for Israel has been large and generous, since 1967 in particular, it has been modulated not to estrange the dominant Arab-Muslim powers. Balancing that double goal has never been simple.

The Soviet Union, in comparison, has often stood on the side of small peoples' liberation struggles against existing state structures. At the very least, Russian rhetorical solidarity was vocal in support of the Kurds in the early 1960s; Mustafa Barzani himself had spent eleven years in exile in the land of communism. Soviet sympathies for the Baluch became part of a broad minority strategy to undermine pro–Western states like Pakistan and Iran (before the 1979 revolution). Not immaterial were the oil and coal of Baluchistan were it to become an independent country just to the south of the Soviet-Afghanistan border upon the collapse of Pakistan.

Likewise, the USSR has cultivated the 'Alawite minority since the early 1970s and served as a veritable guarantor of the regime thereafter. Soviet strategic calculations took into account the valuable port facilities provided by 'Alawite-led Syria for the Russian Navy. Let us not forget Soviet support for Zionism in the years 1947–1948 when Israel's birth received the blessing of Moscow. This Soviet orientation sought British expulsion from the region, and supporting the Jews was a price worth paying. Overall, then, paying lip service to the justice of national liberation struggles and providing them with some assistance converged with promoting Soviet interests in the Middle East as part of a grand strategy against the West. In this fashion, the USSR orchestrates its moves on the side of freedom, and the United States is on the side of status quo order mixed with repression.

Not all Mideast minorities are destined to become majorities or to have their own states. The twenty-first century may turn out to be as dominated by Arabism and Islam as the twentieth century. Some Arabs nonetheless continue to fear the destruction of the Arab world or the invalidation of its pervasive national concept, with the subsequent establishment of small sectarian states — Maronite, 'Alawite, Druze, and so on, in addition to the Jewish one.[14] A vision of historical Greater Syria, to be reconstituted as "a federation of cantons," would provide a return to the cultural diversity of Middle Eastern peoples longing for liberation from the yoke of new or artificial political states.[15] However, Arabism, Islam, and the state system appear sturdy, and ruthless enough when necessary to maintain their geopolitical post–Second World War status throughout the region. There may be little natural rhyme or reason in the configuration of nations to states in the Middle East, but the older indigenous minority peoples are not sufficient in themselves to overturn this reality.

There is a place, nonetheless, to recognize and publicize the condition of the minorities. Many have been engaged in courageous, perhaps futile, campaigns largely unknown to the world. The fighting and destruction in southern Sudan that began in 1955, the Kurdish liberation war from 1961, and the Baluch campaign from the 1970s are three examples of the news blackout and political disinterest that these minority questions have encountered. Even the Armenian genocide from 1915 was understood in all its tragedy only many decades later. The internationalization of Mideastern ethnic-religious conflicts serves to expose local events to a world audience.[16]

With an examination of the minority dimension in the Middle East from a historical and political perspective, other regional topics become elucidated from a new and fruitful vantage point. The minority prism sheds light on questions of Arab unity, the role of Islam, foreign penetration and superpower rivalry in the Mideast, resource allocation, and the Arab-Israeli conflict. It remains to be seen whether decay and dissolution will eliminate the small Middle Eastern peoples from contemporary regional affairs or vitality and recovery will characterize their fortunes.

Notes

Chapter 1

1. The figures are collated from *The Middle East and North Africa 1987,* London: Europa, 1987.

2. Ibn Khaldun, *The Muqaddimah: An Introduction to History,* tr. Franz Rosenthal, vol. I, Princeton University Press, 1967, pp. xxxiv, 18, 21, 23.

3. Carleton S. Coon, *Caravan: The Story of the Middle East,* New York: Henry Holt, 1951, p. 2.

4. Yosef Gotlieb, *Self-Determination in the Middle East,* New York: Praeger, 1982, p. 2.

5. Elie Kedourie, *England and the Middle East: The Destruction of the Ottoman Empire,* Sussex: Harvester Press, 1978, p. 86.

6. Maxime Rodinson, *The Arabs,* tr. Arthur Goldhammer, London: Croom Helm, 1981, pp. 44–45.

7. A. G. Horon, *The Land of Kedem: A Historical and Political Guide to the Near East* (Hebrew), Tel Aviv: Hermon, 1970, p. 22.

8. Coon, p. 158.

9. A. L. Tibawi, *Arabic and Islamic Themes,* London: Luzac & Co., 1976, pt. 1, ch. 7 and ch. 10; pt. 3, chs. 6–7.

10. Charles Issawi, "The Transformation of the Economic Position of the Millets in the Nineteenth Century," in Benjamin Braude and Bernard Lewis, eds., *Christians and Jews in the Ottoman Empire: The Functioning of a Plural Society,* vol. I, New York & London: Holmes & Meier, 1982, pp. 262–63.

11. Elie Kedourie, *Nationalism,* New York: Praeger, 1961, esp. ch. 4.

12. A good exposition on this is in F. H. Hinsley, *Nationalism and the International System,* London: Hodder & Stoughton, 1973, pt. 1.

13. Clifford Geertz, "The Integrative Revolution: Primordial Sentiments and Civil Politics in the New States," in Clifford Geertz, ed., *Old Societies and New States,* New York: Free Press, 1967, pp. 105–57.

14. John Stuart Mill, *Considerations on Representative Government,* Chicago: Henry Regnery, 1962, p. 314.

15. John Emerich Edward Dalberg Acton,"Nationality," in *Essays on Freedom and Power*, London: Thames & Hudson, 1956, pp. 160–61.

16. Alfred North Whitehead, *Science and the Modern World*, New York: Free Press, 1967, p. 207.

17. Benjamin Akzin, *State and Nation*, London: Hutchinson University Library, 1964, p. 23.

18. Myron Weiner, "The Macedonian Syndrome: An Historical Model of International Relations and Political Development," *World Politics*, 23, 4, July 1971, pp. 665–83.

19. William L. Shirer, *The Rise and Fall of the Third Reich*, Greenwich, Conn.: Fawcett, 1960, p. 523.

20. Walker Conner, "The Politics of Ethnonationalism," *Journal of International Affairs*, 27, 1, 1973, pp. 1–21.

21. Colin H. Williams, ed., *National Separatism*, Cardiff: University of Wales Press, 1982.

22. Myron Weiner, "Political and Social Integration: Forms and Strategies," in Eric A. Nordlinger, ed., *Politics and Society*, Englewood Cliffs, N.J.: Prentice-Hall, 1970, p. 201.

23. Gil Carl AlRoy, *Behind the Middle East Conflict: The Real Impasse Between Arab and Jew*, New York: G. P. Putnam's Sons, 1975, pp. 32–35, 157–58.

24. Karl W. Deutsch, *Tides Among Nations*, New York: Free Press, 1979, chs. 2–3.

25. Interesting analyses of this are in Jean Gottmann, ed., *Centre and Periphery: Spatial Variation in Politics*, Beverly Hills and London: Sage, 1980, esp. chs. 1–2.

26. Manfred W. Wenner, "The Arab/Muslim Presence in Medieval Central Europe,"*International Journal of Middle East Studies*, 12, 1980, p. 73.

27. Konstantin Symmons-Symonolewicz, *Nationalist Movements: A Comparative View*, Meadville, Pa: Maplewood Press, 1970, pp. 7, 26.

28. Drawn from José Ortega y Gasset, *The Revolt of the Masses*, New York: W. W. Norton & Co., 1957, pp. 150–56.

29. The seminal work on this is Karl W. Deutsch, *Nationalism and Social Communication: An Inquiry into the Foundations of Nationalism*, 2d ed., Cambridge, Mass.: The M.I.T. Press, 1967.

30. Rupert Emerson, *From Empire to Nation: The Rise to Self-Assertion of Asian and African Peoples*, Boston: Beacon Press, 1962, pp. 46–47. On Rokkan's view, see Gottmann, pp. 198–99.

31. Anthony H. Birch, "Minority Nationalist Movements and Theories of Political Integration," *World Politics*, 30, 3, April 1978, pp. 329–30.

32. Ted Robert Gurr, *Why Men Rebel*, Princeton, N.J.: Princeton University Press, 1971.

33. Crawford Young, *The Politics of Cultural Pluralism*, Madison, Wis.: The University of Wisconsin Press, 1976, pp. 461–69.

34. Lawrence Krader, *Formation of the State*, Englewood Cliffs, N.J.: Prentice-Hall, 1968.

35. Daniel Pipes, "How Important Is the PLO?" *Commentary*, April 1983, p. 19.

36. Crawford Young, p. 427.

37. Arnold J. Toynbee, *Survey of International Affairs 1925*, vol. I, London: Oxford University Press and Humphrey Milford, 1927, p. 389. See also Mordechai Nisan, "The PLO and the Palestinian Issue," *Middle East Review*, 18, 2, Winter 1985/86, pp. 52–61.

38. R. D. McLaurin, ed., *The Political Role of Minority Groups in the Middle East*, New York: Praeger, 1979, ch. 1.

39. Quoted in Elie Kedourie, *The Chatham House Version and Other Middle-Eastern Studies*, London: Weidenfeld & Nicholson, 1970, p. 374.

40. All quotations from Toynbee, pp. 126, 359, 548.

41. William L. Langer, *The Diplomacy of Imperialism 1890–1902*, 2d ed., New York: Alfred A. Knopf, 1968, pp. 159–64.

42. Kedourie, *The Chatham House Version and Other Middle-Eastern Studies*, p. 389.

43. A. Hourani, *Minorities in the Arab World*, London: Oxford University Press, 1947, pp. 109, 118, 122.

44. Edward W. Said, *The Question of Palestine*, London: Routledge & Kegan Paul, 1981, p. 146.

45. Coon, p. 157.

46. Moshe Zeltzer, "Minorities in Iraq and Syria," in Ailon Shiloh, ed., *Peoples and Cultures of the Middle East*, New York: Random House, 1969, p. 13.

47. Pierre Rondot, "Les Minorities en Orient: Danger des 'Solutions' Territoriales," *L'Afrique et l'Asie Modernes*, 107, 4e trimestre, 1975, p. 19.

48. AlRoy, pp. 157–58.

49. Eliezer Be'eri, *Army Officers in Arab Politics and Society*, Jerusalem: Israel Universities Press, 1969, pp. 480–81.

50. Kedourie, *England and the Middle East*, p. 226.

51. Michael C. Hudson, *Arab Politics: The Search for Legitimacy*, New Haven & London: Yale University Press, 1977, pp. 59, 66–68.

52. Abdel Rahim Omran, *Population in the Arab World: Problems and Prospects*, New York & London: United Nations Fund for Population Activities and Croom Helm, 1980, pp. 18, 23–24.

53. Kedourie, *The Chatham House Version*, ch. 11.

54. Jacques Berque, *The Arabs: Their History and Future*, London: Faber & Faber, 1964, p. 260.

55. Said al-Din Ibrahim, "The Orientation of Sociological Studies Towards Unity: Minorities in the Arab World" (Arabic), *Qadaya Arabiyya*, April–September 1976, pp. 5–24.

56. Mahmoud Ayoub, "Dhimmah in Qur'an and Hadith," *Arab Studies Quarterly*, 5, 2, 1983, pp. 172–82.

57. Daniel C. Dennett, Jr., *Conversion and the Poll Tax in Early Islam*, Cambridge: Harvard University Press, 1950, ch. 2, and C. E. Bosworth, "The Concept of *Dhimma* in Early Islam," in Braude and Lewis, vol. I, pp. 37–51.

58. Bat Ye'or, *Le Dhimmi*, Paris: Edition Anthropos, 1980, p. 255 (an English version was later published by Fairleigh Dickinson University Press in 1985).

59. Bernard Lewis, "The Pro–Islamic Jews," *Judaism*, 17, 4, 1968, p. 401.

60. *The Encyclopaedia of Islam*, new ed., vol. III, Leiden: E. J. Brill, 1965,

p. 180. Also Majid Khadduri, *The Islamic Law of Nations: Shaybani's Siyar,* Baltimore: The Johns Hopkins Press, 1966.

61. J. C. Hurewitz, *Diplomacy in the Near and Middle East,* vol. I, Princeton, N.J.: Van Nostrand, 1956, pp. 113–16, 149–53.

62. See Benjamin Braude, "Foundation Myths of the *Millet* System," in Braude and Lewis, vol. I, pp. 69–88.

63. Geertz, pp. 155–57.

64. Jose Casanova, "Legitimacy and the Sociology of Modernization," in Arthur J. Vidich and Ronald M. Glassman, eds., *Conflict and Control: Challenge to Legitimacy of Modern Governments,* Beverly Hills and London: Sage, 1979, pp. 219–52.

65. Fouad Ajami, *The Arab Predicament: Arab Political Thought and Practice Since 1967,* New York: Cambridge University Press, 1981, p. 192.

66. Arend Lijphart, "Consociational Democracy," *World Politics,* 21, 2, January 1969, pp. 207–25.

67. Eric A. Nordlinger, *Conflict Regulation in Divided Societies,* Occasional Papers in International Affairs, No. 29, January 1972, Harvard University, Center for International Affairs.

68. Deutsch, *Nationalism and Social Communication,* p. 186.

Chapter 2

1. Vera Beaudin Saeedpour, "Of Kurdish Spring and Our Own Discontented Winter," *Kurdish Times,* 1, 1, Spring 1986, p. 57.

2. Merhdad Izady, "The Question of an Ethnic Identity: Problems in the Historiography of Kurdish Migrations and Settlement," ibid., p. 18.

3. Quoted in *Kurdish Times,* 1, 2, Fall 1986, p. 64. Also William O. Douglas, *Strange Lands and Friendly People,* New York: Harper, 1951, p. 61.

4. C. J. Edmonds, *Kurds, Turks and Arabs: Politics, Travel, and Research in North Eastern Iraq 1919–1925,* London: Oxford University Press, 1957, pp. 204–05.

5. *Ibn Taimiyya on Public and Private Law in Islam,* tr. Omar A. Farrukh, Beirut: Khayats, 1966, p. 88. The above remark on Abu Muslim appears in Moshe Sharon, *Black Banners from the East,* Jerusalem: Magnes Press, Leiden: E. J. Brill, 1983, p. 204.

6. Arshak Safrastian, *Kurds and Kurdistan,* London: Harvill Press, the Hague: Mouton, 1948, ch. 3.

7. Hamilton Gibb, *The Life of Saladin, from the Works of Imad Ad-Din and Baba Ad-Din,* Oxford: Clarendon Press, 1973, especially p. 16.

8. Safrastian, ch. 4.

9. Kendal [Kurd], "Introduction, Les Kurdes sous l'Empire Ottoman," in Gerard Chaliand et al., *Les Kurds et le Kurdistan: La Question Nationale Kurde au Proche-Orient,* Paris: Françoise Maspero, 1978, pp. 31–68.

10. *The Treaties of Peace, 1919–1923,* vol. I, New York: Carnegie Endowment for International Peace, 1924, pp. 807–08.

11. Dana Adams Schmidt, *Journey Among Brave Men,* Boston: Little, Brown, 1964, pp. 54–57.

12. Kendal, "Le Kurdistan de Turquie," in Chaliand et al., pp. 66–153.

13. Jacob Robinson, *Were the Minorities Treaties a Failure?* New York: American Jewish Congress, 1943, pp. 36, 167, 203–4, 238.

14. Edmund Ghareeb, *The Kurdish Question in Iraq,* Syracuse, N.Y.: Syracuse University Press, 1981, pp. 29–34.

15. Edmonds, pp. 307, 365.

16. Archie Roosevelt, Jr., "La Republique Kurde de Mahabad," in Chaliand et al., 199–223.

17. Patrick Seale, *The Struggle for Syria: A Study of Post-War Arab Politics 1945–1958,* London: Oxford University Press, 1965, p. 62.

18. Chaliand, pp. 248–49.

19. Ghareeb, p. 68.

20. Martin Short and Anthony McDermott, *The Kurds,* report no. 23, London: Minority Rights Group, May 1981, esp. pp. 9–11.

21. Christopher S. Raj, "Iraq: Challenges to Saddam's Regime," *Foreign Affairs Reports,* 32, 2, February 1983, pp. 43–44 (Indian Council of World Affairs); also Chaliand et al., pp. 159–60.

22. Robert D. Kaplan, "Kurdish Guerrillas Continue Their Pressure," *The Wall Street Journal,* August 28, 1986.

23. Short and McDermitt, pt. 2.

24. William E. Hazen, "Minorities in Revolt: The Kurds of Iran, Iraq, Syria, and Turkey," in McLaurin, p. 65.

25. Short and McDermott, pp. 16–17.

26. Ghareeb, p. 181.

27. Peter Shiglett, "The Kurds," in CARDRI (Committee Against Repression and for Democratic Rights in Iraq), *Saddam's Iraq: Revolution or Reaction?* London: Zed Books, 1986, pp. 7–202.

28. "Ou' en est le Kurdistan?" Interview with Ismet Cheriff Vanly in *L'Afrique et l'Asie Modernes,* No. 107, 4 trimestre, 1975, pp. 55–63.

29. *Financial Times* (London), Jan. 7–8, 1986, and *The Guardian,* Jan. 17, 1986.

30. *The Jerusalem Post,* February 26, 1988, April 18, 1988; Scott B. MacDonald, "The Kurds in the 1990s," *Middle East Insight,* January–February, 1990, pp. 29–35.

31. Ghareeb, p. 163, Hazen, "Minorities in Revolt," p. 72.

32. The trial and imprisonment of Dr. Besikci are detailed at length in *Kurdish Times,* Fall 1986, pp. 3–44.

33. Michael M. Gunter, "The Kurdish Problem in Turkey," *Middle East Journal,* 42, 3, Summer 1988, pp. 392–401.

34. *The New York Times,* June 30, 1982.

35. *Kurdish Times,* Spring 1986, p. 8.

36. *South,* November 1987, p. 17.

37. "Helsinki Watch Report" (Special Issue), *Kurdish Times,* 2, 1, December 1987; Michael M. Gunter, "Kurdish Militancy in Turkey: The Case of PKK," *Crossroads,* 29, 1989, pp. 43–59.

38. *Facts on File,* vol. XL, No. 2043, January 1–7, 1980, and No. 2084, October 17, 1980.

39. I am referring specifically to the work of Vera Beaudin Saeedpour,

who established The Kurdish Program in New York City. In a letter addressed personally to the author, she expressed her determination that "there is no way that I shall rest until the cultural survival of the Kurds is assured." I thank her for providing me with material, including the first issues of *Kurdish Times.*

Chapter 3

1. Carleton Stevens Coon, *Tribes of the Rif,* Harvard African Studies vol. IX, Cambridge, Mass.: Peabody Museum of Harvard University, 1931, p. viii.

2. *The Encyclopaedia of Islam,* new ed., vol. I, Leiden: E. J. Brill, 1960, p. 1173.

3. Ernest Gellner, *Muslim Society,* Cambridge University Press, 1981, p. 119.

4. David Montgomery Hart, *The Aith Waryaghar of the Moroccan Rif: An Ethnography and History,* Tucson, Ariz.: The University of Arizona Press, 1976, p. 279.

5. Robert Montagne, *The Berbers: Their Social and Political Organisation,* tr. David Seddon, London: Frank Cass, 1973, p. 41.

6. Seyyed Hossein Nasr, *Islamic Life and Thought,* London: George Allen & Unwin, 1981, pp. 45–46.

7. *The Encyclopaedia of Islam,* p. 1181.

8. Ernest Gellner, *Saints of the Atlas,* Chicago: The University of Chicago Press, 1969, esp. pp. 284–300.

9. Gellner, *Muslim Society,* ch. 4.

10. Bernard Lewis, ed., *Islam from the Prophet Mohammad to the Capture of Constantinople,* vol. II, New York: Harper & Row, 1974, p. 196.

11. Jamil M. Abun-Nasr, *A History of the Maghrib,* Cambridge University Press, 1975, pp. 72–73. Kharijite beliefs appealed to the Berbers, especially the doctrine that non–Arabs could become caliphs.

12. Hart, p. 176.

13. For a fascinating portrayal of husband-wife relations in Kabylia, see Pierre Bourdieu, *Outline of a Theory of Practice,* Cambridge University Press, 1977, chs. 2–3.

14. *Tribes of the Rif,* pp. 132–33.

15. Frantz Fanon, *A Dying Colonialism,* New York: Grove Press, 1965, p. 36.

16. Frantz Fanon, *The Wretched of the Earth,* New York: Grove Press, 1963, p. 45. Here Fanon described the phenomenon without identifying its participants as Kabyle Berbers of Algeria.

17. Gellner, *Muslim Society,* p. 162.

18. See, for example, the portrayal of Kabyle women in Ian Young, *The Private Life of Islam,* New York: Liveright, 1974.

19. Henri Terrasse, *Kasbas Berbères de l'Atlas et des Oasis,* Editions des Horizons de France, 1938, p. 11.

20. Gellner, *Muslim Society,* p. 28.

21. Charles-Robert Ageron, *L'Algérie Algérienne de Napoléon III à de Gaulle,* Paris: Sindbad, 1980, p. 38–39; *The Berbers: Their Social and Political Organisation,* p. 22.

22. *Tribes of the Rif,* pp. 41, 129.

23. David M. Hart, "The Tribe in Modern Morocco," in Ernest Gellner and Charles Micaud, eds., *Arabs and Berbers: From Tribe to Nation in North Africa,* London: Duckworth, 1972, p. 37.

24. *The Encyclopaedia of Islam,* vol. II, Leyden: E. J. Brill, London: Luzac, 1927, p. 599.

25. *The Encyclopaedia of Islam,* vol. I, Leyden: E. J. Brill, London: Luzac, 1913, p. 699.

26. David S. Woolman, *Rebels in the Rif: Abd El Krim and the Rif Rebellion,* Stanford, Calif.: Stanford University Press, 1968, pp. 24–29.

27. Bernard Lewis, *The Arabs in History,* New York: Harper & Row, 1966, pp. 120–22.

28. *The Encyclopaedia of Islam,* vol. I, new ed., Leiden: E. J. Brill, 1960, p. 1176.

29. Ian Lustick, *Settlers and the Failure of British and French State-Building in Ireland and Algeria,* Hanover, N.H.: Dartmouth College, 1984, pp. 28–40.

30. Ageron, p. 119.

31. Mark Twain, *The Innocents Abroad,* New York and London: Harper, 1869, p. 58.

32. The war is vividly related by Woolman, chs. 3–14.

33. See Hart, *The Aith Waryaghar of the Moroccan Rif,* p. 377; Woolman, pp. 217–19.

34. Gellner and Micaud; see Kenneth Brown, "The Impact of the Dahir Berbere in Sale," pp. 201–15.

35. Mohammed Harbi, *Aux Origines du Front de Libération National: La Scission du P.P.A.–M.T.L.D.,* Paris: Christian Bourgois, 1975, pp. 29–38, 114–16.

36. William B. Quandt, "The Berbers in the Algerian Political Elite," in Gellner and Micaud, p. 287. Yet Frantz Fanon hardly mentions the Kabyles explicitly in the two books noted earlier, and this injustice weakens the otherwise authentic treatment he offers of the Algerian revolution. In *A Dying Colonialism* (p. 48) Fanon talked about the vital role of the women in the mountains helping the guerrilla fighters. This was a clear reference to the Kabylia and Aurès, but he never made this clear to the reader.

37. David C. Gordon, *The Passing of French Algeria,* London: Oxford University Press, 1966.

38. Martha Crenshaw Hutchinson, *Revolutionary Terrorism: The FLN in Algeria, 1954–1962,* Stanford, Calif.: Hoover Institution Press at Stanford University, 1978, pp. 22, 32, ch. 3.

39. Jeanne Favret, "Traditionalism through Ultra-Modernism," in Gellner and Micaud, pp. 307–24.

40. *Arab Studies Quarterly,* 5, 1983, p. 39; *Middle East Research and Information Reports,* 1981, p. 9.

41. Rachid Tlemcani, *State and Revolution in Algeria,* Boulder, Col.: Westview Press, London: Zed Books, 1986.

42. *Actuel-developpement,* No. 38, 1980, pp. 25–30; *Awal,* 5, 1989, pp. 1–23.

43. H. J. R. Roberts, "The Economics of Berberism: The Material Basis of

the Kabyle Question in Contemporary Algeria," *Government and Opposition*, 18, 2, Spring 1983, pp. 218–35.

44. *Keesing's Contemporary Archives*, December 12, 1980, pp. 30, 617–18; *The Economist*, May 3, 1980.

45. *Keesing's Contemporary Archives*, October 9, 1981, pp. 31, 121.

46. Hichem Djait, *La Personalité et le Devenir Arabo-Islamiques*, Paris: Editions Du Seuil, 1974, provides an interesting analysis of Arabism and Islam in the Maghreb.

47. Hugh Roberts, "The Unforeseen Development of the Kabyle Question in Contemporary Algeria," *Government and Opposition*, 17, 3, Summer 1982, pp. 312–34.

48. William E. Hazen, "Minorities in Assimilation: The Berbers of North Africa," in McLaurin, ed., pp. 135–55; Quandt, p. 303.

49. Woolman, chs. 14–15; Hart, *Aith Waryaghar*, pp. 421–22.

50. George Thomas Kurian, *Encyclopedia of the Third World*, vol. II, rev. ed., London: Facts on File, 1982, pp. 1243–44.

51. A. Coram, "The Berbers and the Coup," in Gellner and Micaud, eds., pp. 425–30; John Waterbury, "The Coup Manqué," pp. 397–423, ibid.

52. Michael C. Hudson, *Arab Politics: The Search for Legitimacy*, New Haven: Yale University, 1977, ch. 10, pp. 219–29.

53. Robert D. Kaplan, "In Morocco a Berber Face Hides Beneath an Arab Mask," *The New York Times*, June 6, 1982.

54. Mustapha Harzoune of the Association de Culture Berbère in Paris stated that Berbers in Algeria and Morocco do not present a coherent political force, though they exhibit social and cultural vitality (personal communication to the author, December 1988).

55. James A. Miller, *Imlil: A Moroccan Mountain Community in Change*, Boulder and London: Westview Press, 1984, provides a recent investigation of modernization processes in a Berber community.

56. Lewis W. Snider, "Minorities and Political Power in the Middle East," in McLaurin, p. 250.

57. Young, pp. 416–19.

58. Hazen, "Minorities in Assimilation," p. 153.

59. In Gellner and Micaud, pp. 432–36; Abdel Kader Zghal, "Nation-Building in the Maghreb," in Stein Rokkan and S. N. Eisenstadt, eds., *Building States and Nations: Analyses by Region*, II, Beverly Hills and London: Sage, 1973, pp. 337–38.

60. *Middle East Times*, VIII, 4, January 1990, pp. 23–29.

Chapter 4

1. *The Encyclopaedia of Islam*, vol. I, 1913, pp. 627–30.

2. Robert G. Wirsing, *The Baluchis and Pathans*, London: Minority Rights Group, 1981, p. 4.

3. Philip C. Salzman, "Adaptation and Political Organization in Iranian Baluchistan," *Ethnology*, 10, 1971, pp. 433–44.

4. A. V. Rossi and M. Tosi, eds., *Newsletter of Baluchistan Studies*, No. 1, Winter 1982/83, Naples: Instituto Universitario Orientale, p. 3.

5. Robert N. Pehrson, *The Social Organization of the Marri Baluch*, Chicago: Aldine, 1966, chs. 1–2.

6. Warren Swidler, "Economic Change in Baluchistan: Processes of Integration in the Larger Economy of Pakistan," in Ainslie T. Embree, ed., *Pakistan's Western Borderlands: The Transformation of a Political Order*, Durham, N.C.: Carolina Academic Press, 1977, pp. 86–91.

7. For this history, see Wirsing, pp. 4–5; Lucien Vallet, *Pachtounistan et Balouchistan*, Paris: Centre des Hautes Etudes sur l'Afrique et l'Asie Modernes (C.H.E.A.M.), December 1975, pp. 3–6.

8. Baluch fought, for example, in the British Indian army that defeated the Ottomans in the Middle East in World War I. They were identified as Muslims and different from Hindus in that context. Yehuda Litani, "Palestine Periods," *The Jerusalem Post*, December 12, 1986.

9. Ayatullah Khan Baluch, "The Emergence of Baluch Nationalism," *Pakistan Progressive*, 3, 3–4, December 1980, pp. 8–24.

10. Rounaq Jahan, *Pakistan: Failure in National Integration*, New York and London: Columbia University Press, 1972, esp. chs. 2–4.

11. Interview with Murad Khan, representative of Baluchistan People's Liberation Front (BPLF) by Raymond Noat, in *Pakistan Progressive*, p. 27.

12. Selig S. Harrison, *In Afghanistan's Shadow: Baluch Nationalism and Soviet Temptations*, New York and Washington: Carnegie Endowment for International Peace, 1981, p. 48.

13. Ibid., p. 132.

14. Samuel Baid, "Pakistan: Crisis Is Inherent," *IDSA Journal* (New Delhi), 15, 1, July–September 1982, pp. 87–135.

15. *Keesing's Record of World Events*, March 1987, pp. 34, 995–96.

16. Yaacov Vertzberger, *The Enduring Entente: Sino-Pakistani Relations 1960–1980*, The Washington Papers, New York: Praeger, 1983, pp. 107–08; Harrison, pp. 140–41.

17. Quoted by Imtiaz H. Bokhari in "Soviet Military Challenge to the Gulf," *Military Review*, August 1985, p. 61.

18. Elie Krakowski, "Afghanistan and Beyond: The Strategy of Dismemberment," *The National Interest*, Spring 1987, pp. 36–38.

19. Harrison, p. 68.

20. "Debate on the Nationalities Question," in *Pakistan Progressive*, p. 70.

21. V. S. Naipaul, *Among the Believers: An Islamic Journey*, New York: Penguin Books, 1982, pt. 2.

22. Solim Mansur, "Pakistan and the Case of Two-Nations Theory," *The Jerusalem Quarterly*, 38, 1986, pp. 107–24.

23. J. B. Kelly, *Arabia, the Gulf and the West*, London: Weidenfeld & Nicolson, 1980, p. 251.

24. *Pakistan Progressive*, p. 93.

25. Robert D. Kaplan, "The View from Baluchistan," *The American Spectator*, March 1988, p. 23.

26. Avi Plascov, *Security in the Persian Gulf: Modernization, Political Development and Stability*, England: Gower, Aldershot, Hants, 1982, p. 43.

27. Anthony Hyman, "Pakistan: Towards a Modern Muslim State?" *Conflict Studies*, 227, January 1990, p. 10.

Chapter 5

1. Kamal Joumblatt, *I Speak for Lebanon*, London: Zed Press, 1982, pp. 31–33.

2. C. F. Volney, *Voyage en Egypte et Syrie, Pendant les Années 1783, 1784, et 1785*, Paris: Parmantier & Froment, 1825, p. 397.

3. Philip K. Hitti, *The Origins of the Druze People and Religion*, New York: Columbia University Press, 1928, p. 23.

4. *Letter from Lebanon*, No. 12, December 15, 1984 (Jerusalem).

5. The most comprehensive work is that of Silvestre De Sacy, *Exposé de la Religion des Druzes*, Paris: Libraire Orient Edition, 1838, reproduced in Amsterdam: Adolf M. Hakkert, 1964.

6. Peter Gubser, "Minorities in Isolation: The Druze of Lebanon and Syria," in McLaurin, p. 114.

7. Sami Nasib Makarem, *The Druze Faith*, Delmar, N.Y.: Caravan Books, 1974, pp. 105–6.

8. "The Druzes: A People Beyond the Fringe of Islam," *Events*, No. 38, March 10, 1978, pp. 46–48.

9. Joumblatt, p. 36.

10. Gabriel Ben-Dor, *The Druzes in Israel: A Political Study*, Jerusalem: Magnes Press, 1979, p. 74.

11. Joseph T. Parfit, *Among the Druzes of Lebanon and Bashan*, London: Hunter & Longhurst, 1917, p. 4.

12. Henri Guys, *La Nation Druze*, Amsterdam: APA–Philo Press, 1979, p. 182.

13. *The Encyclopaedia of Islam*, vol. II, Leiden: E. J. Brill, London: Luzac, 1965, p. 633; Makarem, p. 112.

14. Salman Hamud Falah, *Ha-Druzim B'eretz-Israel* (The Druzes of Eretz-Israel), M.A. Thesis, Hebrew University of Jerusalem, 1962, chs. 8–9.

15. *The Encyclopaedia of Islam*, 1965, p. 635.

16. Kamal S. Salibi, *The Modern History of Lebanon*, London: Weidenfeld & Nicolson, 1965, pt. 1, chs. 1–3.

17. Guys, *La Nation Druze*, p. 182.

18. Colonel Charles H. Churchill, *The Druzes and the Maronites under the Turkish Rule from 1840 to 1860*, New York: Arno Press, 1973 (orig. 1862), ch. 3–4.

19. T. E. Lawrence, *Seven Pillars of Wisdom*, Garden City, N.Y.: Garden City Pub., 1938, pp. 586, 645–46.

20. Parfit, chs. 3–14.

21. A. H. Hourani, *Syria and Lebanon: A Political Essay*, London: Oxford University Press, 1946 and 1968, ch. 1, pp. 6–15.

22. Safiuddin Joarder, *The Early Phase of the French Mandatory Admin-*

istration in Syria: With Special Reference to the Uprising, 1925–1927, Ph.D. Dissertation, Harvard University, October 1967, chs. 2–5; Toynbee, *Survey of International Affairs,* pp. 408–28.

23. Joarder, pp. 312–13.

24. Ailon Shiloh, p. 24.

25. Patrick Seale, *The Struggle for Syria: A Study of Post-War Arab Politics 1945–1958,* London: Oxford University Press, 1965, pp. 134–36.

26. Eliezer Be'eri, pp. 167–69.

27. See his *I Speak for Lebanon.*

28. Jacob M. Landau, "Elections in Lebanon," in his *Middle Eastern Themes,* London: Frank Cass, 1973, pp. 120–47.

29. *The New York Times,* October 18, 1983.

30. Ben-Dor, ch. 11.

31. Marsha Pomerantz, "The Druze, 1986," *Hadassah,* April 1986, pp. 20–23.

32. Egon Mayer, "The Druze of Bet Ja'an," *Middle East Review,* Winter 1976/1977, p. 27.

33. *Jonathan* (Montreal), No. 9, December 1982, pp. 2, 4.

34. Aharon Dolev, "The Druze Street in Israel Is Excited and Rumbling," *Maariv* (Jerusalem), August 5, 1983.

35. *Maariv,* September 14, 1983.

36. Yosef Goell, "A Question of Loyalty," *The Jerusalem Post,* February 15, 1985.

37. See Egon, pp. 25–28; Miri Gerashi, "Sitting on the Fence," *Pi Haaton* (Jerusalem), No. 4, January 1988, p. 11.

38. Ben-Dor, p. 161.

39. Gubser, p. 131.

Chapter 6

1. Tabitha Petran, *Syria,* London: Ernest Benn, 1972, ch. 1.

2. Peter Gubser, "Minorities in Power: The 'Alawites of Syria," in McLaurin, ed., p. 39; Hourani, *Syria and Lebanon,* p. 97.

3. Jacques Weulersse, *Le Pays des Alouites,* vol. I, Tours: Arrault and Cie, 1940, pp. 45–46, 52–53. *The Encyclopaedia of Islam,* vol. III, Leiden, 1936, pp. 964–65.

4. Claude Cahan, "Note sur les Origines de la Communauté Syrienne Nusayris," *Revue des Etudes Islamiques,* 38, 1970, p. 248.

5. Volney, vol. I, p. 365.

6. Edward J. Jurji, "The 'Alids of North Syria," *The Moslem World,* 29, October 4, 1939, p. 332.

7. Silvestre De Sacy, pp. 567–69.

8. Rene Dussaud, *Histoire et Religion des Nosairis,* Paris: Librairie Emile Bouillon, 1900. This work, claims the author, is based on Nusairi manuscripts.

9. Ignaz Goldziher, *Introduction to Islamic Theology and Law,* Princeton, N.J.: Princeton University Press, 1981 (orig. 1910), p. 228. See also Dussaud, pp. 120ff.

10. Weulersse, vol. I, p. 259, vol. II, fig. 107–08.

11. Hanna Batatu, "Some Observations on the Social Roots of Syria's Ruling Military Group and the Causes for Its Dominance," *The Middle East Journal*, 35, 3, Summer 1981, section III.

12. Petran, ch. 4. See on the general problem of national unity, Michael H. Van Dusen, "Political Integration and Regionalism in Syria," *The Middle East Journal*, 26, 2, Spring 1972, pp. 123–36.

13. Weulersse, vol. I, p. 326; Batatu, p. 341.

14. Hourani, *Syria and Lebanon*, p. 267.

15. Sylvia G. Haim, "The Ba'ath in Syria," in Michael Curtis, ed. *People and Politics in the Middle East*, New Brunswick, N.J.: Transaction Books, 1971, pp. 132–43.

16. Alasdair Drysdale, "The Syrian Armed Forces in National Politics: The Role of the Geographic and Ethnic Periphery," in Roman Kolkowicz and Andrzej Korbonski, eds., *Soldiers, Peasants, and Bureaucrats: Civil-Military Relations in Communist and Modernizing Societies*, London: George Allen & Unwin, 1982, pp. 53–57.

17. Mahmud A. Faksh, "The 'Alawi Community of Syria: A New Dominant Political Force," *Middle Eastern Studies*, 20, 2, April 1984, p. 139.

18. Itamar Rabinovich, *Syria Under the Ba'th 1963–66: The Army-Party Symbiosis*, Jerusalem: Israel Universities Press, 1972, esp. chs. 7–8.

19. William Shawcross, "Playing by the Hama Rules: A Journey in Syria and Lebanon," *Rolling Stone*, Dec. 6, 1984, p. 36.

20. Drysdale, "The Syrian Armed Forces in National Politics," pp. 70–71.

21. Nikolas Van Dam, *The Struggle for Power in Syria: Sectarianism, Regionalism, and Tribalism in Politics, 1961–1980*, 2d ed., London: Croom Helm, 1981, ch. 6.

22. Gerard Michaud, "Caste, Confession et Société en Syrie: Ibn Khaldoun au Chevet du Progressisme Arabe," *Peuples Méditerranéens/Mediterranean Peoples*, 16, July–September 1981, p. 120.

23. Alasdair Drysdale, "The Succession Question in Syria," *The Middle East Journal*, 39, 2, Spring 1985, pp. 255–56.

24. Michaud, pp. 119–20, 124.

25. Alasdair Drysdale, "The Regional Equalization of Health Care and Education in Syria Since the Ba'thi Revolution," *International Journal of Middle East Studies*, 13, 1981, pp. 93–111.

26. Gubser, "Minorities in Power: The Alawites of Syria," p. 43.

27. Annie Laurent, "Syria and Lebanon: The Forged Twins(1)," *Letter from Lebanon* (Jerusalem), 9, November 1, 1984. Also *Letter from Lebanon*, 8, October 15, 1984.

28. Shefi Gabbay, "Assad—Man of Mystery," *Maariv*, April 16, 1984.

29. *The Jerusalem Post*, April 2, 1986 (based on the Parisian *Al-Fiker*).

30. Van Dam, ch. 7; Drysdale, "Syrian Armed Forces," p. 72.

31. Saleem Qureshi, "Political Implications of Fundamentalist Islam," in Janice Gross Stein and David B. DeWitt, eds., *The Middle East at the Crossroads: Regional Forces and External Powers*, Oakville, Ontario: Mosaic Press, 1983, p. 82.

32. Chris Kutschera, "L'Eclipse des Frères Musulmans Syriens," *Les Cahiers de l'Orient*, no. 7, 1987, pp. 121–33.
33. Guy Sitbon, "The Assad System," *Le Nouvel Observateur*, April 30, 1982; Gubser, "Minorities in Power," pp. 44–48.
34. Faksh, p. 150.
35. Edward R. F. Sheehan, "Step by Step in the Middle East," *Foreign Policy*, 22, Spring 1976, p. 42.

Chapter 7

1. Mikhail Kyriakos, *Copts and Moslems Under British Control*, London: Smith, Elder, 1911, p. viii.
2. Fouad N. Ibrahim, "Social and Economic Geographical Analysis of the Egyptian Copts," in *The Copts*, vol. III, Hamburg: European Coptic Union, 1983, pp. 199–202. This work is mainly in German.
3. C. W. Leadbeater, *Ancient Mystic Rites*, Wheaton, Ill.: Theosophical Pub. House, 1986, ch. 2.
4. Shawky F. Karas, *The Copts Since the Arab Invasion: Strangers in Their Land*, Jersey City, N.J.: The American, Canadian, and Australian Christian Coptic Associations, 1985, pt. 1, ch. 3.
5. Otto F. A. Meinardus, *Christian Egypt, Faith and Life*, Cairo: The American University in Cairo Press, 1970, pp. 68–91.
6. Edward Wakin, *A Lonely Minority: The Modern Story of Egypt's Copts*, New York: William Morrow, 1963, pp. 13–14, 153–54.
7. Sir Richard F. Burton, *Personal Narrative of a Pilgrimage to Al-Medinah and Mecca*, vol. I, New York: Dover, 1964 (republication of 1893 ed.), p. 108.
8. Edward William Lane, *An Account of the Manners and Customs of the Modern Egyptians*, London: John Murray, 1860 (1st ed. 1835), pp. 546–49.
9. The Earl of Cromer, *Modern Egypt*, London: Macmillan, 1911, pp. 618–21.
10. Edward Wakin, p. 77.
11. *The Copts: Christians of Egypt*, vol. IX, Nos. 1 and 2, February 1982 (The American and Canadian Coptic Assoc. and Australian Coptic Commission, Jersey City, N.J.), pp. 3, 10.
12. *Minorities in the Arab World*, p. 40.
13. Fred H. Lawson, "Social Origins of Inflation in Contemporary Egypt," *Arab Studies Quarterly*, 7, 1, Winter 1985, p. 53.
14. Leonard Binder, *In a Moment of Enthusiasm: Political Power and the Second Stratum in Egypt*, Chicago and London: University of Chicago Press, 1978, ch. 8.
15. Eric Brodin, "The Christian in Egypt," *Plural Societies*, 9, 1, Spring 1978, pp. 75–76.
16. Bat Ye'or, *Le Dhimmi*, Paris: Editions Anthropos, 1980, pp. 157–60.
17. Y. Masriya, *A Christian Minority: The Copts in Egypt* (reprinted from *Case Studies on Human Rights and Fundamental Freedoms*), The Hague: Martinus Nijhoff, 1976, p. 84.

18. Shelomo Morag et al., *Studies in Judaism and Islam,* Jerusalem: Hebrew University and Magnes Press, 1981, pp. 175–79; Bat Ye'or, pp. 167–68.

19. Henry Laurens, "Le Chevalier de Lascaris et les Origines du Grand Jeu," *Les Cahiers de l'Orient,* 7, 1987, pp. 191–96.

20. Meinardus, pp. 15–16.

21. Doris Behrens-Abouseif, "The Political Situation of the Copts, 1798–1923," in Benjamin Braude and Bernard Lewis, eds., *Christians and Jews in the Ottoman Empire: The Functioning of a Plural Society,* New York and London: Holmes & Meier, 1982, pp. 189–91.

22. Ibid., pp. 195–96.

23. John Marlowe, *Cromer in Egypt,* London: Elek Books, 1970, pp. 265–66.

24. Meinardus, pp. 28–35.

25. Mustafa El-Feki, "A Coptic Leader in the Egyptian National Movement," *International Studies* (Delhi), January–March 1985, 22, 1, pp. 33–58.

26. Y. Masriya, p. 86.

27. Elie Kedourie, *Chatham House Version,* pp. 199–200.

28. Behrens-Abouseif, p. 201.

29. Kyriakos Mikhail, p. 73.

30. Richard P. Mitchell, *The Society of the Muslim Brothers,* London: Oxford University Press, 1969.

31. P. J. Vatikiotis, *Arab Regional Politics in the Middle East,* London: Croom Helm, 1984, ch. 12; "The National Question in Egypt," pp. 240–61.

32. *Army Officers in Arab Politics and Society,* p. 321.

33. C. D. B. Pettit, "The Coptic Christians National Ideology and Minority Status in Egypt," in *The Copts, Christians of Egypt,* 15, 1–2, January 1988, pp. 3–5.

34. *Le Monde,* December 11, 1977.

35. *Valeurs Actuelles* (Paris), May 4, 1987, pp. 30–31.

36. Joseph P. O'Kane, "Islam in the New Egyptian Constitution: Some Discussion in *Al-Ahram,*" *The Middle East Journal,* 26, 2, Spring 1972, p. 137. Important material also in Sami El-Masri, *The Muslim Brothers Under Sadat,* Montreal, 1981.

37. In April 1977 President Carter referred to the 8 million Copts as he welcomed Pope Shenouda in Washington. In September 1986 the Egyptian ambassador to Israel also estimated the Copts at 8 million when he presented his diplomatic credentials to the Israeli president. An ad published by the Coptic Churches in the United States and Canada that appeared in *The New York Times* on May 2, 1983, claimed a Copt population of 10 million in Egypt.

38. Publication of the Coptic Democratic Party, *Al-'Umat Al-Qibtiyya,* September 1985.

39. Ralph de Toledano, "Egypt vs. Christians: Forget About Human Rights," *The Daily Breeze,* February 11, 1986.

40. Much information on these matters is from *The Copts, Christians of Egypt,* the publication of the American and Canadian Coptic Association during the years 1983–1987.

41. Shawky F. Karas, "Egypt's Beleaguered Christians," *Worldview,* 26, 3, March 1983, pp. 13–14.

42. Amnesty International in London reported this case in 1986.

43. *Al-Ahram,* July 23, 1982.

44. *Al-Akhbar,* May 6, 1986.

45. *Al-Ahram,* November 21, 1984.

46. *National Geographic* Magazine, April 1983, pp. 442–46.

47. *Keesing's Facts on File,* vol. xxxi, August 1985, pp. 33, 817–18.

48. Michael Ross, "Islam's Burgeoning Influence, a Growing Challenge for Egypt," *The Gazette* (Montreal), December 28, 1987.

49. Robin Wright, "Militant Islam Gains Ground," *The Nation,* May 23, 1987, p. 677.

50. *Al-Ahaly,* September 9, 1987.

51. John King, "The Fears of Egypt's Copts," *Middle East International,* 305, July 25, 1987, pp. 15–16.

52. *Le Figaro,* April 11, 1980.

53. Rivka Yadlin, "New Images in the Making: Changing Egyptian Conceptions of Self and of Israel," *The Jerusalem Journal of International Relations,* 6, 4, 1982–1983, pp. 98–100.

54. Fouad Ajami, "In the Pharaoh's Shadow: Religion and Authority in Egypt," in James P. Piscatori, *Islam in the Political Process,* Cambridge: Cambridge University Press, 1983, p. 33.

55. Emmanuel Sivan, "The Islamic Republic of Egypt," *Orbis,* 31, 1, Spring 1987, pp. 43–53.

56. "Why the Copts Are Supporting the New Wafd," *Events,* March 10, 1978.

Chapter 8

1. From Xenophon's *Anabasis,* bk. IV, in M.I. Finley, ed., *The Greek Historians,* New York: The Viking Press, 1963, pp. 424, 431.

2. Gerard Chaliand and Yves Ternon, *The Armenians: From Genocide to Resistance,* London: Zed Press, 1983, pp. 3–4.

3. Louise Nalbandian, *The Armenian Revolutionary Movement: The Development of Armenian Political Parties Through the Nineteenth Century,* Berkeley and London: University of California Press, n.d., p. 3.

4. Patrice Brodeur, "Armenians and the 1915 Genocide," *Nitzanim,* 3, Winter 1984/5, The Hebrew University of Jerusalem, The Rothberg School for Overseas Students, pp. 106–09.

5. Frank Leslie Cross, ed., *The Oxford Dictionary of the Christian Church,* London: Oxford University Press, 1958, p. 87.

6. Kevork B. Bardakjian, "The Rise of the Armenian Patriarchate of Constantinople," in Braude and Lewis, vol. I, pp. 89–100.

7. D. S. Margoliouth, *The Early Development of Mohammedanism,* New York: Charles Scribner's Sons, 1914, p. 123.

8. Christopher J. Walker, *Armenia: The Survival of a Nation,* London: Croom Helm, New York: St. Martin's Press, 1980, pp. 38–39.

9. Niyazi Berkes, *The Development of Secularism in Turkey,* Montreal: McGill University Press, 1964, p. 189.

10. Hajop Barsoumian, "The Dual Role of the Armenian *Amira* Class within the Ottoman Government and the Armenian *Millet* (1750–1850)," in Braude and Lewis, vol. I, pp. 171–84.

11. Sir Edwin Pears, *Life of Abdul Hamid*, London: Constable, 1917, pp. 215–16.

12. Heraut Katchadourian, "Culture and Psychopathology," in L. Carl Brown and Norman Itzkowitz, eds., *Psychological Dimensions of Near Eastern Studies*, Princeton, N.J.: Darwin Press, 1977, p. 113.

13. *The Innocents Abroad*, p. 295.

14. Alexander Pushkin, *A Journal to Arzrum*, Ann Arbor: Ardis, 1974, pp. 52, 80.

15. William L. Langer, *The Diplomacy of Imperialism, 1890–1902*, p. 147. Also, Yacus Ercan, "Armenian Claims in the Light of Historical Documents," *Turkish Review Quarterly Digest*, 1, 3, Spring 1986, p. 23.

16. Rohan Butler and J. P. T. Bury, eds., *Documents on British Foreign Policy 1919–1939*, (first series, VIII, 1920), London: Her Majesty's Stationery Office, 1958, pp. 59, 117–18.

17. M. Chahin, *The Kingdom of Armenia*, London: Croom Helm, 1987.

18. Hagop Manadian, *Tigrane II and Rome*, Lisbonne: Imprensa Nacional, 1963.

19. Walker, pp. 38–40.

20. Mesrob K. Krikorian, *Armenians in the Service of the Ottoman Empire 1860–1908*, London: Routledge & Kegan Paul, 1978, chs. 1, 3.

21. Carter V. Findley, "The Acid Test of Ottomanism: The Acceptance of Non–Muslims in the Late Ottoman Bureaucracy," in Braude and Lewis, vol. I, pp. 339–68.

22. Berkes, ch. 8.

23. David Kushner, *The Rise of Turkish Nationalism 1876–1908*, London: Frank Cass, 1977.

24. Nalbandian, p. 62.

25. Chaliand and Ternon, p. 26.

26. William L. Langer, pp. 154–55.

27. *Life of Abdul Hamid*, p. 228.

28. Ch. 10 in *The Chatham House Version and Other Middle-Eastern Studies*, pp. 287–300.

29. Joseph Heller, "Britain and the Armenian Question, 1912–1914: A Study in Realpolitik," *Middle Eastern Studies*, 16, 1, January 1980, pp. 3–26.

30. *Genocide and Collective Responsibility*, symposium held on April 24, 1980, Jerusalem, remarks by Archbishop Shahe Ajamian, p. 4.

31. Ibid., p. 17.

32. Kerop Bedoukian, *The Urchin: An Armenian's Escape*, London: John Murray, 1978, p. 8.

33. Chaliand and Ternon, pp. 69–73.

34. Robert Melson, *A Theoretical Inquiry into the Armenian Massacres of 1894–1896*, 1980.

35. Gwynne Dyer, "Turkish 'Falsifiers' and Armenian 'Deceivers': Historiography and the Armenian Massacres," *Middle Eastern Studies*, 12, 1, January 1976, p. 107.

36. Kerim C. Kevenk, "Armenian Terrorism: Yesterday and Today," *The Muslim World League Journal*, 11, 2, November/December 1983, pp. 61–64.

37. Richard G. Hovannisian, *Armenia on the Road to Independence 1918*, Berkeley and Los Angeles: University of California Press, 1967, chs. 5–6 especially.

38. Richard G. Hovannisian, *The Republic of Armenia, I: The First Years, 1918–1919*, Berkeley, Los Angeles, and London: University of California Press, 1971.

39. *Armenia: The Survival of a Nation*, pp. 263–64.

40. *Documents on British Foreign Policy 1919–1939*, pp. 117–20.

41. Laurence Evans, *United States Policy and the Partition of Turkey, 1914–1924*, Baltimore: The John Hopkins Press, 1965, pp. 75–262.

42. Howard M. Sacher, *The Emergence of the Middle East: 1914–1924*, New York: Alfred A. Knopf, 1969, ch. 11.

43. Richard D. Robinson, *The First Turkish Republic*, Cambridge: Harvard University Press, 1965.

44. Mark Kilbourne Mattosian, *The Impact of Soviet Policies in Armenia*, Leiden: E. J. Brill, 1962.

45. Mikhail Agursky, "The Collapse of Soviet Eurasia," *The Jerusalem Post*, March 4, 1988.

46. *The William Saroyan Reader*, New York: George Braziller, 1958.

47. Interview with George Hentilian, curator of the Armenian Museum, Jerusalem, June 23, 1983.

48. Heraut Katchadourian, pp. 116–24.

49. David Marshall Lang and Christopher Walker, *The Armenians*, London: Minority Rights Group, 1977, p. 15.

50. Paul Wilkonson, "Armenian Terrorism," *The World Today*, September 1983, pp. 346–47.

51. Anat Kurz and Ariel Merari, *ASALA: Irrational Terror or Political Tool*, Tel Aviv University, Jaffee Center for Strategic Studies, No. 2, 1985, esp. chs.3–5.

52. James Ring Adams, "Lessons of Anti-Turk Terrorism," *The Wall Street Journal*, August 17, 1983.

53. Benjamin Netanyahu, ed., *Terrorism: How the West Can Win*, New York: Farrar, Straus & Giroux, 1986, pp. 11–12.

54. Walter Laqueur, *The Age of Terrorism*, London: Weidenfeld & Nicolson, 1987, p. 228.

55. Marcy Agmon, "Defending the Upper Gulf: Turkey's Forgotten Partnership," *Journal of Contemporary History*, 21, 1986, pp. 81–97.

56. *The New York Times*, December 28, 1985.

57. Bruce R. Kuniholm, "Turkey and NATO: Past, Present, and Future," *Orbis*, 27, 2, Spring 1983, p. 427.

58. Michael M. Gunter, "The Armenian Terrorist Campaign Against Turkey," *Orbis*, 27, 2, Summer 1983, pp. 460–61.

Chapter 9

1. Sami Hermes, "The Assyrians in History," *Nineveh* (Berkeley, Calif.), 9, 4, 1986, pp. 4–5.

2. Bailis Yamlikha Shamun, "What's in a Name?" *The Assyrian Star* (Chicago), 34, 1, January–February 1985, p. 9.

3. Henry Charles Luke, *Mosul and Its Minorities,* London: Martin Hopkinson, 1925, pp. 14, 36, 56, 91.

4. Habib Ishow, "Araden or le 'Jardin du Paradis': La Terre et les Hommes dans un Village Chaldéen du nord de l'Iraq," *Études Rurales,* 76, October–December 1979, pp. 97–112.

5. Asahel Grant, *The Nestorians or the Lost Tribes,* Amsterdam: Philo Press, 1973 (orig. 1841), pp. 203–4.

6. *Bet-Nahrain* (Modesto, California), 12, 1, May 1985, p. 19.

7. Grant, pp. 57–58, 74.

8. Robert Brenton Betts, *Christians in the Arab East: A Political Study,* Athens: Lycabettus Press, 1975, pp. 135–36.

9. W. Chauncey Emhardt, Thomas Burgess, and Robert Frederick Lau, *The Eastern Church in the Western World,* New York: AMS Press, 1926 (ed.), ch. 15, esp. pp. 123–24; *The Oxford Dictionary of the Christian Church,* pp. 259–60, 946–47.

10. "Orders and Medals Research Society," *Nineveh,* pp. 9–11.

11. Habib Ishow, p. 100.

12. Grant, Appendix (B), pp. 327–34; Daniel J. Boorstin, *The Discoverers,* New York: Vintage Books, 1985, pp. 128–32.

13. Joseph Najjar, *Les Chrétiens Uniates du Proche-Orient,* Paris: Editions Du Seuil, 1962, pp. 246–47.

14. G. S. Reed, "The Archbishop of Canterbury's Mission to the Assyrian Christians," *The Assyrian Star,* pp. 10–11.

15. John Joseph, *The Nestorians and Their Muslim Neighbors: A Study of Western Influence on Their Relations,* Princeton, N.J.: Princeton University Press, 1961, pp. 27, 32–64.

16. Ibid., chs. 5–6.

17. Arnold Joseph Toynbee, *The Treatment of Armenians in the Ottoman Empire,* London: Hodder & Stoughton, 1916, p. 169.

18. John Joseph, chs. 7–8.

19. David B. Perley, "Whither Christian Missions?" *Nineveh,* pp. 16–23.

20. Stephen Oren, "The Assyrians of the Middle East," *Middle East Review,* 9, 1, Fall 1976, pp. 36–40; "The Assyrian Massacre—1935," *The Copts, Christians of Egypt,* 2, 1–2, June 1984, p. 9.

21. Robert Brenton Betts, pp. 105–7, 144–45, 175–79.

22. Richard Bautch, "Iraqi Christians Languish in Rome," *Catholic Register,* Aug. 28, 1983.

23. *Ashur,* International Bet-Nahrain Democratic Party, The Information Bureau, Modesto, California, March 1987. Ben Daniel has written that 49,000 Assyrians were killed in action in the Iraq-Iran war. *Assyrian Guardian Monthly* (Chicago), October 1990, p. 2.

24. *The Assyrian Quest* (Chicago), 9, 16, January 1987.

25. *Assyrian Guardian Monthly* (Chicago), May 1988.

26. Printed in *Bet-Nahrain,* p. 5.

27. John Joseph, p. 151.

Chapter 10

1. *The New York Times,* May 19, 1980.
2. Walid Phares, *Le Peuple Chrétien du Liban: 13 Siècles de Lutte,* Beirut: Joseph D. Raidy, 1982, pp. 31–45.
3. James A. Bill and Carl Leiden, *The Middle East: Politics and Power,* Boston: Allyn & Bacon, 1975, ch. 3.
4. Volney, vol. I, pp. 370–71.
5. Cross, p. 861.
6. Michel Chebli, *Une Histoire du Liban a l'Epoque des Emirs (1635–1841),* Beyrouth, 1955, p. 36.
7. Kamal S. Salibi, *Maronite Historians of Mediaeval Lebanon,* Beirut, 1959, New York: AMS Press, ch. 1.
8. Iliya Harik, "The Maronite Church and Political Change in Lebanon," Leonard Binder, ed., *Politics in Lebanon,* New York: John Wiley, 1966, ch. 3.
9. Haddad, *Syrian Christians in Muslim Society,* p. 58.
10. For a portrait of a Christian elite clan in Lebanon, see John Sykes, *The Mountain Arabs,* Philadelphia: Chilton, 1968.
11. Frank Stoakes, "The Supervigilantes: The Lebanese Kataeb Party as a Builder, Surrogate and Defender of the State," *Middle Eastern Studies,* 11, 3, October 1975, pp. 215–36; Meir Zamir, "Politics and Violence in Lebanon," *The Jerusalem Quarterly,* 25, Fall 1982, pp. 14–17.
12. Haddad, p. 61.
13. Hourani, *Minorities in the Arab World,* p. 63.
14. John P. Spagnolo, *France and Ottoman Lebanon 1861–1914,* St. Antony's Middle East Monographs, No. 7, London: Ithaca Press, 1977, ch. 9.
15. *Middle East Review,* Fall 1976, pp. 64–65.
16. Cross, p. 861.
17. Salibi, *Maronite Historians,* ch. 1.
18. Najjar, p. 223.
19. Chebli, chs. 9–10.
20. Hurewitz, vol. I, document 58, p. 134.
21. Two historical narratives on these events and later developments are Leila M. T. Meo, *Lebanon: Improbable Nation,* Bloomington: Indiana University Press, 1965, and Kamal S. Salibi, *The Modern History of Lebanon,* London: Weidenfeld & Nicolson, 1965.
22. Colonel Charles H. Churchill, *The Druzes and the Maronites Under the Turkish Rule from 1840 to 1860,* New York: Arno Press, 1973 (orig. 1862), pp. 190–91.
23. Albert Hourani, "Lebanon: The Development of a Political Society," in Binder, pp. 13–29; Meo, ch. 2.
24. Spagnolo, chs. 3–6 especially.
25. Kemal H. Karpat, "The Ottoman Emigration to America, 1860–1914," *International Journal of Middle East Studies,* 17, 1985, pp. 175–209.
26. George Antonius, *The Arab Awakening,* New York: Capricorn, 1965 (orig. 1938), ch. 3.
27. Lyne Loheac, *Daoud Ammoun et la Création de l'État Libanais,* Paris: Klincksieck, 1978, pp. 45, 63–72.

28. Spagnolo, p. 153.

29. Loheac, ch. 3.

30. Salibi, *Modern History of Lebanon,* pp. 173–75.

31. Jacob M. Landau, *Middle Eastern Themes,* London: Frank Cass, 1973, pp. 228–63.

32. Pierre Jemayel, "Lebanese Nationalism and Its Foundations: The Phalangist Viewpoint," in Kemal H. Karpat, ed., *Political and Social Thought in the Contemporary Middle East,* New York: Praeger, 1970, pp. 107–14; *Letter from Lebanon* (Jerusalem) (special Ed.), September 9, 1984.

33. R. Hrair Dekmejian, *Patterns of Political Leadership: Egypt, Israel, Lebanon,* Albany, N.Y.: State University of New York Press, 1975, ch. 2.

34. M. S. Agwani, ed., *The Lebanese Crisis, 1958,* New York: Asia House, 1965.

35. Michael W. Suleiman, "Lebanon," in Tareq Y. Ismael, ed., *Governments and Politics of the Contemporary Middle East,* Homewood, Ill.: Dorsey Press, 1970, ch. 11, pp. 231–50.

36. Jalal Zuwiyya, *The Parliamentary Election of Lebanon 1968,* Leiden: E. J. Brill, 1972.

37. Iliya F. Harik, "Political Elite of Lebanon," in George Lenczowski, ed., *Political Elites in the Middle East,* Washington: American Enterprise Institute, 1975, pp. 201–20.

38. Hussein Sirriyyeh, "The Palestinian Armed Presence in Lebanon Since 1967," in Roger Owen, ed., *Essays on the Crisis in Lebanon,* London: Ithaca Press, 1976, pp. 73–89.

39. Ehud Yaari, "Another Draw in the Lebanon," *New Outlook,* June 1973, pp. 15–19.

40. *The Jerusalem Post,* January 2, 1976.

41. Data from Lebanese authorities and the World Bank, in *Letter from Lebanon* (Jerusalem), 17, 1, April 1985.

42. *The New York Times,* October 18, 1983.

43. Ghassan Tueni, "Lebanon: A New Republic?" *Foreign Affairs,* 61, 1, Fall 1982, p. 93.

44. Sykes, p. 85.

45. Wim Van Leer, "Great Expectations," *The Jerusalem Post Magazine,* July 23, 1982.

46. George Qaram, "The Lebanese Civil War in Perspective," *The Jerusalem Quarterly,* 12, Summer 1979, pp. 52–53.

47. Tueni, pp. 94–98; Zamir, pp. 25–26.

48. Paul A. Jureidini and James M. Price, "Minorities in Partition: The Christians of Lebanon," in McLaurin, p. 182.

Chapter 11

1. Samuel M. Makinda, "Sudan: Old Wine in New Bottles," *Orbis,* 31, 2, Summer 1987, pp. 222–23.

2. *The Strategic Stakes in Sudan,* New York: International Security Council, October 1985, pp. 14–15.

3. Francis Mading Deng, *Africans of Two Worlds: The Dinka in Afro-Arab Sudan*, New Haven and London: Yale University Press, 1978, p. 213.

4. Francis Mading Deng, *Tradition and Modernization: A Challenge for Law Among the Dinka of the Sudan*, New Haven and London: Yale University Press, 1971, pp. 153–54.

5. Dunston M. Wai, *The African-Arab Conflict in the Sudan*, New York and London: Africana, 1981, pp. 18–19.

6. Rafia Hassan Ahmed, "Regionalism, Ethnic and Socio-Cultural Pluralism: The Case of Southern Sudan," in Mohamed Omer Beshir, ed., *Southern Sudan: Regionalism and Religion*, University of Khartoum, Graduate College Pub. No. 10, 1984, pp. 6–59.

7. E. E. Evans-Pritchard, *The Nuer*, Oxford: Clarendon Press, 1940, ch. 3.

8. Deng, *Africans of Two Worlds*, pp. 52–80.

9. Deng, *Tradition and Modernization*, pp. 229–30.

10. Beshir, p. 252.

11. Robert O. Collins, *The Southern Sudan in Historical Perspective*, The Shiloah Center for Middle Eastern and African Studies, Tel Aviv University, 1975, p. 41.

12. Cecil Eprile, *War and Peace in the Sudan 1955–1972*, London: David & Charles, 1974, pp. 27–28; Bona Malwal, *People and Power in Sudan—The Struggle for National Stability*, London: Ithaca Press, 1981, pp. 35–36.

13. *The African-Arab Conflict in the Sudan*, p. 103.

14. Andrea M. Rosenberg, "The Middle East Slave Trade," *Middle East Review*, 9, 2, Winter 1976/77, pp. 58–62.

15. John Laffin, *The Arabs as Master-Slavers*, Englewood, N.J.: SBS, 1982, ch. 5.

16. *Africans of Two Worlds*, pp. 130ff.

17. On Christianity in Ethiopia, see Paul B. Henze, "Ethiopia," *The Wilson Quarterly*, Winter 1984, pp. 103–09.

18. H. A. MacMichael, *A History of the Arabs in the Sudan*, Cambridge: Cambridge University Press, 1922, ch. 1, pp. 160ff.

19. A. J. Arkell, *A History of the Sudan from the Earliest Times to 1821*, University of London, Athlone Press, 1961, esp. pp. 186–220.

20. Robert O. Collins, *The Southern Sudan, 1883–1898: A Struggle for Control*, New Haven and London: Yale University Press, 1962, chs. 1–2.

21. Ronald Robinson and John Gallagher with Alice Denny, *Africa and the Victorians: The Official Mind of Imperialism*, London: Macmillan, 1970, ch. 12.

22. Philip Chol Biowel, "The Christian Church in the Southern Sudan Before 1900," in Mohamed Omer Beshir, ed., *Southern Sudan*, pp. 205–23.

23. Damazo Dutt Majok, "British Religious and Educational Policy: The Case of Bahr El-Ghazal," ibid., p. 236; Mohamed Omer Beshir, *The Southern Sudan: Background to Conflict*, London: C. Hurst, 1968, ch. 3.

24. Bernard Lewis, *Race and Color in Islam*, New York: Harper & Row, 1971, p. 38.

25. Catherine Miller, "Langues et Integration Nationale au Soudan," *Politique Africaine*, 23, September 1986, p. 32.

26. *The Southern Sudan: Background to Conflict*, ch. 6.

27. S. M. Sid Ahmed, "Christian Missionary Activities in Sudan, 1926–1946," in Beshir, ed., *Southern Sudan: Regionalism and Religion*, pp. 241–76.

28. Beshir, *Southern Sudan*, p. 53.

29. Edgar O'Ballance, *The Secret War in the Sudan: 1955–1972*, London: Faber & Faber, 1977.

30. Beshir, *Southern Sudan*, p. 274.

31. Malwal, *People and Power in Sudan*, p. 41.

32. Elias Nyamiell Wakoson, "The Origin and Development of the Anya-Nya Movement 1955–1972," in Beshir, *Southern Sudan*, pp. 127–204.

33. Eprile, pp. 50–51.

34. Deng, *Africans of Two Worlds*, pp. 21–23.

35. Tristram Betts, *The Southern Sudan: The Ceasefire and After*, London: Africa Publications Trust, 1974.

36. Gerard Prunier, "La Guerre Civile au Soudan," *Les Cahiers de l'Orient*, No. 5, premier trimestre 1987, pp. 93–112.

37. "Memo," *Middle East and Mediterranean Outlook*, 11, October 1984, p. 1.

38. *The Economist*, January 14–20, 1984, p. 44.

39. *The New York Times*, May 4, 1986.

40. "Khartoum Loses Its Grip," *South*, May 1988, pp. 31–32.

41. Ann Mosely Lesch, "A View from Khartoum," *Foreign Affairs*, 65, 4, Spring 1987, pp. 807–26.

42. *Sudan*, Country Report, London: The Economist Intelligence Unit, No. 1, 1988, pp. 9–10.

43. *Facts on File*, May 22, 1987, vol. XLVII, No. 2426, p. 375; *Middle East Times* (Nicosia), August 23–29, 1987, p. 7.

44. Mansour Khalid, ed., *John Garang Speaks*, London: KPI, 1987.

45. Salah Abdel Latif, "The Origins and Development of Southern Parties in the Sudan," *Al-Siyasa Al-Dawliyya*, 91, January 1988, p. 84.

46. Ibid., p. 83.

Chapter 12

1. Boutrous B. Ghali, "Egyptian Definitions of Peace," *Middle East Review*, 5–6 (special issue), Fall 1975, p. 25.

2. Max I. Dimont, *Jews, God and History*, New York: Signet, 1966, p. 313.

3. On the tribal theme, see Josh. 7:16ff.; Hanoch Reviv, *From Clan to Monarchy: Israel in the Biblical Period* (Hebrew), Jerusalem: The Magnes Press, The Hebrew University, 1981, ch. 3.

4. Eric Voeglin, *Order and History*, vol. I, Louisiana State University Press, 1969, pt. 3, ch. 7.

5. Yehezkel Kaufmann, *The Religion of Israel*, tr. Moshe Greenberg, New York: Schocken, 1972. The point is stressed in Maimonides (HaRambam), *Laws of Idolatory*, ch. 1, in his *Mishne Torah*.

6. Norman H. Snaith, *The Distinctive Ideas of the Old Testament*, New York: Schocken, 1964.

7. Albrecht Alt, *Essays on Old Testament History and Religion*, tr. R. A. Wilson, Garden City, N.Y.: Doubleday, 1968, pp. 103–71.

8. Maimonides' famous philosophic work is *The Guide for the Perplexed* and Rabbi Hirsch's is *Horeb: A Philosophy of Jewish Laws and Observances.*

9. Solomon Grayzel, *A History of the Jews*, Philadelphia: Jewish Publication Society of America, 1970, p. 45.

10. Shalom Spiegel, "On Medieval Hebrew Poetry," in Louis Finkelstein, ed., *The Jews: Their Religion and Culture*, 4th ed., New York: Schocken, 1971, pp. 82–120.

11. Arthur Hertzberg, ed., *The Zionist Idea*, New York: Harper & Row, 1966, p. 161.

12. Bat Ye'or, *Dhimmi Peoples: Oppressed Nations*, Geneva: Editions de l'Avenir, 1978, pp. 17–18.

13. See James Parkes, *A History of the Jewish People*, Middlesex: Penguin, 1967.

14. George Adam Smith, *The Topography, Economics and Historical Geography of Jerusalem*, Jerusalem: Ariel (orig. pub. in 1907), p. 12.

15. Josephus, *The Jewish War*, tr. G. A. Williamson, Middlesex: Penguin, 1959, p. 377 (Excursus II).

16. H. H. Ben-Sasson, ed., *A History of the Jewish People*, Cambridge, Mass.: Harvard University Press, 1976, ch. 14.

17. Moshe Pearlman, *The Maccabees*, London and Jerusalem: Weidenfeld & Nicolson, 1973.

18. Cecil Roth, *A History of Jews*, rev. ed., New York: Schocken, 1970, chs. 7–10.

19. Werner Keller, *Diaspora: The Post-Biblical History of the Jews*, London: Pitman, 1971, p. 54.

20. Jacob Neusner, *From Politics to Piety: The Emergence of Pharisaic Judaism*, 2d ed., New York: Ktav, 1979.

21. Keller, pp. 102–237.

22. Joshua Trachtenberg, *The Devil and the Jews: The Medieval Conception of the Jew and Its Relation to Modern Antisemitism*, New York: World, Philadelphia: The Jewish Publication Society of America, 1961 (orig. 1943).

23. Hillel Bavli, "The Modern Renaissance of Hebrew Literature," in Finkelstein, ch. 7, pp. 228–63.

24. Prince Serge Dmitriyevich Urussov, *The Kishinev Pogrom—Memoirs of a Russian Governor*, New York: Bergman, 1970 (orig. 1908).

25. Arthur Gilbert, *The Vatican Council and the Jews*, Cleveland and New York: World, 1968; Arnold Foster and Benjamin R. Epstein, *The New Anti-Semitism*, New York: McGraw-Hill, 1974.

26. Hava Lazarus-Yafeh, *Some Religious Aspects of Islam*, Leiden: E. J. Brill, 1981, ch. 6.

27. Charles Cutler Torrey, *The Jewish Foundation of Islam*, New York: Ktav, 1967 (orig. lectures in 1933).

28. S. D. Goitein, *Jews and Arabs: Their Contacts Through the Ages*, 3d rev. ed., New York: Schocken, 1976.

29. Philip Khuri Hitti, *The Origins of the Islamic State* (in Arabic, *Kitab Futuh Al-Buldan* by al-Baladhuri), New York: AMS Press, 1968, chs. 1–2.

30. Moshe Perlmann, "The Medieval Polemics Between Islam and

Judaism," in S. D. Goitein, ed., *Religion in a Religious Age*, Cambridge, Mass.: Assoc. for Jewish Studies, 1974, pp. 103–38.

31. Rose Lewis, "Maimonides and the Muslims," *Midstream*, November 1979, pp. 16–22.

32. Bernard Lewis, "The Decline and Fall of Islamic Jewry," *Commentary*, June 1984, pp. 44–54.

33. See Gershom Scholem, *Sabbatai Sevi: The Mystical Messiah 1626–1676*, London: Routledge & Kegan Paul, 1973.

34. A remarkable Israeli analysis of this is in Moshe Ben-Yosef (Hagar), *Cultural Coercion* (Hebrew), Sifrei Mossad Lehafatzat Ha-Sefer Ha-Tov, 1979.

35. V. D. Segre, *Israel: A Society in Transition*, London: Oxford University Press, 1971, p. 39.

36. Amnon Rubinstein, *The Zionist Dream Revisited: From Herzl to Gush Emunim and Back*, New York: Schocken, 1984, p. 184.

37. *Ben-Gurion Looks Back in Talks with Moshe Pearlman*, New York: Schocken, 1970, pp. 22–23.

38. Barbara W. Tuchman, *Bible and Sword: How the British Came to Palestine*, London: Macmillan, 1983.

39. Amnon Cohen, *Palestine in the 18th Century*, Jerusalem: The Magnes Press, The Hebrew University, 1973.

40. Samuel Katz, *Battleground: Fact and Fantasy in Palestine*, New York: Bantam, 1973.

41. Yehoshua Ben-Arieh, *The Rediscovery of the Holy Land in the Nineteenth Century*, Jerusalem: The Magnes Press, The Hebrew University, 1983, pp. 102–08.

42. See Laurence Oliphant, new ed. by Rechavam Zeevy, *Haifa or Life in the Holy Land 1882–1885*, 1887, Jerusalem: Canaan, 1976, pp. 140, 153, 205.

43. J. C. Hurewitz, *Diplomacy in the Near and Middle East: A Documentary Record 1914–1956*, New York: Octagon, 1972, p. 48.

44. Itzhak Galnoor, *Steering the Polity: Communication and Politics in Israel*, Beverly Hills, London, New Delhi: Sage, 1982, p. 90.

45. Dan Horowitz and Moshe Lissak, *Origins of the Israeli Polity: Palestine Under the Mandate*, Chicago and London: University of Chicago Press, 1978, chs. 2, 6.

46. Israel Eldad, *The Jewish Revolution, Jewish Statehood*, tr. Hannah Schmorak, New York: Shengold, 1971.

47. Norman A. Stillman, *The Jews of Arab Lands: A History and Source Book*, Philadelphia: Jewish Publication Society of America, 1979, p. 207.

48. On rock throwing, see William Shaler's report in *Sketches of Algiers*, Boston, 1826, pp. 66–67, quoted in David Littman and Bat Ye'or, *Protected Peoples Under Islam*, Geneva: Centre d'Information et de Documentation sur le Moyen-Orient, 1976, p. 10; Goitein, p. 76; Lewis, "The Decline and Fall of Islamic Jewry," p. 44; Stillman, p. 84.

49. Elie Kedourie, "Minorities," in *Chatham House Version*, pp. 315–16.

50. Charles S. Liebman and Eliezer Don-Yehiya, *Civil Religion in Israel*, Berkeley: University of California Press, 1983.

51. Jacob M. Landau, "Hebrew and Arabic in the State of Israel: Political

Aspects of the Language Issue," *International Journal of the Sociology of Language,* 67, 1987, pp. 117–33.

Chapter 13

1. Yonatan Ratosh, *Hebrew Peace: 1967 and What Next?* (Hebrew), Tel-Aviv: Hermon, 1967.

2. Horon, *The Land of Kedem.*

3. Shimon Peres, *David's Sling,* New York: Random House, 1970, p. 286.

4. Efraim Inbar, "Israel and Lebanon: 1975–1982," *Crossroads,* 10, Spring 1983, pp. 42–43.

5. Haim Rigbi, *The End of Zionism or the Doom of Arabism* (Hebrew), unpub. manuscript, Tel-Aviv.

6. Benjamin Netanyahu, "How Central Is the Palestinian Problem?" *The Wall Street Journal,* April 5, 1983.

7. Claude Khoury, "The Case for Lebanese Neutrality," *Monday Morning* (Beirut), December 13–19, 1982, p. 37.

8. *The Jerusalem Post,* November 29, 1982.

9. *Letter from Lebanon,* 7, October 1, 1984.

10. Efraim Inbar, "Israeli Strategic Thinking After 1973," *The Journal of Strategic Studies,* 6, 1, March 1983, p. 47.

11. "Interview with Mohamed Sid-Ahmed," *SAIS Review,* 3, Winter 1981–82, p. 53.

12. Noam Chomsky, "The Middle East and the Probability of Nuclear War," *Socialist Review,* 70, July-August 1983, pp. 24–25.

13. "Redrawing the map of the Middle East," *Events,* 37, February 24, 1978, p. 11.

14. Oded Yinon, "Strategy for Israel in the 1980s," *Kivunim* (Hebrew), February 1982, pp. 49–59.

15. *The Wall Street Journal,* December 8, 1982; *Middle East International,* September 3, 1982; the *Review of Palestine Studies,* a PLO journal, also summarized the Yinon article in French in its Autumn 1982 issue.

16. Grant, *The Nestorians or the Lost Tribes,* pp. 31–33.

17. 2 Kings 17:6; 1 Chron. 5:26.

18. A. Avihail and A. Brin, *Haovdim Be-eretz Ashur* (Hebrew), Jerusalem: Agudat Amishav, 1981.

19. Henri Noach, "In Pursuit of the Lost Ten Tribes: An Odyssey to the East," *Forum,* 61, Spring 1988, pp. 40–45.

20. N. Slousch, "Les Juifs En Afghanistan," *Revue du Monde Musulman,* Paris, Tome Quatrieme, 1908, pp. 502–11.

21. Fredrik Barth, *Political Leadership Among Swat Pathans,* London: Athlone Press, 1975, p. 21.

22. Itzhak Ben-Zvi, *The Exiled and the Redeemed,* 2d ed., Jerusalem: Yad Yitzhak Ben-Zvi, 1976, p. 214.

23. Matthew Stevenson, "Traveling the Afghan Archipelago," *The American Spectator,* February 1984, pp. 11–14.

24. Ben-Zvi, bk. I, ch. 3.

25. Schmidt, *Journey Among Brave Men*, p. 152.

26. Coon, *Caravan*, p. 140.

27. Arieh Lova Eliav, *Taba'ot 'Edut* (Rings of Faith), Tel Aviv: Am Oved, 1984, pp. 156–64.

28. *Facts on File*, 40, No. 2082, October 3, 1980, p. 735; Alouph Hareven, "With a Handful of Israelis in the Kurdistan Mountains," *Maariv*, October 10, 1980.

29. Reported by Jack Anderson in *The Washington Post*, September 17, 1972; Marion Woolfson, *Prophets in Babylon: Jews in the Arab World*, London and Boston: Faber & Faber, 1980, pp. 219–20.

30. Yosef Gotlieb, "The Kurdish Connection," *The Jerusalem Post*, December 10, 1986.

31. Raphael Israeli, "Back to Nowhere: Morocco Revisited," *The Jerusalem Quarterly*, 34, Winter 1985, p. 8.

32. *The Heterodoxies of the Shiites According to Ibn Hazm*, tr. Israel Friedlander, New Haven, 1909, p. 49.

33. Ignaz Goldziher, *Muslim Studies*, vol. II, London: George Allen & Unwin, 1971, p. 283.

34. M. Shokeid, "Jewish Existence in a Berber Environment," in *Les Relations entre Juifs et Musulmans en Afrique du Nord XIX–XX Siècles*, Paris: Centre National de la Recherche Scientifique, 1980, pp. 62–71.

35. Related to the author by Louis-Jean Duclos, French official in Morocco in the 1950s, presently at the Foundation National des Sciences Politiques in Paris.

36. Dorothy Willner, *Nation-Building and Community in Israel*, Princeton, N.J.: Princeton University Press, 1969, ch. 7, esp. pp. 301–02.

37. Related to the author by his student, Dawn Feldman, May 1985.

38. Coon, *Tribes of the Rif*, pp. 21, 54–55, 63, 135–37, 144–45.

39. Robert N. Pehrson, (comp. Fredrik Barth), *The Social Organization of the Marri Baluch*, Chicago: Aldine, 1966, ch. V, esp. pp. 61–65.

40. Zev Garber, "Jethro, Father-in-law of Moses: Summary of Biblical and Rabbinical Material," *Forum*, 50, Winter 1983/84, pp. 58–62.

41. *Counterpoint* (Jerusalem), March 1985, p. 4.

42. This is from Benjamin of Tudela's travel record published in Tel Aviv: Sifriat Poalim, 1984. Quoted in Gabriel Ben-Dor, *The Druzes in Israel: A Political Study*, Jerusalem: The Magnes Press, The Hebrew University, 1979, Introduction.

43. Yosi Walter, "The Legend of the Hasbaya Governor," *Maariv* (Hebrew) (Tel Aviv), July 30, 1982.

44. Mixed feelings were reported by Ben-Dor, pp. 161, 227, n. 71.

45. *New Middle East*, 56, May 1973, p. 7.

46. *Le Pays des Alaouites*, vol. I, p. 62.

47. Dussaud, p. 40, n. 3.

48. Alasdair Drysdale, "The Succession Question in Syria," *The Middle East Journal*, 39, 2, Spring 1985, p. 250.

49. Zeev Schiff, "Sharon's Vision in the U.S.A.," *Ha'aretz* (Hebrew) (Tel Aviv), November 8, 1987.

50. Haim Shapiro, "Between a Rock and a Hard Place," *The Jerusalem Post Magazine*, November 29, 1985.

51. Charles Burney and David Marshall Lang, *The Peoples of the Hills: Ancient Ararat and Caucasus,* London: Weidenfeld & Nicolson, 1971, p. 204.

52. Yavuz Ercan, "Armenian Claims in the Light of Historical Documents," *Turkish Review Quarterly Digest,* 1, 3, Spring 1986, p. 15.

53. Yaacov Caroz, *The Arab Secret Services,* London: Corgi, 1978, p. 14.

54. Braude and Lewis, vol. I, p. 309.

55. Gideon Rafael, *Destination Peace: Three Decades of Israeli Foreign Policy,* London: Weidenfeld & Nicolson, 1981, p. 132.

56. Gunter, p. 462.

57. *The Jerusalem Post,* April 26, 1985.

58. Meron Benvenisti, *Jerusalem: The Torn City,* Jerusalem: Isratypset, 1976, p. 258.

59. Isaiah 19:24.

60. Ibid., 17:13.

61. *The Nestorians or the Lost Tribes,* pt. 2, chs. 10–18.

62. 1 Kings 5:26.

63. Barry Rubin, *The Arab States and the Palestine Conflict,* Syracuse, N.Y.: Syracuse University Press, 1981, ch. 2.

64. Neil Caplan and Ian Black, "Israel and Lebanon: Origins of a Relationship," *The Jerusalem Quarterly,* 27, Spring 1983, pp. 48–58, quotation from p. 56.

65. Shabtai Teveth, *Ben Gurion and the Palestinian Arabs: From Peace to War,* Oxford and New York: Oxford University Press, 1985, p. 182.

66. Oded Yinon, "Peace and Its Hope — Israel's Peace Policy 1948–1984," *Kivunim* (Hebrew), 33, November 1986, p. 114.

67. Moshe Sharett, *Yoman Ishi* (Personal Diary), Tel Aviv: Sifriat Maariv, 1978, entry from Feb. 27, 1954, p. 377.

68. Ibid., entry from May 16, 1955, p. 996.

69. Interview with Shula Cohen, former Jewish resident of Beirut, August 1988.

70. *Monday Morning* (Beirut), January 17–23, 1983, esp. 37–39.

71. A. J. Arkell, *A History of the Sudan from the Earliest Times to 1821,* University of London, The Athlone Press, 1961, pp. 196–97, fig. 24 opposite p. 192.

72. Wai, *The African-Arab Conflict in the Sudan,* pp. 138–39.

73. Tudor Parfitt, *The Thirteenth Gate: Travels Among the Lost Tribes of Israel,* London: Weidenfeld & Nicolson, 1987, ch. 5; *Yediot Aharonot,* Tel Aviv, August 3, 1990 (Interview with Adnan Khashoggi).

Chapter 14

1. Arnold J. Toynbee, *Survey of International Affairs 1925,* vol. I, London: Oxford University Press & Humphrey Milford, 1927, p. 23.

2. D. S. Margoliouth, *The Early Development of Mohammedianism,* New York: Charles Scribner's Sons, 1914, p. 134.

3. Patricia Crone, *Slaves on Horses: The Evolution of the Islamic Polity,* Cambridge: Cambridge University Press, 1980, p. 78; Herbert Mason, *Two Statesmen of Mediaeval Islam,* The Hague and Paris: Mouton, 1972, p. 110.

4. Hisham B. Sharabi, *Nationalism and Revolution in the Arab World*, Princeton, N.J.: Van Nostrand, 1966, p. 3.

5. Manfred W. Wenner, "The Arab/Muslim Presence in Medieval Central Europe," *International Journal of Middle East Studies*, 12, 1980, p. 73.

6. *The Muqaddimah*, vol. I. ch. 2, p. 302.

7. Baron De Montesquieu, *The Spirit of Laws*, tr. Thomas Nugent, London: George Bell and Sons, 1878, ch. 18.

8. Ignatz Goldziher, *Muslim Studies*, vol. I, ed. S. M. Stern, Chicago: Aldine, 1966 (orig. 1889), chs. 1–4.

9. Adeed Dawisha, *The Arab Radicals*, New York: Council on Foreign Relations, 1986, pp. 32–34.

10. Friedrich Nietzsche, *The Will to Power*, ed., Walter Kaufmann, New York: Vintage, 1968, p. 58.

11. Joshua Prawer, *The Latin Kingdom of Jerusalem: European Colonialism in the Middle Ages*, London: Weidenfeld & Nicolson, 1972.

12. Mordechai Nisan, "The Search for an Israeli Ethos," *Global Affairs*, 2, 3, Summer 1987, pp. 147–61.

13. Miles Copeland, *The Game of Nations: The Amorality of Power Politics*, London: Weidenfeld & Nicolson, 1970, p. 163.

14. Mohamed Heikal, *The Return of the Ayatollah: The Iranian Revolution from Mossadeq to Khoumeini*, London: Andre Deutsch, 1983, p. 207.

15. Samir Amin, *The Arab Nation*, tr. Michael Pallis, London: Zed Press, 1978, p. 103.

16. Marvin G. Weinbaum, "The Internationalizations of Domestic Conflict in the Middle East," *Middle East Review*, 20, 1, Fall 1987, pp. 31–42.

Index